Economic and Social History of England 1770—1977
New Edition

Economic and Social History of England 1770—1977
New Edition

R. B. Jones

Longman

Longman Group Limited
London
Associated companies, branches and representa-
tives throughout the world

© Longman Group Ltd 1971, 1979

First published 1971
New Edition 1979
ISBN 0 582 33058 0

Printed in Hong Kong by
Sheck Wah Tong Printing Press Ltd

Contents

1 · The Great Changes   1
England between the 1770s and the 1880s   1
The problem of population   2
Causes of the population increase   4
Changes in the distribution of population   8
Living conditions of the masses   9

2 · Trade and wealth   11
Mercantilism   11
Foreign trade and empire   12
Smuggling   15
Slave trade   16
How the increased wealth promoted the
  Great Changes   19

3 · The Great Changes:
    the countryside   23
Farming in the early part of the eighteenth
  century   23
The agricultural improvers   25
Enclosure   28
Rural poverty   30
The Speenhamland System   32
The gang system   35
Agricultural trade unions   35
High farming   36

4 · The Great Changes:
    the shrinking provinces   39
The turnpike trusts   40
The engineers   41
The coaching industry   42
River transport   44
Disadvantages of river transport and the
  coming of canals   45
The effects of canals   47
Disadvantages of canals   48
The railways   49
The development of the lines   53
The navvies   54

The railway mania   54
The impact of the railways   57
The steamship   58

5 · The Great Changes:
    the industrial inventions utilised   62
The domestic system   62
Changes in textiles   64
The iron industry   68
The coal industry   70
The steel industry   71
The steam engine   72
The development of machine tools   74
Other industries   76

6 · The Great Changes:
    new methods of industrial organisation   77
The entrepreneurs   77
Josiah Wedgwood   79
The Great Exhibition, 1851   81
Slumps, and trade cycles   83
Nineteenth-century banks   84
Limited liability   85

7 · Some political consequences of the
    Great Changes   87
The rise of laissez-faire   87
Free trade   88
Repeal of the Corn Laws   90
Government regulation revives   92
Climbing boys   93
Factory Acts   94
Working conditions in the mines   97
The truck system   98

8 · Some social consequences of the Great
    Changes:
    the new towns   99
Condition of the urban poor   101
Cholera   104

Public health reformers 106
Reform of local government 108
Housing the poor 109
Rural local government 111

9 · The life of the wealthy, and others, during the Great Changes 113
Country houses 113
Parks 115
Country life 116
Press gangs 120
Town life 121
The spas 122
Prisons 124
Police 126

10 · Religion during the Great Changes 129
The Methodists 130
The Evangelicals 133
The Oxford Movement 134
Christian Socialism 135
'Heathen' England 135
The Salvation Army 136

11 · Education during the Great Changes 139
The Poor 140
Sunday Schools 141
Denominational schools 141
Mechanics' Institutes 142
Grammar schools 144
Public schools 145
Women's education 146
The growth of a national system 147
Universities 153

12 · Working-class movements during the Great Changes 154
The demand for parliamentary reform 154
Corresponding societies 155
The Luddites 156
Disturbances after the war 157
Owenism and the trade unions 159
The Poor Law 160
Chartism 162
New model trade unions 164
The Co-operative movement 166

13 · Taking stock 168
The new electorate and the collectivist state 168
The 'Great Depression' 170
Foreign competition 171
British failures 173
The pattern of trade 175
Balance of trade and balance of payments 176
The crisis in agriculture 176

14 · The appearance of twentieth-century society 179
Emancipation of women 180
Changes in towns 184
Gas and electricity 186
Developments in transport 187
Recreations 189
Mass communication 193

15 · The widening scope of government 196
The writers 198
Regulating the conditions of the workers 200
Labour exchanges 202
Care of children 203
Social security 203
Old-age pensions 204
National Insurance Scheme, 1911 205
'War Socialism': 1914–18 205
Provision of cheap housing 207
Destruction of the Old Poor Law 209

16 · The 'Humbler Orders' become Governors 213
The new unionism of the 1880s 213
The rise of the Labour Party 216
The Fabians 217
The great strike movement 219

17 · The changing nature of Britain's trade 224
Tariff Reform 224
The steps to protection 225
The new economics 228
The Second World War 229
The economic crises after the war 230
The Common Market 235
The problem of agriculture 238

18 · The managerial revolution 241
The old staple industries 241
The new industries 242
Changes in the structure of industry, 1880s to 1970s 246
The Government and industry 248
Trade unions since 1927 252

19 · The common man and the Welfare State 255
War socialism, 1939–45 255
The evacuation 259
The Welfare State takes shape 259
Beveridge Report, 1942 260
Social legislation after the war 261
1951: the Festival of Britain 263
Housing 263
New Towns 267
Education in the twentieth century 271
Changes in local government since the war.. 276
Mass media and the consumer society 278
Transport changes 282
Greater leisure 286
Problems of adjustment 288

20 · The 1970s: a watershed 292
Population changes 293
New-Commonwealth immigrants 295
Sex equality 297
A new permissiveness or a classless society? 297
Problems of Government and industry 299
Britain and the E.E.C. 308

Further Reading 312

Index 316

Maps
1 The changing distribution of population in the eighteenth century 7
2 Empire and trade in the eighteenth century 14
3 Principal areas of eighteenth-century enclosure 30
4 Inland waterways 45
5 English railways about 1850 52
6 The European Economic Community and COMECON 233
7 Pollution 246
8 New Towns 269
9 The new local government authorities (1974) 277
10 Motorways, 1978 284
11 National Parks and Long Distance Footpaths 287
12 The changing distribution of population in twentieth-century England 292
13 Oil in home waters 305

Graphs
1 Population growth and emigration 3
2 Birth and death rates 4
3 Growth of foreign trade in the eighteenth century 12
4 Movement of wholesale prices 1770–1870 31
5 Poor relief and wages movements 34
6 English railway developments 55
7 (a) Consumption of raw cotton 65
   (b) Growth rate of textile industry 65
8 (a) Employment in textiles 67
   (b) Numbers of power looms in use 67
9 Pig iron and coal production 69
10 The relationship between certain machine-tool makers 74
11 The distribution of the labour force (1851–1871) 83
12 The price of bread in London (1770–1930) 92
13 Different rates of growth of major industrial towns 102
14 Real wages and retail prices, 1850–1905 170
15 (a) Coal 172
   (b) Steel Production, U.S.A., Germany and U.K. 172
16 Export of cotton piece goods, 1820–1900 175
17 The changing pattern of British exports 175
18 The trade gap and the balance of payments, 1860–1914 177
19 New houses completed, 1900–77 208
20 Prices and wages, 1850–1945 220
21 Days lost by strikes and numbers of unemployed, 1891–1939 221
22 Imports and exports (by category), 1900–64 224

23 Balance of trade, 1900–64   226
24 The declining value of the pound,
    1967–77   231
25 Growth rate of Common Market Countries
    contrasted with that of Great Britain,
    1952–66   234
26 Comparison of imports and exports by region,
    1900–76   234
27 The changing structure of the British
    national produce   240
28 The changing distribution of employment
    1966–75   240
29 The industrial structure of the United
    Kingdom, 1907–55   241
30 Trade union membership, 1900–77   252
31 Numbers of full time students, 1900–75   275
32 Growth of road transport, 1900–76   283
33 Greater Leisure
    (a) Weekly hours worked by full-time
    adult manual workers, 1950–77   287

(b) Annual paid holiday, 1966–76   287
34 (a) Population growth, birth and death
    rates   293
    (b) Age structure of the population,
    1881–2001 (estimated)   293
35 Populations of the conurbations, 1951–74   295
36 Wages and salaries
    (a) Average weekly earnings (hourly paid),
    1966–77   298
    (b) Average salaries (non-manual),
    1970–77   298
37 Working days lost by industrial action,
    1965–77   299
38 Total unemployment, 1966–77   301
39 Balance of Trade 1970–77   302
40 Retail prices, 1962–78   303
41 Balance of payments, 1955–77   304
42 (a) Industrial growth   308
    (b) Britain's changes in GNP compared
    with other countries   308

Acknowledgements

For permission to reproduce illustrative material we are grateful to the following:

Aerofilms Limited, pages 28, 99, 209, 265, 270, 275, 286; Barnaby's Picture Library, pages 282, 285; Bodleian Library Oxford, pages 3, 22; Building Research Establishment photograph, page 264; Brighton Art Galleries and Museums, page 69; BBC Copyright, page 276; Trustees of the British Museum, pages 6, 76, 119; British Railways London Midland Region, page 51; British Vacuum Cleaner Co Ltd, page 181 (below); Cambridge University Library, pages 117, 185; Central Press, page 290; Central Electricity Generating Board, page 242; City Engineer and Surveyor's Office Sheffield, page 266; Decimal Currency Board (1971), page 235; Department of Environment Crown Copyright, page 114; Greater London Council Photograph Library © pages 149, 150, 272; Crown Copyright. Controller of Her Majesty's Stationery Office, page 256 (left); Cartoon by Les Gibbard as appeared in *The Guardian* 27. 2. 1975, page 237; Guildhall Art Gallery, City of London, page 267; Illustrated London News Picture Library, front cover and pages 161, 163, 197, 201; International Computers Limited, page 244 (above); A.F. Kersting, page 115; Keystone Press Agency, pages 283, 288; City of Kingston Upon Hull Museums and Art Galleries, page 17; Leicester Museum and Art Gallery, page 54; London Transport, page 187; Cartoon by David Low, by arrangement with the Trustees and the London *Evening Standard*, page 229; Mansell Collection, pages 101, 118, 126, 129, 174, 189 (below); The Metrication Board, page 309; National Buildings Record, page 68; The National Trust, Claudon Park, near Guildford,

page 18; Nottingham Museum and Art Gallery, page 33; Press Association Ltd, page 289; Punch Publications Ltd, pages 82, 134, 181 (above), 188; Radio Times Hulton Picture Library, pages 43, 49, 59, 107, 110, 111, 113 (above), 123, 137, 139, 142, 147, 155, 171, 180, 182, 183, 190, 192, 195, 196, 202, 203, 206, 207, 210, 213, 215, 219, 223, 239, 244 (below), 255, 257, 258, 259, 261; The University of Reading Museum of English Rural Life, page 27; Reyrolle Parsons Ltd, page 186; Runcorn Development Corporation, Cheshire, Photo: Brian Williams, page 268; Photo: Science Museum of London, pages 44, 70; Crown Copyright. Science Museum of London, page 194; Shell Photographic Service, back cover and page 306; Chris Steele-Perkins, page 280; Tony Stone Associates Ltd, London, page 251; Syndication International, page 292; U.K. Atomic Energy Authority, page 243; Union of Shop, Distributive and Allied Workers, page 200; United Press International, page 279, 281, 296; Upper Clyde Shipbuilders Ltd, page 61; Victoria and Albert Museum. Crown ©, page 81, 113 (below); The Wellcome Trustees, page 105; George Wimpey and Co Ltd, page 284 (above); C.H. Gibbs-Smith, *The Great Exhibition of 1851*. Victoria and Albert Museum, H.M.S.O. 1950, page 37; J.F.C. Harrison, *Learning and Living 1790–1960*. Routledge and Kegan Paul, 1961, page 143; E. Royston Pike, *Human Documents of the Victorian Golden Age 1850–75*. Allen and Unwin 1967, page 214; A.R. Scmoyen, *The Chartist Challenge*. Heinemann 1959, page 163; E.S. Turner, *Roads to Ruin*. Michael Joseph 1950, page 60; Fig 107 by D.E. Woodall from *A History of Technology Vol 4* edited by Charles Singer, E.J. Holmyard, A.R. Hall and Trevor I. Williams, Clarendon Press, based on Plate XI in Farey's *Treatise of the Steam Engine*. Publ. London 1827, page 73.

1 · The Great Changes

*England between the 1770s and
the 1880s*

Walk down Oxford Street from Marble Arch. On both sides there are big shops; some are part of a great national chain of stores, some sell only one type of goods, some are department stores. Occasionally you catch a glimpse of a small shop, a one-man store. Many people are hurrying in and out of the shops. They are from all walks of life and are all fairly well dressed, the women in dresses or skirts bought from the stores, the men in suits or jackets bought 'off the peg', and all the clothes are cheap because they were made in big factories producing a great quantity of the same type of article. Everyone is in a hurry, but it is a very orderly crowd and you might not even see a policeman. Certainly it will not occur to you to notice that the street is clean and well surfaced and that there are powerful street lights every few yards. But you will notice the constant stream of traffic passing quickly, obeying immediately the many traffic signals. As you pass Oxford Circus you will remember the Underground, where electric trains run to a strict time-table, quite impossible for the red double-decker buses that pass down the roadway. People are hurrying because they must be back at work at a set time, whether it is at an office, shop or factory. The clock dominates their lives. At the end of Oxford Street is St Giles's Circus and there you will find a gigantic tower block of glass and concrete, where, before 1847, were the 'Rookeries', one of the worst slums in England.

Friedrich Engels, described them

'It is a disorderly collection of tall, three- or four-storeyed houses, with narrow, crooked, filthy streets, in which there is quite as much life as in the great thoroughfares of the town, except that here, people of the working class only are to be seen. . . .

The houses are occupied from cellar to garret, filthy within and without. . . . But all this is nothing in comparison with the dwellings in the narrow courts and alleys between the streets . . . in which the filth and tottering ruin surpass all description. . . . Heaps of garbage and ashes lie in all directions, and the foul liquids emptied before the door gather in stinking pools.'

In 1847, a new road (New Oxford Street) was cut through these slums to relieve traffic congestion. The traffic then was horse-drawn and the crossing-sweeper was constantly in demand to clear a path across the roadway. The road was cobbled for the horses and the street lighting was poor, oil lamps were widely used although gas had been available for forty years (the electric light was still forty years away in 1847). The people on this new street would be definitely of the working class and their clothes would be coarse in comparison with our own. The suits would be 'factory made', but a close glance would show that most men had only one working suit: their wages were low and a stout cloth lasted a long time, especially if it were *fustian* (a sort of corduroy which had become almost a symbol of the working man in the 1840s). You would feel less inclined to walk unconcernedly along this street as along the Oxford Street of today. But the people would still be hurrying, for their lives, too, were dominated by the clock. And they had little leisure to walk over the green fields that then lay towards Camden Town, Hampstead and Paddington.

But if you were to go back a further hundred years, it would be quite a different world. Wander through the more fashionable parts of Georgian London; buy a pint of milk fresh from a cow tethered in St James's Park; see the liveried servants walking behind their mistresses, and note the great gulf between the life of the rich and that of the poor, a gulf of which the poor seemed scarcely aware. The clothes would be quite different. The knee breeches, waistcoats and jackets of the gentlemen and the dresses of the ladies were specially made by very skilled hands. The poor would be shabbily dressed in different kinds of cloth and styles, and most of their children would be without shoes. People's manners were different, too, for it was a rougher England. Shopkeepers would not lay out their wares as freely as they do now, for theft was a common thing even though the penalty was hanging. And you would be in danger as much from petty thieves as from rich, riotous young men, like the Mohocks and Corinthians,

'every night employed in roasting porters, smoking cobblers, knocking down watchmen . . . breaking windows. . . . One could hardly find a knocker at a door in a whole street after a midnight expedition of these *beaux esprits.*'

The smell would be different, too. You would probably find the stench unbearable on a hot day, for you would never have come across such conditions. But the people would not be hurrying in the same way: life was more leisurely, much less organised, and not dominated by the clock. It would be a way of life easily recognisable by a visitor from Tudor times.

What has happened in these two hundred years since the 1770s has been a complete change in the way of life brought about by a whole sequence of social, economic, industrial and political factors. No one planned this change; no Act of Parliament made it possible and no army of civil servants worked out its details. The factors that produced the changes were beyond the control of the governments of the day—developments in technology and business organisation; expansion of markets at home and abroad; pressure of population; growth of big towns—all these created problems that the world had not experienced before.

It was the Victorians who, without experience to guide them, struggled manfully to find the answer to these problems. It was a triumph of adjustment to new conditions: we did not suffer the bloodshed of a violent political revolution, like the French or the Russians. The answers that the Victorians stumbled upon have to a great extent framed the society of today. Some of them were political, like the extension of the *franchise* (the right to vote)—democracy as we know it today is much less than a hundred years old, for all that Westminster is called 'the Mother of Parliaments'. Some were economic, like the changing structure of business organisation; some were social, like the gradual development of state education, better housing and the extension of social services. Above all there was a change in people's attitude of mind. Those who lived through these changes only dimly understood the nature of what was happening. If we can come to understand how these changes occurred, it may help us to understand and to adjust ourselves more quickly to the equally big changes that are going on around us today.

The Great Changes since the mid-eighteenth century are usually referred to as the *Agricultural* and *Industrial Revolutions*. These are useful names: but it is utterly wrong to think of the changes coming quickly. Like most of the real problems in history, there is no simple answer to the question, 'When did the changes start and when did they finish?' By the 1770s they were under way and by the 1880s they had produced a society of an obviously modern structure. It is for this reason that we are looking at the period of the Great Changes over a hundred years.

The problem of population

The most important happening of the eighteenth century was the 'population explosion' (see *graph 1*). Since Tudor times the population had been gradually increasing, but suddenly, about the 1770s, it leapt forward with a really tremendous increase, and it has continued to grow. This 'explosion' really divides the modern world from the past, for it fundamentally altered conditions of life for everyone.

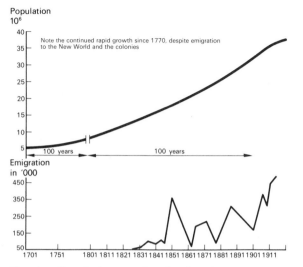

Graph 1 *Population growth and emigration*

The study of population is called *demography*, and historians are becoming particularly interested in it because it helps to explain many social and economic changes. Unfortunately, before 1801 there was no official count of the population, and records, like parish registers and bills of mortality, were not always kept, so that it is difficult to gain a clear picture of what was happening in different parts of the country. However, we do have a number of surveys, often carried out by Treasury officials anxious to discover the number and wealth of families for purposes of defence, trade and taxation.

One of these was by Gregory King, whose survey of English society in 1696 has proved to be fairly accurate. His estimate of the population of England and Wales was $5\frac{1}{2}$ million, and his survey revealed a society dependent upon agriculture and trades closely associated with farming rather like the economies of under-developed countries in the Third World today. There was a huge gap between the wealthy and the poor, and there were nearly three million living on the verge of poverty, who in bad times had to be helped by gifts of money, clothing or food from the parish 'poor box', which the parish had to provide out of the *poor rate* levied on all land owners in the parish (see *page 31*). This was known as 'out-door relief', because the *paupers* (people receiving relief) continued to live at home and did not have to enter a special poor house. King also showed that most people lived in the countryside, especially in the Home Counties, East Anglia and the West Country. The North was sparsely populated. Although London was huge by the standards of King's day (some 675,000), we would have found the old market-towns the size of villages today. Cities like Bristol and Norwich, then thought big, had only 25,000 inhabitants, and Manchester less than 10,000.

But there was a good deal of controversy in the hundred years following King's survey about the size of the population, and in 1798 the Rev. Thomas Malthus published his very influential *Essay on the Principles of Population as it Affects the Future of Society*. He argued that it was a natural thing for population to grow, but that it was held in check by

A bill of mortality. Before the census of 1801, evidence for population studies comes from various tax returns, parish registers and bills of mortality. There was no check on their accuracy and it was not until 1836 that the cause of death had to be registered.

diseases, plagues, famine and war. If these checks did not operate, then the population would rapidly outstrip the natural resources available to it and a disastrous famine would result. When they read the book many feared Britain's population might soon face such a famine and it was partly this fear that prompted the Government (then fighting a major war with France) to accept John Rickman's idea of conducting a *census* in 1801 to reveal just how big the population was. The first census showed the population of England and Wales to be over nine million (a big increase since King's day), and the Government decided to hold a census every ten years.

Causes of the population increase

Why there was so huge an increase in so short a time is a question that has puzzled demographers for many years, for the evidence available is uncertain, unreliable and difficult to interpret. There are several theories, but as research adds to our picture, it is becoming clear that local differences and factors affecting particular areas were of considerable importance, so that it is dangerous to make sweeping generalisations.

A great deal of discussion has ranged round the question whether the *birth rate* (the ratio between births and total population) was increasing and the *death rate* (the proportion of the population dying each year) decreasing. Clearly, if more people were being born and surviving to become parents in their turn, the population would increase. During the eighteenth century the birth rate probably rose to a peak in the 1770s, declining slowly until it fell sharply in the 1870s, but the figures before the 1840s are unreliable. At the same time, the death rate fell especially steeply after 1770, and continued to fall thereafter, except for the generation between 1810 and the 1840s (see *graph 2*). This shows why the population increase should have been so marked in the 1770s, but neither the birth nor the death rate by themselves explain the increase, they are only indications of what was happening. We must look beyond statistics for an explanation;—to the har-

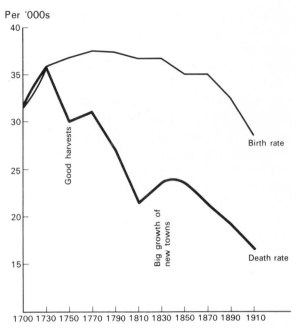

Graph 2 *Birth and death rates*

vest, for example, for it is a fact of life for an economy dominated by local agriculture. When harvests were poor (as at the beginning of the eighteenth century) the weaker infants and old folk died; the stronger survived to be parents in their turn. When harvests were good (as in the 1750s) more children would survive to add to the number of potential parents in due course.

Older writers used to point to improvements in medicine as the answer, and it is worth examining some of the evidence. Doctors, especially in Scotland, received a much better training as the eighteenth century progressed. The medical profession then was very different from what we know today, there being, broadly, three types of doctors. First there was the *physician*, a gentleman, probably a graduate of Oxford or Cambridge, wealthy, well connected, and—if you were lucky—he might know something about medicine. Then there were the *surgeons*. These became 'respectable' during the century so that they ceased to be classed with 'barbers and bloodletters'. The great Scottish medical schools did much to improve their training and skill, and many a young Scotsman became a naval surgeon (there was ready employment in the navy, the pay was good and he might well save enough to buy a partnership with a physician). This is why the British navy had the best doctors in the world on their ships, and their skill in tending wounds not only saved the navy from a serious recruitment problem, but raised their own status to that of 'gentlemen' (even if they continued to make up their own medicines!). The third group were the *apothecaries*. Some had a little medical training, but they were largely restricted to dispensing medicines and giving advice to the poor. Of course there were many 'quacks' who made a living out of the Englishman's addiction to patent medicines like Godfrey's Cordial, Mother Bailey's Quieting Syrup and a host of elixirs reputed to cure every imaginable disease. Many of the medicines contained harmful drugs in dangerous quantities and were a real danger to children. Doctors relied on these medicines, too, and they often also had recourse to such 'old wives' tales' as this, taken from a recipe of 1841 and intended for children suffering from ague fever:

'A spoonful of flower, peper, made mustard, half spoonful soup. Mix all together in four parts, put one to each wrist, let it ly on till next fit comes, then take off and lay on the other an hour before fitt comes, until it is dry.'

Or this one for adults:

'Half of bark, dram Venice treacle, 15 grains Salt of Wormwood, 15 grains powder of snake root, to be made into three parcels, to be taken three nights on going to bed.'

Clearly, the improvement in medicines available was not remarkable! (although quinine and some other drugs were introduced during the eighteenth century). And not all doctors were as well trained as the Scots surgeons. There were also too few doctors and many villages without one—even if his services could be afforded. Improvements in training and medicines would help wealthy patients in Bath or Kensington, but not the poor in Lancashire or Staffordshire, the very areas where the population was expanding rapidly.

It was the same with surgery. Anaesthetics were not in general use until at least 1847, when Dr Simpson of Edinburgh used chloroform. Surgeons had to be quick and skilful, with nerves of steel and a calm indifference to the cries of the patient. A leg would be amputated in under two minutes. For such an operation, the patient could be made drunk and insensible to the pain; but this was not possible for a stomach complaint or a gall bladder (a quite frequent operation). Even when the surgeon had done a good job, the poor fellow might die because there was no real knowledge of antiseptics. Dr Lister's antiseptic spray was first used in 1867: even so, the senior surgeon of University College Hospital, London, said in 1874, 'Skill in performance has far outstripped success in result.'

Dr William Smellie did much to improve midwifery during the eighteenth century. When his methods became widely known and practised, they must have done much to reduce infant mortality. But the 'population explosion' had occurred long before his improvements could have had much effect. In 1749 the first 'lying-in' hospital was founded in London for mothers to have their babies. Others were founded soon afterwards. Many of the patients were favoured servants of the well-to-do who subscribed to the hospital. Even so, it remained generally true that it was safer to have your child at home, for a very large number of babies died in hospitals from different infections, especially puerperal fever, of which doctors were ignorant until the later nineteenth century. Hospitals were places to avoid. In 1700 there were five public hospitals in the country and St Bartholomew's and St Thomas's in London. By 1800 there were over fifty hospitals in the country. This was highly desirable, yet Florence Nightingale, that great hospital reformer, as late as 1870, wrote in a manual for nurses, 'the first requirement of a hospital is that it should do the sick no harm.' It was a long time before the control of *sepsis* (poisoning of wounds) and infection was understood, and a long time before the big city general hospitals made a substantial contribution to the population increase. Smaller hospitals, with fewer beds and fewer problems, like those at

'The wonderful effects of the new inoculation'—a cartoon by James Gillray

York, gave patients a far greater chance of leaving them alive.

Perhaps *inoculation* was the only significant development in eighteenth-century medicine that immediately affected the death rate. It was used to combat the widespread killing, or at best disfiguring, disease of small pox. It was introduced by Lady Mary Wortly Montagu in 1721 on her return from Turkey and at first the drastic method of keeping children in an over-heated room with a small-pox sufferer was used. Soon the practice of injecting the small-pox virus from a small-pox victim was adopted. It was not always effective and sometimes proved fatal, and as there was much opposition from doctors it was 1746 before the first London Small-Pox Hospital was opened. However, the practice of inoculation spread and there were cases of whole villages being inoculated when there was

a small-pox scare. In 1765 Robert Sutton, a surgeon at Framlingham Earl, Suffolk, developed a simple and much less risky technique using a needle to introduce the virus. After 1798, Dr Edward Jenner's technique of *vaccination*, using the virus from a cow-pox sufferer, introduced into a small cut, became popular and proved more effective than Sutton's method. Even so, there was tremendous opposition from medical opinion and the general public. But small-pox as a killing disease was wiped away fairly quickly: vaccination became compulsory in 1853.

Since we can find little convincing evidence from developments in medicine to explain the population explosion in the 1770s we must look to other social factors. The fall in death rate was most marked in the rural areas and it was also obvious in London. On the other hand the growing industrial areas of the North showed a conspicuously high birth rate. It seems that families engaged in industry at this time had far more children than families engaged in agriculture: there were many jobs that children of five or six could do, and this itself was a strong inducement to have more children in order to bring more money in—many of the eighteenth-century schools that provided some basic instruction for the poor laid great emphasis on tasks that would earn money and lead to a training in a trade. Young people in towns were marrying at an earlier age and this meant more chance of children, because women are more fertile in their late teens and early twenties than in their late twenties. Such early marriages were possible because wages were better in the towns. Also the practice of apprenticeship was changing. It had been usual for apprentices (and often farm labourers, too) to 'live-in' at their master's house—it was cheaper for them and gave their master almost complete control of their time. Normally they could not marry until their apprenticeship was ended, and often not for some years afterwards. But during the eighteenth century fewer apprentices 'lived-in' and so they might marry ear-

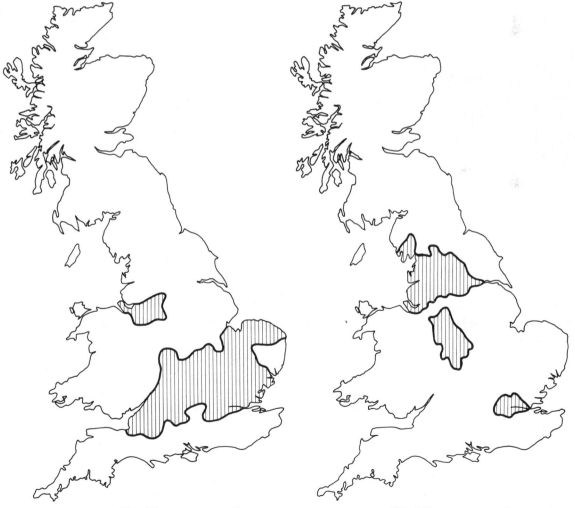

1701 : 100 persons per sq. mile   1801 : 200 persons per sq. mile

Map 1 The changing distribution of population in the eighteenth century

lier. The traditional pattern of apprenticeship was changing, too, and fewer young men were prepared to suffer starvation wages for at least seven years before entry to a trade: this left them freer to marry young. There seems, also, to have been a very high illegitimacy rate in the growing towns.

Perhaps the most effective explanations are the simplest. After 1709 there were years of bad harvest and high prices but nothing approaching famine in Britain. There was plenty of disease, but no great epidemic after the 1740s, and the wars in which we were engaged, right up to that of 1914, did not cause the loss of very many British lives. The checks that Malthus had indicated did not operate. There was also a definite rise in the standard of living during the eighteenth century, and the standard, despite rising costs and serious inflation in the 1790s, was maintained. The rural areas and the growing industrial towns were helped by local improvements in transport facilities that made it easier not only to get an increased supply of foodstuffs, but to ensure that it was a *regular* supply even in winter. More food was being produced and a great deal imported so that people in general were eating a better, fuller and more varied diet than before. Tea and sugar, luxuries in 1700, had become necessities by 1800. Soap and clothing was becoming cheaper and people were cleaner, had some change of clothing, and the use of night-wear and underclothing was becoming commoner. Better personal hygiene and a better diet must have helped keep disease at bay. Housing was getting better for more sections of the population and as coal became cheaper and more plentiful more families kept warmer in winter. In the towns dispensaries did much good work among the poor, providing better medicines and giving good advice.

In London especially, gin drinking was a great abuse, causing much drunkenness and many deaths. (There was a popular saying, 'Drunk for a penny, dead drunk for two pence, clean straw for nothing.') But in 1751 a heavy *excise duty* (a tax on goods produced at home) was imposed and gin drinking declined because the cost of gin rose. William Hogarth produced a famous series of cartoons on 'Gin Alley', illustrating the evil effects of gin drink-

ing, in contrast to 'Beer Street' where good healthy beer was drunk (pure tap water was scarcely obtainable by the poor).

Changes in the distribution of population

During the eighteenth century there emerged a quite different distribution of population from that recorded by King (see *map 1*). Instead of the Cotswolds and East Anglia (the old wool areas) being the most densely populated areas after London, the North and West Midlands became 'growth areas'. Once again it is not easy to account for this. One thing is certain: hordes of families were not driven from the land by the agricultural revolution to seek work in the 'industrial north' (a phrase King simply would not have understood). In fact, more people travelled south than moved north, so that the higher density of the north was due to a higher birth rate.

People have always moved from place to place to find work. But before the railways they normally moved only a few miles. As we learn more about local conditions in the eighteenth century, we can see what was happening in the different regions. The biggest growth area was round London. Here people seemed to move in waves over short distances. People living near a growing town would move into it, those living in villages further away would then move into the villages the first people had left. In this way a continual movement of people took place involving large numbers (Middlesex seems to have absorbed about 400,000 during the century).

Something like this was happening in Lancashire, the second biggest growth area, where the great towns of Liverpool and Manchester acted as magnets. There was also considerable Irish immigration. Lancashire developed cotton factory towns later in the century, and many small villages became big towns. Oldham, for example, was a village of some 400 people in 1760: in 1801 it had over 20,000 people. The same growth was true of other Lancashire towns. A similar type of growth was true of the West Midlands, where Birmingham and Coventry, relying on the metal and other trades, attracted waves of people.

But in the wool areas of the West Riding, despite the big towns of Leeds and Bradford, the normal pattern of development was by large industrial villages, relying at first upon expanding the domestic system (see *page 62*). The same was true of the coal and iron areas of Staffordshire. It was the nineteenth century before really big towns were common in these areas.

The countryside also saw an increase in population density during the century, despite the continual movement into neighbouring towns. But the population increase was most marked in the new towns, despite the bad conditions experienced there.

The eighteenth century was prosperous and the economy was expanding. The population explosion helped to increase that prosperity, both by providing an ample supply of labour and, since the workers earned wages, an expanding market for goods and food. Where population growth and economic expansion go together, prosperity results.

Living conditions of the masses

In the long run, the period of the Great Changes saw an immeasurable improvement in the standard of living. In the short run, however, that improvement was often very far from obvious for lower-paid workers. In those new towns during the 1820s and 1830s conditions were very bad indeed for the poor and this was reflected in the death rate. Reforms in public health followed (see *page 106*), but it was not simply a question of standards of living: it was also a question of a way of life.

Before the Great Changes there had been prosperity, although it had not been shared by very many. England had been a land of villages where people lived their whole lives, for few travelled more than a few miles. The local squire was normally a humane father figure to whom all turned for advice—after all, his family had occupied the manor for generations and he had the habit of forgetting that his tenants owed him rent if the harvest was bad. His wife and daughter would lead the social life of the area and visit the sick, perhaps teach in the Sunday School. There was a clear social division between the few wealthy families and the poor, but they all lived close to each other; rarely would one find a village where the poor all lived in one part. The village was a community in a very real sense, and its very smallness gave it its special character—a character that remained throughout Victorian England, despite the Great Changes.

But move to the new towns. That was a different world. Accommodation was scarce and expensive; 'home' for a family of six might be a single room in the basement or attic. Country villages knew poverty and lacked sanitation, but with open country and fewer people around this mattered less. The crowded tenements, without water or drains, built so close together as to make ventilation impossible, brought a filth and stench to the poor parts of towns that was degrading in the extreme. There was no local squire in the towns and no one to visit the sick. Employment was easier to get throughout the year and wages were higher than in the country, but there were no kitchen gardens, and food could be expensive. In the growing textile towns of Lancashire the mill-owners lived in great houses: their many employees crowded into slums in a lower part of the town. Even in Birmingham, where masters and men lived on close social terms, the better-off moved out to create the middle class suburb. Instead of the close-knit community of the villages, classes were divided by their earning power. It was in the towns that class war arose and it was this that led Karl Marx to develop his theory of the communist revolution. Many writers, perhaps sentimentally, deplored the passing of village community life. Carlyle put the point clearly, 'Our life is not a mutual helpfulness . . . it is a mutual hostility. We have profoundly forgotten everywhere that *Cash-payment* is not the sole relation of human beings; we think . . . that *it* absolves and liquidates all engagements of man. "My starving workers?" answers the rich Mill-owner: "Did not I hire them fairly in the market?

Did I not pay them, to the last sixpence, the sum convenanted for? What have I to do with them more?" '

Those moving from the countryside had to get used to quite new conditions immediately. The biggest change for them was the 'tyranny of the clock'. Machinery worked to set hours. For the first time ever, workers who had been used, within reason, to choosing their own hours of work, had to be present to begin work when the factory siren or bell went. Today we are so used to time-tables that it is difficult for us to realise how keenly country folk, and skilled craftsmen, felt the new discipline. At Phoenix Mill, Manchester, in the 1840s,

'a worker who is 3 minutes late loses a quarter of an hour's pay, while anyone who is 20 minutes late loses a quarter of a day's pay. An operative who does not arrive at the factory until after breakfast is fined 1s on Monday and 6d on other days.'

Employers found that heavier penalties were essential for Monday mornings, since the old practice of keeping 'Saint Monday' (see *page 63*) was so well established. A shilling fine was crippling to an operative, and he was in no position to argue with his employer. Indeed, so defenceless were the workers that it was soon necessary to pass factory acts to protect them (see *page 94*).

As factories belched grimy smoke and ugly towns sprawled, it is easy to see why many writers should have deplored the Industrial Revolution and looked back to a romantic non-existent 'merrie Englande'.

' "There were yeomen then, Sir," explained a character in Disraeli's novel *Sybil*, "the country was not divided into two classes, masters and slaves; there was some resting-place between luxury and misery. Comfort was an English habit then, not merely an English word." '

But it is very easy to forget how very bad conditions were in the countryside, and even easier to exaggerate the bad conditions in the towns. In 1696, Gregory King, remember, had found over half the people living on the edge of poverty, even with the low standard of living then experienced. It is not the least of the achievements of the period of the Great Changes that conditions of this nature passed away for ever.

No one would have understood the expression 'national economy' in the eighteenth century, for business and industry were run on a local basis. But during that century there developed a series of inter-related changes that from the 1770s produced the rapid and continual social and economic changes that characterise modern society. No simple explanation is possible for this 'take off into self-sustained economic growth'. The population explosion at a time of rising wealth produced a ready labour force and an expanding market for consumer goods, for although their wages were low, many more people were earning more and spending more. Improvements in agriculture and transport, the expansion of the coal industry and the introduction of new methods of production and of business organisation all helped to release the expanding wealth of Victorian England. There were years of depressed trade and a dreadful famine occurred in Ireland in the 1840s, but prosperity was the key note of the nineteenth century, and by 1851 we were so far ahead of our rivals that we had become 'the workshop of the world' and proved it at the Great Exhibition in the Crystal Palace (see *page 81*). At the same time we were producing a new type of industrial society, one with clear barriers between social classes, but one in which it was possible for men of capacity and vigour, given good luck, to rise to a high position. Perhaps it was this capacity to mould a new and open society that made Britain uniquely suited to blaze the trail of what we call the Industrial Revolution.

Within about a hundred years, from the 1770s to the 1880s, the whole pattern of life in Britain, and to a great extent her landscape, changed fundamentally. Elizabeth I would have found much to recognise in the England of 1770. Elizabeth II would be able to recognise much of her own world in the England of 1880. Between these years lies a gulf, a gulf out of which emerged the modern world, a gulf that was the age of the Great Changes.

2 · Trade and wealth

In the conditions of the eighteenth century, the population increase was essential before any massive economic growth could take place. But increasing wealth was also necessary before every citizen could enjoy the greater number of different goods and services which is the sign of economic growth. How this wealth became available is difficult to explain, both because of the complexity of relationships in any economic situation, and because the sources available for the eighteenth century are few and unreliable. But we can point to certain indications. Of these the most apparent was the increase in trade throughout the century, and especially in the 1780s.

Mercantilism

Before the nineteenth century governments feared to allow merchants to trade where they liked, lest they drained the country's supply of gold. So they imposed *tariffs* (customs duties) and other government regulations to *protect* manufacturers from foreign competition. Every trading nation sought to develop its own system that was as self-sufficient as possible. As early as 1581, a pamphlet made the point clearly:

'We must alwaies take care that we bie no more of strangers than we sell them . . . for so we sholde empoverishe our selves and enrich them.'

For this reason a country's empire was vital, for colonies served as a source of raw materials and a market for manufactured goods so that it was less necessary to trade with other countries. Indeed, one traded with another 'system of trade' only when it could not be avoided; and then countries endeavoured to balance their purchases with sales to the same value, for otherwise purchases had to be in gold (*bullion*), and they believed that paying out gold meant draining away wealth, for they equated

gold with wealth. So, anxiety to balance one's foreign trade was a feature of eighteenth-century commercial policy for any 'system of trade'. And, since bullion was clearly a proof of wealth, countries tried to restrict its export and to acquire as much of it as they could.

'The two principles being established, however, that wealth consisted in gold and silver, and that those metals could be brought into the country which had no mines only by the balance of trade, or by exporting to a greater value than it imported, it necessarily became the great object of political economy to diminish as much as possible the importation of foreign goods for home consumption, and to increase as much as possible the exportation of the produce of domestic industry.' (Adam Smith, *Wealth of Nations*).

It was not that governments believed there was only a fixed amount of trade to be had: they merely had no intention of helping a rival. So they protected their own trade and tried to make themselves self-sufficient. Commercial relations for trading nations became very important, and commercial concessions became a branch of diplomacy. A favourable trade treaty was at least the equivalent of an important military victory.

Transporting goods overseas (the carrying trade) cost money and in the seventeenth century the Dutch had been our principal rivals for carrying goods. In order to restrict merchants paying bullion to our commercial rivals we had passed the *Navigation Acts* (1651 and 1660) requiring British trade to be carried in British ships. The Acts were also intended to strengthen the mercantile marine:

'The great object of the Navigation Act is naval strength; it sacrifices commercial speculations to strengthen our marine,' wrote Lord Sheffield in 1783. 'It is the basis of our great power at sea, and gave us the trade of the world: if we alter that Act, by permitting any state to trade with our islands, or by suffering any state to bring to this country any produce but its own, we desert the Navigation Act and sacrifice the marine of England.'

This was an important point: the navy was never large enough for the many tasks it had to perform, and in war time the Government relied on using merchantmen. A strong merchant fleet was essential, too, in order to maintain a supply of sailors. There were never enough sailors, and the press gangs (see *page 120*) that terrorised ports to gain men had to be supplemented by 'impressing' merchant sailors, often on the high seas.

Although it was never worked out into a full policy, the Government did regulate trade by a whole series of Acts of Parliament that protected home industry and impeded the natural expansion of trade. Adam Smith called this the 'mercantile system' and in *The Wealth of Nations*, published in 1776, the year of the American Declaration of Independence, he attacked the 'system' as one contrived by merchants for mercantile ends. He advocated freeing trade from restrictions in order to allow it to expand naturally:

'We trust with perfect security that the freedom of trade, without any attention of government, will always supply us with that which we have occasion for.'

During the nineteenth century, Adam Smith's views, which are called *Free Trade* views, were adopted and it became fashionable, especially because of the great prosperity of that century, to scoff at Mercantilism as the invention of men who lacked a proper understanding of economic policy. But it would be wrong to adopt this view: remember that in the eighteenth century few disagreed with mercantilism and that the great age of deliberate mercantile policy (1650s to 1780s) was an age of great economic expansion, slow by later standards, yet solid to the core. It was also a time of great expansion in empire. There is also a curiously modern ring about their concern for a balance of trade, when we recall the balance of payments crises of the 1960s.

Foreign trade and empire

It was during this period of mercantile policy that Britain ceased to be a country with a staple export— wool and wool products. Colonial trade was responsible for this, and by 1760 about 40 per cent of our trade was colonial and this was rapidly expanding because the Navigation Acts kept our colonies a captive market for our goods and increased the variety of goods exported—nails, axes, firearms, coaches, clocks, saddles. This *diversification* of exports acted as an important spur to some of our most basic industries, and has its place in the causes of the industrial revolution, for the expansion in foreign trade after 1740, and especially in the 1780s (following the American War), is truly remarkable (see *graph 3*).

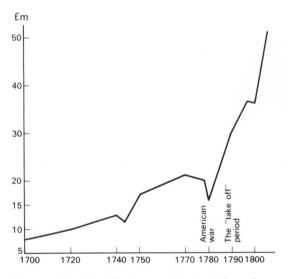

Graph 3 *Growth of foreign trade in the eighteenth century*

In the British eighteenth-century system of trade there were three inter-locking sections, each supplementing the other. The oldest was Europe and this did not expand very much. The next was trade with India and China, dominated by the East India Company in London that managed to maintain so strong a monopoly that it was not until 1814 that Liverpool was permitted to trade direct with India. This trade brought pepper, spices, indigo, saltpetre, silk, calicoes, China porcelain and China tea, and expanded considerably during the century. China tea (tea from India and Ceylon did not begin to compete until the nineteenth century) in Charles II's reign (1660–85) was kept locked in tea caddies: in George III's reign (1760–1820) it was becoming the national beverage. Some people strongly disapproved of the tea-drinking habit: Jonas Hanway (famous for his work for sweep boys, see *page 93*) declared

'the vast consumption and the *injurious effects of tea*, seemed to threaten the lives of the common people equally with *gin*; *suicide* would not be so frequent, nor held in so little detestation, if a better diet than *tea* were in fashion.'

But there was no double of its popularity. Sir Frederick Eden in 1797 noted:

'Any person who will give himself the trouble of slipping into the cottages of Middlesex and Surrey at meal times, will find that in poor families tea is not only the usual beverage in the morning and evening, but is generally drank in large quantities at dinner.'

The third great part of the trade system was the colonial, designed to supply raw materials and food not produced in Britain, in exchange for surplus manufactured goods (see *map 2*).

'By the establishment of colonies in distant countries, not only particular privileges but a monopoly was frequently procured for the goods and merchants of the country which established them.'

This part of our trade system was expanding at a phenomenal rate. Most of the colonies fitted neatly into our trade pattern without imperilling British manufactures—the Royal Africa Company which controlled the slave trade across to the sugar plantations dove-tailed perfectly. But the North American colonies, although they were invaluable as sources of naval timbers and stores, tended to compete in agriculture and manufactured goods. Lord Sheffield put the point simply:

'It was not in the interests of England to raise colonies of farmers in a country which could only produce the same articles as England did.'

Since they were denied free access to our markets, and to those in the Empire as well, the Americans became smugglers and later were to achieve their independence (in 1783) because they resented their political and especially their economic dependence on Britain. But in 1770 few men thought there was anything wrong with subjugating colonies economically to the mother country by means of the Navigation Acts that *enumerated* the items that colonists could export to Britain. After all, they argued, the mother country had to be re-imbursed for defending and governing the colonies. What lay behind the great drive for empire in the eighteenth century was that colonies were essential to complete the trade system. The eighteenth-century empire was 'a businessman's world, a world of dockets, of ledgers, of bills of sale'. In 1739, the Elder Pitt, the greatest imperialist of the age, had declared: 'When trade is at stake it is your last entrenchment: you must defend it or perish.'

France was our greatest eighteenth-century trade rival and we fought her for the possession of an extensive empire. By 1763 (Treaty of Paris) we had reached the apex of our fortunes, gaining Canada and the vast area of the Ohio from France, Florida from Spain and defeating the French and their allies in India.

If colonies fitted into the trade system easily (like the West Indies, getting slaves from Africa and sending sugar to Britain), things went well. If they did not the colony suffered. Ireland was the best example, for her industry and agriculture were rigorously controlled lest they compete with Britain's. The American colonies, unable to get satisfaction from George III's government, broke away to form the United States of America (1783) (however, they found they still were compelled to trade with Britain, indeed our trade with U.S.A. rose from £14 million in 1784 to £40 million in

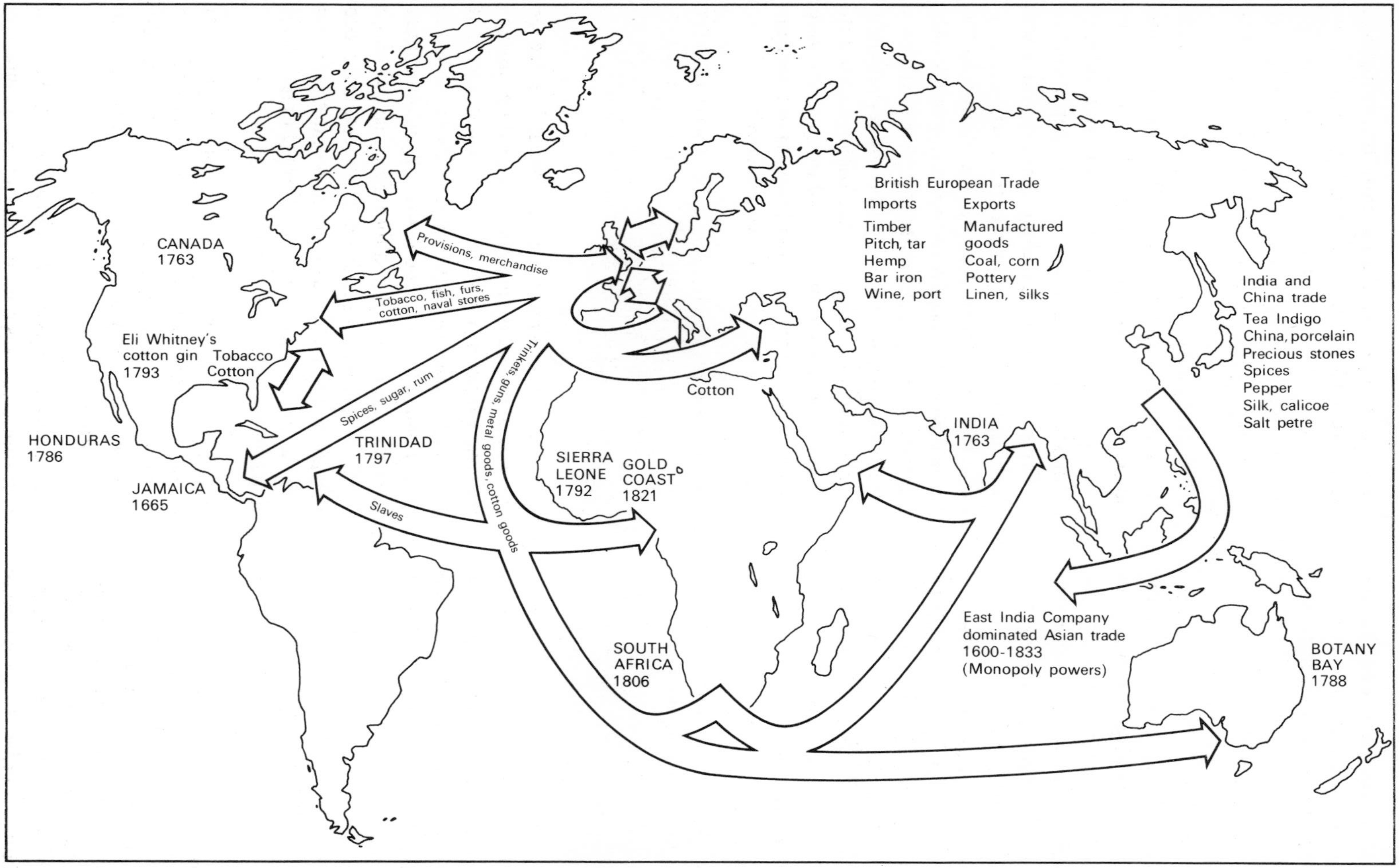
CANADA 1763
Provisions, merchandise
Tobacco, fish, furs, cotton, naval stores
Eli Whitney's cotton gin 1793
Tobacco
Cotton
HONDURAS 1786
JAMAICA 1665
Spices, sugar, rum
TRINIDAD 1797
Slaves
Trinkets, guns, metal goods, cotton goods
SIERRA LEONE 1792
GOLD COAST 1821
Cotton
SOUTH AFRICA 1806
British European Trade
Imports
Timber
Pitch, tar
Hemp
Bar iron
Wine, port
Exports
Manufactured goods
Coal, corn
Pottery
Linen, silks
INDIA 1763
India and China trade
Tea Indigo
China, porcelain
Precious stones
Spices
Pepper
Silk, calicoe
Salt petre
East India Company dominated Asian trade 1600-1833 (Monopoly powers)
BOTANY BAY 1788

Map 2 Empire and Trade in the eighteenth century

1800). At the end of the great war with France between 1793 and 1815, we emerged with a larger empire and an unchallenged position in world trade.

Smuggling

Mercantilism meant heavy duties, and the Government hoped to earn a great deal from the tariffs they imposed. Unfortunately, the heavier the duty, the greater was the inducement to smuggle goods into the country to sell at a lower price than goods that had paid the duty. Smuggling increased as trade and the demand for goods increased, so that the eighteenth century was the great age of coastal smuggling. Adam Smith remarked that smugglers had become the principal importers of English goods into France and of French goods into England. Mockingly, Macpherson (*Annals of Commerce*, 1760) quoted some figures:

'Can we suppose that England this year bought goods from France only to the value of £37 in return for goods to the amount of £209,946?'

Here, then, was one of the biggest concerns of the century. It was a measure both of the rising prosperity and of the rising demand for goods that typified the trade pattern of the century. Smugglers might well be gentlemen, and in any case their activities were regarded as perfectly normal by the local inhabitants, who asked no questions. It was the most natural thing in the world for Parson Woodforde to write (1777),

'Andrews the smuggler brought me this night about 11 o'clock a bagg of Hyson Tea 6 lb. weight. He frightened us a little by whistling under the parlour window just as we were going to bed.'

The Government tried hard to stop smuggling, for they were losing a lot of revenue. Perhaps as much as 25 per cent of imports were smuggled in the 1770s. But prosecutions often failed because witnesses were not forthcoming, or because juries refused to convict. There were never enough revenue men, and quite a number (for they were badly paid) were in league with the smugglers themselves. However, occasional pitched battles were fought between them, for, whatever the romance surrounding midnight landings in Dorset coves, smuggling was a dangerous game that might well end on the gallows.

The Navigation Act made the Americans smugglers and it was well known that the foggy fishing banks off Newfoundland provided a convenient rendezvous for illegal trade in 'enumerated' articles brought by New Englanders for transport direct to foreign ports without touching England. At home some 200,000 gallons of brandy were seized, and it was estimated that for every ounce of tobacco the revenue men impounded, a pound was illegally distributed. Tea was the biggest item smuggled. For every pound seized, three hundredweight escaped the revenue. In 1784, the Younger Pitt calculated that some thirteen million pounds were imported, of which only about five million pounds paid duty, and Adam Smith commented:

'All the sanguinary laws of the customs are not able to prevent the importation of the teas of the Dutch and Gottenburgh East India companies, being somewhat cheaper than those of the British company.'

Hawkhurst in Kent was an established centre for tea smuggling and the local magistrates and customs men were quite intimidated. The tea was landed at night and carried by small groups of horse riders to inland towns or to London, away from the danger of seizure, and well placed for a ready sale through local wholesalers who disposed of lots of 1,000 pounds at a time. It was hidden in church vestries and in cellars, even in the Fleet Prison itself. Sometimes there were 'duffers'

'who have coats in which they can quilt a quarter of a hundredweight of tea, and bring it to London in that manner undiscovered, and these duffers supply hawkers, who carry it about the town and sell it to the customers.'

In London shops tea was sold at about 5s a pound, although there was a tax on it of 4s 9d a pound!

To have ended smuggling by repression would have meant a whole army of revenue men always on duty and would have cost far more than the massive revenue lost through smuggling. The idea of bonded warehouses, stores into which goods were imported direct, to be released only when the appropriate duty had been paid, begun in 1709 and extended by Walpole in the 1720s and by the Younger Pitt in the 1780s, did not alter the situation very much, because there were never enough warehouses for the amount of trade, nor did all the ships enter harbour to unload. Smuggled goods were frequently landed by rowing boats whilst the merchantman lay at anchor in the roads. To prevent this, Pitt brought in a 'Hovering Act' in 1784, but this meant naval patrols and was expensive to enforce. What brought the age of smuggling to an end was the change in tariff policy. By lowering tariffs it was no longer worthwhile taking the risks of smuggling, and by cutting the tariff the Government found that a greater revenue was returned with far less trouble than when the tariff was high. There was little place for smuggling in conditions of 'Free Trade' (see *page 88*).

Slave trade

The slave trade was one of the great sources of eighteenth-century wealth for it grew to enormous proportions. It was not only that Negro slaves were valuable 'merchandise' (Britain earned some £15 million from slaves in 1783–93), but they supplied the necessary manual labour on the sugar plantations of the West Indies and Brazil, and later on the cotton fields of the southern states of America (especially after 1793, when Eli Whitney invented the cotton gin). This labour force was made the more necessary, for the demand for sugar and cotton grew tremendously throughout the century.

The British were the principal 'slavers' because the trade fitted so closely into their trade pattern. Basically this pattern was triangular so far as the Atlantic was concerned. Cheap cloth, trinkets, domestic hardware from Birmingham and raw rum from New England would be transported to the

Guinea coast of Africa and there exchanged for slaves. When the slave ships were full they would sail for the West Indies—this was the infamous *Middle Passage*. In the West Indies they were sold in exchange for sugar and raw materials that were transported back to England either directly or via the American colonies. Although this is too simple a picture of the actual trade pattern, it illustrates the vital commercial importance of the slave trade. In 1760 slaves cost about £20 in Africa and fetched anything from £40 when they reached Jamaica, the principal American market. Their prices rose steeply in the next hundred years. It is no wonder that men found it a profitable investment—Britain dominated it (Portugal was her nearest rival), for the Asiento Treaty of 1713 with Spain had given her the right to supply a minimum of 144,000 slaves at a rate of 4,500 a year, the King receiving 25 per cent of the profits.

The trade was ostensibly in the hands of the Royal Africa Company, although there was much competition from privateers and other nationals (especially the French), and the dues it exacted from traders were intended to pay for the upkeep of forts and trading stations and for protection against the French. In the middle of the century a new Company of Merchants Trading to Africa was formed to run the trade, managed by a committee of nine, three from London, Bristol and Liverpool. These three ports dominated the trade and it was said that 'there is not a brick in the city (of Bristol and of Liverpool) which is not cemented by the blood of a slave'.

Probably seven million slaves were shipped across the Atlantic during the century, at least half in British ships. In 1771, for example, Britain transported 50,000 slaves in 188 ships, of which twenty-three came from Bristol, fifty-eight from London and 107 from Liverpool. Liverpool came to dominate the trade. At the beginning of the century she was still regarded as an out-port of Chester, at the end she was second only to London, and her harbour works were gigantic.

With so much money and future profits tied up in slavery, the trade had many defenders. They argued that the trade was essential to British prosperity; that slaves enjoyed in captivity conditions superior to what they experienced at home; that they had the chance to save their souls by becoming Christians; that they had been saved from a worse slavery in Africa itself; that only Negro slaves could work in the hot sun of the plantations; that if Britain withdrew from the trade, others would take her place. But as our industrial production rose and our trade became more diversified, the importance and profitability of the slave trade diminished, and this may well be a reason for its abolition.

The case against the slave trade was based on grounds of morality: it was wrong to treat a human being as a beast of burden. There were humanitarian grounds because of the great cruelty that characterised the capture of slaves and their imprisonment while awaiting transport to the Americas. In the plantation, cruelty again was common, especially where slaves were numerous, because of the fear of a revolt and it can be said that slavery debased the owners as much as it did the victims.

During the eighteenth century there was a growing humanitarianism and slavery's inhumanity repelled an increasing number—the many floggings, breaking up of slave families, and, above all, the horrors of the Middle Passage. Here the slaves were manacled to each other to prevent mutiny or attempts to jump overboard. As they were so valuable, captains would crowd them between decks 'like books on a shelf'. There exists a famous model prepared for the House of Commons demonstrating the way in which slaves were stowed away: conditions were very bad. Most slave ships were of 120–150 tons, about 80–90 ft long, perhaps 25 ft wide. They had a crew of eight officers and twenty-four men, who always feared risings among the slaves (there were often 300 aboard, though 'cargoes' of 500 were recorded). The Middle Passage took about five weeks, unless they were becalmed. The slaves were brought up on deck daily for exercise and in order to swab down the 'shelves' they occupied, but in rough weather they were simply left to roll. If a slave became very ill he was probably thrown overboard, and occasionally the death rate was very high. But slaves were valuable, and captains, who got a commission on sales, would take reasonable care of them: some captains boasted that they never lost a slave in the Middle Passage. Yet, as Wilberforce said, they were 'stowed so close that there is not room to tread among them . . . the stench is intolerable'.

Thomas Clarkson, one of a group of humanitarians who fought to end slavery, made a collection of leg-shackles, hand-cuffs, and wedges used to open a slave's mouth so that he could be forcibly fed if he tried to starve himself to death.

Manacles for slaves

Wilberforce's model slave ship

We must not exaggerate the suffering, however, for life was then also very hard for the ordinary seaman. The suffering of the Middle Passage is intolerable to us—but it was not always as bad as might be experienced in a man o'war; one must keep a sense of proportion in making judgements in history. Conditions on the plantations were not always unbearable: indeed, the poor white labourers of Maryland and Virginia, who had agreed to work on set conditions for a fixed period (*indentured labourers*), and who did not represent capital, as the Negro did, often suffered worse conditions than the slave. Some slaves were lucky enough to become nurses, coachmen, house-servants and were treated, if not with respect, at least with consideration.

At the beginning of the century, it had been fashionable among wealthy London families, to have Negro slaves as footmen and pages. Perhaps there were 15,000 slaves in England. But as fashions changed many became destitute and were absorbed into the worst slums—they were known as 'St Giles blackbirds'. Others were ill-treated, imprisoned in their master's houses, paid no wages. Advertisements for those who had escaped were common, like this one of 1770:

'Run away on Wednesday the 28th. ult., and stole money and goods from his master, John Lamb,

A Negro servant at a society gathering

Esq., an indentured black servant . . . whoever apprehends him and brings him to his master . . . shall have 10 guineas . . . N.B. He is also the property of his master, and has a burnt mark L.E., on one of his shoulders.'

Others were openly sold—this advertisement is from the *Gazetteer* for 1769:

'For sale at the Bull & Gate, Holborn, a chestnut gelding, a trim whisky and a well-made, good tempered Black Boy.'

It was by discovering the actual sufferings of such 'Black Boys' that Granville Sharp decided to take up the cause of Abolition. It was due to him that the famous Somerset Case was brought in 1772. By this famous judgement, Lord Mansfield made the sale of slaves illegal in England:

'The state of slavery is of such a nature, that it is incapable of being introduced on any reasons, moral or political, but only by positive law, which preserves its force long after the reasons, occasion and time itself from whence it was created, is erased from memory. It is so odious, that nothing can be suffered to support it, but positive law. . . . I cannot say this case is allowed or approved by the law of England: and therefore the black must be discharged.'

In order to relieve the condition of the destitute slaves who had lost their employment in England, a Committee for Relieving the Black Poor was founded in 1786 and in the next year 441 Negroes were sent off to found the free colony of Sierre Leone.

The man chiefly associated with the abolition of slavery is William Wilberforce, a fashionable young man who experienced a deep religious conversion, and who devoted his considerable fortune and abilities to the cause of Abolition. His 'Bill to End the Slave Trade' was rejected in 1789, despite the support of Pitt, Fox, and Burke, for many vested interests were represented in the House of Commons. He re-introduced the measure each session thereafter, despite the intervention of war (1793–1815) that spoiled the chance of many reforms, and

in 1807, with the support of Fox, he secured the passing of a measure that banned the slave trade. But it was not until 1833, the year of Wilberforce's death, that slavery was abolished within the British Empire—£20 million was paid by the British taxpayer in compensation to the slave owners. Slavery remained elsewhere, and for thirty years afterwards the Royal Navy kept a watch to intercept ships illegally trading slaves. Actual engagements occurred, when the shot injured many of the slaves between decks; sometimes the 'slave-runner' would throw slaves overboard in barrels in the hope that the naval ship, whose captain received a bounty on each slave liberated, would stop to pick the slave up, and so let the pursued ship escape.

In Wilberforce's capable hands the Anti-Slavery League became one of the best 'pressure groups' of any age. It agitated continually, used different methods in different parts of the country, distributed information sheets untiringly, published cartoons, held public meetings and raised subscriptions from rich and poor alike. Its methods were extensively copied by subsequent movements because of its obvious skill and success. It stands as a great tribute to the humanitarian spirit of nineteenth-century Britain, prepared, at considerable financial cost, to put herself at a disadvantage commercially with her rivals in the name of common humanity. But it comes as something of a surprise to discover that Wilberforce himself, anxious to free slaves 3,000 miles away, should be indifferent to the frightful conditions of the workers and child-labourers in the County of Yorkshire, which he represented in Parliament.

How the increased wealth promoted the Great Changes

An expanding empire, a booming foreign trade, extensive smuggling and an embarrassingly prosperous slave trade were all signs of the prosperity the eighteenth century enjoyed. But at home there had to be a sufficient quantity of produce and manufactured goods to support the expanding trade. This meant changes in agricultural methods and industrial techniques, which in turn required money (usually in the form of gold or silver coins) to be available. Some of this money came from profits in agriculture (for agriculture was the major industry of the eighteenth century), which would be used to buy more land or beasts (adding to the farmer's *capital*), or to purchase consumer goods, or to lend to a business friend or a trading firm or bank (which is called an *investment*). In any case the profit would be used in a way that would help the *flow of goods* and so add to the demand for goods. Much was invested in improvements in transport, vital to the expansion both of agricultural and industrial production. In the second half of the century, rising prices also increased the profitability of farming.

Another source of money for investment was the profits on trade. Unlike most European countries, Britain had had no internal customs duties (taxes paid on goods passing from one region to another) since the Union with Scotland in 1707. This encouraged internal trade. It helped foreign trade, too, already expanding during the century, especially to the empire. Fabulous fortunes were made in India, from whence merchants and administrators returned to buy an estate, enter Parliament (lest the means by which they had acquired their wealth be too closely examined), live extravagantly and still have money left over for investment. These wealthy men were called 'nabobs' and they made a considerable impact on eighteenth-century society. London merchants, both great and small, benefited from the port being a great emporium of colonial trade, a centre for re-exporting goods, and a huge *market* in itself for consumer goods (economists call a market any place or situation in which buyers and sellers can get together).

Imports of new goods created new demands which home manufacturers were quick to supply, for example, the Lancashire cotton industry, the 'chinaware' porcelain of Chelsea and Bow' and Derby.

Trade also raised the standard of living by making what were once luxuries into necessities (in 1700 only 10,000 tons of sugar were imported, by 1800 this had become 150,000), and by making more goods generally available. Incomes rose during the century, but whilst the rich continued to grow richer, the poor failed to raise their incomes very much during the second half of the century. This meant that some people felt worse off as the century proceeded, but also that greater wealth was available to act as a spur (economists would say a *multiplier*) to the demand for food, goods and services. So the 'redistribution of incomes' in favour of the rich helped the expanding economy.

Many of the great industrialists found the money they needed for expansion from their own resources, for their businesses were often of a relatively small scale and needed only a little money to make steady progress (a good example is the steel firm of Walkers at Rotherham). They lived frugally, 'ploughed back' their profits and borrowed from friends. But to build a new factory or acquire a big machine (like a steam engine) required more money than could easily be borrowed from local prosperous men. Here the banks helped, for *interest rates* (the price paid for borrowing money) were low and money was not expensive to borrow. But industry had to compete with other areas of investment, like enclosure, housing, ship-building, turnpike trusts, canals, even with the Government National Debt.

Business methods were improving throughout the country, especially as people got used to the idea of selling goods over a wide area, and of adjusting their finances so that they could meet heavy expenses in the future and allow credit to favoured customers. Double-entry book-keeping, learnt from the Dutch, was becoming common and trained clerks were often employed to give better management of affairs. As yet few firms used commercial travellers, but the great potter Josiah Wedgwood was already pioneering new methods of marketing (see *page 80*). As the supply of gold and silver coin was limited, there was not always enough money in circulation to meet requirements, for this reason some traders and industrialists minted their own, like Wilkinson (see *page 69*). In many cases *promissory notes* were issued by bankers and businessmen (this is why today's bank notes say 'I promise to pay') who promised to pay in cash (or *redeem*) the amount of the note. If they came from a reputable firm they would pass from hand to hand, just like money, and some firms existed to purchase good notes at a profit (this is called *discounting*). Traders and manufacturers often allowed their major customers to purchase goods on credit. Repayment terms varied, and this is why it became customary to offer a discount for cash purchases or for prompt settlement of accounts. But it meant that manufacturers needed sufficient money in hand to tide them over until payments came in. They also wanted to borrow money on easy terms—and low interest rates and easy credit made this possible.

Banks developed rapidly in the second half of the century to meet this demand; they oiled the wheels of commerce. The Bank of England (1694) occupied an important place, but it usually dealt only with great merchants—its Notes were usually of too high a value for the ordinary manufacturer. Other banks were founded in London, independent of the Government, and known as 'private banks'. But in 1716, James Wood opened a 'country bank' at Bristol, the first of its type, to help supply money to local businessmen. Many more were founded after 1760 and by 1793 there were 60 in London and nearly 400 in the country. Philanthropists, anxious to 'help the poor help themselves', encouraged the founding of local savings banks—by 1828 these had a capital of £14 million. For the most part country banks were family concerns, often begun by corn merchants or wool merchants, like the Gurneys of Norwich, or goldsmiths, like the Vaughans of Gloucester. Quakers and Dissenters (Protestants not members of the Church of England) played a prominent part. But many of the banks had insufficient funds, and they could fail. They helped the flow of money and helped to direct it where it was most needed, for the major changes in industrial methods often had to wait until sufficient money was available. After 1826 corporate banks, commanding greater funds, were formed (see *page 85*) and were one of the principal means by which industry was so rapidly advanced in the 1830s and 1840s.

Bank loans were usually for short periods only. Longer term credit was achieved through the development of the Stock Market. Brokers (men dealing in the shares of companies) became important in the eighteenth century, often meeting for business at Jonathan's Coffee House in Change Alley. By 1773, the Stock Exchange had its own premises and thirty years later it issued its first List of Companies in whose shares it was prepared to deal. The great development in *shares* (one purchases a part share in a firm in the hope of gaining a profitable *dividend*, or share of the profit) and *debentures* (securities issued in return for long-term loans, paying a fixed rate of interest), provided useful methods of raising money quickly and conveniently. At the same time insurance was becoming important, providing 'cover' against different types of 'risk', like loss of cargoes in storms, or of goods in fires. Insurance companies soon became important investors, for they used the money subscribed by their policy-holders to invest profitably in the money markets of England and those abroad. Life assurance (where the policy-holder is guaranteed an agreed sum should he die during the period of the policy, and should he survive receives back his subscriptions with interest) became important during the eighteenth century and a number of important Life Offices which exist today began at this time (their concern to determine the likely length of life of policy-holders explains why a number of businessmen were interested in demography in the 1780s and 1790s). Insurance against fire and other risks (where the policy-holder only gets a return on his subscriptions if he has occasion to make a claim) was well established by the beginning of the century—the bigger companies often employed their own fire-fighting bands to put out fires in property belonging to policy-holders. You can still see the signs used by companies to identify their subscribers on the walls of eighteenth-century houses.

Manufacturers and merchants could use a whole variety of ways to borrow money and there soon grew up a class of people (called *rentiers*) whose investments were so extensive and profitable that they were able to live comfortably off their dividends (an example of *unearned income*). The British were also investing heavily abroad, especially in India and in the sugar plantations, thus laying foundations of even greater wealth in the nineteenth century. In addition, because investments were so comparatively safe in Britain, many foreigners were prepared to invest here. By the early years of the nineteenth century, London had replaced Amsterdam as the world centre for international banking and loans. This brought great profit to individual banking houses and also improved our world trading position, helping us to become the 'workshop of the world'. Already, in the 1770s Matthew Boulton of Soho had been able to raise £8,000 in Amsterdam, and at that time he was still quite a humble Midlands businessman.

No single cause can be produced to explain the 'take off into self-sustained economic growth', but this chapter has brought together some of the important factors that helped to launch this development and so begin the Great Changes.

A Sun Life Insurance sign. The Sun Life Office was a well-known insurance firm. Note the firemen's tools and the old fire engine

3 · The Great Changes: the countryside

We are so familiar with towns and factories today that we often overlook agriculture as one of our major industries; but two hundred years ago it was the prime industry of the country. The whole life of the countryside turned on the farming tasks of the changing seasons, and the traditional crafts (weaver, blacksmith, thatcher, miller) were all dependent on agriculture. Villages were local communities that enclosed the lives of most common folk and their deep-seated deference for the landed gentry is easy to understand. Landed wealth was then to a great extent the measure of social influence and power. M.P.s had to own an estate, and successful businessmen, whether or not they sought a political career, lost no time in buying an estate.

In the eighteenth century, agriculture dominated the economy and its increasing prosperity was one of the factors that assisted the Great Changes. For there was something in the nature of a transformation in agricultural methods that brought increased crop yields and better livestock as well as a change in the landscape of the Midlands—a transformation that has been called the *Agricultural Revolution*. In part, this reflects the growing wealth of the country in general and of the gentry and small farmers in particular, but it was also a response to the growth of population, for every year there were more mouths to feed.

Farming in the early part of the eighteenth century

It is very easy to forget that there are vast regional differences of soil and climate that determine the different types of farming carried out in Britain today. In the eighteenth century, these regional differences were even more pronounced, and it is always dangerous to generalise about agricultural conditions in the country as a whole.

Two hundred years ago very much less land was cultivated than today; extensive, undrained marshes were frequently to be found in the valleys and there were huge areas of uncultivated poor soils— 'wastes', as they were called. Most of these wastes were brought into cultivation by 1850. The biggest contrast to today would be the landscape of the Midlands, East Anglia and the South, for there the medieval Three Field (or *Open Field*) system of agriculture was still carried on. Each village would be surrounded by several huge fields without wall or fence. The fields were communally owned, and they were divided into 'strips' of land belonging to individual villagers, each of whom had their strips scattered throughout the fields so that everyone would get a share of the good and the poorer land available. Each field grew one crop a year, varying according to a strict rotation, and often one whole field lay fallow for a whole season so that the soil should not become impoverished, for there was a shortage of manures. Village beasts grazed on this fallow land, and on the meadows that produced the hay for their winter fodder. Beyond the meadow was the Common where villagers had a *common law right* to graze their beasts free of charge. Often poor farmers would build a shack on the Common, grow vegetables and graze beasts for a living. These were known as *squatters*.

In medieval times this open field system had been important and valuable as it provided enough food for the village and it was regarded as what we would call *subsistence farming* (growing just enough to live off). But by the eighteenth century farming had become a profitable business. The great land lords let out their farms for *rent*, and their tenant farmers often were prosperous men. There were also a large number of quite well-off farmers who owned their farms, some with large holdings and a significant number with small farms.

However, because this ancient system of open-field farming almost entirely disappeared between the 1750s and the 1850s, it has become the custom to regard it as bad and wasteful. It is easy to think of the disadvantages of open-field farming. It had been devised for subsistence farming so that villages could continue to feed themselves without impoverishing the ground. The sequence of crops and times of ploughing, sowing and harvesting were determined by a majority decision of the village, or by custom, so that enterprising farmers could not experiment, while the obligatory fallow year reduced productive land sometimes by as much as a quarter. A bad farmer who let weeds take a hold was a positive menace. Between the strips were *balks* to divide the holdings and give access to different parts of the field, but they wasted a great deal of productive land. Again, much time was wasted walking from one holding to another, especially when carrying tools (machines were a rarity). Common pasturage for beasts meant that diseases spread quickly—liver rot in sheep, and cattle plague caused extensive losses in the 1760s that might have been avoided with separate grazing. An Oxfordshire farmer commented, 'some years within living memory rot has killed more sheep than the butchers here'. Selective breeding was impossible in these conditions, and as the supply of hay was limited, many beasts had to be slaughtered in the autumn and their meat salted down (thus producing a monotonous diet) while those surviving were wasted and undersized by the following spring. It is easy to accept Arthur Young's view: 'The old open-field school must die off before new ideas can become generally rooted. . . . Without inclosures there can be no good husbandry.' Enclosure of each person's holdings, consolidated together (see *page 28*) was to be the answer.

But this picture is altogether too general and too simple. Heavy clay areas *were* very backward, but it would be quite wrong to suppose that the open-field system was moribund. As we read more local studies we find that it could be surprisingly flexible and enterprising. Within the great fields themselves and on the commons, enclosures of a sort had appeared early in the century, and it proved quite

possible in some localities for enterprising farmers to introduce new crops into their strips (as was the case in parts of Oxfordshire). New fields were being brought into cultivation. More flexible rotations, the cultivation of the fallow fields and 'closes' pastures for better breeding and dairying, were all to be found. The open fields themselves, especially in the lighter soils, had been shrinking for some time. Laxton in Nottinghamshire is famous as one of the few surviving examples of open-field agriculture, yet half its land had already been enclosed by 1691. It was quite common for farmers to exchange strips in order to consolidate their holdings: once 'enclosure' became widely practised farming would greatly profit.

But progress in farming, by its very nature, is a very slow business. Nor was the open-field system the only one. It was unknown in Wales and much of the North. In the West Country and in Kent farms had been enclosed since the early middle ages. Enclosure by itself was not the key to good farming: one does not think of Kent and the West, still less of Wales and the North, when one thinks of agricultural improvement. In backward areas very primitive methods continued to be used until the 1880s. But, by and large, eighteenth-century farmers were vigorous men who achieved a substantial increase in production. Wheat harvests rose from 29 to 50 million bushels during the century with yields up by 10 per cent, the acreage increased by 25 per cent. We exported up to a quarter of the crop during the early part of the century, but by the 1770s we were importing wheat —here is the effect of the rising population, and of a rising standard of living, for our workers demanded a white wheaten loaf and not the 'black' bread of the Continent. Prices, low and depressed in the early years of the century, began a long-term increase in the 1740s that reached a peak in the Napoleonic Wars: this, with the better harvests in the middle years of the century, encouraged farmers to break-in new land and to adopt better methods to increase their yields.

Local market towns, prosperous and often expanding, are another indication that eighteenth-century agriculture was profitable. Regional fairs attracted local merchants and farmers from different areas of the country and, as Defoe shows us, regional cheeses had a big sale, especially in the larger towns. London called Stilton cheese the 'English Parmesan' and it was brought to table

'with the mites, or maggots round it, so thick, that they bring a spoon with them for you to eat the mites with, as you do the cheese.'

River transport helped considerably, because of the bad state of the roads, and as the means of transport improved some regions began to *specialise* (concentrate production) in particular crops or in stock breeding. The picture of agriculture in the early eighteenth century is of extensive trade in wheat, cheese, cider, meat; this is evidence of an agriculture working on developed capitalist lines; it was no longer a question of most farmers producing for subsistence only. Capitalist farming was *not* introduced by the 'agricultural improvers'.

No better indication of this can be given than the great droving industry. There were certain well known 'fattening areas' to which drovers, already developing many different and identifiable local breeds, would drive their beasts to be fattened for slaughter. London was, of course, the great market. Drovers from Scotland walked their herds down the Pennines, the Welsh drovers crossed the Midlands (those from Anglesey literally swam the Menai Straits, the leading beast drawn by a boat and the rest tied to the tail of the one in front). Frequently drovers risked sums of up to £10,000, indeed, some drovers were actively concerned with the development of early banks, making full use of *bills of exchange*,—if disease caught the herd, or if there was a fall in market price the drover and his backers could be ruined. In any case, 15 miles a day 'walked off' several pounds of good meat. It was a tough life. The Scottish drovers lived on black puddings made from the blood they drew from the cattle as they moved south. They went by well known routes, remembered today by pub names like 'The Drovers' Rest', the cattle grazing on the autumn stubble. They would buy (and acquire) more cattle on the way (villagers were wise to drive their herds to a safe distance until the drovers had passed). Many drovers' ways led into Norfolk (St Faiths, just north of Norwich, was a recognised 'fattening area' for the London market). London needed some 300,000 quarters of corn, 75,000 cattle and 500,000 sheep a year: no wonder Norfolk prospered. By 1760 at least 80,000 cattle and 150,000 sheep, most bound for Smithfield, were annually crossing the Cheviots. But for all the money tied up in droving, this was not the way to breed better beasts for better meat, milk and wool.

The agricultural improvers

By this time we have realised three important things that help us put into perspective the agricultural changes known as the 'Agricultural Revolution'. First that there are always vast differences in agricultural practice because of different soil and weather conditions. Secondly, changes in husbandry (farming methods) emerge slowly and are successful only in those areas that are suited to them. Thirdly, eighteenth-century farming was vigorous in the prosperous areas. It follows that none of the great names of the 'agricultural revolution' can be regarded as originating a new system, since they were building on the unremembered work of many generations of experimenters. Also the 'new methods' took several generations to be generally adopted. This is why 'evolution' is a better word to use than 'revolution'.

Some of the improvers were great lords, like the Bedfords, the Earls of Egremont, the Marquis of Rockingham at Wentworth Woodhouse, Lord Braybrook (stockbreeding at Audley End), Sir John Sinclair on his Scottish estates. But it would be wrong to think that the aristocracy were in the forefront of the changes. For all their interest in farming, they were primarily concerned to raise the rental of their estates and often used quite conservative methods. William Marshall, a remarkably accurate observer of the agricultural scene, complained that they were often indifferent to new methods, whereas the merchants and industrialists who had just bought estates were often noted for the enthusiasm with which they invested in improvements. The real improvers were the local country gentry and wealthier tenant farmers with long leases whose security of tenure encouraged them to invest in the land so that an increasingly more prosperous tenancy might be handed on to their sons. As they travelled the country on business or to a spa (see *page 122*) or to Parliament, these mildly prosperous men would note down methods that had been successful elsewhere and experiment with them on their return home. The Midlands contained many of these improving farmers whose farms varied from 200 to 500 acres, and who took full advantage of the opportunity provided by enclosure. Arthur Young, an intrepid traveller and observer of the agricultural scene, noted:

'I am well acquainted with the progress and present state of English agriculture in all parts of the kingdom; and can venture to assert, that we owe the extension of every great and beneficial practice, such as marling, turnips hoed, carrots, clover, sainfoin, water meadows, drilling and horsehoeing beans, dibbling pease on layers, etc., etc., all to great farmers; and whatever further improvements we may look for, must be gained by the same means.'

By 'great farmers' he meant the local gentry with money, experience and unbounded self-confidence. Smaller farmers rarely followed their example: they had little income from farming and were often simply ignorant of the new methods.

The improvements can be divided into three groups: better husbandry, with better fertilisers, crops and rotations; better breeding methods; better machines. In each case certain men are especially remembered, not because they were responsible for the changes, but because they were the effective popularisers of the new methods. Many of the methods were adopted from Dutch experience —especially in East Anglia—and experiment had been going on since the early seventeenth century. Water meadows (where the pasture was flooded for a short period to make the grass grow luxuriously) appeared then and the turnip had been a garden crop in Elizabethan times. Rotations with careful manuring that avoided the necessity of the fallow year were already in use in Charles II's reign (like the one that was to become the famous Norfolk Four Course rotation), and manuring was extensively practised—a survey by the Royal Society in 1664 showed that 'lime, marl, chalk, salt, pigeons' dung, shovellings of streets, courts, ponds, ditches' were being used.

Viscount Townshend, a leading minister of George II, quarrelled with Walpole and was dismissed in 1730. Retiring to his Norfolk estates at Raynham, he followed the improving methods of his neighbours. But he was a great public figure and gave publicity to his methods. For this reason he has been credited with developing the *Norfolk Four Course rotation* (turnips, barley, clover, wheat grown in successive seasons) which avoided the fallow year and used marl as a manure. The light sandy soils of Norfolk were good for turnips which provided useful winter fodder for cattle. Norfolk farmers had no need of Townshend to tell them this, yet he has earned the nickname 'Turnip Townshend'. Had that quarrel in 1730 gone the other way, we might have had 'Turnip Walpole'. Incidentally, the turnip had its limitations as a winter fodder, and was unsuitable for sheep if grown on heavy clay soils. Other root crops used were swede, kale, potato (the mangel wurzel, good on heavy soils, came in the next century). However, the Norfolk rotation method proved popular for light soils and Townshend deserves to be remembered for promoting its use. It always helped to know that a great lord recommended a particular method. Two generations later, George III similarly encouraged new methods, lavishing great care on his model farm at Windsor.

The same can be said of Thomas William Coke of Holkham, Norfolk, created Earl of Leicester. He came from a long line of improvers and on his model farm at his great country seat of Holkham, he held sheep shearings and agricultural shows from 1788 onwards that did much to advertise new and

Sheep shearing at Holkham Home Farm

different methods. His family was well known as excellent land lords whose farmers had long leases with every inducement to use improved methods. Often strict instructions as to the rotations, marls and manures to be used were written into the conditions of their leases. In this way the Coke family ensured effective and profitable farming even on their estates far away from Holkham. Coke of Holkham deserves his reputation (the Duke of Bedford at Woburn Abbey copied his sheep shearings), but he was no originator. It is true that the income from the Holkham estate doubled from £12,332 in 1776 to £25,789 in 1816, but this was at a time of rapidly rising rents and it is important not to exaggerate the increase—some responsible writers have quoted figures that are patently absurd when illustrating the impact of his improvements.

If Coke is to be dislodged a little from his pedestal, so must Arthur Young. He was not a successful farmer, but he did travel a great deal and was a magnificent journalist. His brilliantly written *Tours* of Britain and France did much to promote improvements and enclosure; so did his *Annals of Agriculture* (1784-1809) for which George III wrote under the pen-name of his shepherd, Ralph Robinson. But Young was often far from accurate: his enthusiasm

led him to exaggerate. William Marshall was more reliable and deserves to be better known. Another writer of consequence was Nathaniel Kent, whose *Hints to Gentlemen of Landed Property* appeared in 1775. It is difficult to gauge the influence of writers, for their books were often read by improvers and not by those who still used traditional methods. But the Government was on the side of the improvers and established the Board of Agriculture in 1793 with Sir John Sinclair as President and Arthur Young as Secretary with £400 a year and an official residence. The Board did useful propaganda work and offered advice on subjects from drainage to pig-feed. It began a survey of the agricultural resources of each county (Young wrote six himself). It was a pity that the Board was dissolved in 1822 as an economy measure. Several agricultural societies were founded at this time, including the Bath and West (1777) with its own experimental farm, the Dishley Society (1783) and the Smithfield Club (1798). There were many local agricultural societies, and the interest that the landed gentry took in agricultural improvement is apparent from the libraries they built up in their country houses.

Robert Bakewell is the great name in stock-breeding. He was a tenant farmer who, after a long

struggle, made his farm at Dishley Grange (Loughborough) the centre of outstanding breeds of sheep,
cattle, horses and pigs (although he achieved less
success with these). His methods were not original,
for the Midlands 'abounds, and has for many years
abounded, with intelligent and spirited breeders'
(as William Marshall, the agriculturist, wrote in
1790). Amongst these were George Culley and the
Colling brothers of Ketton, Rutland, whose shorthorn cattle were to supersede Bakewell's longhorn
breed (a shorthorn breeder's book was produced in
1822 by Coates). Bakewell, however, was the most
successful: in 1760 he had charged 16s a season for
the use of his rams, by 1786 he was choosing his
clients from all parts of the country and renting out
his prize rams at 400 guineas for a third of a season!
His most famous ram was called 'Two-Pounder'
because it looked like the barrel of a cannon. He did
not use scientific methods but he took great care in
developing those characteristics he thought important and he had a museum in which he kept
skeletons of selected beasts and joints preserved in
brine. The working class provided the biggest
market for mutton and preferred it fat, so Bakewell
concentrated on heavy fat joints. One wit commented, 'Mr Bakewell produces beasts that no one
can afford to buy to provide meat that no one can
bear to eat.' Pedigree stock-breeding became possible
because of the work of these eighteenth-century
breeders. Jonas Webb, for example, developed the
famous Southdown sheep; and the cow, in 1700
regarded as a draught animal, was now bred for the
increasing dairy industry, and for meat—as Bakewell
himself put it, 'You cannot eat bone, therefore give
the public something to eat.'

During the eighteenth century many agricultural
machines were developed, but none was widely
used until after 1815. The normal tools were of
wood and wrought iron, often crude and inefficient.
Both the normal size of farms and the abundance
of cheap labour stood in the way of machinery, and
it was not until the end of the century that iron
became cheap enough for mass production (see
page 69). Jethro Tull is often credited with a
prominent place among the improvers, but, again,
he was not alone. His famous horse hoe and seed

Medieval strips still visible today

drill, which sowed seeds in rows rather than being
wastefully scattered by hand, were not produced
commercially for a hundred years after their
invention (his book, *Horse Hoeing Husbandry* (1731),
failed to get them widely used) and hand sowing,
even on light soils was normal throughout the
century. There were many other inventors—the
thresher is attributed to Andrew Meikle (1786) and
once it was adopted it rapidly replaced hand
threshing (this was a factor in the rural revolt of the
1830s—see *page 34*), but corn was still being
threshed by hand in 1850 near Brighton. In 1780
Ransome of Ipswich produced his famous plough
and his works were to become a centre for agricultural machinery. But mechanisation was a feature
of 'High Farming' (see *page 36*): the massive
increase in yields during the eighteenth century was
achieved without reducing the labour force, or
going over to machines.

Enclosure

The rural landscape of the Midlands today was
largely produced by the enclosures of the eighteenth
century. You can often see, especially in Leicestershire, the lines of the old strips cutting in different
directions across the fields. Many of the village
roads were laid out at the same time: you can
recognise them by the broad verges and the sudden
right-angled turns, where the road had come to the
edge of an original field.

Enclosure is the consolidation of strips usually
grouped together, under individual ownership into
actual fields. Such changes had been going on for a

A contemporary Award map of the Barsby and South Croxton area, Leicestershire, showing enclosures (1798)

long time, but there was a great increase in pace as prices rose during the century. If villagers agreed, the strips could easily be grouped together into fields by consent at a village meeting. Owners who refused had to be bought out and this took time. Prosperous farmers, large and small, were keen to hasten the process and turned for aid to Parliament: what was new in the eighteenth century was the growing number of private enclosure acts. Until the General Enclosure Act (1845), each village had to have its own act. It cost money to have the bill prepared and presented to Parliament, and then the actual cost of the enclosure had to be met. But it was clearly worth it, for there were very many acts passed: incomes rose rapidly from the advantages of better farming and stock breeding to be gained from consolidated farms. At the same time many of the 'wastes' were brought into cultivation, especially during the Napoleonic Wars and in the nineteenth century. A further reason for the enclosure acts was the opportunity to 'commute' (convert into a cash payment) the ancient tax paid in kind to the clergy, called the *tithe*. It had always been troublesome, especially in bad years, and a convenient clause in the Enclosure Act provided for a set sum to be paid instead.

Enclosure Acts		Acres enclosed by Act of Parliament	
1730–59	212	1727–60	74,518
1760–89	1291	1761–92	478,259
1790–1819	2169	1793–1815	1,013,634

The peak period was 1801–1811 when 1013 Acts were passed. Enclosure continued throughout the nineteenth century. Many of the later Acts were more concerned with enclosing the remaining commons and wastes than the open fields.

Parliament appointed commissioners to make a survey and produce an Award on the basis of existing ownership, parcelling out the new fields between actual owners. (The maps that were produced may be seen at your Local Records Office.) These commissioners were important landowners, but they seem to have done a very fair job and rarely was there a substantiated case of unfairness. Many commissioners were professional surveyors, for the profession was just beginning to establish itself and the enclosure movement helped it considerably. The basis of the Award was ownership: tenants did not own the land they occupied and 'squatters' had even less title to their land. Certainly the squatters suffered, for they were unprotected even by a tenancy agreement, and the common

Division between low wage
south and high wage north

Map 3 Principal areas of eighteenth-century enclosure

erected. The Board of Agriculture estimated that the average cost per acre in 1790 was 28*s* (8*s* 6*d* for the Act, 10*s* for the Commissioners and 9*s* 6*d* for fencing). However, since interest rates were low, it was not difficult to raise loans, especially as many of the costs involved could be spread over a number of years. Costs varied according to the village, but there is a good deal of evidence to show that small farmers could pay the cost of enclosure. Where soils were good, the small farmer prospered, especially in Derbyshire and Warwickshire. He is with us still.

Most of the improved methods did not have to wait for enclosure before making their appearance, and, despite the progress made elsewhere, some backward areas, even when enclosed, continued to use the methods and rotations of medieval times. But, although it is possible to exaggerate the effects of enclosure, it was the most obvious of the agricultural changes. The Midlands landscape was transformed rapidly, and corn production shot up (we were able to feed our increased population during the French Wars 1793–1815). A new vigour was brought to farming, especially where better transport facilities and a big market (like a nearby growing town) were also present.

Rural poverty

Enclosure did *not* create a massive army of rural poor compelled to flock to towns in search of work. Many writers at the time condemned enclosures on these grounds—Oliver Goldsmith's *Deserted Village* and Cobbett's writings are good examples. There may well have been cases of exploitation and dispossession, but only where beef was profitable did the arable acreage shrink and the number of jobs available decline. Otherwise, enclosure *increased* the jobs. As soon as fencing was done, there were buildings and roads to make. The new methods themselves often needed more men per acre than before (the turnip was a great source of employment) and many more acres were under cultivation. In 1801 there were 697,353 families engaged in farming: in 1831, at a time when the new towns were growing

grazing ground was greatly reduced. Certainly a great opportunity to make specific provision for the poor was lost (very occasionally a village school was provided for), and so much common land passed into private ownership that nineteenth-century enclosure acts actually created or preserved commons to allow the public access to open spaces.

It was once thought that enclosure meant the end of the small farmer. But detailed study has shown that their number had declined in the early eighteenth century but rose during the main period of enclosure. It is true that the cost of enclosure was heavy, for not only was there the Award, but fences, new roads and new farm buildings had to be

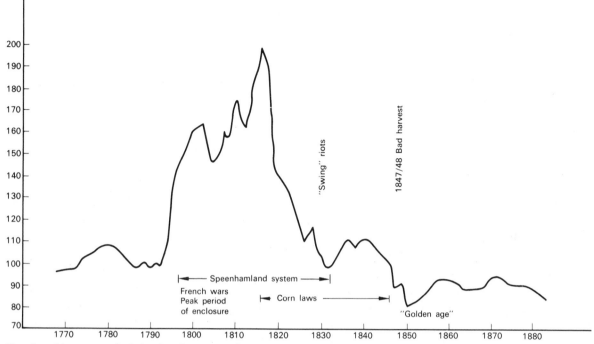

Graph 4 Movement of wholesale prices 1770–1870

considerably, this had risen to 761,348. The great drift from the land had to wait for the railways: between 1841 and 1901 urban and colliery districts attracted some three million people, while rural areas lost some four million. *This* was the time of population movement, not the age of enclosure.

Enclosure did not cause rural poverty for it was worse in Kent, Dorset and Somerset none of which had been affected by enclosure. The problem became more acute in the eighteenth century for several reasons. People were more aware of it, for the gap between rich and poor widened considerably; there were also more people, and the poor labourers tended to remain in villages where there was too little work available (except at harvest time when even the vicar joined in). Economists call this *under-employment*. In the north, agricultural wages were high because there was competition for labour from the growing industrial areas. Also, where there was well-established domestic industry (see *page 63*) families were often cushioned against the worst effects of rural poverty, especially as the early industrial changes (see *page 64*) led to an increase in

the use of domestic labour. But throughout the south there was serious unemployment and widespread poverty. Prices were rising and when war with France broke out in 1793 they rose in a steep inflationary spiral (see *Graph 4*). This was also the main period for enclosure: no wonder contemporaries blamed enclosure for bad conditions!

Poverty is no simple thing: it has many causes and there are many different types of poor—old people, mental defectives, widows, orphans, bastards, the chronically ill, the seasonally unemployed, and the lazy. Since Elizabethan times, the poor law had required parishes to look after their own poor and to levy a poor rate for the purpose of supplying relief (see *page 3*). But parishes had limited resources and in bad years a high poor rate could prove an intolerable burden for poor farmers. Parishes tended to deal with the problem in their own way. In 1722 an act permitted them to build work-houses and to offer relief only to those prepared to enter them—this assumed that the poor were merely idle, and not all parishes were prepared to take this harsh view. In 1782, Gilbert's Act permitted parishes to join together to form 'unions' in order to provide poor relief more efficiently (though few parishes availed themselves of the opportunity). Normally, poor relief had been a seasonal thing, depending on the work available in the fields and barns, but as the population rose and wages failed to keep pace with prices, more families found themselves in need of poor relief during most of the year. Private work-houses and alms-houses existed, though not always where they were most needed and never in sufficient numbers.

The problem of poverty was aggravated by the fact that families normally did not leave over-crowded villages in search of higher wages (in the North, for example), but remained frequently unemployed and always wretchedly paid (economists call this *immobility of labour*). The 1662 Settlement Acts restricting poor relief to those who had been born, married or apprenticed within the parish for seven years, probably was a principal cause of this immobility. Some people preferred to walk miles to and from work in order to preserve their 'Settlement', and there are many stories of parishes trying to prevent more people claiming settlement. Mothers in labour would be hustled off lest the child be a charge on the parish, and the very ill were sometimes deposited outside the parish boundary, lest the parish have to pay for their burial (an act of 1795 forbad this 'forcible removal'). Paupers without a settlement were sometimes chased off and cottages were pulled down lest they be occupied by a pauper family that might then claim relief. Couples from different villages were sometimes forcibly married, lest the bastard that had been conceived become a charge on one parish. But there were exceptions to the general immobility, and local studies are revealing that the old idea of a southern stagnant population may need reassessing in some respects.

The Speenhamland System

The practice of giving allowances in aid of wages was quite widespread, but the inflationary year of 1795 led the Berkshire magistrates to regularise the practice into an actual system (called the Speenham-

land System because they happened to meet at the Pelican Inn, Speenhamland, near Newbury). Their system of an allowance proved so popular that it was widely adopted by 1797. Money from the poor rate was to be used to supplement wages on a sliding scale according to the cost of bread:

'When the Gallon Loaf of Second (quality) Flour, weighing 8 lb 11 oz shall cost 1s,

Then every poor and industrious man shall have for his own support 3s weekly, either produced by his own or his family's labour, or an allowance from the poor rates, and for the support of his wife and every other of his family, 1s 6d.'

The allowance varied with the cost of bread. It was not a minimum wage, for this would not allow for differences in need arising from differing sizes of family. It was a starvation level allowance, a response to low wages and under-employment, designed to keep the poor alive in a very bad year. No one dreamt that the next twenty years would see a massive rise in prices that would make poor relief a continuing necessity every year: but at least the Speenhamland System saved many from utter destitution for it was a humane attempt to meet a growing difficulty. With many local variations, it was applied over many counties in southern England and the Midlands, but scarcely at all in the North where wages were higher. (There were many other expedients adopted, like the *Labour Rate*, labourers were sent round to ratepayers who employed whoever they wished, paying a set wage per man, the best workers costing more; and the *Roundsman System* where paupers were sent in turn to farmers who paid a part of their wages and the parish the rest. Both these systems were dying out by 1830.)

The Speenhamland System had many disadvantages. It provided no incentive to work hard since any extra wage merely reduced the allowance made by the parish. As prices rose the cost of the system rose, so that some small farmers, especially in the bad years after the Napoleonic War, went bankrupt because of the high Poor Rate, while bigger farmers who employed more labour were subsidised. However, Dr Blaug has recently demonstrated that the increase in poor rate was not due to the Speenhamland System, but to rising prices, for the 'Speenhamland' counties increased their expenditure in much the same proportion as did the counties that did not apply the System. Furthermore, counties were ceasing to apply the System during the 1820s.

The effect on the labourer himself was worse than on the small farmer. He had to depend on charity perhaps throughout the year, although able-bodied and anxious to work. The bachelor might get by with only a small subsidy, but the man with a large family had to have much more help. Many rate-payers firmly believed that the System encouraged labourers to marry early and have large families because of the extra allowance that might be available for the bigger family—Malthus, among others, was loud in his complaints against improvident and early marriage on this score. But in fact allowances were normally paid only for the third and subsequent child, and then in accordance with the amount of child labour available in the village. Despite what contemporaries said, the System was not 'a bounty on indolence and vice'. However, the ancient view that the unemployed were idlers who should be treated with severity, grew as the cost of relief rose. One can scarcely blame the men of the time who knew nothing of economics and little about statistics, if they failed to recognise that surplus and immobile labour and high prices were the real problems. Instead they blamed the workers whom they could actually see and Arthur Young, in a famous passage took them to task for it:

'For whom are they to be sober? For whom are they to save? For the parish? If I am diligent shall I have leave to build a cottage? If I am sober, shall I have land for a cow? If I am frugal, shall I have an acre of potatoes? You offer me no motives, you have nothing but a parish officer and a workhouse. Bring me another pot!'

Bad harvests and high prices after the war brought a fresh series of disorders, riots and rick-burnings. Many labourers were driven to desperate measures and poaching became widespread. The land lords replied with the severe Game Laws of 1815, for with the disturbed economic conditions after 1815 and the return of soldiers and sailors to swell the army of unemployed, there was even greater fear than in the 1790s of revolution. Game was restricted to 'gentlemen' and could neither be sold nor consumed by the other ranks of society unless received as a gift from a landlord. Farm labourers, however, had starving families and poaching became something of an organised activity, with a state of violence touching almost upon civil war between labourers and gamekeepers, especially in Kent. Buckshot, spring guns that killed or maimed any who touched them off, whether poacher, child or squire, mantraps that either dug into the flesh obliging the limb to be amputated, or simply bruised and held the poacher, and gangs of armed gamekeepers were common. High Court judges defended the Game Laws:

'I say that a man has a right to keep people off his lands in order to preserve his game. . . . If you do not allow men of landed estates to preserve their game you would not prevail upon them to reside in the country. Their poor neighbours will thus lose their protection and kind offices.'

All convicts sentenced under the Game Laws were liable to *transportation* (although fewer were actually transported than is commonly supposed). Better conditions and the legalised sale of game after 1831 brought a decline in poaching; but the gamekeeper remained, as W. H. Hudson explained at the end of the century, to tell the labourer 'to keep to the

Mantraps of the Regency period

road and sometimes to ask him, even when he is on the road, what he is looking over the hedge for'.

Crisis came in the early 1830s, at the time of the passing of the First Reform Act (see *page 158*). The years after 1815 were difficult ones for farmers working the heavy soils (although those on the light soils did well). The high Poor Rate did not help the small farmer, and the economic slump of 1826 added to his difficulties. The 1829 harvest was poor and farmers faced a serious situation, while their labourers faced wage cuts. Suddenly and spontaneously in 1830 there broke out 'the last revolt of the rural poor'. It began in Kent and usually took the form of a demand for an extra 3*d* or 6*d*, accompanied by strikes. The Home Counties, the West Country and East Anglia were affected; ricks were burnt,

overseers of the poor evicted in all the indignity of the parish cart, and the new threshing machines that had come in since 1815 were broken. There were rumours that a 'Captain Swing' organised the riots, but there does not seem to have been any deliberate organisation. The Home Secretary, Lord Melbourne, reacted vigorously; nine labourers were hanged and over 400 transported and imprisoned. The climax came with the Tolpuddle Martyrs (see *page 160*). It was under stress of these conditions that Edwin Chadwick, Nassau Senior and others examined the old Poor Law and produced the Report that led to the abolition of the Speenhamland System by the Poor Law Amendment Act of 1834 (see *page 160*).

But gradually the problem of under-employment was ended, partly by the greater mobility achieved through railways, partly by the growing prosperity of Victorian England. It was not easy for a farm labourer, with no knowledge of anything but farming, to quit a neighbourhood where his family had lived for generations. But they began to leave their villages as the century wore on. Many emigrated, helped by emigration societies like that at Petworth formed in 1831 (although the middle class who supported these societies were often thought to be more interested in reducing the poor rate than in assisting the labourer!).

As incomes of farmers rose during the first half of Queen Victoria's reign, those of the labourers did not greatly improve (see *Graph 5*). In higher wage regions things were better, but the southern labourer, even in a re-built cottage, might be worse off than his grandfather. Even at the beginning of the present century, rural poverty caused labourers to lead unbelievably hard lives. Homes could be damp and ill-lit, where six lay abed together and even 'bread and scrape' ran out, while the stench of the family's defecations pervaded the whole of childhood.

In the year of the Great Exhibition (1851), Sir James Caird, a leading agriculturalist, gave this picture of a Wiltshire labourer:

'After doing up his horses he takes breakfast, which is made of flour with a little butter and water "from the tea kettle" poured over it. He takes with him to

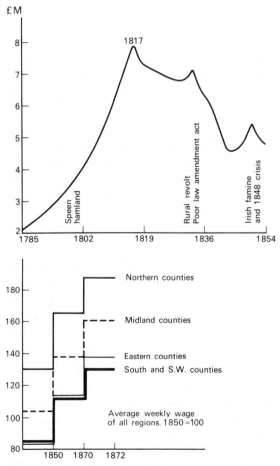

Graph 5   Poor relief and wages movements

the fields a piece of bread and (if he has not a young family and can afford it) cheese to eat at mid-day. He returns home in the afternoon to a few potatoes, and possibly a little bacon, though only those who are better off can afford this. The supper very commonly consists of bread and water. The appearance of the labourers showed, as might be expected from such a meagre diet, a want of that vigour and activity which mark the well-fed ploughman of the northern and Midland counties.'

But improvements did occur, even in Wiltshire, less in terms of higher wages, than in terms of 'fringe benefits' like allotments, better cottages on the bigger estates, village schools and cottage hospitals. Nevertheless, when Devon labourers in 1866 got 7s 6d a week to live in hovels and had to take unsaleable cider as part of their wage, whilst their wives got 7d a day and were sometimes required to work as a condition of their husband's employment, can it be wondered, that the second half of the century saw an exodus from the rural areas and a massive increase in emigration?

The gang system

One of the ways in which the surplus agricultural labour was used, especially in the eastern counties, was by the pernicious gang system which began in the 1820s. Gang masters would recruit their gangs from near-destitute labourers and their families. A master provided a form of employment, although it meant perhaps a 14 hour day with a seven-mile tramp there and back. The pitiful wage he paid was further reduced by deductions for food and transport, and he was often able to maintain his gang by getting families to incur debts to him which they could never repay. In short, they became little better than his slaves. Children were also employed and the conditions were brutalising and degrading: immorality and illiteracy was the normal condition of whole families. The evidence as to the character of the gang masters seems to be almost wholly bad. A Report on the Gangs in 1867 describes the masters as

'men whom the farmers are not willing to have in their regular employ; men who belong to the class of "catchwork labourers"; in most cases men of indolent and drinking habits, and in some cases men of notorious depravity; as a rule, unfit for the office they undertake.'

Farmers found it cheaper to hire a gang for a short period rather than be put to the expense of building cottages and maintaining permanent labourers. By the 1860s the outcry against the conditions of the gangs led to the Gangs Act of 1867, which required the licensing of gangs and forbad child labour. This, together with migration, compulsory schooling after 1875 and the widespread use of labour-saving machinery gradually ended the gang system.

Agricultural trade unions

From the 1840s onwards, the condition of the farm worker in most parts of the country was improving slowly, the more so because the surplus labour was leaving the villages. Those remaining could afford to adopt a more independent attitude to their employers. There were signs of growing thrift among them, like the development of savings banks and friendly societies through which they tried to insure against periods of illness, the cost of funerals and for old age. Trade Unionism was growing among them, and this was a conspicuous sign of improved conditions, for farm workers were rarely together for any length of time, and labourers were frequently 'tied' because their house went with their job. Successful unionism began in Kent in 1866, and by 1871 was strong in other southern counties. Local strikes at harvest times often secured a temporary wage increase. The movement changed in character when in 1872 some Warwickshire labourers asked a well known skilled labourer, and Primitive Methodist lay-preacher, Joseph Arch, to help them. His idea was a National Union of farm workers. In his autobiography, he wrote:

'I had pondered over it when at work in the wood

and the field; I had considered the question when I was hedging and ditching; I had thrashed it out in my mind when I was tramping to and from my day's toil; and I had come to the conclusion that only organised labour could stand up, even for a single day, against employers' tyranny.'

His union was to be a peaceful one intent on co-operation, its slogan was 'Defence, but not defiance'. Nevertheless it met with violent opposition, threats of dismissal and actual dismissals, evictions and lock-outs by farmers. Here was material for a conflagration. But Arch preached co-operation, self-improvement and temperance— many of the union's leaders were Methodist lay-preachers. By 1873 he claimed a membership of 20 per cent of all agricultural labourers. It ran its own newspaper and secured wage increases immediately. But protest was violent from local squires and vicars, who were amazed that their labourers could actually make speeches and behave like full-grown citizens. The few squires and vicars who welcomed the Union were shouted down and lock-outs and 'blackleg' labour soon put the union funds in jeopardy. But the Union had come too late, for American competition (see *page 177*) was already making its presence felt. The great lock-out of 1874 convinced many farmers of the advantage of machinery in economising with the use of labour. Also the farmers' hold over the labourer's tied cottage, and the lack of suitable local leaders to sustain the rapid growth of the Union began to tell, and by 1879 the movement had failed. Wages fell and labourers returned to their customary submissiveness. Arch himself turned to politics, demanding the vote for the agricultural labourer—which was achieved in 1885, the year in which he was returned to Parliament.

High farming

Sir James Caird used this name for the heavy investment in farm improvements to secure higher output that occurred in the 1850s: it was during this time, the very time that Britain's industrial output was dominating the world, that our farming was at its most prosperous.

The thirty years that followed Waterloo are generally regarded as difficult years for farmers. In 1813 the bumper harvest had brought corn prices crashing down, so that the farmers who had invested in improvements and in breaking-in new land during the war had difficulty meeting their commitments. The high Poor Rate was also a burden, and, in order to ensure that the market price of corn would not remain ruinously low, and that English production would continue at a high level, the land-owning House of Commons in 1815 passed the Corn Laws that prevented the import of foreign corn until British wheat reached 80s a quarter. Much has been written about the Corn Laws, often derived from the prejudiced arguments of the Anti-Corn Law League (see *page 90*). Certainly the Laws protected the British wheat farmer, and may have kept the price of corn high in some years—but there was little fear of a flooding of corn from Europe, since Europe no longer had the surplus she once enjoyed. Also, 'sliding scales' by Huskisson in 1829 and Peel in 1842, allowed corn to be imported in increasing quantities, as the price moved nearer to 80s a quarter. But the Corn Laws became the centre of a great campaign to free trade of all protective tariffs (see *page 88*) and they were repealed in 1846. Not all farmers had favoured the Corn Laws, for those working light soils found their cost low and their profits from mixed farming substantial. Even in the grain growing areas, despite financial difficulties in the 1820s, production grew considerably and farmers seemed to be investing in more productive techniques in order to guard against falls in prices.

The growing urban market and the increased spending power of urban workers greatly extended agricultural sales. Machinery was gradually coming in now, and transport improvements, notably railways, made it possible to carry goods quickly and cheaply over a wide area. A more scientific interest in farming was developing. Fertilisers were becoming more sophisticated; phosphates had been used since 1795, later Peruvian guano and Chilean

Agricultural machinery at the Great Exhibition, 1851

nitrate were introduced and after 1860 potash was imported from Germany. In 1823 bone for bone fertiliser was imported to the value of £14,450: in 1837 it had risen to £254,600. Liebig's epoch-making book, *Organic Chemistry in its Application to Agriculture and Physiology* (1840), was surprisingly widely read. In 1843 Sir John Lawes founded the agricultural research station at Rothamsted. The Royal Agricultural Society began in 1838 and in 1845 Cirencester Agricultural College was founded. Here was evidence of vitality that typified the high farming methods of the 'golden age' (1850s–70s) as Lord Ernle called it. By the early 1840s a machine was producing 20,000 feet of clay piping a day, and this made the draining of heavy clay soils cheaper—Fowler's 'mole' plough was a popular exhibit at the Great Exhibition (1851). Government loans at very favourable rates were available for farm improvements, and Professor Clapham estimated that in this 'golden age' over £24 million had been invested in draining, building and fertilisers.

The importance of railways for these improvements cannot be over-emphasised. Produce was moved vast distances at previously unimagined speeds: dairying became possible on heavy clay soils simply because the milk could be transported to London. The droving industry disappeared and stockbreeding, beyond the wildest dreams of Robert Bakewell became possible. Bulk delivery, of fertilisers and cattle food, was common, and machines could now easily be transported. American reapers, the thresher, the steam plough, drills and mowers, some quite cheap, were appearing even on the smaller farms. One entry in the catalogue of the Great Exhibition read:

'The most remarkable feature in agricultural operations of the present day is undoubtedly the rapid introduction and use of small portable steam engines for agricultural purposes, especially noticeable in connection with the combined threshing, straw-stacking and dressing machines, unknown until the last two years, on account of the non-efficiency of "horse-power" application to the working of such apparatus.'

One farmer in 1859 purchased a steam plough, disposed of his oxen, and, by grubbing up his hedges reduced his fields from thirty-six to nine, thus reducing his cultivation costs by a third. New seeds and rotations were experimented with. But the biggest change of all was that new methods were being experimented with by small cultivators as well as the bigger farmers. Sir James Caird noted in 1878:

'The change has not been in any considerable progress beyond what was then the best, but in a general upheaval of the middling and worst.'

But there were still farmers continuing medieval methods.

This period of high farming was one of intense investment, of the use of machinery that brought more land into cultivation, reduced labour costs and raised production. It was a period of rising prices, too, and there was as yet no serious competition from abroad: Free Trade and the repeal of the Corn Laws, contrary to the arguments of wheat producers, ushered in the period of greatest prosperity in British agriculture before the 1950s. This was the period of Surtees and Mr Jorrocks, and of the sure 'cosy' world of the prosperous farmers of Trollope's novels.

Much of the heavy investment never paid for itself. Ironically enough, the railway, which had done so much for high farming, destroyed it in the 1870s. Allied with the steamship, they opened up the prairies and Mid-West, where much development had been concentrated after the American Civil War and the war with Mexico, and transported vast quantities of cheap corn to Europe. So complete a change in the source and cost of supplies drove European countries to return to protection. Britain did not, and her farmers could not compete. The age of the 'Great Depression' had begun for them (see *page 176*). Fortunately during the period of high farming there had been a great increase in livestock and dairy produce. Some farmers were able to shelter a little while by going over to meat production: but in the 1880s refrigeration meant that cheap frozen meat and dairy produce cut their market, too.

4 · The Great Changes: the shrinking provinces

Only a brave and unusual man would have set out on a tour of Britain at the beginning of the eighteenth century. Daniel Defoe, author of *Robinson Crusoe*, did just this, and his Journal is a useful source of information about his times. Of course, people would walk to neighbouring villages or towns, but they never travelled far without good reason. For one thing, they lacked the money and leisure for anything but essential travel, for another, the roads were so very bad. As a result, communities were very local, and whole regions were strangers to each other.

During the century this changed, and the 'provinces' and growing towns became less isolated from each other. This was partly because there were more people, partly because the standard of living was rising and encouraging merchants and pedlars to transport more goods to supply their customers' demands. Naturally, this led to improvements in transport. But it is impossible to say which came first, for each locality developed at its own pace. Some localities attracted quantities of merchandise whatever the state of the roads: others had to wait for better transport before attracting more goods. But it only takes a moment's thought to realise how vital a factor in the expansion of industry and commerce was ease of communication. It was essential to the Great Changes.

Merchants wanted to distribute the merchandise from trade with the Empire and abroad; farmers wanted to extend the market for their products; manufacturers needed more and varied raw materials; and all depended on transport. Transport costs were so important to manufacturers that they sometimes determined the siting of their works, for if the value of goods is low in relation to their weight (like coal, iron ore, timber, china clay) they would only be transported far if cheap transport were available—London's coal, for example, came direct from Newcastle by sea. In Defoe's day, iron masters would 'stock-pile' coal during the dry summer months because they would never get supplies through in winter: and one of the biggest problems of inland colliers was the accumulation of unsold coal at the pit head throughout the winter. Once better transport was available the production of goods could increase rapidly for the market was expanding: the country's economy could leap forward. By 1815 foreign visitors were commenting on the excellence of our transport services: no wonder we were a whole generation ahead of our competitors in industry and commerce.

In Defoe's day, pack-horses were the norm. Merchants led a line of horses (sometimes asses) tied one behind the other, with baskets strapped to their sides. Some of the roads they travelled had a paved causeway in the centre and the bridges they crossed were narrow and hump-backed with triangular recesses in the walls for pedestrians to shelter from the passing beasts. Carts normally had to cross rivers by fords, for they were often massive things drawn by a team of cows, oxen or horses, that made ten miles on a good day, provided their wheels did not sink into the ruts of the roadway, or they did not meet another big cart without room to pass. Coaches were rare then and did not normally run in winter (the first coach of Spring was welcomed with flowers). In 1700 it took a week on the Great North Road to get from London to York—it was cheaper and probably more comfortable to walk! Defoe commented that the clay roads of the Midlands were almost impassable to travellers and the sheep and cattle made them 'sloughs and holes which no horse could wade through'. Carts and coaches would skirt roads to avoid getting stuck (the main Exeter road across Salisbury Plain was reputed to be half a mile wide with ruts!). This was the age of the highwayman. Roadside gibbets might creak with the weight of a hanged highwayman, chained lest body-snatchers sell the corpse to medical schools, but the highwaymen were not deterred, for there was slow-moving valuable booty to be had. It was not fear of the gallows, but the increasing speed of road transport that ended the reign of the highwayman.

The turnpike trusts

Parishes, by an Act of Parliament of 1555, were required to look after their own roads. But parishes were often quite small and in any case did not wish to repair roads for the benefit of passing travellers. And so the roads were not properly kept. The bigger parishes elected an unpaid Surveyor of the Highways who could call out villagers for six days' unpaid statute labour on the roads each year. County Magistrates could fine villages at *Quarter Session* courts for failing to maintain roads, but this did not often happen, and most repairs meant merely tipping rough stone into the deeper ruts or holes.

By Defoe's time the idea of empowering a group of people (called a *Trust*) to raise money from local landowners to pay for better road repairs had become popular. Each Trust required a private Act of Parliament because it was given the right to levy a toll on road users to defray expenses, and normally the King's Highway was free for all to use. A gate or bar was placed at each end of the stretch of road covered by the Trust, with a spiked gate for pedestrians, from which the name *Turnpike* comes. A toll-bar cottage stood beside the gate and the toll

A toll-bar cottage in Rutland

keeper had to be tough, for many sought to use the road without paying for it—especially local people who now had to pay for what they had formerly used free of charge. Minor riots, sometimes resulting in the burning of toll gate and cottage, were common and occasionally troops had to be called out. However, because some Trusts did very good work, Parliament continued to create new ones, despite much local opposition. In 1773 a General Turnpike Trust Act simplified the procedure for creating new Trusts and regulated important matters like the provision of bridges and milestones.

Growth of Trusts

1748	150	Trusts
1770	530	,,
1820	1100	,,

Some of the larger, more efficient Trusts maintained road surfaces of such quality that contemporaries were full of extravagant praise—sometimes with justification, for the roads between London and the university towns of Oxford and Cambridge carried the famous 'flying coaches'.

'The Benefit of these turn-pikes appears now to be so great,' wrote Defoe in 1726 'and the People in all Places begin to be so sensible of it, that it is incredible what Effect it has already had upon Trade in the Counties where it is more compleatly finished: even the Carriage of Goods is abated (i.e. reduced) in some Places, 6d per hundred Weight, in some Places 12d per hundred.'

But turnpikes did not always mean better roads. At times, indeed, it meant paying now for struggling through the same old ruts. The Trusts were not obliged to use a fixed part of their receipts on maintenance and many were too small to be effective and either would not or could not pay wages that would attract road builders who knew their business. Macadam (see *page 42*) complained in 1820:

'The *formation* of roads is defective in most parts of the country; in particular the roads round London are made high in the middle, in the form of a roof, by which means a carriage goes upon a dangerous slope, unless kept on the very centre of the road. These roads are repaired by throwing a large quantity of unprepared gravel in the middle, and trusting that, by its never consolidating, it will in due time move towards the sides.'

Some Trusts were simply too poor, others were too short in length and there were sometimes stretches of unimproved road between Trusts, even on the main roads of the country. In 1820 there were only 22,000 miles under the Trusts out of a total of some 125,000 miles of road. Long journeys were frequently expensive because of the numerous tolls. Arthur Young can be forgiven his ill-temper travelling upon a Turnpike to Wigan in 1770:

'I know not, in the whole range of language, terms sufficiently expressive to describe this infernal road. To look over a map, and perceive that it is a principal one, not only to some towns, but even whole counties, one would naturally conclude it to be at least decent; but let me most seriously caution all travellers who may accidentally purpose to travel this terrible country, to avoid it as they would the devil. . . . They will here meet with ruts that I actually measured four feet deep, and floating with mud. . . . I actually passed three carts broken down in these 18 miles of execrable memory.'

Nevertheless, great improvements were made by some Trusts, especially between the 1780s and the 1830s. The growth of traffic on main routeways both increased revenue for the Trusts and necessitated a good surface. Enclosure awards (see *page 29*), requiring local roads to be laid out, often got more local traffic moving, and by the 1780s a great deal of merchandise of all types was being moved. Some Trusts amalgamated and with the bigger revenue were able to afford outstanding surveyors. Gradients were improved for the horses, the main roads frequently taking a bold course away from villages, with only toll-cottages and inns beside them for some miles. In Lancashire and the West Riding (both industrial 'growth areas') new roads were cut to link growing and new towns. Many bridges were built, often without humps, and quite broad enough

for them to be still in use today and carrying now a quantity and weight of traffic of which the builders never dreamt. By 1838 the Trusts were spending £51 a year per mile as against the parishes' £11. It is a little ironic that the Trusts should have been gradually taken over by local authorities—most had been wound up by 1888, the year of the County Council Act (see *page 111*). County Councils are today responsible for roads that are not motorways.

The engineers

The amalgamated Trusts gave a wonderful opportunity and we were fortunate to have at that moment several truly remarkable engineers whose efforts made the principal road network of Britain the best in the world for its time. To some extent a pattern had been set by General Wade's military roads in Scotland, built after the 1715 rebellion, but their gradients were so steep that drovers avoided them. It was different with the first great road builder, John Metcalfe, 'Blind Jack of Knaresborough', who, although blind from the age of six, lived an active life, and as a carter of merchandise knew the ways over the Pennines well from years of tapping with his stick. He gained his first commission in road building in 1765 when he built three miles of the Harrogate to Boroughbridge road. By 1792, the year he retired aged seventy-three, he had built 180 miles of road in the Pennines and several bridges. Despite the difficult country he contrived good gradients for horses. He insisted on good drainage and where the road crossed boggy ground he would 'float' the road on hurdles of brushwood (a technique George Stephenson was to follow, see *page 51*). His construction was first to dig a trough and lay a foundation of large stones with smaller ones above to form the surface which had a steep camber to allow quick drainage into the deep ditches on either side of the road.

These roads earned high praise, but they did not compare with the achievement of Thomas Telford. The son of a Scottish shepherd, he was apprenticed to a stone mason, but journeyed to London in search of work, which he found as a mason building Sir

William Chambers's additions to Somerset House in the Strand. His work and intelligence soon made him an adviser to noblemen interested in building and he was soon launched upon a career that was to make him one of the most outstanding civil engineers of his age. Both he and Metcalfe were examples of self-taught geniuses whose success came from hard work. The early years of the Great Changes are studded with outstanding men who achieved real success without formal technical education. Their early struggles and successes, heavily romanticised by Samuel Smiles in *Self Help* and *The Lives of the Great Engineers*, became the ideal of the Victorians.

Telford had decided views on road-building. His foundations and drainage methods were far superior to Metcalfe's, and he planned his roads as far as possible to avoid any gradient greater than 1:40, and made cuttings and embankments to achieve this. He preferred direct routes, crossing rivers with fine bridges, and avoiding towns as much as possible. In 1786 he was Surveyor of the Shropshire Roads, but his greatest achievement as a road-builder was the London to Holyhead Road. He carried it over the Menai Straits in 1826 by a remarkable suspension bridge with a span of 500 ft, the longest for some years. The bridge had to be 100 ft high because the Admiralty required this for shipping clearance. Telford's roads were magnificent constructions, but they were so expensive that only the wealthiest Trust could afford them. Alone, Telford's roads could never have given Britain her fine road system.

It was John Loudon Macadam who supplied the answer—a cheap but very effective way of road building. He paid most attention to the road surface—provided the road was well drained—and he achieved a firm surface by successive layers of finely graded stones, the top layer being small enough to be held in the mouth. It was not an original method, for the French engineer Trésaguet had used it in 1764, but it was cheap and effective, and soon many roads were 'Macadamised' (tar asphalt—'tar macadam'—did not come in until the 1860s). In 1815 he was Surveyor of the Bristol Roads

and made possible the high speed of coach travel that so pleased Dickens' Mr Pickwick in the 1830s. An advocate of the amalgamation of Trusts into larger, more economical units, Parliament granted him £10,000 for his surface method. As the coaches dashed along his roads on fine days they raised vast clouds of dust—when the motor car came it was vital to tar-macadam the roads!

The coaching industry

The fine new roads created a quite new 'service' industry that has touched the popular imagination (think how many Christmas cards have been inspired by it)—coaching. The coaching inn with its stables, out-houses and (often) low, flat arch, is easily recognised today. In its yard there would be a frantic bustle when the coach arrived; the breakfast room with its great fire—and bay window so that travellers could see when the coach was ready to depart—would fill up, then the coach would be ready and the passengers on top, clinging to their perches, would have to duck as it swung under the arch on its way to the next stop.

Coaching was the product of better road surfaces that allowed for very high speeds. Coach designs and methods of springing them rapidly improved, and the provision of horse teams became an art, for a bad team could overturn a coach when travelling at speed. They had to be of a size and to have the same stride, or the coach would be difficult to steer. The pace setter was usually the first right hand horse—called the parliamentary horse, because it was illegal to gallop with a coach, and the pace setter was therefore a *very* fast trotter. The second pair were heavier 'wheelers' as they were called. Coaches carried six passengers inside and more on top, where the luggage was stored in a great net. They carried the Royal Mail because of their speed (which was itself a pretty safe guarantee against highwaymen). This idea had originated from John Palmer of Bath. The post boy sat at the back of the coach to blow his horn warning of the coach's approach. He might also carry a gun. But the dominating figure, in his huge greatcoat, was the

The yard of a busy coaching inn in the 1820s

coachman, highly skilled and respected: the fastest coaches (which kept to a very close time-table) were driven by men who had great followings of 'fans' who would turn out to watch them hurtle down the road. But if you were travelling 'on top' you had better wrap up well, or you might (as some did) freeze to death in winter.

Travel by coach was not cheap, and for long distances tickets had to be supplemented by money for meals and tips and perhaps a night's stay. Each big coaching inn was a 'stage' (every five to fifteen miles) at which horse-teams were changed: if it were a fast coach, everything had to be ready. A whole service industry grew up round coaching—coach-builders, horse-dealers, inn-keepers, drivers, guards, grooms. The great coaching days were from about 1820 to about 1840, when there were about 3,000 stage coaches using some 150,000 horses and employing about 30,000 people. In 1830, 300 coaches a day passed Hyde Park Corner Turnpike and about forty left down the Brighton Road. Speeds of 10 mph were achieved (greater speeds would have killed horses if maintained for any time), and 100 miles covered in a day. In 1750 it took four days for a coach to reach York from London: in 1836 only twenty hours.

It was a colourful, picturesque period, but damp,

cold and inconvenient for travellers, even inside the coach. However, the stage coaches popularised the idea of travel as a normal thing. It was ironic that at the very moment of their triumph their business was about to be destroyed by railways—although they continued to serve remote areas, if only as 'feeders' to the railway stations. The whole economic life of the country was speeded up by better roads. Commercial travellers went by coach carrying samples, instead of carrying actual goods for sale, like pedlars. Wagons replaced pack-horses, and fast vans brought perishable goods to London—though at a price, for they rarely covered more than twenty-five miles because of the expense of 'staging' with heavier cart horses. Bulky goods were still very difficult to transport.

Steam carriages were experimented with at this time. A French engineer, Cugnot, had devised one in 1769, but it proved a costly failure. William Murdoch (see *page 76*) had experimented with one at Redruth in Cornwall, when representing the firm of Boulton and Watt. But it was Richard Trevithick who produced the first real steam car in 1801, called 'Puffing Devil'. In 1802, he drove a bigger version from Cornwall to London, reaching 12 mph. This proved his invention effective, but people feared steam cars would explode. They were heavy, too,

A late nineteenth-century traction engine

and had to carry a lot of coal or coke, and as their weight damaged road surfaces, they had to pay very heavy tolls. So they were not popular. But Walter Hancock of Stratford in Essex in 1831 ran a steam carriage for hire and in 1827 Goldsworthy Gurney was running a steam coach between London and Bath. Improved models of steam coach, by Summers and Ogle, reached as much as 32 mph. But, like the stage coaches, they were overtaken by railways. However, they survived longer, not only to become steam rollers, but to become the great traction engines of the late nineteenth century, which brewers, iron founders and others concerned in moving very heavy weights where there were neither canals nor railways, found valuable and economical to use. They were important in agriculture, particularly for steam ploughing teams and threshing teams, and they remained popular with fair-ground owners well into the middle of the present century.

River transport

At the same time as Turnpike Trusts were amalgamating and bringing on the great coaching days, river transport and canals were adding a further improvement to the means of transport. England is well served by navigable rivers—the Thames was the busiest, and the Severn and the rivers flowing into the Wash opened up a vast hinterland (Kings Lynn was an important port), but perhaps the fastest growing area was served by the Mersey and the rivers from Yorkshire and the Midlands that drained out at the Humber. Midlands heavy goods would normally go all the way round by the Trent and Humber, and then by sea to London (though perishables would go by road). Throughout the century much money and ingenuity had been expended to improve the rivers and to make them navigable higher up stream. Weirs and sluice gates were constructed to control depth and speed of current, locks were built and rivers straightened. In Cheshire, Lancashire, the West Riding and Derbyshire, the improvements meant that coal and other heavy goods could be moved more easily. In 1755, improvements to the Sankey Brook to connect St Helens with the Mersey culminated in the passing of an Act of Parliament for the building of a canal.

Disadvantages of river transport, and the coming of canals

Improved river transport helped those towns on or near the improved river, but not necessarily those in the countryside beyond. Canals, of course, could go across country and link towns in the same way as roads. Rivers tended to be unpredictable as to their currents so that mud and sand banks could easily shift in bad weather and the water level rise or fall according to the season. Strong currents could make it difficult to pull up stream, and floods could easily wash away the tow path beside the river. Many smaller rivers had fords or low medieval bridges, or mill weirs that simply prevented further navigation, and even the largest rivers tended to meander a good deal. Canals offered an easy answer, for they could be reasonably straight, maintaining a regular level, carrying trade to and from hitherto isolated areas, without low bridges or fords. They could carry heavy goods cheaply and to some sort of schedule, if a slow one—wagoners could never keep to a time-table because they could never be certain of completing a journey without mishap. There was nothing new about canals, but so many were constructed in the years between 1760 and 1830 that a revolution in transport was effected.

It required only an adventurous man to build a canal that paid for itself to release the demand for canal transport both to earn money, improve transport and so increase production. This man

Map 4 Inland waterways

was the Duke of Bridgewater, a romantic and unusual figure who spent much of his time and his fortune on his estates. His coal mines at Worsley were frequently flooded because of bad drainage; his coal could sell at 10d per horse load at the pit head, but in Manchester, where the coal was sent, it cost 1s 8d because of the incredible expense of pack horse transport (40s a ton) or even by river (12s a ton). In 1737 an attempt to improve Worsley Brook failed and Bridgewater adopted an audacious plan of his estate manager, John Gilbert, to link the many channels within the mine into a canal at a set level, and then tunnel out to the hill-side and continue the drainage channel, now a canal, to Manchester. This would drain the mines and supply a continuous water supply to the canal, as well as permitting coal barges to load virtually at the coal face. Gilbert introduced Bridgewater to James Brindley, as the man capable of building the canal, a man with no formal training, but a highly skilled millwright (the eighteenth-century version of the mechanical engineer) who had a reputation for solving difficult problems. He would simply retire to bed until he had hit upon a suitable solution: this was how he hit on the idea of 'puddled clay' as the lining for the canal to ensure that there was no *seepage* (water seeping out of the channel). With Bridgewater and Gilbert in 1759 he visited London and by his direct replies and practical demonstrations rapidly convinced the Parliamentary Committee and an Act was passed permitting the building of the canal for transport of goods and passengers.

The Bridgewater Canal not only launched the canal age; it solved many of the problems later engineers had to face, both in proper drainage and water supply and in the provision of locks. The major work was the Barton Aqueduct (completed in 1761) over the River Irwell, where the canal was carried over the valley, in a stone channel lined with puddled clay, thus avoiding the necessity of a series of complex locks. It was acknowledged as a wonder of the age. Arthur Young noted in 1770, in language betraying that he was unacquainted with common technical terms:

'The effect of coming on to Barton Bridge, and looking down upon a large river, with barges of great burthen sailing on it; and up to another river, hung in the air, with barges towing along it, form altogether a scenery somewhat like enchantment, and exhibit at once a view that must give you an idea of prodigious labour; for the canal is here not only carried over the Irwell, but likewise across a large valley, being banked up on each side in a surprising manner, to form a mound for the water, and the channel also filled up to the usual depth.'

Despite his huge fortune, Bridgewater was almost bankrupted by this canal because of the cost of construction. However, he was able to sell coal at

$3\frac{1}{2}d$ a cwt. at his wharf at Castlefield, Manchester, and was thus able to recoup the cost by selling huge amounts to manufacturers and vast numbers of poor people. Soon the canal paid for itself and brought prosperity to Worsley, where the Duke built many houses for his works people.

In 1762 he was allowed to extend his canal to the Mersey at Runcorn (the extension was opened in 1776, after Brindley's death) and in due course Bridgewater reaped a huge fortune (£100,000 a year by 1800). Many local landlords followed his lead and built canals. Between 1758 and 1801 some £13 million was invested in canal building. Many canals were intended to bring down the cost of coal, and this is why coal production rose so rapidly at this time, for the coal could be transported easily and cheaply most of the year.

But Brindley was more than an engineer. He dreamt of a time when there would be a great national network of canals that would link different parts of the country and so get commerce moving throughout Britain. He planned a 'grand cross', linking the river systems of the Thames, Severn, Mersey and Trent. It was an ideal that was eventually achieved long after his death: but it showed his vision, for most men thought in purely local terms and could not see so clearly the benefit to the country of a national system of waterways.

Another man of vision was Josiah Wedgwood, a potter of genius (see *page 80*) who was concerned to get china clay from Cornwall and flintstone from Hull to his pottery in Stoke, cheaply and in quantity, and to transport his finished pots and china without breakages. With Bridgewater and Brindley he planned the Grand Trunk Canal (opened 1778) linking the Mersey and Trent (he sited his Etruria pottery beside the canal during its construction). This involved digging seventy-six locks and constructing the Harecastle Tunnel, nearly two miles long. This was Brindley's masterpiece (though he did not live to see it finished in 1777). He sank shafts along the route of the tunnel and dug out from them, leaving the shafts to serve as ventilation shafts for the finished tunnel, a technique copied by later engineers, whether for canal or railway. A contemporary merchant wrote:

'Gentlemen come to view our eighth wonder of the world, the subterraneous navigation, which is cutting by the great Mr Brindley who handles rocks as easily as you would plum-pies, and makes the four elements subservient to his will. He is as plain a looking man as one of his own carters; but when he speaks, all ears listen, and every mind is filled with wonder at the things he pronounces to be practicable. . . . The clay he cuts serves for bricks to arch the subterranean part.'

Brindley was not the only great canal builder. Others were Rennie, Jessop, and especially Telford, who, although possessing Brindley's experience (Brindley had to experiment on his own), far surpassed him in his expertise, judgement and daring. Where Brindley's canals meandered to keep to one level as much as possible, Telford's (like his roads) took a definite course, with deep cuttings, embankments, tunnels (as at Sapperton) and aqueducts, the most remarkable of which was the Pont Cysyllte (1795–1805) on the upper reaches of the Ellesmere Canal, where the canal is carried in a continuous iron trough over nineteen great arches. Telford was engaged on many major canals, including the great Caledonian. He was also important for constructing new harbours; for our expanding trade and better internal transport meant that more goods were being shipped. Between 1753 and 1830 some 380 acres of wet docks were dug, notably at Liverpool, Bristol and London, and on the Clyde.

By 1830 most of the canals were complete and we then had some 4,000 miles of canals that had cost some £20 million to build. It had been a remarkable engineering achievement with the locks and tunnels and inclined planes, where barges were carried in a cradle up a steep slope by steam power, and lifts. All this was to be invaluable to the engineers who built the railways. The teams of men who built the canals were called navigators, or 'navvies', and their successors were to build the railways (see *page 54*). The amazing thing was the speed at which the canals were built. Many people, often with no interest in the canal beyond the profit it made, invested in new

Pont Cysyllte Aqueduct, showing the arches and trough

ventures—£60,000 was subscribed in an hour in 1792 for the Rochdale Canal. This flood of capital to build so many canals has been called the *canal mania* of the 1790s. Some of the canals were badly built and lost water from seepage; others lacked an adequate water supply on the highest reaches, so that they were gradually drained dry (Brindley had always ensured a good supply of water to the top stretch of a canal, even at the cost of constructing reservoirs to provide the water). Some canals proved useless; others failed to pay for themselves. By 1811 a canal was either prosperous or not. In 1825, the year of the Stockton to Darlington Railway, the average canal dividend was 6 per cent, but the most successful paid 28 per cent.

The effects of canals

The canal mania gave a great boost to the idea of the small investor parting with a little money, which made a vast sum when many investors contributed —railways were to reap the full advantage of this, and the limited liability company (see *page 85*) was to develop under special laws to safeguard the small investor. Agricultural areas gained especially because heavy loads of manure, lime and marl could now easily be carried, and so could loads of grain. Tramways often fed canals with produce. Coal was the principal raw material transported and the importance of this for the industrial revolution cannot be exaggerated. Iron masters benefited because lime and ore weighed heavy—and so did iron plates. Where loads were heavy and bulky, canals had an immediate advantage over roads, and together they released a massive industrial potential, stimulating trade, influencing the siting of factories and towns—Stourport, Worcestershire, and Shardlow, Derbyshire, were virtually created by the canals. Even before the canal mania, Thomas Pennant commented (1782):

'The cottage, instead of being half covered with miserable thatch, is now covered with a substantial covering of tiles or slates, brought from the distant hills of Wales or Cumberland. The fields, which before were barren, are now drained, and by the assistance of manure, conveyed on the canal toll-free, are clothed with a beautiful verdure. Places which rarely knew the use of coal are plentifully supplied with that essential article upon reasonable terms; and what is of still greater public utility, the monopolisers of corn are prevented from exercising their infamous trade; for, communication being opened between Liverpool, Bristol, and Hull, and the line of canal being through counties abundant in grain, it affords a conveyance of corn unknown in past ages.'

Disadvantages of canals

Brindley's great vision of a national system of canals was never achieved and this in itself was a hindrance to the growing industrial economy of the country. But the greatest disadvantage was the lack of a common design for the canals. Most had been built piecemeal to meet local demand and conditions. They were of different sizes and their locks varied. This was crucial, for the size of the smallest lock determined the size of canal boat that could get through that particular canal. The Midlands canals had small locks which meant narrow barges with living conditions of some squalor; the Yorkshire canals had bigger locks and used bigger barges—too big to penetrate the Midlands systems. Goods travelling north or south had to be reloaded into other craft wherever the different sized canals met, and this increased costs and transit times. Even when two canals were of the same size they did not always communicate, so that there was the same problem of reloading to get from one system to the

The Filton flight of locks

other. The small boats themselves added to transport costs because they could only carry a limited tonnage.

Canals did not increase the speed of transport. Again it was the locks that caused the trouble. They were a cheap and convenient way of changing the canal level, but they could take only one barge at a time and this meant long delays—and fights over who should get into the lock first. Delays meant deliveries suffered and only the Forth Canal carried any quantity of passenger traffic. Lock fees were expensive and added to transport costs. Few canal companies were carriers and most of the barges were run by self-employed bargees or very small barge companies; many of them were inefficient, content to plod along behind an ancient horse at a slow walking pace. The bargee led a forgotten, nomadic life (in the 1850s there were some 44,000 adults and 72,000 children, mostly illegitimate, living on the canals 'innocent of sanitation, religion or education'). Some canal carriers tried to speed travel by using 'fly' boats with frequent changes of strong horses (the great removals firm of Pickfords began in this way) but it proved very expensive. Sometimes the canals were badly maintained, for banks were continually crumbling under the wash from the 'wall of water' pushed up by the bows of barges, and seepage, especially on the upper levels, was common.

Tolls were collected at locks. They provided the income of the canal company and helped to pay for ordinary running expenses and maintenance as well as to pay off the loans that had been raised when the canal was being constructed. Few companies reduced the tolls as the loans were redeemed, indeed some tried to increase them—to such an extent that they provoked resistance from their customers (the Soar Navigation in Leicestershire had to cancel an increase in tolls for this very reason). By 1830, people were looking for cheaper and more efficient forms of transport. This came with the railways, but although they overtook the canals, it was some time before the canals were doomed, and the violent competition between them showed that canals still had a rôle to play. The Third Report on Railway Communication (1840) noted:

'carriers using wagons and vans on roads cannot successfully compete with a railway.... The canals, however, still retain their business, and, having reduced their charges, continue to be used for the carriage of goods, in cases especially where the weight gives them some advantage over railways. As far as regards the heavy merchandise, it appears probable that the canals will always secure the public against any unreasonable demands on the part of the railway companies.'

The railways

Railways produced the most profound change of the nineteenth century, for there was scarcely an area of Victorian life that was not touched by them. The economic and social life of the community was altered beyond recognition and the whole pace of life was affected.

The idea of moving heavy loads along prepared roadways is very ancient. From Tudor times in collieries and quarries (especially in Northumberland and North Wales) 'tramways' were common; these were pathways packed with ashes taking

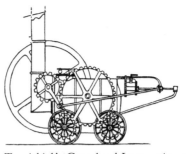

Trevithick's Gateshead Locomotive, 1805

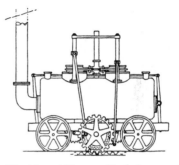

Blenkinsop/Murray Rack Locomotive, 1812

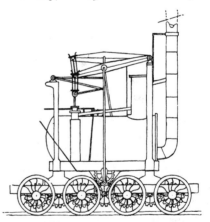

William Hedley's Wylam Locomotive, 1813

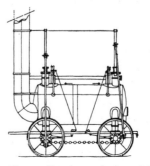

George Stephenson's second Killingworth Locomotive, 1816

wooden rails set in stone 'sleepers'. Horses could pull heavy loads along quite steep inclines in this way. By the 1760s the tramways were being made more level by cuttings and embankments and iron rails were being introduced. Sometimes they were open to the public, who used their own wagons and horses on them, a practice continued by the early railways. Various methods were used to prevent iron wheels slipping off iron rails, the most popular being to cast the rail with a flange that would hold the wheel and allow ordinary cart wheels to be used, so that road vehicles could use the rail tramway without difficulty (the modern method of flat rails and flanged wheels seems to have originated with William Jessop in 1788). But the iron was brittle and frequently broke under heavy weights—it was not until 1820 that John Birkinshaw produced a stronger wrought iron rail that became the standard for the later railways. As late as the 1820s, rail roads were built for the sole purpose of allowing horses to pull wagons along the rails. But as steam locomotives became more reliable, it proved impracticable to continue with horse-drawn wagons on the same rails, and railway companies soon took over the complete responsibility for supplying the wagons for both goods and passenger services on their lines.

By this time the locomotive was already born. Trevithick produced one that ran between the Pen-y-Daren Iron Works and the Glamorgan Canal in 1804, but its weight broke the rails. He made another for the Wylam Colliery in Northumberland. Several other inventors produced locomotives, including William Hedley whose heavy engines ran beside George Stephenson's cottage. George Stephenson was no more the father of the locomotive than James Watt was the father of the steam engine. But by 1814, Stephenson had produced the *Blücher*, a powerful and impressive locomotive.

Stephenson was an engine-wright, without formal education, but an engineer of genius and a man of great character. In 1822 he was asked to survey a route for a railway between Stockton and Darlington and he proposed the use of locomotives, although the management had thought of using only horse-drawn wagons. As it was, part of the line was considered too steep for locomotives and stationary winding engines were used. The line was opened in 1825 and Stephenson's *Locomotion* worked well (although it had to be repaired frequently during its working life). It was only a very local line, used primarily for getting coal away from the collieries of Pease, one of the principal backers. Passenger services were provided by private operators who hired the use of the lines and used their own coaches—normally drawn by horses. The Stockton and Darlington Railway was opened on 27 September: *The Times* reported it only on 4 October, and then only in a report quoted from the *Newcastle Courant*. England was not agog at the new development. Stephenson's second railway changed all this. Again it was another local line, but this time it was between Liverpool and Manchester, two of the most important cities in the country, and it was opened in a blaze of publicity in 1830. The Railway Age had arrived.

Oddly enough, the scheme for this railway (Liverpool–Manchester) arose out of the excessive charges made by the Bridgewater Canal Company. The prospectus of the Railway Company (1824) complained:

'The average length of passage (on the canal), including the customary detention on the wharfs, may be taken at 36 hours. . . . The average charge upon merchandise for the last 14 years has been about 15s a ton. By the projected railroad, the transit of merchandise between Liverpool and Manchester will be effected in four or five hours and the charge to the merchant will be reduced at least one third. . . . It is not that the water companies have not been able to carry goods on more reasonable terms, but that, strong in the enjoyment of their monopoly, they have not thought it proper to do so. . . . *It is competition that is needed.*'

(It was, of course, to be a different story later, when the railways sought to destroy competition from the canals.)

Stephenson began surveying the route in 1824, and for the first time encountered the savage opposition that was to be the common experience of railway builders for the next ten years in those areas where railways were a novelty. Gangs of men (and women) set on the survey teams and broke the theodolites, local farmers used guns on them and much of the work had to be carried on by night. Only on Chat Moss, where the team had to work with boards strapped to their boots for fear of sinking in, were they undisturbed. Stephenson crossed this barrier using the hurdle and rubble technique he had learnt from John Metcalfe.

Since it had not been decided whether to use horses, stationary engines (a steam engine housed beside the line drawing wagons along by a rope) or locomotives (although Stephenson demonstrated that stationary engines were twice as expensive and

far slower and more inconvenient than locomotives), the Directors decided to hold the Rainhill trials (1829) in order to allow locomotives to prove their powers. The *Rocket*, built by Robert Stephenson at his Newcastle works, won the contest and future railways were built for locomotives. But people still preferred other means of travel, as Creevey said in 1829:

'I had the satisfaction, for I can't call it *pleasure*, of taking a trip of five miles in (the locomotive machine), which we did in just a quarter of an hour . . . it is really flying, and it is impossible to divest yourself of the notion of instant death to all upon the least accident happening . . . sparks of fire are

The day compartment of Queen Victoria's train, built in 1869

aboard in some quantity: one burnt Miss de Ros's cheek, another a hole in Lady Maria's silk pelisse, and a third a hole in someone else's gown. Altogether I am extremely glad indeed to have seen this miracle, and to have travelled in it. Had I thought worse of it than I do, I should have had the curiosity to try it; but, having done so, I am quite satisfied with my *first* achievement being my *last*.'

At first public opinion was hostile to the railways. It was not because the companies had to acquire land for their lines—the canal companies had already familiarised people with this practice—but the railway cut a gash upon the countryside that was not disguised with water. Noise, foetid gases, sparks and smoke annoyed people, but above all it was the speed. The *Quarterly Review* (1825) commented:

'What can be more palpably absurd than the prospect held out of locomotives travelling twice as fast as stage coaches?'

People genuinely feared that the human frame could not stand the strain of travelling at a mile a minute (six times faster than the fastest stage coach), and confidently predicted that cows would yield sour milk or go dry at the shock of the sudden appearance of a train. Birds flying overhead would die, smoke would kill trees and make lambs be born black, while years of drainage work would be ruined by the diversion of water courses consequenting on the building of embankments. Game would be destroyed, livestock harmed and the beauty of a parkland permanently disfigured by locomotives. Behind these objections lay a mass of vested interests that fanned the blaze of protest. Canal companies and coaching and turnpike interests united with landowners. They wrecked the first Stockton to Darlington railway bill, and the Fellows of Eton College obliged the Great Western to avoid Eton and Windsor and prevented a station being built at Slough for some years, lest their boys' morals be imperilled. Huge sums had to be paid in compensation and 'inducement' to landowners that made the British lines the costliest to construct in the world (and made it profitable for landowners to

Map 5 English railways about 1850

protest). The purchase of land for the London to Birmingham line cost £6,300 per mile and the Great Western £6,696. When the advantages of railways were realised, the Duke of Bedford restored £150,000 and Lord Taunton £15,000. Those towns which had refused the railway lived to regret it: Stamford remained for a century a dreamy market town, whilst Peterborough became a great railway centre and a prosperous engineering city. Much of the wilder opposition was hushed when the young Queen Victoria chose to go by rail. She recorded of her first journey from Windsor to London, 'half an hour free from dust and heat and I am quite charmed with it'. Soon a special train was built for royal journeys. In place of hostility, the railways were soon to inspire unbounded confidence in Britain's industrial wealth and power. In 1851, E. P. Hood was able to write:

'Within the last half century, there have been performed upon our island unquestionably the most prodigious feats of human industry and skill witnessed in any age of time or in any Nation of the Earth.'

The development of the lines

At first the lines were local but very soon there developed a pattern of lines radiating from London and with a heavy concentration in the West Midlands and in Lancashire. The railways emphasised the importance of the capital and the principal termini were soon established (London Bridge in 1836, and King's Cross in 1850). The two predominant railway builders were Robert Stephenson and I. K. Brunel. The former's major achievement was the London to Birmingham line, which included the Kilsby tunnel. It was a mere 2,398 yards long, not to be compared with Brunel's Box Tunnel (3,195 yards) or Joseph Locke's Woodhead Tunnel (5,280 yards). What makes its construction memorable is the discovery of a quicksand that flooded the mine and took nineteen months of pumping to drain. Had he had access to the Grand Union Canal surveys, his route would have been changed, but the survey was not made available. The line also had the Tring cutting and the Wolverton embankment and cost £5½ million.

Isambard Kingdom Brunel was an engineer of genius whose design for the Clifton Suspension Bridge at Bristol was chosen in preference to one by Telford. In 1833 he was commissioned to build the line from London to Bristol, which involved the construction of Box Tunnel (1836–41) acclaimed a wonder of the age, especially as there was a fairly steep incline towards Bath on the track. For several years, trains stopped so that travellers could travel by coach and reboard the train lower down, in order to avoid the 'dangers of the tunnel'. The line

was opened in 1841 and cost £6½ million, over twice as much as was originally estimated.

The greatest demands for railways came from the North and the Midlands and here Stephenson's lines were built: he followed his father's practice and adopted the 'coal wagon gauge' (4 ft 8½ in) that was common in Northumberland (he also continued to use stone sleepers after wooden ones had been proved to be most effective). This conservatism in approach was not Brunel's way. By careful experiment and calculation he decided that a 'broad gauge' of 7 ft provided the best conditions for speed and comfort. As the northern lines gradually approached the Great Western, it rapidly became obvious that a clash of interests would develop. If once the broad gauge was built in the Midlands, there would be both a duplication of lines and a race for freight and passengers that would mean cutthroat competition that might well endanger lives and property, and ruin the major companies. The very speed of railway development made the clash more likely, and business and financial interests indulged in heavy 'in-fighting' trying to keep Brunel's gauge out of the Midlands.

Stephenson's 'standard gauge' won the race to build the line from Birmingham to Gloucester (although Brunel had reached Gloucester from Bristol), and Brunel demanded a trial of the two gauges. The two tracks between Paddington and Didcot and York and Darlington were chosen and the broad gauge justified everything Brunel had said in its favour as superior to the 'standard'. But to widen the standard would mean broadening all the track already laid and reconstructing tunnels, bridges, embankments and cuttings, whereas the broad gauge could easily be converted by introducing an inside rail. So the Gauge Act of 1846 required the standard gauge to be used in all future main railways, although the Great Western maintained its own gauge, whilst introducing the interior rail. Now rolling stock and engines of both gauges could run over the broad gauge and Britain had the advantage of a national system of railways (unlike her canals). The last broad gauge train ran in 1892 from Paddington to Penzance.

The navvies

The motorways of today are largely built by machine, but the railways, for all the movement of earth they involved, were largely built by man-power. This was provided by the navvies, skilled labourers and bricklayers (for lining tunnels and building bridges). They were well paid, but the life was rough and nomadic and the work dangerous. Drunkenness and debauchery that terrorised the villages of rural England was the result.

The navvies were generally employed by a contractor for a specific job—a cutting or a section of line. These contractors (many of the smaller ones were former navvies) often made fortunes, and some, like Thomas Brassey or Samuel Morton Peto, were noted for their concern for their men and for safety precautions. The navvies were often local men (especially for the Great Western, which offered a great relief from rural poverty), but Scots and Irish labourers were common in the North. Local accommodation was inadequate for them, and they lived and slept as best they could (those who constructed the Woodhead Tunnel built stone huts for themselves). Since they were often some way from shops and especially since they were hard drinkers, truck shops (see *page 98*) were common and the truck system much abused.

As with mining, the nature of their work made them something of a race apart, and few 'outsiders' dared investigate their conditions, although there were some missionaries. Fights were frequent, they terrorised the neighbourhood, exchanged their women-folk and had wild orgies on pay days; but there was a certain comradeship, they helped each other and ran sick clubs for themselves and their fellows. Elementary precautions were often ignored (especially in blasting tunnels) so deaths were frequent; but it was worse for the navvy who had an accident—a disabled man would be discarded without compensation.

The railway mania

The railway age is generally thought to have ended in the 1860s, but nearly as many miles of line were built after then as before: but it is one thing to build 10,000 miles of track in a generation that had never known the railway nor witnessed construction on such a scale before, and quite another, merely to add 10,000 miles to tracks already laid. During the Great Changes people got used to completely new conditions remarkably quickly, so that by the 1870s the railway had become a part of daily life. For this reason we still think of the second generation of the nineteenth century, the generation of the stage

Navvies beside their railway workings

coach, as the railway age. A vast amount of money was invested in railways by both great and small—witness to the tremendous prosperity of Victorian England (see *graph 6*). There were in fact two 'manias' or 'booms', 1835-7 and 1844-7, when the money invested rose to fabulous sums.

Each of the booms was followed by a new and disturbing feature—a severe trade slump, partly aggravated by bad harvests, but largely due to a sudden loss of confidence. The slump of 1847 was remarkably severe and developed into the first world-wide financial crisis of the modern era, involving both U.S.A. and Europe—it was no coincidence that 1848 was the 'year of revolutions'. But, unlike the major slumps of the twentieth century, that of 1847 was followed by an amazingly rapid recovery, illustrating the bouyant economy of the period.

Very rapidly local sources of finance were over-taken by the resources of the London Stock Exchange, which became the centre of railway speculation. It was not only for efficiency and to attract more freight and passengers, but also to attract more investment that the early local lines tended to amalgamate. The promoters of big national rail systems were not thinking of the national good, they were concerned to make a fortune. Chief amongst them was George Hudson, a York draper, who came to be called the 'railway king', for at one time he controlled a fifth of the railway system of the country. Such great power enabled peculiar pressure to be put on Parliament during the 'battle of the gauges'. But Hudson's financial management was unsound: he paid high dividends out of capital, not profits, and purchased the shares of rival companies with the capital of others. In the

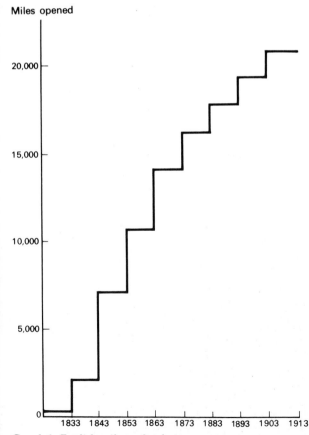

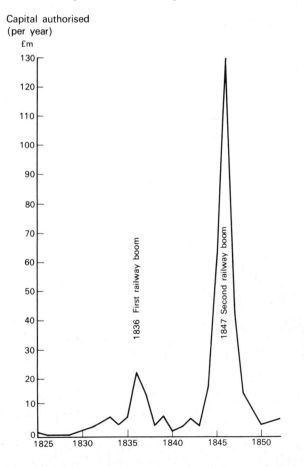

Graph 6 English railway developments

great slump of 1847 his railway empire was shown to be a house of cards and many small investors lost their money. An enquiry exposed his methods, and he chose to live abroad.

Believing that monopoly in any form was inherently bad (a view we regard as quite mistaken), Parliament was concerned at the tendency towards amalgamation. Lord Seymour's Railway Act (1839) set up in 1840 a Railway Department at the Board of Trade to supervise railway companies (especially their safety regulations) through Government inspectors. W. E. Gladstone (later to be a great prime minister) in 1844 was responsible for an important Railway Act which made it possible for the State to take possession of private companies if within twenty-one years (by 1865) they had failed to comply with the Board of Trade regulations. The threat of 'nationalisation' was never brought into effect and, indeed, it is surprising to come across it at this date (see *page 248*). However, the companies set up a Railway Clearing House that from 1850 onwards arranged conditions of through-carriage between different lines.

Gladstone was also interested in passenger travel. Not all railway companies consented to carry passengers because of the additional costs required. On the passenger lines, first-class fares were high, for the relative comfort (especially compared with coach travel); second-class passengers had fewer comforts, but normally a roof over their heads (although one company provided neither windows nor proper sides); third-class passengers frequently travelled in open trucks, sometimes on trains composed of empty wagons and livestock wagons, for third-class carriages were not always coupled to passenger trains. Some of their trucks actually distintegrated on the track. Time tables were rarely published 'lest it place an obligation on the companies' as one director put it, and the first edition of Bradshaw's famous railway guide (1839) gave no indication of times of arrival. Gladstone's 1844 Act provided for a 'parliamentary train' requiring each company to run one train a day along the length of their lines at a charge of 1d a mile. This meant cheap travel was possible for those in lower income groups —Gladstone often travelled 'third-class' himself in order to test conditions. The Act itself indicated what had been going on:

'Such train shall travel at an average speed not less than 12 mph for the whole distance . . . including stoppages. The carriages in which passengers shall be conveyed . . . shall be provided with seats, and shall be protected from the weather.'

In this way rail travel for poorer people was made bearable—that it should require an Act of Parliament is a shrewd comment both on people's attitudes and on the conditions of travel prevailing in other means of transport.

The Welland Viaduct

The impact of the railways

The railways epitomised the Great Changes. Their sheer physical impact, surpassing that of the canals, not only announced that the profession of Civil Engineer had arrived, but seemed to alter the whole aspect of the countryside—'your railroad mounds, vaster than the walls of Babylon', complained Ruskin. Who can doubt that the Victorians were fascinated by the new monuments they built—the great embankment at Chippenham, for example, or the Mersey viaduct at Stockport. Today the Severn, Medway and the new Forth bridges excite far less notice.

From the first men were aware that they were experiencing more than a transport revolution. An observer of the Liverpool to Manchester line in 1830 commented:

'Parliamentary Reform must follow soon after the opening of this road. A million persons will pass over it in the course of this year, and see that hitherto unseen village of Newtown; and they must be convinced of the absurdity of its sending two members to Parliament, whilst Manchester sends none.'

Rail travel brought the classes together, not only because they mingled on station platforms, but because from train windows working class housing (especially that near to marshalling yards) could be observed by the upper classes, perhaps for the first time. 'I fear it has a very dangerous tendency to equality,' complained Lord de Mowbray in Disraeli's *Sybil*.

Speed of travel caught popular imagination, for the whole pace of life was affected. People, goods, letters could move more quickly and in greater quantity than ever before, and this simply increased the number of things that could be done in a day. Rowland Hill persuaded the Government in 1840 to adopt the penny postage, instead of charging the receiver of a letter according to the distance carried. It lost money at first, but in a few years paid dividends for the Post Office and for commerce; and it was made possible by railways. So was the movement of police and troops, as the Chartists were to discover (see *page 163*). In war, the side that commanded the railways won—as witness the American Civil War and the Austro-Prussian War, in the 1860s.

To us the pace of their life was slow, but to them it was still a novelty that was either exhilarating or exasperating—Frederick Harrison complained: 'we are whirled about, and hooted around, and rung up as if we were all parcels, booking clerks or office boys.' Standard time was introduced. The appearance and nature of towns was changed. As passenger services developed, the suburb was created and the commuter 'city worker' appeared, travelling his twenty miles to work in half an hour. The agricultural market town that accepted the railway became a thriving expanding area, those that refused railways ossified. Swindon and Derby suddenly spread outwards as vast railway towns, and Crewe was transformed from a village of 203 in 1841 to a town of 18,000 in 1871.

Cheap day tickets, as well as the 'parliamentary train', meant that poorer people were able to enlarge their lives by occasional trips, and, as working class purchasing power increased, the great seaside resorts like Blackpool were created, and middle-class resorts like Bournemouth grew in size. Scarborough became the Brighton of the North. The new fashion of a holiday beside the sea for the whole family became possible, even for the lower middle classes. Public schools owed a great deal to railways, which permitted big schools to be established in remote areas. Travel had become an everyday thing.

Provinces were no longer strangers to each other and the old slow rhythm of country life was affected. The clock played an increasingly dominant part in daily life—trains had to run to a rigid schedule. For the first time, farm labourers in the west country became aware of alternative work and of different rates of pay. Canon Girdleston at the cost of great unpopularity from squires and farmers, arranged for distressed agricultural labourers to move to higher wage areas:

'Many of the peasants of North Devon were so ignorant of the whereabouts of the places to which they were about to be sent (in Kent and in northern counties), that they often asked whether they were going "over the water"!'

It was now that the exodus from the countryside began. At the same time, railways made 'high farming' possible (see *page 37*) enlarging the market both for perishable foods (speed was the vital factor here) and for other products. Even livestock could easily be carried quickly over many miles. Market gardening and fruit growing expanded, and fish ports like Grimsby became important. The building trade was greatly assisted, and Midland bricks and Welsh slate produced the rash of nineteenth-century housing visible today. Traditional local materials were now used only for expensive building.

'From 1850 onwards, every kind of material was poured on to the unprotesting soil: harsh red bricks, sometimes glazed; in the north, yellow-green brick from Three Counties near Hitchin; slates, pantiles, green tiles; stucco, artificial stone and concrete,' complained an historian of Middlesex, where the changes were first apparent.

The railways created a vast fund of employment, and increased production in vital industries like iron and heavy engineering both for the rails and the rolling stock. Coal production soared, both for industry and locomotives and for the domestic market—by 1880, six out of nine million tons of London coal came by rail. The great bulk of merchandise that could be carried greatly enlarged both the market and the production of consumer goods.

There was an expansion of light as well as heavy industries; railways helped to make us the 'workshop of the world'. Canal companies tried to compete by cutting freight rates (the Erewash Canal, Nottingham cut its rates for coal from 1s to 4d a ton, the Grand Junction from 9s 1d to 2s 0¼d a ton for coal from Birmingham to London). But it was in vain and the canals in due course were taken over.

In business and commerce, railways hastened the coming of full limited liability (see *page 85*) and helped to familiarise the small investor with the Stock Exchange, thus releasing vast stores of capital for investment. Experience in forming and running very big companies was rapidly gained. George Hudson, for all his faults, ushered in the company promotion ideas that were to lead to the commercial giants of this century. Abroad, our railway builders earned us vast sums (Brassey constructed nearly 4,500 miles in three continents) which strengthened our economic predominance and laid good foundations for the future. The hinterland of ports was immeasurably increased and big harbour works began. Together with the steam ship, a revolution in the speed and quantities of world trade was begun; and it was one that damaged our farming (see *page 177*).

The steamship

The traditional wooden sailing ship was predominant until the 1870s. This was because the nineteenth century sailing ship (especially the clipper, first developed in U.S.A.) was fast and profitable, partly because early steamships were unreliable and partly because of natural conservatism. But in the 1870s even the clippers, at the peak of their achievement, were overtaken by the superior technology of the steamship.

William Symington had launched a double-hulled paddleboat on the Forth-Clyde canal in 1788, but it was in 1802 that the first effective steamship was launched, on the same canal. It was the *Charlotte Dundas* and had a paddle-wheel at the stern. The boat worked well and Lord Bridgewater ordered eight such vessels for his canal; however, the fear of the great wash undermining the canal banks destroyed a future in canals for the steamboat. So it is Robert Fulton (also a Scot) who is often credited with being the father of the steamship with his *Clermont* paddleboat that had its trials on the Hudson River, U.S.A. in 1807. Many different types appeared in the next twenty years, including Henry Bell's *Comet* (1812), but they were built for

One of the attempts to launch Brunel's steamship the Great Eastern

the smooth waters of big rivers, not the open seas. Also, they consumed a great deal of coal and so had little cargo space. But bigger boats were being built, although they carried sails as well (as much for extra leeway as for lack of confidence in the engines!). The *Savannah*, that made the first paddleboat crossing of the Atlantic (1819) used her engines for only eighty hours in twenty-four days, but the *Sirius* made the crossing in 1838 carrying heavy cargo and using her engines throughout.

Brunel was interested in the steamship: his idea was to continue his great railway line to Bristol by constructing a great steamship to cross the Atlantic. His first was the *Great Western* twice the size of the *Sirius*, built to conventional design with a wooden hull. Between 1838 and 1846 she did the crossing in a fortnight each way, regardless of contrary winds. His second ship, *Great Britain* (1843) incorporated two big changes: she was driven by propellers instead of paddle-wheels, and her hull was of iron (so that she proved indestructable when she lay a

wreck on the Irish coast in 1846). Brunel's third ship was the incredible *Great Eastern* begun in 1854 at Millwall, London. After weeks of effort to launch her, she eventually launched herself on an exceptionally high tide in 1858. For some years she was the biggest ship afloat. She had four screw engines and four paddle engines with a crankshaft weighing forty tons (the biggest forging then seen, for which Nasmyth's steam hammer (see *page 75*) was used). But she was a commercial failure, partly because there were as yet too few passengers continually crossing the Atlantic to fill her 4,000 berths each time, partly because no solution was then available for the problem of running her engines economically. However, she proved a valuable means of laying the Atlantic cable in 1866. (After an inglorious period as a coal-bunker in the Falkland Islands, she has been restored as a museum, moored permanently at Bristol.)

Steamers had obvious advantages over sail, for they could run to a regular schedule and were not becalmed. The Post Office, by awarding contracts to steamship companies to carry mail to various parts of the Empire for these reasons, laid the foundation of several great ocean liner companies —the Cunard Steamship Company (1839) gained the contract for the North Atlantic mails, which was worth a million pounds a year by 1860. Iron hulls, as John Laird of Birkenhead showed in 1828, were stronger and lighter than wooden ones of the same size (they became even lighter when made of steel, after the Bessemer and Siemens processes had made steel cheaper and available in bulk in the 1870s). They could be made much bigger, too, and lasted longer than wooden ships—but they were slow to develop and it was not until the 1850s that iron replaced wood, and the screw the paddle. The first steam ships were propelled by paddles, but the advocates of screw propulsion were anxious to show the superiority of their method. At last the Admiralty held a trial (1843) to determine which method was the best. A paddleship and a screw-driven ship were tied together and ordered to steam away in opposite directions. The screw succeeded in pulling the paddle after her at a speed of two knots and this settled the matter conclusively. By the 1890s steel had replaced iron. But the need to carry sufficient coal obliged the building up of a succession of coaling stations around the world, and at first reduced the space available for cargo. In 1854 John Elder's compound engine reduced fuel consumption by half, thereby increasing cargo-space, and in 1881 the triple expansion marine engine proved a great advance in power and fuel economy. In 1884 Parsons produced the steam turbine, a revolutionary engine that was capable of the unprecedented speed of 34 knots. Against such speeds the sailing clipper could not compete, although it had reached a peak of technical development and efficiency. The opening of the Suez Canal in 1869 also contributed to the demise of the clipper, for sailing-ships had to be pulled through it because of contrary winds, and thus the shortest route to the East and India was really closed to them.

The building of iron and then steel ships meant a shift of ship building from its traditional sites in the

This Punch *cartoon of a coffin ship shows the ship owner 'dicing with death'*

South to the industrial North with its coal, iron and mechanical expertise: Clydeside, Tyneside, the Mersey and the Durham coast, unheard of in the days of wooden ships, were now the giant shipyards. London never recovered her ship building after the slump of 1866.

To finance the building and sailing of big ships, large firms were necessary that required first-rate management as well as considerable investment, so that something of a revolution in the running of the shipping industry came with the steamship. Specialist marine engineering firms developed whose expertise was to be an example to the world. Bigger ships meant bigger docks, and here Britain had a considerable advantage over continental ports at first: at the moment that the steamship was winning its fight for recognition, our future rivals, U.S.A. was engaged in Civil War, and still producing splendid sailing ships, because of the supply of timber on her Atlantic coast, Japan was only just

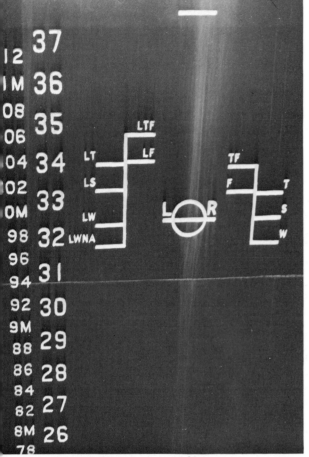

Plimsoll line markings on a cargo ship

countries could take advantage of new methods, too.

The great emigration of people from Europe to U.S.A. was only possible in so short a time because of the size and speed of the steamship. However, it was often no easy thing to travel the high seas without money. Many emigrants had barely enough money to pay for the bare 'steerage' ticket, so that they would begin the voyage with no resources only to find that their ticket did not include food during the voyage. In sailing-ships this could be simply the cause of death, for there were cases of starvation on board, even when ships were not held up. The plight of steerage passengers was such that the Passenger Act was passed in 1855 which provided for Government inspectors to ensure that there was not overcrowding and that passengers had sufficient food to last them the voyage. Conditions were better on the steamships simply because voyages were quicker. To some extent, too, the steamship helped to limit another abuse, that of the 'coffin ship' that did so much to make death by drowning a common fate for sailors in the early nineteenth century. Samuel Plimsoll devoted his public career to securing legislation to end both the 'coffin ship' and the over-loading of ships. Ship owners, many of them small owners with perhaps only one or two boats, were content to send out unseaworthy ships that were often overloaded, but were also heavily insured, in order to get the maximum profit. If the ship reached its destination, it would earn a good profit, if it foundered the insurance company would pay the owner (not the families of the drowned sailors). If sailors refused to sail in a ship because it was unseaworthy or overloaded, they could be (and were) sent to jail. Plimsoll's campaign was bitterly opposed by ship owners on the grounds that their profits would be ruined and our competitors would gain our trade if restrictions were imposed. But, after a great struggle, the Merchant Shipping Act was passed in 1876, allowing for Government regulation of shipping and the placing of a 'Plimsoll line' at the maximum loading point of the ship. As sail gave way to steam, the evil of the rotten ship grew less.

beginning to modernise, and Germany was engaged on wars of unification until 1870. For this reason we had at first no great competitor and so became ship builders to the world and we held nearly half the world tonnage at the end of the century. This earned us considerable sums of foreign currency. However, our competitors soon wiped away our advantage.

The steamship completed the railway revolution by releasing a massive increase in world trade which the sailing-ships were not capable of carrying. The expansion of trade increased our prosperity and the import of great quantities of raw materials and food reduced the cost of living. Every one benefited from this in terms of cheaper goods and more employment, but, of course, the farmers suffered and manufacturers soon came to realise that other

5 · The Great Changes:
the industrial inventions utilised

The most obvious of the Great Changes was the Industrial Revolution, the transformation of industry from small to large-scale. It meant the decline of old and the appearance of new industrial areas, and the growth of huge towns where before were tiny villages. Above all, it meant the appearance of factories where often large numbers of workers were compelled to work set hours at repetitive tasks, servicing machines that *mass produced* great quantities of goods to be sold all over the world. It meant, in effect, the change of the economy of the country from one based on agriculture, to one based on industry.

But the industrial revolution is no simple process: it is a tangled web, and we have already found some of the threads that made it. The demographic explosion created both a labour force and a ready market for cheap goods, and the expanding overseas trade extended that market and brought in more raw materials. The growing wealth provided the money necessary for investment in machinery and the improvements in transport made mass production economic by allowing cheap distribution of raw materials and finished goods. As markets grew, both at home and abroad, many inventions were produced to reduce costs by producing goods at greater speed with fewer workers.

The industrial revolution depended on these inventions. But they are only a part of the whole process: in a sense they are the last threads in the web. An invention that works is only valuable if it can be put to effective use. Leonardo da Vinci invented many marvellous things, even a tank and a flying machine; but few of them were taken up. If he had invented a lunar space-ship, it would have mattered little, because no one could have made it work for 400 years. It is not the invention, but its exploitation that matters.

For this reason we cannot date the industrial revolution from the appearance of an important invention. We must look for the time when the invention was applied in a way that really changed things. Economic historians distinguish between *invention* and *innovation*, for innovation, the applying of the invention on a big scale, is the important thing. There was a gap between the inventions that made technological change possible, and the time when they were applied on a big scale by businessmen (*entrepreneurs*) who grasped their significance and exploited them. Sometimes this time gap was short: it depended on circumstances. The French Wars (1793–1815) probably held back innovation in a number of fields; in other cases, exploiting an invention had to await technological changes; sometimes the sheer magnitude of the changes took time to accomplish. Innovation was probably most apparent in the Railway Age.

The domestic system

Before the nineteenth century, nearly all industrial processes were small-scale and carried on at home or in tiny forges. Eventually, this was swept away by the *factory system* (although the boot and shoe industry around Northampton was domestic until the 1890s), and because of the ugly, smoky industrial world that resulted, many writers began to look back to a time when they imagined people lived pleasant lives in pretty villages, taking a craftsman's pride in their work. When we read of the suffering of workers in nineteenth century towns, it is easy for us to fall into the same error ourselves. The reality of life for workers in pre-industrial Britain could be very harsh indeed, even when many were able to gain some money and food from part-time farming and so to some degree were cushioned against times of bad trade.

There were many ways in which the domestic system of industry could be organised. The most familiar pattern was in the wool districts of Gloucestershire and Wiltshire, where fine cloths were produced. The weavers usually owned their looms, and worked at them often in the upper storeys of their cottages (you can recognise the weavers' cottages from the windows). But they were dependent on merchants who visited them to leave a supply of wool sufficient to be worked into a set length of cloth. On his next visit the merchant would leave more wool and take the finished cloth to sell in the market towns. But *he* decided the price he paid the weaver. Indeed, he controlled the whole process of production, for he had the money to buy the wool the weaver needed. The weaver was probably more exploited than the factory hand. He was merely the *out-worker* of the merchant, compelled to do the merchant's bidding. Ill-feeling was widespread and sometimes there were riots over the prices paid. There was a touch of class war, too, between the wealthy clothier who considered himself a gentleman, and the isolated poor weavers dependent on his agents for their livelihood. In 1757 Dean Tucker observed:

'The master . . . however well disposed himself, is continually tempted by his situation to be proud and over-bearing, to consider his people as the scum of the earth, whom he has a right to squeeze whenever he can; because they ought to be kept low and not to rise up in competition with their superiors.'

Weavers complained of the prices offered; merchants complained that weavers filched materials. The weavers said merchants deliberately left less wool than was needed for the piece to be worked, and then imposed a fine for dishonest or poor work. If he felt inclined the merchant might pay in kind, not cash, and the weaver, up to his ears in debt to the merchant, could not refuse. Few merchants did not reap the full reward of their favourable position, while weavers, isolated in small villages, had few opportunities to present a united front. Bad labour relations and exploitation did not come in with the factory system. And what was true of the West of England cloth industry was probably more true of the *nailers* and *filers* of the west Midlands, engaged

on producing nails by hand, of the hosiery workers of the east Midlands, and the knife makers of Sheffield. However, the weavers of the wool and worsted areas of the West Riding of Yorkshire (many of whom were also part-time farmers) had greater independence and may well have been more prosperous than elsewhere.

If trade were bad, or he fell ill, the domestic worker had no money to tide him over: he got into worse debt. But the merchant had money and could store finished cloth until the market was favourable. He was cushioned against bad trade, for the burden of it fell immediately on his outworkers with their idle looms, particularly where the weavers actually owned the looms, for then the loss from idle machines was theirs and not his. It was an improvement for workers to be in a factory when trade was slack, for the owner would keep his machinery running at a loss, producing for stock. In this way, his workers got short-time until the market picked up, and he bore the expense. The domestic system market was limited and there was a constant danger of over-production bringing prices down: this was no longer a problem in the railway age. Changes of fashion would ruin domestic workers, for their range of product was narrow (when men stopped wearing knee breeches the Leicester stockingers were badly hit). The factory system allowed much more flexibility.

Hours were not regular in the domestic system. If the agent were late bringing wool or iron rods for nails, valuable production time was lost, which meant more debts. But when materials were to hand, a worker decided his own hours. Many worked up to eighteen hours a day for three or four days, so that they could earn enough to relax in a drunken orgy at the weekend. This was the origin of *Saint Monday* (and even of Saint Tuesday!). Small wonder, therefore, coming from such a tradition, they should find the tyranny of the factory clock an intolerable burden. But they got rapidly used to it.

Children were exploited under the domestic system, working long hours (and this continued after hours and conditions for children in factories had been regulated). Their parents were severe task-masters and they set them to work almost as soon as they could walk, helping with simple tasks. Children too small to help were a nuisance to busy mothers, who, 'having no time to attend to their families, or even to suckle their offspring, freely administer opium in some form or other to their infants, in order to prevent their cries interfering with the protracted labour by which they strove to obtain a miserable subsistence'. As a teenager the child would be apprenticed to a trade for seven years and be in danger of continued exploitation, if his master were oppressive. As he aged, prematurely, even as a master-craftsman (especially if his eyesight failed him) he might well end his days in the parish poor house. 'They all go there when they cannot see to work,' commented William Hutton, who began life as a stockinger but ended as a famous eighteenth-century Birmingham bookseller.

Domestic workers in growing towns were as badly housed as factory workers. In 1840, a Government report on distress among hand-loom weavers noted:

'With regard to health, having seen the domestic weaver in his miserable apartments, and the power loom weaver in the factory, I do not hesitate to say that the advantages are all on the side of the latter.'

That same year a report on the nailers stated:

'I never saw one abode of a working family which had the least appearance of comfort or of wholesomeness, while the immense majority were of the most wretched and sty-like description.'

These are extreme examples, for life was not always so hard, but they serve to show that stories of a 'merrie Englande' which the factory system destroyed are fables. It is worth remembering that the appalling conditions in early factories were the more bearable because workers were already very well used to distress—and that the men who grew wealthy from the sweat of factory workers, unlike the prosperous merchant of an earlier day, did much to improve the workers' lot.

Changes in textiles

For centuries wool was our principal industry, but by 1800 two things were happening. First the cotton industry was growing at so amazing a rate that it came to dominate English textiles for a century and more, and secondly, the traditional textile area of East Anglian worsteds was disappearing and the West of England cloth industry was shrinking, whilst Lancashire and the West Riding of Yorkshire were growing rapidly. The development of the power-driven machinery in factories made this possible. The first such factory, using water-power, was the Lombe brothers' silk factory at Derby (1719). Other silk mills were opened in Macclesfield and Congleton, but the silk industry remained small-scale and Lombe's importance is that the organisation of his mill was closely followed by Arkwright some fifty years later.

It is difficult to explain why cotton raced ahead. One reason is that more raw cotton became available as the Southern States of U.S.A. expanded their cotton fields using slave labour, and this supply increased phenomenally when Eli Whitney, in 1793, developed a cotton gin which speeded up the cleaning of the raw cotton. Another is that the spinning section of the work was extremely slow and used a lot of domestic labour, indeed it had scarcely changed since medieval times; but a series of inventions (often the product of a long line of technical improvements) revolutionised the whole spinning industry. Although the inventions could be used for most of the textile industry (wool, silk, linen or cotton), they were taken up first in the cotton industry. Perhaps this was because it was a relatively new industry and so had far easier opportunities for growth; but the most likely explanation is the simplest—once the problem of the supply of raw cotton and the problem of the speed of spinning and weaving in quantity had been overcome, there were better entrepreneurs in the cotton industry, capable of realising the potentialities of the situation.

However, the first invention that is generally recorded, John Kay's *flying shuttle* (1733), speeded

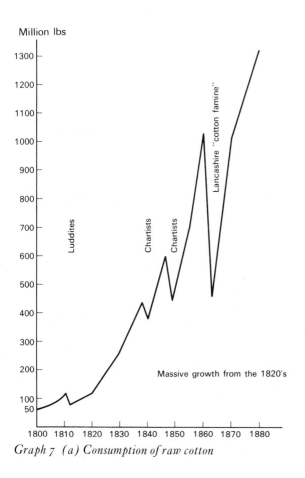

Graph 7 (a) Consumption of raw cotton

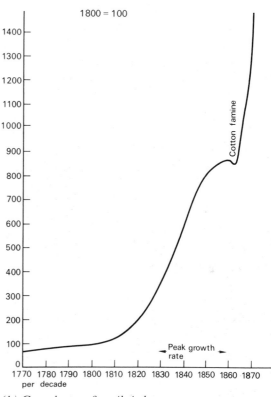

(b) Growth rate of textile industry

the process of weaving, and thus accentuated the difference between weaving and spinning. It allowed the weaver to pass automatically his shuttle from side to side of the loom, and as it could easily be applied to broad looms, it meant an increase in broad cloth. It also meant that a quicker way of spinning was urgently needed. In 1738 Lewis Paul developed a *roller spinning* machine, although it was not fully taken up until the end of the century. In 1748 he and John Wyatt developed a *carding* machine (the process of preparing cotton fibre for spinning). Then, in 1764 came James Hargreaves's *spinning jenny* (patented 1770), which allowed a spinner to spin several threads at once. Here was the answer to the bottle-neck that had developed in spinning and was holding back the weaving industry. Later versions of the machine added greatly to the number of threads that could be spun, and the machine was widely adopted—some 20,000 were in use by 1788.

But none of these machines brought in the factory system, for they were all used by domestic workers. Furthermore, cotton goods remained coarse, for cotton thread was only strong enough to carry the warp (the perpendicular threads), the weft (the horizontal threads in the cloth) being linen. The real change came with Richard Arkwright's *water frame* (1768), a water-powered spinning machine which produced a thread strong enough for the warp as well as the weft. This made cotton goods virtually a new product. But the carding process was still done by hand and so was slow and costly; in 1775, after many others had tried, Arkwright produced a *rotary carding machine*. The mass production of cotton yarn was now possible, and in 1779 the revolution in spinning was completed by Samuel Crompton's *mule*, which spun many threads at once, but as fine and as strong as any that could be bought in the East. British cotton goods could now compete in the quality market as well as in the

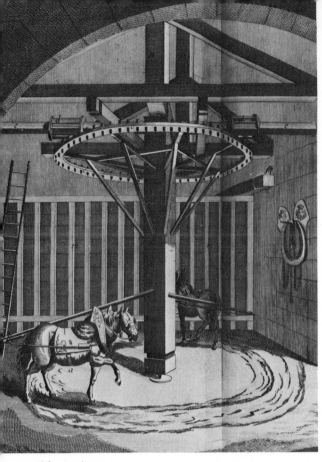

A horse gin

working-class market—for here a revolution in cleanliness resulted; working class women now discarded the petticoat quilted with horsehair and leather, 'worn till they drop to pieces from dirt', in favour of cotton garments.

Conditions were ripe for mass production, too. Indeed, Arkwright's *water frame* brought in the factory system for cotton spinning, first at Nottingham, where a horse gin provided the motive power, then at Cromford (1771) using water power. With Jedediah Strutt, he opened a factory at Belper (1773) and in 1780 he opened the biggest textile factory to that date at Manchester, employing 600 people. Water power was the motive force of the new factories, so they tended to be sited near swift streams that did not slacken in dry summers (for example in the dales of the Pennines and in Southern Scotland). Sometimes the water wheel was of gigantic size—one at Bolton was 62 ft across and cost £5,000: it was a rare thing for a common weaver to become a big mill-owner! Soon, the steam-engine (see *page 73*) provided the power, so

that mills were sited on coal measures, and this confirmed the development of the southern Pennines as the new textile area of the country.

The bottle-neck was now, it seemed, in weaving. The difficulty was the complex nature of the loom which did not easily lend itself to water or steam power. In 1784 the Rev. Edmund Cartwright produced his *power loom*, which proved it was possible to use water, and later steam, power for weaving. But the machine was crude and it was some years before it could be used on any commercial scale. Also, the weavers resisted the idea of factories, preferring the relative freedom of the domestic system. Indeed, with so much machine-spun yarn available, the hand-loom weavers entered a 'golden age'. Young men were encouraged to become skilled weavers because of the good money that was earned (in 1811 there were some 200,000 weavers). Thirty years later, they were to pay for their heady prosperity. As the power loom was brought into factories, especially after 1820, weavers found it progressively more difficult to compete and their numbers dropped steadily after 1830 (see *graph 8*). It comes as no surprise to find the surviving, suffering hand-loom weavers among the more obvious recruits to Chartism (see *page 163*).

The fate of the weavers shows how slow was the process of transforming the textile industry into factory production, and it is a warning against dating the industrial revolution too early. (Indeed, in 1830 the great majority of all workers were still outside the factory system.) The period of maximum growth in textiles was between 1830 and 1860 (see *graph 7b*): it was then that steam power replaced domestic labour among the weavers and brought textile production within the factory walls. It was a very favourable moment for the mill owners. They purchased new machines: the old, out-dated, slow hand-looms belonged to the weavers. The weavers lost their independence and were left with obsolete machines as well. It was at this moment, too, that the home market was expanding rapidly because of railway transport and the rising prosperity of the country. In the second half of the century the cost of machines rose, and so did that of labour and of

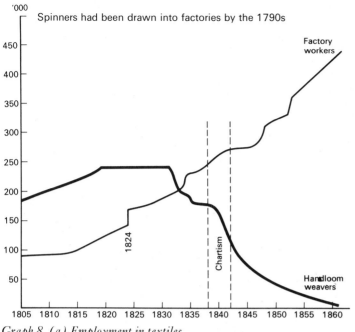

Graph 8 (a) Employment in textiles

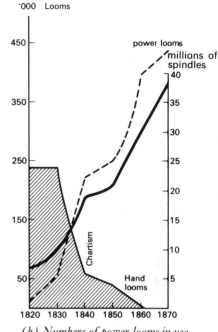

(b) Numbers of power looms in use

raw material: it was then that overseas markets, especially the Empire, became essential to our expanding production (see *page 174*).

But, however remarkable the growth of cotton, we must not exaggerate its place in the *national income* (a convenient measure used by economists to include all goods and services available at any one time). In 1811 it produced only about 4·5 per cent of the national income and less people were employed in it than in our relatively small armed forces. As the pace of transformation to factory production increased after the 1820s, it began to draw greater supplies of coal and iron, but it never had the pervasive effect of railways. It was localised (sited) in Lancashire because of the great port of Liverpool and the commercial centre of Manchester; because of nearby coal supplies; because there was cheap transport available by land and water, and because the soft, lime-free waters of the rivers were good for processing. The traditional flax and linen industries were already there and there was an ample supply of labour, both from the increasing population (Lancashire was a great growth area in the eighteenth century) and from Irish immigrants across the Irish Sea.

The woollen industry was different. The process at least, that of fulling, had been carried out in mills powered by water since pre-Tudor days, but the industry as a whole was slow to change from the domestic system. In the West Riding, entrepreneurs were slow to turn to new methods because they found the domestic organisation profitable. It was some time before high-speed weaving machinery could be applied to wool and although the carding process had been mechanised by 1800, no effective combing machine (for the worsted cloth) was available until that of G. E. Donisthorpe and Samuel Cunliffe-Lister (1851). This made it possible to produce an adequate supply of wool already processed, sufficient to justify large-scale production. It was at this time, too, that large quantities of Australian wool were becoming available. Before 1850, most of the growth was in worsteds, and Bradford rapidly replaced Norwich as the main centre; but wool-cloth took the lead in the 1860s when the power-loom was being introduced into wool factories. The proud, independent, handloom wool weavers were soon eclipsed, although a few hung on into the twentieth century, especially those producing high quality cloth. It was fortunate for the

Wrought-iron gates at Trinity College, Oxford, 1715

industry in the 1860s that its supplies did not come from U.S.A., as did cotton, for the American Civil War badly interrupted supplies and faced Lancashire with a 'cotton famine' that caused widespread unemployment, suffering and severe losses.

The iron industry

What was true of cotton was also true of iron production. The industry was transformed at the end of the eighteenth century by new techniques and there was a change in its location and method of organisation that enabled it to be one of the major growth leaders of the nineteenth century.

Iron smelting has been a skilled craft since the days of primitive man, but its methods were involved and expensive and had remained traditional until the eighteenth century. Charcoal was used to smelt the iron ore in a *blast furnace*, and certain *cast iron* goods could be made by tapping the furnace direct. Most iron, however, was run off into moulds as *pig iron*, which, because of its impurities and brittleness, had to be treated in the *forge* and made into *bar iron* from which most products were made. The bar iron could be rolled

in slitting mills into rods for those most wretched of domestic out-workers, the nail makers. It could also be worked up into most beautiful *wrought iron* work of great delicacy.

The fuel traditionally used was charcoal, so that the industry was confined to forest areas where ores occurred. But it was already declining in the Weald of Sussex, although it was strong in the Forest of Dean, Shropshire, Staffordshire and in the Pennines. It was already organised on capitalist lines, for the plant was expensive and stocks had to be maintained. However, it only produced about half our needs, the rest coming from Russia, Sweden and, increasingly during the eighteenth century, from North America. This was because charcoal was expensive, the ores near the best charcoal areas were giving out and transport of ores was virtually impossible because of their great weight and the lack of adequate means of carrying them. The streams that powered the forge hammers often ran low in summer, so that production was badly affected. Clearly, before expansion could take place, three things were needed: an alternative source of fuel and of power, and better transport facilities.

Coal supplied the first need, the steam-engine the second and canals the third. But coal produced very bad quality iron, and it was not until an effective method of removing the impurities had been discovered that coal could be used. Abraham Darby used coal, converted into coke, at his Coalbrookdale works in Shropshire as early as 1709. His local ores and coal produced low quality cast iron and other manufacturers elsewhere found that their supplies produced very inferior iron because of the chemical constituents of the raw materials. It was only after many experiments by Abraham Darby II, that Coalbrookdale was able to produce pig iron that could be forged into bar iron. This was in 1749, and production began to expand wherever coal and iron ore of the right type occurred together—South Wales, Shropshire, Staffordshire, South Yorkshire and the Scottish Lowlands. At the same time the charcoal areas declined rapidly.

Production increased rapidly after 1776 when

and rolled into bars. This produced high quality iron quickly and cheaply. It was now possible for iron production to increase tremendously (see *graph 9*). The only major development in the next sixty years was Neilson's hot blast (1828) which economised on fuel in the furnace.

So many new uses for iron were now developed that the 1790s have been called the years of 'iron mania'. It was Abraham Darby III who demonstrated the potentiality of iron as a building material by constructing in prefabricated sections that great monument of the industrial revolution, the first iron bridge (1779). Telford took up the idea, even planning a single-spanned iron bridge to replace London Bridge. New textile factories were often constructed with iron frames—it was cheaper and stronger than conventional methods—and iron was used in new country houses like Eaton Hall. Iron now replaced wood in many machines (John Horrocks's power looms at Stockport (1803) were wholly of metal). John Wilkinson produced iron

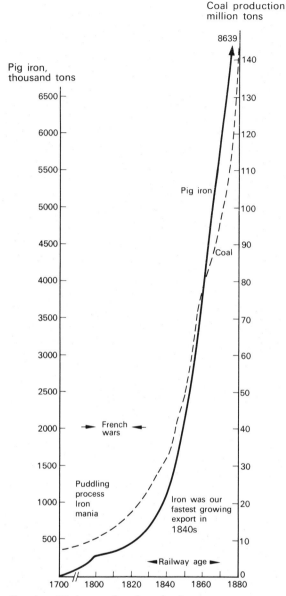

Graph 9 *Pig iron and coal production*

Ironwork at the Royal Pavilion, Brighton

John Wilkinson greatly improved the blast in his furnace by using a steam-engine to work his bellows instead of a water wheel, and the victory of coke over charcoal was guaranteed by the *puddling process* developed in 1784 both by Peter Onions at Merthyr Tydfil and Henry Cort at Fontley, near Fareham. Cort patented the process, removing the impurities in the furnace by stirring the molten pig iron with a puddling rod; it was then run off, cooled

Telford's design for London Bridge

furniture and an iron ship: he was buried in an iron coffin and designed an iron tomb. Cannon and shot were required in quantities during the French wars and the industry supplied the need; but it was the railway age that developed the full potentiality of the industry, and the iron ship ensured that the demands made in the middle of the century would be continued.

The expansion in iron production was neither as sudden nor as dramatic as that of cotton, but it had far greater impact. Coal and transport were directly affected and the civil and mechanical engineers became recognised as professional men. Our capacity to mass produce iron kept us ahead of our competitors for two generations; it boosted wealth and employment and acted as a spur to other industries. It was the prototype of modern industry, for it was large-scale with large sums invested in plant and raw materials; also the larger firms (the Crawshays of Cyfartha, the Guests of Dowlais, the Wilkinsons) had works combining the mining of coal and ore, the smelting of iron and rolling it into bar iron for immediate use, or casting prepared shapes for immediate sale. This method of controlling the whole range of the stages of production in one locality under a single management is called *vertical integration*.

The coal industry

Coal production rose from about $2\frac{1}{2}$ million tons in 1700 to 11 million in 1800. This was partly due to increased wealth allowing people to buy more coal, partly to more people buying coal, partly to the use of the steam-engine to provide motive power in factories, partly to the new demands of the iron industry, but above all to the improvements in transport that made it possible to move coal even from the areas which were not served by navigable rivers. The nineteenth century was to see a phenomenal growth, and this meant far deeper mines and a big development in mining techniques.

Northumberland was the principal coalfield of eighteenth-century Britain, simply because of the easy river and sea transport. Coal was hauled on wagon-ways to *staiths* (loading quays) where *keels* (barges) carried it to the ports to be re-loaded on *colliers*, the coastal vessels that carried the coal to London. Other coalfields were in South Yorkshire and Lancashire (to be important for textiles in the nineteenth century), the Midlands, Forest of Dean, South Wales and Somerset.

The mines were small, and there were great differences in methods and in quality of coal between the coalfields. Few mines penetrated far underground because of the dangers of explosion, flooding and falling roofs. Since the mines were mostly small concerns, few could afford expensive equipment, and the lack of mechanical aids certainly held back production. But improvements were made. The Newcomen steam-engine was used to pump water out of workings and this allowed deeper mines to be sunk. Trap-doors and fans, operated by boys, helped to ventilate the levels and move dangerous gases; special fires were lit under shafts to help ventilation by getting warm air to rise out of the pit and occasionally two shafts were used, one for fresh cold air to descend, the other for warm foul air to rise (but it was the 1870s before the Government forced mine owners to construct proper ventilation shafts). In 1815 Sir Humphrey Davy produced his miners' safety lamp (George Stephenson produced his 'Geordie' lamp the same year) and this made for safer mining by reducing the danger of explosion from naked lights. Winding gear long remained primitive, and in many pits the descent and ascent with coal was made by ladder. But the greater use of steam-engines and the use in the nineteenth century of wire ropes made bigger and more efficient mines possible. Before 1800 there were pit ponies underground pulling wagons on rails to the shaft bottom, and this practice was widely used in the nineteenth century. There was little use of mechanical power underground, largely because of the cost and difficulty of installing it in the narrower galleries, and because of the plentiful supply of human labour—indeed, the gigantic increase in coal production during the nineteenth century (see *graph 9*) was gained largely by sweated labour, not greater mechanical power. But this immense increase in production made the industrial revolution possible, and the development of canals and railways secured the opening up of inland coalfields on a big scale.

The steel industry

Steel is an *alloy* (mixture) made from iron, carbon and other materials and has many advantages over iron. But, although it has been made for centuries, it was always very expensive and could only be made in small quantities. In the later nineteenth century steel underwent the same changes which took place in the iron industry in the later eighteenth century, so that by 1900 it had replaced iron as the principal metal and economic barometer of the nation's prosperity.

Sheffield had become the centre of the industry, and the Sheffield masters were both secretive and conservative in their methods. German steel was preferred both because it was cheaper and better. But by 1740 a Doncaster watchmaker, Benjamin Huntsman, perfected a *crucible* process of steel-

making, producing very high quality steel, though the process was lengthy and no less expensive than existing methods, so that it was adopted only slowly. Nevertheless, as the demand for steel increased, its production, in Sheffield, Birmingham and Newcastle slowly increased.

It was Sir Henry Bessemer who did for steel what Cort had done for iron. The Bessemer *converter* (1856) produced molten steel by burning off the impurities and carbon from pig iron by blasting air through the molten metal by means of *tuyeres* (chimneys). Large quantities of steel could quickly be converted from the molten iron. Two difficulties prevented the new method changing the steel industry overnight. The metal produced was too brittle—but Robert Mushet overcame this by adding a little manganese to the molten pig iron. Secondly, the British ores contained a high proportion of phosphorus that prevented high quality steel being made. The non-phosphoric ores of Cumberland were rapidly exhausted and this meant heavy imports of ores from Sweden or Spain if the process were to be continued. There was every need to continue it, for Bessemer had opened up a new era for steel: hitherto it had been used for high-quality work, now it was to be used on a large scale and to replace iron. In 1862 he exhibited the first steel nails ever made and laid the first steel rail at Camden Goods Station. The following year steel was used for ship-building.

But the difficulty over phosphoric iron remained, and Sir William Siemens's *open-hearth* process (1867) did not solve it. His method, burning out impurities by a flame applied to the surface of the molten metal, was cheaper and easier than Bessemer's; it was also easier to determine the quality of the resultant steel, and it was possible to use scrap metal as well as ore, which was cheaper. The phosphorus was removed by Sidney Gilchrist Thomas (1878) who lined the furnace with dolomite limestone which extracted it from the pig iron. The phosphorus, and other wastes withdrawn from the furnace, was useful as a fertiliser (an example of a *by-product*). At first, British steel makers were slow to take advantage of the Gilchrist Thomas process, but the Germans used it extensively in the Lorraine ore field and so did Andrew Carnegie, in the U.S.A. Both countries surpassed us in steel production before 1900. But after the process was taken up here, our steel production expanded so rapidly from 1880 onwards that it replaced iron as the principal metal produced (in 1877 the Board of Trade had permitted its use in bridge construction).

These nineteenth-century developments produced major shifts in the location of the steel industry, first to the port areas (South Wales, Middlesbrough and the Scottish Lowlands) to take advantage of foreign ores that were imported in bulk for thirty years after the Bessemer process, and later to the low quality phosphoric ores of Lincolnshire and Northamptonshire. The full

impact of the new methods was felt only in the twentieth century—a further indication of the time-lag between invention, innovation and full exploitation.

The steam engine

The steam-engine was the vital link in the industrial revolution, but it is easy to exaggerate the speed with which it was adopted and the part played by James Watt personally.

The principle of the steam-engine had been known for centuries, but Thomas Savery made it effective with his engine of 1698. It was used for pumping water from mines: it was neither very efficient nor economical to use. In 1711 Thomas

The Bessemer converter

Newcomen produced a superior type of engine that could pump water from a considerable depth, thus making deeper shafts practicable. It was still very extravagant of fuel, but it proved popular and many improvements were made to it, but James Watt's improvements made it in effect a new engine.

Watt was unusual among the great inventors of his day in having something of a scientific training. In 1757 he was given the task of repairing a demonstration Newcomen engine used by Glasgow University. Appreciating its inefficiency, he set himself to design a more effective model and by 1765 had produced an engine with a coal consumption half that of Newcomen's. He achieved this by incorporating a separate condenser cylinder which avoided cooling the main cylinder repeatedly (the principal cause of the Newcomen engine's inefficiency). The research work had brought him into heavy debt and he was lucky to be invited to the Carron Works by Dr Roebuck, who was interested in using the new machine in his coal and iron workings. Roebuck, however, went bankrupt in

1773 and Watt was again lucky to be taken into partnership by Matthew Boulton of Soho, Birmingham, who had already been experimenting with steam-engines on his own account. By 1775 the firm of Boulton Watt had produced the steam-engine that was in due course to revolutionise the principal industries of the country. The accurately bored cylinders were supplied by John Wilkinson from his Bilston works. But the engine was still confined to pumping operations: if it were to be used to drive machinery, it would need to convert the pumping operation into a rotary motion. In 1781 James Pickard patented a simple crank and flywheel for this purpose, and so Watt, on the suggestion of his assistant, William Murdoch, patented his *sun and planet* gear (1781) which had to be used until Pickard's patent ran out. In order to ensure that the piston was always vertical when turning a shaft, Watt devised the elegant *parallel motion* (1784). The third major development was the *centrifugal governor* (1787) that regulated the speed of the engine so that it turned wheels at a

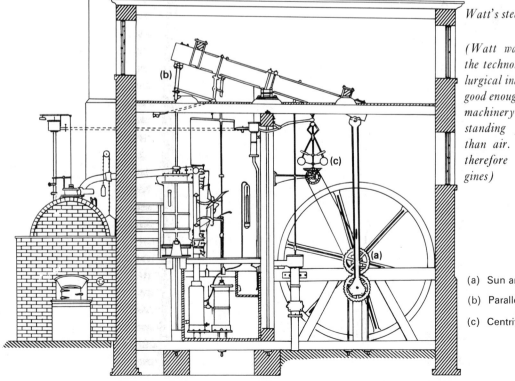

Watt's steam engine

(Watt was convinced that the technology of the metallurgical industry was not yet good enough to construct safe machinery capable of withstanding pressures greater than air. His engines were therefore 'atmospheric' engines)

(a) Sun and planet gear (1781)

(b) Parallel motion (1784)

(c) Centrifugal governor (1787)

consistent speed, necessary for driving machinery.

The new engine was revolutionary, for it could be used in textile mills, breweries, flour mills, potteries and other industries.

Watt's patent ended in 1800, by which time there were some 1,200 steam-engines (321 made at Soho). Thereafter, other manufacturers began producing engines in competition with the Soho works. But it is easy to exaggerate the impact of steam power: by 1850 it is estimated that steam-engines in factories were producing no more than 500,000 h.p., and the vast majority of firms were too small to afford an engine, or only a small one at best. The great period of steam power is really the second half of the century, and much of the steam power then produced came from the railway locomotive. But steam-engines meant that factories were no longer dependent on water power, so that mill towns began to spread away from rivers and since the proximity of coal was important, the concentration of factories in the 'industrial north' and Midlands was strengthened.

The development of machine tools

Watt's steam-engine did a great deal to launch the profession of mechanical engineer, and the industrial changes of the future were to depend to a great extent upon the skill of these men. Mass production techniques depend upon machines whose working parts can be quickly and exactly replaced when they become worn, so that the machines have to be produced to an absolute standard, for otherwise the parts would not fit. Such accuracy is possible only with machines, for however skilled the craftsmen, it is unlikely that one man would exactly reproduce the work of another with the desired precision. Consequently, engineers have been driven to make *machine tools*, machines to make machines. This was a really revolutionary development, for until the late eighteenth century, craftsmen usually designed their own machines and tools—even screws, so that it was often necessary to bore out and re-make screws when machines were repaired With machine tools any size of object can be worked

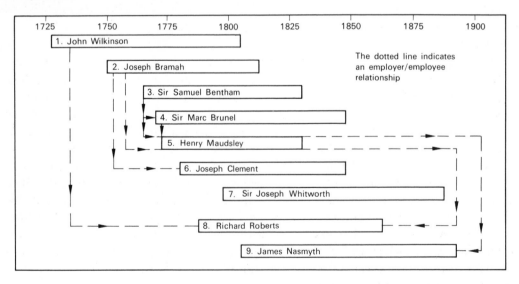

1. Wilkinson invented the accurate boring machine
2. Bramah invented a whole range of machine tools
3. Bentham invented wood working machinery (Inspector General of naval works)
4. Brunel invented block-making machinery for naval dockyards
5. Maudslay introduced the slide-rest for lathes and the screw-cutting lathe
6. Clement built a metal planer and manufactured taps and dies
7. Whitworth leading tool manufacture, standardised screw threads
8. Roberts improved the lathe
9. Nasmyth invented the steam hammer, shaper, index miller

Graph 10 The relationship between certain machine-tool makers

to an accuracy unattainable by hand, at great speed and with remarkable economy.

We have already met John Wilkinson, whose ability to bore cylinders with great accuracy made it possible for Watt to produce his steam-engine. A second figure of consequence was Joseph Bramah whose works at Pimlico trained many prominent engineers. (*Graph 10* shows the close relationship between many of the machine-tool makers of the period.) His own craftsmanship can be seen in the gates of Marble Arch. His machines included the basic principle of the modern self-flushing water closet (1778) which was just being introduced into wealthy houses, a machine for numbering bank notes that enabled the Bank of England to dismiss 100 clerks, and, of course, his famous burglar-proof lock that remained unpicked between 1784 and 1851. His assistant Henry Maudslay made many of the parts for this lock, and he opened his own shop in 1797 where he gained fame by devising the specialised tools required to produce naval pulley-blocks of great accuracy for Sir Marc I. Brunel. By 1808 he had produced 160,000 blocks using his machines and ten unskilled men—traditional methods would have required 110 highly skilled men. Here was a sign for the future: a new age in productive industry was dawning.

Joseph Clement, who patented the domestic water tap, and who frequently was given jobs other engineers found beyond them, was trained by Bramah and Maudslay. He did much work on the problem of accurate screw-cutting. Sir Joseph Whitworth was also trained in the same school as a precision engineer. By 1851 he had an international reputation, and his micrometer, capable of measuring to a millionth of an inch, was a star exhibit at the Great Exhibition: but, despite the pioneering work of these tool-makers, precision engineering, the basis of large-scale, mass production industry, did not properly appear until the later nineteenth century. Whitworth persuaded the Board of Trade in 1880 to adopt standard measurements (*gauges*), especially for screws, and his work for the interchangeability of machine parts greatly advanced the techniques of mass production methods. He

Nasmyth with his steam hammer

was also notable for his researches into 'work study' in order to get the best layout for his machine shops. These ideas were developed in the twentieth century, largely by foreigners: our rivals produced the revolutionary machines of the present century.

James Nasmyth was also trained by Maudslay and was the inventor of a series of precision tools. His two most remarkable were a safety ladle (1838) allowing large quantities of molten metal to be accurately poured by precise mechanical control, and the famous steam-hammer (1839) used to forge the huge paddle shaft of the *Great Britain*. The catalogue of the Great Exhibition (1851) stated:

'This steam hammer is capable of adjustment of power in a degree highly remarkable. While it is possible to obtain enormous impulsive force by its means, it can be so graduated as to descend with power only sufficient to break an egg shell.'

Such machines were to lay the foundation of a

highly sophisticated engineering industry that was to make the developments of the twentieth century possible. The tool-makers deserve to be remembered along with the Watts, the Stephensons, the Darbys.

Other industries

There were so many industrial changes in the hundred years after 1770, that it is only possible to mention the 'pace-setters'. The pottery industry was transformed, to a great extent by Josiah Wedgwood (see *page 80*), making it possible to mass produce pottery and fine china and thus work a social revolution on a gigantic scale.

The chemical industry also made great strides during the period. We have already seen it in relation to iron and steel, but it made an immeasurable contribution to textiles by simplifying the finishing process for cloth with the use of chlorine (its bleaching powers were discovered by Berthollet in 1785). In 1797 the Tennant Works at Glasgow began producing chloride of lime for bleaching. Within a generation they were the biggest chemical works in Europe. Other works for manufacturing sulphuric acid and alkalis were founded at the end of the eighteenth century, especially in the west Midlands, St Helens, Lancashire and on Tyneside, as more uses were developed. The great salt field of Cheshire made Widnes the centre of the soda industry (essential for soap-making on any scale). The glass industry also consumed massive supplies of soda, and the dyeing industry made persistent demands on industrial chemists.

Coal gas produced a completely new industry that was to effect a massive social revolution in providing light and heating. In England the man primarily responsible was William Murdoch, Watt's assistant, and in due course Soho became the centre for producing gas plant—the works were illuminated by gas to celebrate the Peace of Amiens in 1802. Murdoch's idea was to have individual gas plants for each main consumer, but the idea of a central factory producing gas that was distributed by

A cartoon poking fun at the products of the National Light and Heat Company

pipeline to consumers, domestic or industrial, came from Albert Winsor, who established a National Light and Heat Company (1804) and lit Pall Mall in 1807. Much of the practical work involved in making coal gas safe for domestic use and passing it through miles of pipes, was done by Samuel Clegg, who had been apprenticed at Soho. The process of producing and purifying coal gas released a number of valuable by-products like tar, creosote and ammonia. At the same time, the demand for miles of metal piping and for coal, acted as a spur to other industries.

The industrial changes we have discovered produced a great range of goods in quantities and at prices that would have been inconceivable in 1770. Mass production methods did not happen overnight, but they introduced a totally different type of industrial economy and helped to underline the new society that was emerging throughout the period of the Great Changes.

6 · The Great Changes: new methods of industrial organisation

Studying an historical period is rather like visiting a building site where a big block of offices is being constructed. For quite a time there will be nothing but a hole with men occasionally doing things at particular points: it does not seem to make much sense. But suddenly you will see that the foundations of the steel frame of the building have been laid, and the frame itself will begin to rise. From that moment each stage of the building process will be understandable. Now that we today are a hundred years away from the period of the Great Changes, we can begin to understand what was really going on: the building is taking shape.

We know that in this period a new economic structure was appearing. The traditional agricultural based economy was being replaced by one based on large-scale industry which depended not merely upon the needs of a local community, but upon the opportunities to supply markets all over the world. Raw materials and food stuffs came increasingly from overseas and our exports to foreign markets grew. Consequently our economy could be immediately affected by disturbances in world trade and by trade slumps that tended to occur in cycles (see *pages 83*). Today we can see what was happening, but the businessmen of the time did not have this advantage for they could not see the overall plan of the foundations they were laying. But they laid sound foundations and their achievement is a tribute to their hard work and willingness to experiment.

The common people were changing, too. They were better behaved. Despite the huge new towns with their bad crowded conditions, the big disturbances of nineteenth-century Britain were more orderly and less vicious than those of the previous century. Francis Place wrote:

'Look even to Lancashire. Within a few years [of the 1820] a stranger walking through their towns was "touted" . . . and sometimes pelted with stones. "Lancashire brute" was the common and appropriate appellation. Until very lately it would have been very dangerous to have assembled five hundred of them on any occasion. Bakers and butchers would at least have been plundered. Now a hundred thousand people may be collected together and no riot ensue.'

The crowd that gathered on St Peter's Field in 1819 (see *page 158*) was dressed in Sunday clothes. Instead of cudgels it bore banners.

Among the 'labouring classes' there was emerging a new self-consciously 'respectable' group of skilled workers (*artisans*) and clerks upon whom the new forms of industrial organisation depended. They were, by the middle of the century, better housed, better fed, better educated than their grandparents. With the development of railways they were developing a taste for occasional travel as well. Some of them emigrated to make fortunes or live ordinary lives in virgin lands in the Empire and North America. It is important to remember that behind the great industrialists, lay a mass of keen workers whose part in creating the new society that was emerging cannot be chronicled, but must not be forgotten. And behind the artisans and clerks lay another huge mass of workers upon whose labour the achievements of the nineteenth century depended.

The entrepreneurs

Economists call businessmen who take the risks of developing their businesses *entrepreneurs*. The engineers and manufacturers who made their fortunes creating nineteenth century industry are good examples. They exploited inventions and *innovation* depended on them (see *page 62*). In many cases, they had to work out quite new problems of management. Too little attention has been paid to the history of business management, partly because of the lack of sources available, but one of the keys to understanding the industrial revolution lies here.

Most of the early managers were not labourers, but sons of families with some business experience. Out of 130 industrialists prominent between 1750 and 1850, barely a third rose from humble working class or small tenant-farmer backgrounds. The rest could lean on established family skills to solve the problems posed by the new inventions. Of these, the factory system itself posed the most. Never before had it been necessary to maintain a large and *permanent* labour force, and to organise, control, recruit and train it. The Brasseys, Petos and Cubitts, whose control of railway navvies was legendary, rose to the occasion—but they were construction men engaged on jobs that had a completion date. A factory simply went on consuming labour as it produced goods. Here, merchants who had controlled a long chain of domestic workers had some experience to lean on. Benjamin Gott, a West Riding factory master, reported in 1828:

'I was brought up as a merchant and became a manufacturer rather from possessing capital than understanding the manufacture. I paid for the talent of others in the different branches of manufacture.'

But once a labour force had been recruited, trained and disciplined to keep the regular hours required by the machinery, a continual supply of labour was needed that had to be trained and often re-trained. Wedgwood found he had to train his own skilled men to use the machinery he introduced. In machine tool making, the lack of skilled men was a great hindrance: the early firms were very small, and 'poaching' was common, for it gained a skilled worker and *really* damaged a rival.

Many of the new factories were small, especially those in London and in Birmingham. The larger ones enjoyed *economies of scale* (they could buy their raw materials more cheaply in bulk, the cost of supplying motive power to machines was less per machine than in small works and they could afford

to engage specialist staff for particular work). As factories grew in size, the expense of purchasing materials and machines grew beyond the resources of family firms, so many became companies, often with limited liability (see *page 85*).

Several industries found it more economical to contract some of the work to particular firms. The railways did this on a grand scale when they contracted with a firm of navvies to build part of the line. Even within factories contracting was possible, and in the early cotton factories the 'scavengers' (who cleaned machines) and piecers were often directly employed by the spinners and not the factory owner—in 1833 about half the child labour in cotton was employed in this way. In pottery works (even in Wedgwood's Etruria), the throwers and furnace men employed their own children for casual labouring jobs. But sub-contracting like this was only a temporary solution to the labour problem raised by concentrating production within a factory. It was wide open to abuse and could not continue when factories began to grow in size.

If factories were to grow beyond the point at which the owner knew all his employees, a disciplined labour force had to be created. This itself was an achievement. The Crawshays at the Cyfarthfa Works, for example, employed 1,000 men in 1804, some 1,500 in 1812 and over 5,000 in 1830. In 1799 one of the biggest water wheels in Britain, measuring 50 ft and costing £4,000, had been installed there: by 1830 this was supplemented by eight steam-engines. And what was true of the Cyfarthfa Works was also true of other South Wales works, like the Guests's at Dowlais, or the Pen-y-Daren Works, and elsewhere, as at Coalbrookdale, and the great Carron Works. Such a growth, largely occurring *after* the Napoleonic War, brought out a further problem of management. To manage an eighteenth-century iron works involved skill and technical expertise, but to manage the Cyfarthfa Works of 1830 required administrative gifts beyond anything demanded in the eighteenth century.

Iron works were often examples of *vertical integration* in which the mining of coal and ores, smelting and the casting of particular products were all carried on within the same site. A similar process was appearing in the major engineering firms, where the second generation of entrepreneurs organised their factories on a fully planned basis, with each section concerned with a particular part of the production process. This *rationalisation* of production was particularly developed at the great Soho factory by the sons of Boulton and Watt, who took over the factory after 1795. They developed a really modern planned factory technique, with careful and elaborate costing, using machine tools with interchangeable parts, and ensuring a smooth flow of production so that their machines were neither over-burdened nor lying idle. Nasmyth's foundry at Manchester was another good example:

'The whole establishment is divided into departments, over each of which a foreman, or responsible person, is placed, whose duty is not only to see that the men under his superintendance produce good work, but also to endeavour to keep pace with the productive powers of all the other departments.'

Such advanced planning was unusual and most factories struggled on in a hand-to-mouth way. Many entrepreneurs lacked technical knowledge and merely followed blindly where others led. This was often the case in family firms, where the second and third generation failed to develop the work of their predecessors to new conditions. It was partly for this very reason that Britain lost her world lead in engineering towards the end of the century. Even today courses in Business Studies are in their infancy and regarded with unjustifiable suspicion.

Mass production methods needed careful organisation, and this meant that a good manager was essential. Industrial management is a product of the industrial revolution. If firms were to grow in size, they simply had to cope with the problems posed by mass production. Managers had to teach themselves the principles of accountancy—not merely to check that bills were properly paid, but to be able to fix prices with some certainty of the cost of producing goods. Prices were often decided without even thinking of the production costs involved. Here Josiah Wedgwood was exceptional, for he devised a system of accounts that helped him manage his works by indicating in advance what stocks needed re-ordering, and which sections of the works ran at a profit and which at a loss.

Many entrepreneurs were men of ruthless character, indifferent to the fate of their workpeople. But some, often the torch bearers of innovation, had a keen interest in the welfare of their employees. These were often men who had built up big concerns; men like Strutt of Belper, Gott of Leeds, Fielden of Todmorden, or the Guests of Dowlais, were builders of communities. Arkwright, less an inventor than an entrepreneur of genius, cherished an ambition to accumulate enough capital to pay off the National Debt. The most remarkable was Robert Owen, who created a new community at New Lanark Mills and demonstrated that one could still become very wealthy quickly whilst providing excellent working conditions, good housing, schools for one's workers' children, and creating a community of good will. Like Sir Robert Peel at Bury, he limited the working day for he regarded his employees not as slaves of the steam-engine but as people. His contemporaries feared to cut hours lest it cut production and profit. It was 1847 before a ten-hour day was achieved (see *page 96*) and even then it affected only a small part of industry. Manufacturers firmly believed that their profit came from the labour of the last hour worked, but Robert Gardiner of Preston put the point well in 1845:

'All the arguments I have heard in favour of long-time [working] appear based on an arithmetical question—if 11 produce so much, what will 12, 13 or even 15 hours produce? This is correct, as far as the steam engine is concerned, whatever it will produce in 11 hours, it will produce double the quantity in 22. But try this on the animal horse, and you will soon find he cannot compete with the engine, as he requires both time to rest and to feed.'

Josiah Wedgwood (1730–1795)

Wedgwood perhaps best exemplifies the achievements of the early entrepreneurs, not only discovering answers to new problems that were to set the pattern for the future, but uniting the world of manufacturing and sales with that of fashion and high society. His grasp of the real nature of the problems with which he was faced, and the modern ring of his answers, is truly remarkable.

He was fortunate in being born at a time when many improvements were being introduced, both in industry and in transport. He put himself at the van of these improvements so that the domestic pottery industry was transformed in his life-time into an industry whose products were to work a social revolution by supplying the poorer classes with sufficient pottery at a price they could afford. The new green glaze, creamware, black basalt and jasper he made his own were all available to his competitors, but Wedgwood developed them, and, as his success grew he was soon employing professional artists in a successful bid to capture contemporary taste, especially by copying classical moulds and motifs—the cast of the Portland Vase is the outstanding example here.

He was outstanding, too, for his use of machinery. In order to grind his materials he installed a Boulton-Watt steam-engine in 1782. He had four by 1800, by which time he was actually printing the painted decoration on his ware. His Etruria works became 'a model of minute division of labour and the development of factory discipline and control' (which he probably copied from Boulton with whom he had a close friendship through the Lunar Society). His scientific management ensured a smooth flow of work and a well constructed pattern of production that made the most effective use of his machines and skilled workers. Like Robert Owen, he was concerned also to develop the self respect of his employees and to encourage further effort by means of incentives. It is no surprise that Wedgwood should leap ahead of his rivals, some of whom may have been even more skilled than he: it is more of a surprise that his fellow potters should in 1775 reject a scheme for establishing an experimental works for the benefit of the industry as a whole.

Romantic stories of Wedgwood hobbling through his works breaking pieces of inferior workmanship

saying, 'This won't do for Josiah Wedgwood!', pale before the real achievements of the man. And yet his most important contribution lay not in the field of factory production, but in marketing and salesmanship. It was by developing techniques of a peculiarly modern character in this field that he was able to transform a domestic industry producing rough earthenware for a local market into a modern factory industry producing china that rivalled the great European houses.

Wedgwood led the Potteries in mass production methods, but it is quite wrong to think of him supplying the cheap mass market. His competitors did that. He sold his ware for what the nobility were prepared to pay for it, and he was quite happy to lose smaller orders because his prices were too high. Proudly displaying on his bills and notepaper the title Queen's Potter, he willingly undertook unreasonably expensive and difficult commissions of which others fought shy (like a table service of 1,282 pieces with over 1,000 original paintings for Catherine the Great of Russia in 1773) because of their advertisement value throughout the courts of Europe. He encouraged nobles to visit his works and accepted their smallest orders, and they repaid him by introducing his name to foreign monarchs —'Conquer France in Burslem' was his slogan. In order to break through the chain of middlemen and sell direct to his public, he opened showrooms in London, Bath and Dublin. It became the height of fashion to visit the rooms, and ladies could decide upon the designs of their own table-ware. Leading artists (many were his own personal friends) were employed, and he produced pattern books for the direction of his craftsmen. Special exhibitions were arranged, and no public event, whether Wesley preaching, or Chatham dying in the House of Lords, was absent from his ware. London and provincial newspapers ran editorial copy and carried advertisements for him, and some foreign journals did so, too. But hand-bills were too 'common' for his showrooms.

When orders fell off, he began paying up to half the cost of transport and accepting orders on extensive credit. Later he began accepting orders by correspondence, sending out the goods with a 'satisfaction or return' guarantee (much in the way that a modern *mail order* firm works). In 1777 he began to use travelling salesmen effectively. Clearly, his genius lay in marketing, and it was not too much of an exaggeration to call him 'Vase Maker General to the Universe'.

The Great Exhibition, 1851

The early entrepreneurs launched Britain upon a new career as the leading industrial nation. Our production of consumer goods was expanding phenomenally, and our markets were growing all over the world. To help those markets expand further, industrialists advocated Free Trade (see *page 88*) for they were confident of beating their competitors in any market. Their confidence was caught by the slogan that Britain was the 'workshop of the world'.

The idea of holding a huge exhibition, both to demonstrate our commercial supremacy and to gain new orders, was very popular among certain businessmen, and eventually a private company was formed to stage the whole exhibition. A powerful committee, headed by Albert, the Prince Consort, organised a national competition for the design of a hall for an exhibition 'uniting the industry and art of all the nations of the earth'. The idea of an international exhibition not only underlined our massive industrial lead, but encouraged international trade and (an idea close to the heart of free traders) promoted international harmony and peace.

With great courage the committee chose Joseph Paxton's design. It was novel, daring and incredibly simple—and it demonstrated the skill and capacity of British technology, for it applied directly to a public building the principles the railway builders had developed in building iron bridges. It was a gigantic glasshouse supported by massive iron pillars and cross pieces. All its measurements were divisible by twenty-four so that it could be entirely prefabricated. Nearly 300,000 panes of plate glass were used (a tribute to a growing industry, for sheet glass had only been introduced into England in 1832). Built at incredible speed, enclosing within it the great elms in Hyde Park, it was, and has remained, the symbol of an age: it was moved to

The Crystal Palace in 1851. Joseph Paxton's original design was altered somewhat by the commissioners. The barrel vault that gives it the distinctive appearance was added at the suggestion of the great Victorian architect, Barry

Sydenham, Kent, in 1853–4 and was destroyed by fire in 1936.

But in 1850 it had many enemies. People objected to the building; to the international character of the Exhibition, believing all foreigners to be rogues and thieves; to the danger of riots and revolution because of the numbers of working class people who might assemble. Others objected to the simple novelty of the idea. They were led by the eccentric M.P. Colonel Sibthorpe:

'That miserable Crystal Palace, that wretched place, where every species of fraud and immorality will be practised. . . . Let [the Britisher] beware of man traps and spring guns—they will have all their food robbed—they will have a piebald generation, half black, half white; but I can assure them that my arm at least will be raised to prevent such violation. They might look for assassinations—for being stabbed in the dark; but careless of that, I am determined to pursue an even, straight-forward course, and I would say that the dearest wish of my heart is that that confounded building called the Crystal Palace should be dashed to pieces.'

The Great Exhibition amazed everyone with its success. It was open for 141 days and had over six million visitors. Part of the reason for its success was the daring decision eventually to issue tickets at one shilling to allow the common people to visit it (daring because of genuine fears of revolution, for it was only three years since the great Chartist meeting on Kennington Common (see *page 164*) when London had been prepared for civil war).

The Exhibition came at a propitious moment, for a generation of great prosperity lay ahead and it became a symbol of British greatness and prosperity. *The Times* (2 May 1851) caught the popular emotion on the opening day:

'It was felt to be more than what was seen, or what had been intended. Some saw in it the second and more glorious inauguration of their sovereign; some a solemn dedication of art and its stores; some were more reminded of that day when all ages and climes shall be gathered round the Throne of their Maker.'

But it was even more than this: it demonstrated that there was the possibility of a new community in which provinces were no longer strangers to each other. Railways ran special exhibition trains at excursion rates from all over the country and the roads round Hyde Park were crammed with coaches and horse-omnibuses. The rich were genuinely surprised to see how well dressed and orderly were the 'respectable' working classes—even those from the industrial north whom previously they had ignorantly supposed to be scarcely civilised. *Punch* put it well:

'Let anyone who wishes to be instructed as to the character of the industrial classes of England and London especially, go to the Exhibition and watch how they behave themselves. He will see them well-dressed, orderly, sedate, earnestly engaged in examining all that interests them, not quarrelsome or obstinate but playing with manifest propriety and good temper the important part assigned to them at this gathering of the nations.'

A Punch *cartoon of the poor visiting the Great Exhibition*

Slumps, and trade cycles

In 1851 Britain was not yet the industrial nation we would recognise today, for the vast majority of her firms were very small, many producing almost upon an individual craftsman basis. One reason for this was the difficulty of raising the money required to finance a factory geared to mass production. Local blacksmiths outnumbered workers in iron foundries and works, and more men worked with horses than on the railways (see *graph 11*). But the next generation was to see a great development of factory production, aided especially by the development of *limited liability* (see *page 85*).

Our foreign trade continued to expand, and to manufactured goods we now added the export of machinery, particularly textile machinery. Our merchant fleet grew to help transport our exports and bring in imports—indeed our imports were far greater than our exports and became more so as cheap food was made available in the 1870s. An excess of imports over exports is called an unfavourable *balance of trade* and ours was at least £70 million by the 1880s. This would have caused serious difficulties in paying for all the imports had we not also had a huge income from investments overseas. These foreign investments (some £1,200 million in 1875) were in railways, mines, shipping and loans for all kinds of public works like building harbours,

roads, bridges, dams etc., mostly in the Americas or in India. In their turn, the investments encouraged a flood of orders for new machines and consumer goods to supply markets opened up by new railways and steamships, and so they helped industry at home as well. Our shipping earned huge sums for transporting goods and the City of London became not only one of the most important ports of the world, but the international financial centre for banking and insurance. Lloyds, the great corporation for insuring risks of all kinds, had a network of marine insurance agencies throughout the world, and merchants of all nations recognised the value of their merchandise travelling 'A1 at Lloyds', properly and effectively insured. The income from foreign investments, shipping, banking and insurance charges is called *invisible earnings*. At this time our invisible earnings were so great that they entirely concealed the fact that we imported so much more than we exported. We had no difficulty paying for the imports because our earnings were so great that we had a very favourable *balance of payments*. A good deal of the prosperity in the second half of the nineteenth century rested on the favourable balance of payments and the City of London became perhaps the most important international money market in the world, with international bankers anxious to trade in pounds sterling.

But despite the fact that it was a period of tremendous growth, there were crises from time to time when the growth suddenly stopped. Indeed, throughout the nineteenth century short periods of poor trading, or trade slumps, were so regular that economists were soon talking about the *cyclical theory of trade*. Trade increased overall, but every ten years or so there was a sudden loss of business confidence; order books fell, stocks were unsold and workers went on short time or were laid off until trade picked up again. There is no simple explanation for this phenomenon. Business confidence seems to have been the crucial factor, for whenever businessmen were confident of the future, a boom period was released which ended as confidence flagged. This tendency of businessmen to act in common was a feature of industrialism accentuated

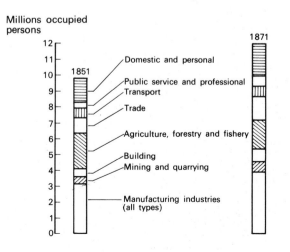

Graph 11 The distribution of the labour force (1851–1871)

by the speed of transport and the expanding market for goods. Trade was fast becoming international, no longer confined to local and national markets. This helped mass production because it meant a huge market for goods. Manufacturers began increasingly to *specialise* (to concentrate upon one product). This meant manufacturers came to depend completely upon other manufacturers for the supply of machinery, vital parts or materials. If there was a sudden depression in one industry it spread rapidly to others, causing a loss of business confidence and bringing on a slump (leading to a *cyclical downswing* in trade, i.e. a temporary loss of trade and profits). The profitability of foreign markets, on which we were coming increasingly to depend, played their part in this tendency of trade to follow an up-swing, down-swing pattern: if a foreign market was disturbed by a war or some natural disaster it might affect productive industry in Britain. Another factor was the relative instability of the agricultural market, even in prosperous Britain—a bad harvest raised food prices which meant less money for consumer goods and so sales fell off, production followed suit and unemployment resulted. This was the case in 1837–42 and 1846–8. Yet another factor was the supply of credit—manufacturers found it difficult to raise money for investment and purchasing future stocks unless there were boom conditions where business confidence was high. Individual employers could do nothing to control these cycles; they cut their losses in a slump and waited for the next boom. The effect on the employees was often catastrophic, especially if the slump was a deep one, for they had to take wage cuts, go on short time, or they might even lose their jobs, their sole means of livelihood, through no fault of their own. One way of avoiding this was to emigrate in search of better things in the USA or the Empire, and there was a distinct relationship between depressions and emigration. For the majority who remained at home, a slump meant considerable distress. It was not much comfort to a starving, unemployed weaver to be told that he was living through a period of unexampled prosperity in the long term, despite his merely temporary discomfiture!

Until the level of production and the standard of living was so high that workers remained above the poverty line even in times of depression, most workpeople had an insecure time. This was their fate throughout the hey-day of Victorian prosperity. Businessmen, too, were left to weather their storms as best they could.

The international character of trade was underlined by the 1857 slump, partly resulting from the dislocations caused by the Crimean War (1854–6). It began with the collapse of some American banks that caused the bankruptcy of some leading Liverpool and Glasgow firms, and it spread to the iron trade and so to Europe. But recovery was amazingly rapid. The last big slump of the period was in 1866 following the failure of the leading financial house of **Overend and Gurney** and aggravated by the Austro-Prussian War. Thameside ship-building never recovered from the depression, and important railway contractors failed, too, including Peto and almost the great Brassey himself. Various companies revealed evidence of mismanagement and there was a general feeling of uneasiness at the apparent lack of trustworthiness in some parts of the business world. But recovery was again rapid, helped by the quick expansion of the American market. This time the boom lasted until the later 1870s when came a slump that helped to lose Disraeli the 1880 election and heralded the period known as the 'Great Depression' (see *page 170*).

Nineteenth-century banks

The efficiency of the banking system came under fire because of the persistent slumps, and it is hardly surprising to see at this time both the amalgamation of many country banks into larger units and (despite *laissez-faire* views) the extension of Government regulation through the Bank of England.

The two principal weaknesses of early nineteenth-century banks were the limitation of partners to a maximum of six, which tended to prevent the building up of reserves large enough to carry them through crises; and the lack of control over note issue.

Country Banks
No. of Banks

1784 — 119	1815 — 699	1835 — 411
1798 — 312	1825 — 544	1840 — 332
1809 — 799	1830 — 439	1842 — 311

There were sixty-two Private Banks in London in 1832.

The financial crisis of 1825 saw the closing of eighty country banks and in 1826 the Government allowed the formation of joint stock banks provided they were sixty-five miles outside of London, and permitted them to issue notes of over £5 in value. These became the banks of the new industrial areas. In 1833 the Government permitted joint stock banks to be formed in London without restriction as to the numbers of partners—but they were not allowed to issue notes. From this time the bigger banks began to open branches in provincial towns and thus facilitated the flow of credit to business and commerce. By the same Act (1833), Bank of England notes became legal tender.

Sir Robert Peel's Bank Charter Act of 1844 was the most important measure of the period. This brought the issue of notes ultimately into the hands of the Bank of England: no new note-issuing banks were to be formed, and those then issuing were to be restricted to their current issue, while the Bank was to take over the issue of any bank ceasing to issue notes or amalgamating. (But it was not until 1921 that the last note-issuing bank ceased to issue notes.) The Bank of England was divided into two separate departments, the Banking Department for ordinary business and the quite separate Issue Department permitted to make a *fiduciary* issue of £14 million in notes backed by the Bank's own holding of Government securities, and above this figure all notes were to be backed by gold bullion actually in the vaults of the Bank. A weekly account was to be published.

These measures helped to strengthen the banking system and may have helped to lessen the severity of the impact of the slumps (although they were not effective enough in 1847, 1857 and 1866 when the Bank Act had to be suspended). The 1844 Act did not make the Bank of England a central bank, but after the serious crisis of 1866 it quickly withdrew from ordinary commercial banking. As the century progressed, private and country banks were absorbed by the joint stock banks, a process accelerated by the increasing use of the cheque for ordinary commercial purposes. In 1854 the joint stock banks joined the London Clearing House in order to facilitate payments between banks by cheques drawn on the Bank of England, where banks had now to keep a proportion of their reserves.

The working classes, meanwhile, were making use of savings banks—it was a sign of their thrift and growing 'respectability'. In 1861 Gladstone, the Chancellor of the Exchequer, proposed to open a Savings Bank as part of the service offered by the Post Office in recognition of this thrift and 'respectability'. There was some opposition and it is worth quoting a Mr Crossley:

'Working men were often very much afraid to let their masters know that they were saving money from a notion that it would lead to a reduction of their wages, and under the present system the masters were very often concerned with banks and could know exactly how each man's account stood. By this new arrangement each account would be secret.'

Limited liability

Important changes in company law occurred at this time, permitting the formation of companies big enough to raise sufficient money to finance large-scale industry and so advance mass production and increase trade. These changes eventually permitted the formation of limited liability companies, in which people could invest a set amount by purchasing shares or taking up debentures, but if the company failed they would lose only what they had invested and the rest of their property would be untouched—in other words their liability for debts incurred by the company in which they had an interest would be limited to the amount they had invested. If investors were liable to meet the whole debts of a company, then it would be very difficult to raise money through the Stock Exchange, and this had certainly held back industrial development in the past. But the development of canals and of railway companies, of shipping firms, of gas and water companies to supply cities, to say nothing of insurance companies and banks, all of which needed to raise a great deal of money, created a demand for limited liability companies that would enable them to draw upon the great wealth represented by the small savings of a host of families.

The system was open to abuse, especially as the small investor might know nothing of the firm in which he was investing, and there was a good deal of resistance to limited liability on the grounds that it was an immoral avoidance of individual responsibility—'a disreputable subterfuge for evading the payment of debts'. But after a series of government enquiries a number of Acts of Parliament between 1855 and 1862 extended the principle of limited liability. It was a great triumph for the middle classes and released a vast store of money into investment that provided capital for expansion and proved a powerful stimulus to the growth of industry—and of stockbrokers. It created a class of *rentiers* living on dividends from investments, and allowed firms to equip themselves for mass production. At the same time it hastened what has been called the 'managerial revolution' (see *page 241*).

7 · Some political consequences of the Great Changes

The rise of 'laissez-faire'

Most nineteenth-century thinkers believed in competition and private enterprise. Their main slogan came from the ideas that French economists had popularised before the French Revolution—*laissez-faire*—meaning that governments should take as little part as possible in matters of trade and commerce, leaving them to entrepreneurs who, through the action of free competition, would ensure progress and profit and provide the public with the best products at the cheapest prices. The belief was so strong that even in the very different conditions of today, we hear echoes of it. It was quite different from the views of eighteenth-century businessmen, who believed in Mercantilism (see *page 11*). It was an extremely influential view in politics as well as in commerce and industry, and it became so widely established probably because it was associated with rising prosperity at a time when we were several leaps ahead of our rivals.

There were a number of important writers in the second half of the eighteenth century whom we call the 'classical economists' who preached *laissez-faire* views. Adam Smith was the most important. His book, *An Inquiry into the Nature and Causes of the Wealth of Nations*, was published in 1776 and in it he attacked the mercantilist theories of his day on the grounds that they restricted trade, discouraged enterprise and confined the natural expansion of wealth. He advocated the repealing of government regulations controlling trade, so that it could expand without the hindrance of any artificial barriers. Many informed men of his generation had come to similar conclusions to those of Smith, but his book was so well written and so powerfully argued that it became the bible of the Free Trade school of thought. He argued that the entrepreneur needed the spur of competition to keep him vigorous:

'Every individual is continually exerting himself to find out the most advantageous employment for whatever capital he can command. It is his own advantage, indeed, and not that of society, which he has in view. But the study of his own advantage naturally, or rather necessarily, leads him to prefer that employment which is most advantage to the society.'

Here was the philosophical justification for free competition: society would benefit in the end. The Government should confine itself to a minimum of tasks, like preserving public order and defending the country from invasion. Businessmen would do the rest.

Other economists developed Smith's theme, especially the Rev. Thomas Malthus, whose views on population we have encountered (see *page 3*). David Ricardo had perhaps the greatest impact on economic theory among the economists of the early nineteenth century, for in his *Principles of Political Economy and Taxation* (1817), he developed his 'labour theory of value' (the value of goods and services is directly proportional to the labour expended on them—and thus the fewer people employed, the cheaper would be the goods) and demanded that commerce should be liberated so that Britain might have access to the world's food supplies and markets. Jeremy Bentham also had a great influence (one that extended to reforms in many fields beyond economics). He favoured applying what he called the *principle of utility* to all institutions demanding to know whether they were effectively fulfilling their functions according to a yardstick he devised in the form of a popular slogan 'the greatest happiness of the greatest number' (it was called the *felicific calculus* because it was applied by his supporters to so many things with an almost mathematical precision). His followers, the Benthamites, or *Utilitarians*, had a tremendous impact on the nineteenth century, particularly because so many were among the vigorous and incredibly hard-working reformers of the period. Many of the classical economists have been accused of being heartless theoreticians because they based their ideas on economic laws and seemed indifferent to the fate of ordinary people who might be badly affected by the forces of economic change. In actual fact, they were men with a highly developed social conscience, struggling to put forward new ideas and at the same time to do battle with the gigantic problems created by those very forces of economic change in order to find the most effective solution.

Throughout the period of the Great Changes, economists advocating *laissez-faire* urged the dismantling of economic regulations and the withdrawal of government influence as far as was practicable. In fact, as we shall see, things worked out rather differently from what they anticipated. But the first and most obvious point of their attack was the citadel of Mercantilist theory that, through its regulations, *protected* trade and businessmen.

Free trade

Free trade means the removal of all artificial restrictions on trade, such as tariff barriers (import and export duties), monopolies (where one company is given the exclusive right to trade in a particular commodity or area), and the close control of colonial trade represented by the Navigation Acts (see *page 11*). The Free Traders believed that trade would expand indefinitely, given the opportunity to do so. It was a confident belief that appealed especially to the new industrialists who wanted wider markets for their goods. Cotton manufacturers, particularly, favoured free trade and gave a powerful leadership to the movement to achieve it during the nineteenth century. They were known as the *Manchester School*, and their leader was Richard Cobden. His views went beyond problems of commerce, for he confidently predicted that free trade would bring peace as well as prosperity, for free competition would remove economic grievances between nations. Free competition, too, would remove ineffective firms, so that the whole community would benefit and

enjoy both cheapness and sound quality.

But there were many interests that opposed the lowering of tariffs. Manufacturers who feared foreign competition; bankers fearing loss of business to foreign banking houses; shippers who relied on the Navigation Acts (however imperfectly enforced) to fill their ships with British goods; Government agents, who saw no practical alternative to indirect taxation as a source of revenue; and farmers who wanted to protect their British market from cheap imports; all resisted moves to free trade. Only manufacturers, confident of outstripping all rivals, were anxious for the end of protective measures.

The Younger Pitt, leading minister from 1783 to 1801, was greatly influenced by Adam Smith's views. He first modified the navigation system to allow certain colonial ports to trade direct with foreign countries. Then he simplified and reduced tariffs—this was partly to make smuggling unprofitable. In 1786 he secured a mutual reduction of tariffs with France by the Eden Treaty. But no very great progress to free trade had been made by 1793 when the war with France began. War and the economic crises to which it gave rise, prevented any further progress. At the end of the war, in 1815, the Corn Law was passed, preventing the import of foreign corn until British corn had reached the famine price of 80s a quarter. This protected the British farmer from a possible influx of foreign corn that would have brought down the price and so ruin many small farmers.

But a new spirit of confidence was rising, not only amongst industrialists, but among merchants, too. It was well expressed in 1820 by a petition of some London merchants for 'free imports without retaliation, and no duty except for revenue'. Already the East India Company had lost its monopoly of the trade with India in 1813 (it lost that of the China trade in 1834). The Levant and Royal African Companies were relieved of their monopolies in 1821. This new spirit was personified by William Huskisson (President of the Board of Trade 1823-7), perhaps the first minister who could properly be called a doctrinaire free trader. He permitted the export of machinery and allowed skilled workers to emigrate if they wished to do so. Protective tariffs were reduced to a maximum of 30 per cent on imports of manufactured goods, and raw materials were allowed in at a much lower tariff. In 1823 the Reciprocity of Duties Act permitted ministers to make tariff treaties with any country willing to accept a mutual tariff reduction, and, despite the opposition of shipping interests, in 1825 Huskisson modified the Navigation Acts (they were repealed in 1849). He even produced a sliding scale for corn prices so that small imports of corn could be allowed as the price rose, rather than holding imports until the limit had been reached. The sliding scale was introduced in 1828 (it was to be extended by Peel in 1842) and is important because it affected the Corn Law of 1815, protecting the British farmer, which the landed interest was determined to maintain. Free Trade was 'in the air' and our commerce expanded—especially with Latin America, for in 1823 the Foreign Secretary, Canning, had recognised the new Republics being declared there, partly to secure our trade with them.

The Whig governments between 1830 and 1841 left tariffs alone, partly because they were concerned with other reforms, partly because trade was expanding in the early 1830s, and partly because from 1837 to 1842 a severe slump occurred. This slump encouraged demands for a further reduction of tariffs to encourage trade: a Committee on Import Duties (1840) revealed that 1,146 articles were liable for duty, and yet 94·5 per cent of the total tariff revenue came from only seventeen of them. In 1841 Sir Robert Peel became Prime Minister, at the head of a powerful Tory (now called Conservative) ministry. He set himself to the task of restoring prosperity after the slump, and his great Free Trade Budget of 1842 reduced the tariff on imported manufactured goods to 20 per cent, on partly manufactured goods to 12½ per cent and on raw materials to 5 per cent; and he withdrew the remaining duties on manufactured exports. All this seriously affected the revenue, and therefore, as a temporary measure, until the rapid expansion of trade had brought as much money under the surviving duties, as under the old ones, he re-introduced *Income Tax*. Pitt had introduced this direct tax on a person's income in 1799 as a war measure. It had been very unpopular, even though it was a light tax, and was abolished in 1816. Now it was re-introduced at sevenpence in the pound on incomes over £150. Much encouraged by the results of his 1842 Budget, Peel extended the free trade policy in his Budget of 1845 by removing all remaining export duties and further reducing import duties. The following year, Peel was involved in the repeal of the Corn Laws (see *page 91*).

In his free trade policy, Peel had been assisted by W. E. Gladstone at first Vice-President, then President of the Board of Trade. Gladstone admired Peel immensely and he continued the free trade policy when he became Chancellor of the Exchequer in 1853. He had hoped to abolish income tax, but the Crimean War (1854-6) prevented him. Gladstone proved to be a brilliant financier and his budgets were models for all to follow. The 1853 budget fixed a maximum duty of 10 per cent on manufactured imports and lowered the few remaining import duties on foodstuffs like tea, cocoa and fruit. Most of the remaining duties were removed by his 1860 Budget, which left a small duty for revenue purposes only on forty-eight items. That year Richard Cobden negotiated a free trade treaty with France for a reduction of tariff on wines and spirits in return for a French reduction in their tariff on imported British coal, iron, machinery and certain textiles.

By 1860 Britain had become a free trade country, the few remaining duties being merely for revenue and served no protective purpose. There was no danger at this time of our industries suffering from this policy, because we had no rival. Prosperity grew and people began to associate free trade with expanding wealth. But the wealth expanded because the world trade situation was entirely favourable to us. Things changed in the 1880s and from then onwards a rising demand for a return to protection to save industry and agriculture from foreign competition culminated in the rejection of free trade finally in 1932 (see *page 227*).

Repeal of the Corn Laws

During the eighteenth century, trade in corn had been regulated by various corn laws. As the century wore on, we exported less corn and imported more, but during the French Wars (1793-1815) our imports of corn were drastically cut and we had to produce sufficient corn for our own needs. It was greatly to the credit of British farmers and their new agricultural methods (see *page 26*) that they were able to do this. But when peace came at last, farmers feared that an influx of cheap corn from the continent would undersell them in the market and ruin many of them. Parliament, composed of landowners, therefore passed the Corn Law of 1815, which prevented the import of foreign corn until British corn had reached the famine price of 80s a quarter. This protected the farmer. There were sound reasons for this protection even though the threat of a glut of cheap foreign corn was not great, for Europe no longer enjoyed a surplus. Farmers had invested much money during the war and needed to be sure of their income in order to meet their interest payments: the Poor Rate was crippling for small farmers, and as prices began to fall many talked of the years of the 1820s and 1830s as years of agricultural depression. M.P.s were themselves landowners: so were most of the electorate, and no government was prepared to touch the Corn Law, despite David Ricardo's advice to let in cheap food.

Now, as most people at the time felt that the Corn Law kept bread prices abnormally high at a time when it was the staple item of the diet of the poor, it is not surprising that the Corn Law became the symbol of the oppression of the poor by the landed interest. At the same time, industrialists in the north wanted a greater say in government—and the Reform Act of 1832 (see *page 158*) did not open much of the political world to them. They recognised that the growing wealth of the nation was based on industrial enterprise and they were anxious that they, and particularly their sons, should enter political life as easily as did the squirearchy. They hoped to gain a political power appropriate to their wealth, and to get future governments to adopt policies more in keeping with a country whose industrial power was expanding so rapidly. Free trade was one of their principal aims: the Corn Law represented protection. Thus two factors were involved in the attack on the Corn Law; a demand for free trade and a demand by wealthy industrialists for political equality with the landed interest.

The attack was organised by the Anti-Corn Law League and its centre was, appropriately enough, Manchester. The League began in 1838 with Archibald Prentice, George Wilson, President for most of the League's life, and J. B. Smith as the three men chiefly responsible for the League's success. Richard Cobden, often thought to be the main figure behind the League, came to prominence only after 1840, especially when he was elected M.P. for Oldham (1841). In 1841, Cobden secured the support of John Bright, one of the finest orators and moral leaders of the century. Together, both in the country at large and in the House of Commons, they pressed the case for a repeal of the Corn Law.

The Anti-Corn Law League was one of the best organised pressure groups of the century. It modelled itself closely upon Wilberforce's Anti-Slavery League, and, with a thoroughness appropriate to Lancashire businessmen, it used every available means of spreading its views. Lectures were delivered according to a well prepared schedule; literature and propaganda was distributed liberally; petitions were organised; demonstrations held; cheap transport by rail and cheap postage by Rowland Hill's Penny Postage (1840) were put to good effect; and almost every means adopted in modern public relations campaigns were used. One of the most telling arguments they used was to present the anti-corn law issue as a moral campaign for human betterment.

The League had a number of advantages. The movement of opinion was towards free trade and the League was well supported by industrialists who regarded their subscriptions as money well invested. One Liverpool merchant was disarmingly frank in 1842:

'He had gladly given his £100 for the next year to

accomplish the objects of the League; he had hopes he was promoting his own individual good to no small extent by extending Free Trade principles; he was not ashamed to avow his belief, that his £100 subscription would bring him back a hundred times £100, if the objects of the League should happen to be attended by success.'

The support of wealthy men gave an aura of respectability and reasonableness, so important in the politics of the time. The League's chief rival as a movement for popular support was the Chartist movement (see *page 163*) which conspicuously failed to attract this type of 'respectability'. The Chartists argued, with good cause, that the League's interest in the cost of bread sprang from a wish to reduce wages, not from a concern for the welfare of the poor. It was no wonder that the two movements were hostile: but the League benefited because of Chartist failures. Finally, under Cobden's direction, the League concentrated solely on the negative aim of *repeal*, thus attracting support from all those who saw the Corn Law as an obstacle to reform, without having to worry about the disagreements that existed between their different supporters.

The League argued that food prices were kept artificially high by the Corn Law, and that the protected landed interest grew rich out of the hardship it imposed on the poor. Because foreign countries could not send us their corn, they could not earn the money to buy our goods, so trade suffered because of this artificial barrier. The League's propaganda made a huge impact, especially with posters showing the 'Big Loaf' that would come with free trade, once the Corn Law was repealed. Indeed, they were so successful in their propaganda, that they convinced their contemporaries that *they* repealed the Corn Law, and historians have often accepted their arguments uncritically. Many of these arguments were demonstrably unsound, such as the suggestion that the Corn Law kept prices artificially high (see *graph 12*).

But the story of the League was not one of continual success, and in reality it was often in danger of collapse from lack of funds. When the 1841 election returned Peel with the Conservatives committed to defending the Corn Law, it had a real struggle to continue. Peel, who had already been blamed for breaking his party over the Roman Catholic Emancipation issue of 1829, would not be likely to risk his political future tampering with anything so emotionally charged as the Corn Law. However, Peel was a free trader, and by about 1843 he had come to accept that the law should be repealed, but he would have done nothing himself, for he had no wish to break his party. It was the Irish famine, induced by the failure of the potato crop in 1845 that forced the repeal of the Corn Law. It was not the Anti-Corn Law League. Obliged to act to prevent the Irish famine causing many deaths, Peel at first tried to get the Whigs to form a ministry to repeal the Corn Law. But the Whigs could not, so Peel returned to power at the head of a new ministry of younger men to carry repeal in 1846. His supporters, among whom was W. E. Gladstone, were known as 'Peelites'. Tory agriculturalists found a spokesman in Benjamin Disraeli who rose again and again to attack Peel for betraying the very interest that he had been returned in 1841 to defend. But party unity was less important to Peel than the chance of saving life, and he carried repeal at the cost of his own political career and the unity of his party. Shortly afterwards, Peel was defeated and compelled to resign. For the next twenty years, largely because of the collapse of the Conservative party in 1846, there was confusion in British politics with no clear division between the parties until the emergence in the late 1860s of Gladstone's Liberal Party and Disraeli's Conservative Party.

In all this, the League had played small part: but it took the credit for repeal, and seemed (although it was wound up at a triumphal banquet in 1846) to take the credit for the prosperity of the next thirty years, based on the free trade it had advocated. The Corn Laws were never re-imposed (indeed, Disraeli converted the Conservatives to free trade in his Budget of 1852); and the collapse of British agriculture, so confidently predicted by the protectionists, did not follow. Instead the thirty years after 1846 were years of great agricultural prosperity, known as *High Farming* (see *page 36*).

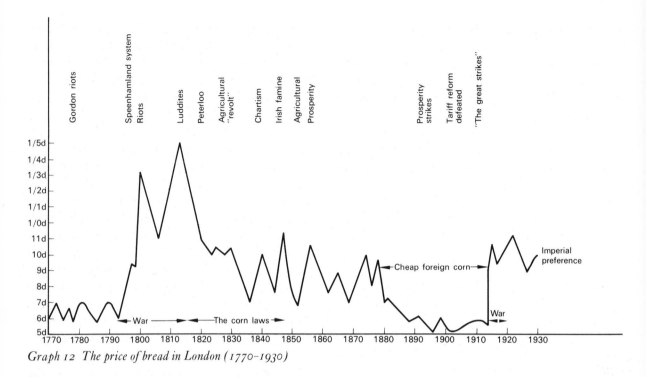

Graph 12   The price of bread in London (1770–1930)

Much has been written about the repeal of the Corn Laws, especially as three of the greatest prime ministers of the century, Peel, Disraeli and Gladstone, were intimately concerned with the crisis. At the time it seemed a great watershed, and it was certainly a victory for free trade. But was it so great a victory for the industrial interest? The landed interest, strengthened by an influx of money, and enlarged by intermarriage with industrialist families, continued to dominate British politics until the twentieth century. The Second Reform Act (1867), which gave the vote to urban artisans, was still twenty years away: and when it was passed the industrialists were already being absorbed into the Establishment, partly by marriages, but more particularly by educating their sons at the new public schools then becoming a great social force for the wealthy (see *page 145*).

Government regulation revives

If the growth of free trade meant the withdrawal of many Government regulations in the name of free competition, it did not mean that all Government regulation was withdrawn. Indeed, one of the strangest things about the nineteenth century was that, although its slogan was *laissez-faire*, Government regulation grew in the social and industrial fields. This was for a number of reasons. The growth of large-scale towns and factories produced a mass of problems that were only too obvious because of the numbers involved. Bad conditions were nothing new, and when these conditions concerned individual families in the domestic system, or particular areas of bad housing, they could conveniently be ignored. They were. But when vast areas of new towns were dreadful slums, or large numbers of workers were recognised as being obliged to work in bad conditions, it was more difficult to ignore the problem. And because the numbers of people involved were so large (a consequence of the demographic revolution) only the Government could effectively handle the matter. Early nineteenth-century conditions for the workers were not necessarily worse than ever before: they were just more obvious, and something had to be done to protect people from exploitation. This meant an expansion of Government regulation at the very moment that *laissez-faire* views were bringing in free trade. In social and industrial matters, 'in absolute form, the doctrine of *laissez-faire* was never accepted or given effect in this country' (W. H. B. Court). Indeed, if one takes a long view of English history, over several centuries, Government regulation is normal: it was the nineteenth century that was unusual. The 1830s and 1840s were the key decades for this revival of regulation. Inspection and enforcement by government inspectors became the rule, although it was not always possible to do more than scratch the surface of problems.

By the 1870s the Government was deliberately assuming responsibility for deciding the nature of contracts of employment between masters and men, and for the well-being of citizens. This meant recruiting an army of civil servants:

'officers and commissioners not merely requested and secured, they even anticipated legislation which would award them the widest discretion and independence. . . . There could be no doubt now that the limit of State activity was imposed, not so much by individualism, contract, free trade or any other notion, as by the paucity of the human and physical resources at the executive's disposal.' (Macdonagh).

The amazing thing is that contemporaries failed to realise the significance of what was happening. In a world declaring its belief in *laissez-faire*, where governments were not expected to interfere, Government administration was beginning to encroach in an effective way upon the lives of ordinary citizens. This expansion of Government regulation was to lead to what we call the *collectivist state* (see *page 168*) in which the State (Government) assumes extensive responsibility for the protection of those who cannot protect themselves, and provides for its citizens in order to make their lives easier.

Climbing boys

There was nothing new in using boys to sweep chimneys. But during the period of the Great Changes many more houses were being built with narrow flues which it was difficult to enter to clean. It was still the fashion to send youngsters of either sex up the chimney with a brush: they made a better job, especially where there were corners for the soot to lodge upon. Many housewives preferred a climbing boy to any other means of chimney cleaning. So, a hundred years ago, one would have met sweeps in town streets, their brushes and bags carried by children, sometimes their own, sometimes 'apprentices' usually sold to them for virtual slavery by parish officers or by parents. If a child showed any disinclination to ascend, a beating was usually enough, failing that a threat to return him to his parents would persuade him to climb. If he got stuck by his clothes he would be pulled down and sent back, beaten and naked, or a dry straw fire lit beneath him to encourage him to greater exertions. Sores on the knees, elbows and back did not always heal quickly, and the child's knees and legs frequently became deformed both because of the constant straining for a foothold, and because of the heavy bag of soot he had to carry. Ears, eyes and throats were constantly sore, and skin complaints were common—the worst being 'chimney sweepers' cancer' for which the only relief was the surgeon's knife. If a child stuck too tightly he was pulled down by a rope, or, if it could not be avoided, the brickwork was opened to release what by then would be a corpse. It was not unknown for sweeps to be sentenced to hard labour for causing deaths.

In the eighteenth century a philanthropist, Jonas Hanway, began to awaken the public conscience to the conditions under which these children worked and lived, but his Act of 1788 was not enforced. By the end of the century there was a Society for Superseding the Necessity for Climbing Boys that tried to popularise the use of mechanical brushes. The boys climbed on nevertheless. Oliver Twist would have become a sweep's lad had he not shown himself so terrified that the magistrate refused to approve the indenture of the 'apprenticeship'. Dickens's novel was published in 1838 and may have helped the passing of the 1840 Act that prohibited the employment of climbing chimney sweeps under the age of 21 (when they were too big for climbing). But this Act, too, was ineffective for it lacked means of enforcement.

It was Lord Shaftesbury who achieved effective legislation. He was helped by the widespread humanitarianism of the nineteenth century, by the earnestness of many affected by the Evangelical Revival (see *page 133*), by books like Charles Kingsley's *The Water Babies* (1863) and by his own remarkable powers of advocacy. In 1863, a Commission on Children's Employment was told by a master sweep:

'The usual age at which boys begin now is from six upwards. I myself began a little over five. They are generally the children of the poorest and worst behaved parents, who want to get rid of them and make a little money by it as well. It is as bad as Negro slavery, only not so well known.'

Another told how the boys would 'sleep black':

'I have gone to bed with my knee and elbow scabbed and raw, and the inside of my thighs all scarified; we slept 5 or 6 boys together in a kind of cellar with the soot bags over us, sticking in the wounds sometimes; that and some straw were all our bed and bed clothes; they were the same bags as we had used in the day, wet or dry. I could read, and we used sometimes to subscribe for a candle to read by when we were in bed. I have seen the steam from our bodies so thick as to obscure the light so that I couldn't read at all. . . . I have been for fifteen months without being washed except by the rain: why, I have been almost walking away with vermin!'

A child died in 1875 after sweeping a flue in an asylum near Cambridge. *The Times* thundered 'whoever deliberately authorised and permitted the employment of this unfortunate boy, are morally guilty of murder'. Public opinion had changed, and Lord Shaftesbury was able to pass an Act that was effective because it could be enforced. By 1875, after all, fewer chimneys were being built that could be swept by boys, and better machinery was available for cleaning: perhaps technical improvements and developments in building rather than

humanitarianism ended the era of the climbing boy.

The example of climbing boys illustrates Parliament, if somewhat unwillingly, interfering with the freedom of private contracts of employment because of the exploitation of defenceless children. It is one example among many.

Factory Acts

Factory Acts regulating the conditions of work of employees were necessary because the concentration of large numbers of people in factories made bad working conditions the more obvious, so that it was no longer possible not to notice them, as had been the case with the domestic system.

The early factories offered much better wages than could be earned on the land, but the first generation of factory workers had to get used quickly to a new way of life. They had to adjust themselves to the speed of the machines, which were too expensive to be kept standing idle. Improved machinery often required little skill on the part of the actual operative, and employers frequently preferred child-labour, both because it was cheapest and because there was often a labour shortage in certain areas. Few employers showed much concern for the welfare of their workers: they had no wish to reduce their profits, and they had struck a bargain with their workers when they took them on and saw no reason to modify it. It is easy to blame the employers; but remember that they, too, were in a totally new situation. Who had assumed responsibility for workers' welfare under the domestic system? No one in particular. It took time for them to realise that with factories and larger, concentrated working forces, they had acquired a new responsibility of welfare as well as wages for their workers. It took Government action to compel them to recognise this.

Conditions were worst in the small mills (the vast majority), where the employer, concerned for profit margins, was not inclined to indulge any sentimental interest in the conditions of his workers. The 1833 Factory Report noted:

'It is of the old and small mills that the report pretty

uniformly is—dirty; low roofed, ill-ventilated; no conveniences for washing or dressing; no contrivance for carrying off dust and other effluvia; machinery not boxed in; passages so narrow that they can hardly be defined; some of the flats so low that it is scarcely possible to stand upright in the centre of the rooms.'

Severe discipline, enforced by beatings or dismissals or fines (one shilling for opening windows or for singing at work, two shillings for keeping the gas burning too long), added to the long hours and the risks of industrial injuries and diseases, for which no one gained compensation—but then, who had ever had compensation under the domestic system? The most dangerous thing in textile mills was the driving belt, especially if it had been joined by buckles. If you were caught by it, you would be hurled several times against ceiling and floor. Engels, Marx's friend, quoted a Report of 1836:

'The unfavourable influence of mill-work upon the hands are as the following: 1. The inevitable necessity of forcing their mental and bodily effort to keep pace with a machine moved by a uniform motive power. 2. Continuanace in an upright position during unnaturally long and quickly recurring periods. 3. Loss of sleep in consequence of too long working hours, pain in the legs, and general physical derangement. To these are often added low, crowded, dusty or damp work-rooms, impure air, a high temperature and constant perspiration.'

But there were good employers, even among small factory owners. There is so much evidence of bad conditions that it is easy to exaggerate them.

Child-labour, of course, was high on the list of abuses. But then, the domestic system exploited children, too; and parents were often rougher task-masters than employers. During the eighteenth century there was a clear abuse of child labour, especially of pauper children. As early as 1738 an enquiry into the increase of the poor noted:

'A most unhappy practice prevails in most places to apprentice poor children, no matter to what master

provided he lives out of the parish; if the child serve the first forty days we are rid of him for ever. The master may be a tiger in cruelty; he may beat, abuse, strip naked, starve, or do what he will to the poor innocent lad, few people take much notice, and the officers who put him out the least of anybody.'

Chimney-sweeps were an obvious source of 'apprenticeship' for 'parish boys' and the new mills in Lancashire, short of labour and prepared to ask few questions, especially as they were so far away from London, proved an even more profitable means of relieving the poor rate in London parishes. Batches were sent off to what might be slave labour, with boys tending machinery in shifts of up to fifteen hours so that the few beds the employer provided were never left unoccupied, whilst machinery worked throughout the day. Entirely free from supervision or regulation, these hostels of mill boys were dens of corruption and degradation: floggings were inflicted as often to keep children awake as to punish them. If an apprentice escaped, he could be pursued and obliged to return.

Various Acts tried to prevent this trafficking in pauper children. Robert Owen and Sir Robert Peel, two wealthy employers who were humanitarians, secured the passing of the Health and Morals of Apprentices Act (1802), often referred to as the first factory act. It applied solely to cotton mills, limiting the hours of work to twelve, forbidding night work and requiring children to receive some form of education. But it was totally ineffective, for its enforcement was left to local magistrates (or Justices of the Peace), who, if they were prepared to inspect at all, were favourable to the mill owners. A second Act in 1819 was no more successful. In 1816 the apprenticing of pauper children more than 40 miles from their home parish was forbidden, but the problem of pauper apprentices was not ended until the system was abolished in 1844. What cured the evil was not legislation, but the growing number of parents and children seeking employment, whom the mill owner did not have to trouble to house and feed. More abundant labour, however, did not improve conditions of work.

In 1830 the *Ten Hours Movement* was launched by John Fielden of Todmorden, and Richard Oastler. Their campaign for a ten hour working day was vigorous and Oastler's letter in the *Leeds Mercury* of October 1830, contrasting Wilberforce's concern for the Negro slave with his indifference towards mill workers in his own parliamentary constituency of Yorkshire, caused a sensation:

'Let truth speak out, appalling as the statement may appear. The fact is true. Thousands of our fellow-creatures and fellow-subjects, both male and female, the miserable inhabitants of a *Yorkshire town* (Yorkshire now represented by the giant of anti-slavery principles) are this very moment existing in a state of slavery, *more horrid* than are the victims of that hellish system *"colonial slavery"*. . . . The very streets which receive the droppings of the "Anti-Slavery Society" are every morning wet by the tears of innocent victims at the accursed shrine of avarice, who are *compelled* (not by the catwhip of the Negro slave-driver) but by the dread of the equally appalling thong or strap of the over-looker, to hasten, half-dressed, *but not half-fed*, to those magazines of British infantile slavery—*the worsted mills in the town and neighbourhood of Bradford*!!!'

They hoped to reduce the hours of children and women, and so of men, for the mills could not function without female and child labour then employed. Their spokesmen in the House of Commons were Michael Sadler and Ashley Cooper, Lord Shaftesbury. But the manufacturers argued that they would be ruined if costly machinery were kept idle by reducing working hours, and their bill failed. However, a Royal Commission was set up, and its Report obliged the passing of Althorp's Factory Act, 1833, the first *effective* one. It applied to all textile mills except silk, and disallowed the employment of children under nine years old, reduced the working day for those between nine and thirteen to nine hours a day, and for young persons aged thirteen and eighteen to twelve hours a day. There was to be no night work for anyone under eighteen. Two hours' education a day under the care of the employer had to be provided for children,

and there was to be a break of one and a half hours for meals during the day. What made it effective was the provision of Inspectors. At first there were only four of them, but their numbers were later increased. The fact that they were appointed at all makes the 1833 Act a landmark in nineteenth-century legislation. No longer were Acts of Parliament to be words on paper: they were to be enforced. The inspectors, indeed, soon found that manufacturers were not applying the act, or doing so in a ridiculous way, like holding education classes in the boiler house during meal breaks. The threat of prosecution, however, gradually got the act enforced, and the compulsory registration of births (1836) eventually made it possible to determine a child's age. Unlike the J.P.s, the inspectors were experts in their job.

The Ten Hours Movement continued to agitate, and in 1844 Shaftesbury secured an act disallowing the employment of children under eight years old, reducing the working day of children between eight and thirteen to six and a half hours and the working day for women to twelve hours. To prevent argument, a public clock, clearly visible, was to be provided (although fear of dismissal prevented many noticing how the hands were put back as the time limit approached!). Dangerous machinery was to be fenced in, and machines were not to be cleaned when in motion. Employers adopted a shift system, making it possible for them legally to keep their machines running throughout the day. But the triumph of the Ten Hours Movement came with the 1847 Factory Act which limited the hours of women and young persons to ten in any one day and to fifty-eight during the week. Even so, by the 'relay system' some employers were able to keep their machinery in production throughout the day, and therefore a compromise was reached by the 1850 Act that allowed for a ten and a half hour day, but prohibited the relay system. These acts applied to a part of the textile trade only, not to industry as a whole. Other trades, for the moment, fell outside factory regulations.

The *Report of the Children's Employment Commission*, 1863, revealed the need to protect employees in other trades. In the potteries, for example, extensive use was made of child labour (often directly employed by the operatives themselves). Bronchitis and other respiratory diseases and lead poisoning from the glazing vats were so prevalent as to demand legislation. The Lucifer (self-lighting) Match, the simple invention of the 1830s that produced a social revolution in its own right, was manufactured in frightful conditions, often at first on a domestic scale. Fortunately, by the 1870s most of the smallest and worst manufactures had disappeared, but some 1,800 children and 850 adults were still concerned. The worst complaint was 'phossy-jaw' where the entire jaw rotted away because of phosphorus poisoning. One of the witnesses before the 1863 Commission reported seeing

' . . . one who had lost his jaw. "You could take his chin and shove it all into his mouth." Has known several die from "phosphorous in their inwards". Has known eighteen or twenty lose their jaws. . . . Some are seized in four or five months.'

The 1864 Factory Acts Extension Act extended factory legislation to include potteries, match works and fustian cutting shops. In 1864, also, Gladstone extended the powers of factory inspectors. Later, in 1867, the regulations were extended to all premises where more than 50 were employed and the Workshops Regulation Act regulated conditions in workshops employing less than 50 people. By this time factory legislation was so complex that it was simplified into a code of factory procedure by Richard Cross's Consolidated Factory Act (1878). Further sanitary and safety requirements were added by the 1901 Factory Act, and the twentieth century has seen continual improvements without the violent opposition from factory owners that accompanied the nineteenth-century reforms.

There were good employers who applied the factory acts and provided even better conditions: but there were others who had to be forced by the full power of parliament. This showed the failure of laissez-faire to provide proper working conditions. As the nineteenth century wore on the workers

gradually became stronger to resist the exploitation of some employers, especially with the development of trade unions (see page 164).

Working conditions in the mines

Many mines still remained small or controlled by small firms who could not afford expensive equipment, and, as with the factories, it was in the smaller mines that the worst working conditions were to be found. It was very rare indeed to encounter a mine owner, even a great mine owner, who cared much about the condition of his work people. A long tradition of bitterness dominates the history of coal mining: it is a long, hard story, as hard and unsentimental as the life of a miner. The mine owner often owned the miner's cottage and turned them out if they would not work on his conditions. He would bring in 'black-legs' to break strikes and there were frequent fights with them, with the police, even with the military. Sudden death in the pit was accepted philosophically: this tended to cut miners off from other workers. The mines were often isolated geographically, and as miners lived rough and violent lives, few outsiders knew how bad their conditions were, for few dared to visit them. Miners were an isolated and depressed class of people, and their conditions probably worsened as deeper mines were sunk without proper safety precautions.

The Report on Mining Conditions in 1842 made the public aware for the first time of these bad conditions. Women and children were often employed underground; babies of four were 'trappers', working their shutters in total darkness and alone, 'were it not for the passing and re-passing of the coal carriages, this would amount to solitary confinement of the worst order'. Older children and women would sometimes cart coal, occasionally crawling on all fours, sometimes pushing wheelless tubs of coal through soft clays and water along low passages. Women and girls would carry up to three hundredweight of coal, bent double, climbing the ladders of the shafts at the risk of dropping coal on those below. Debauchery and brutality was common and elementary safety precautions lacking. Accidents were too frequent to be recorded, and as the miner's food was meagre and his hours long, few survived into their late forties.

One of the Commissioners, Dr Southwood Smith (see *page 106*) suggested illustrating the report and this made a great impact on public opinion. The Mines Act (1842) followed. Women and boys under ten were not allowed to work below ground—but inspectors to enforce the Act were not appointed before 1850. It is amazing that mine owners were able to prevent inspection for so long, when the need for inspection was so great. Indeed, regulations for greater safety came very slowly. It was 1862 before all mines were required to have two shafts for ventilation (and much later before this was enforced). Various regulations about the employment of youths below ground were made in the 1860s and 1870s, but it was 1881 before the Home Secretary was empowered to hold inquests when fatal accidents occurred, and 1896 before safety regulations concerning the use of explosives in mines appeared. That mining safety regulation lagged behind that for factories, was probably because fewer children and women were involved; but the legislation showed the growth of Government regulation.

The truck system

In the eighteenth century there was often not enough actual coinage of the realm available for industrialists to pay their workers in cash. Many iron masters cast their own tokens that often were accepted in the locality as though they were coins of the realm. But most employers fell back on the 'truck system', the practice of paying wages partly in cash and partly in tokens to be exchanged for specific goods, or goods to a specific value at a local *tommy shop*. If the employer did not actually own the tommy shop, he would have a big interest in it. In isolated villages, mills, mines, and for the navvies, there was sound sense in the arrangement: but it was obviously open to abuse. The employer could

gain a huge profit from his tommy shop, where prices were often 25 per cent higher than those in comparable shops in the same area, and the workers were obliged to go to the tommy shop because their tokens could only be exchanged there. He could intimidate too, for, even if wages were paid in cash, workers would be well advised to visit the tommy shop if they valued their jobs. Wages were sometimes irregularly paid, or workers temporarily laid off or put on short time, and at such periods, workers had no alternative but to run up a sizeable bill at the shop for more-than-usually-expensive necessities. So notorious were the abuses of 'truck', that a Truck Act was passed in 1831, and another in 1841, designed to curb the worst forms of exploitation. But the system remained a major problem into the 1870s, and was only ended partly by rising prosperity and partly by the growing self-assertiveness of the workers who could find more alternative employment, or bring trade union pressure to bear, and partly by the development of co-operative stores (see *page 166*). The wholesale exploitation by truck left a long and bitter memory and it is alive today in wages legislation providing for hourly-paid staff to be paid in cash if they demand it.

In the same way as with conditions and hours of work in factories and mines, the Truck Acts show nineteenth-century governments prepared to interfere with what the employer would call his 'freedom of contract' with his workers, in order to ensure that defenceless people should not be exploited. This extension of Government was not confined to industry, for it was also a feature of the development of business (limited liability companies, for example), of the new Poor Law of 1834, of the changes in local government, especially in the second half of the century, and in the field of education. In view of this, we must be careful not to think of the nineteenth century as a century in which *laissez-faire* dominated the government of the country, although many writers of the time give this impression.

8 · Some social consequences of the Great Changes: the new towns

Today English towns sprawl, so that the countryside to most people is either moorland and hills, or the strip of land between towns glimpsed from the motorway. But it was not always so. Indeed, only since 1851 have more people lived in towns than in the countryside.

In the eighteenth century, towns were either great ports like Bristol, the growing Liverpool, or the huge metropolis of London, or they were much smaller market towns of merely local importance. In the cities some remarkable pieces of town planning were produced, like the Bath crescents or the Nash terraces in London. These were in the wealthier parts of the towns, parts that were always well built. But conditions were always bad in the poorer parts.

As the period of the Great Changes wore on, towns grew bigger and many lost the close link with rural life that had been the feature of even the metropolis, when green fields lay between Euston and Highgate, and cows grazed in St James's Park, so that one could buy really fresh milk. 'When I

Bath's eighteenth-century crescents, seen from the air

was a child,' noted a writer in the 1860s, 'in every city of the kingdom and even in London, an easy walk would take a man into quiet fields and pure air. We did not live in a pall of smoke, and a yellow fog . . . a prison . . . of brick and pavement.'

Towns changed, and so did the relationship between people. In the small market town there was a sense of community, despite differences in wealth, for most families were known to each other. Except, perhaps, in Birmingham, among the small masters who continued to live with their work people, this close contact was broken down in the new industrial towns, and many people might experience an acute sense of loneliness and isolation. Charles Dickens put it well: 'a man may live and die in London . . . his existence a matter of interest to no one save himself'.

Local conditions determined the way towns developed. In the South there were fewer factories: in parts of the Midlands and the North, villages sprawled outwards, often into each other, so that there was an 'industrialising' of the countryside, rather than the building of a town. Even today the townships between Nottingham and Derby, almost a continuous succession of buildings, are separated by sudden patches of green fields. Occasionally, the fields around growing towns could not be purchased for building, especially if they carried pasture rights for the freemen of the town. Nottingham was the best example of what has been called this 'cowocracy'. In the eighteenth century it was a graceful town, but the expansion of knitware brought mills and the need to build more houses. But the burgesses would not allow the surrounding fields to be built upon, lest they lose their pasture rights. And so the population crowded into the narrow space of the town: eventually enclosure saved the city, but by then the damage was done, as a report of 1845 to the Health of Towns Commission demonstrated:

'I believe that nowhere else shall we find so large a mass of inhabitants crowded into courts, alleys and lanes as in Nottingham, and those, too, of the worst possible construction. Here they are so clustered upon each other, court within court, yard within yard, and lane within lane, in a manner to defy description.'

Steam-power and factories changed the nature of towns. There were massive buildings and smoke clouds, and workers had to be housed as near as possible to the works; hours were long and a minimum time had to be spent on travel, and as many jobs were casual, workers had to be 'on the spot' to get them. So houses crowded round factory yards in rapidly built terraces: speculative jerry-building was the hand-maiden of working-class housing. Factories tended to be in the lower parts of valleys, often near a canal. The land was cheaper here, but it was low and marshy, difficult to drain. For workers' houses adequate draining was not required. The word 'slum', perhaps derived from a regional word 'slump' or wet mire, first appeared in the 1820s. This was a time of expensive building materials and when it was not always easy to raise money for housing. A high proportion of the rent of a house is intended to cover interest charges, so that a rise in interest rates meant a drop in size and quality of houses.

The railways brought many changes. Cheaper building materials and the siting of factories away from valley bottoms helped raise housing standards slightly. But the noisy, smoky areas round stations and marshalling yards and beside the lines were left for slum areas: the long viaducts provided archways that were used for storage, workshops and even housing. But the building of local lines meant the appearance of the commuter and the growth of suburbia where lower middle-class clerks lived pale and 'respectable' lives, like Mr Pooter in *The Diary of a Nobody*. These were the areas of fashionable church-going, of Victorian families struggling to maintain two servants in a mean pretence of social ease, sometimes imposing on defenceless girls conditions and hours of work quite as bad as any to be found in factories or even the mines.

The factory town drove out the countryside: it also drove a deep cleavage into society. Class consciousness, itself largely a product of the sociological changes of this period, was accentuated by the way towns grew. For the first time the wealthy lived in areas, often suburbs, at some distance from working-class areas. There developed a degree of hostility between the classes that had not existed before. It was to play a great part in the development of working class self-assertion in education, religion, local government and national politics. Intellectuals were well aware of what was happening. Mrs Gaskell explained it in *North and South* through the person of a mellow southerner reacting sensitively to a northern city:

'I see two classes dependent on each other in every possible way, yet each evidently regarding the interests of the other as opposed to their own; I never lived in a place before where there were two sets of people always running each other down.'

Condition of the urban poor

We remember the nineteenth century as an age of appalling conditions in towns. We ought to remember it as the time when men recognised that the appalling conditions in which the poor had always lived were no longer acceptable. Better conditions for the urban worker is a nineteenth and twentieth century cry: it should have been that of the previous five hundred years.

THE CROWDED STREETS.

Boy. "NOW, MISSUS, THERE'S NO BUSSES, KITCH 'OLD OF MY HARM, AND I'LL TAKE YER OVER!"

The crossing sweeper

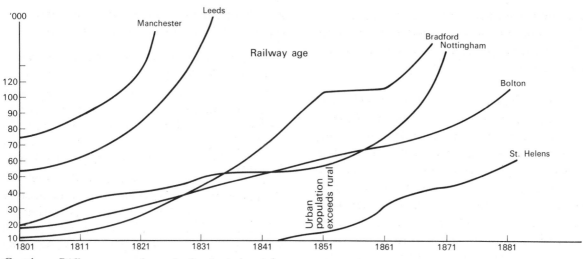

Graph 13 Different rates of growth of major industrial towns

Some villages today lack proper sanitation, but this is not immediately noticed because few people are involved. Towns always presented a greater problem, simply because of their greater size. In the streets of the wealthy, the crossing-sweeper was there to clear a way across the well laid cobbles. They were not there in the poorer areas. These areas had their distinctive smell. It had always been there, but it suddenly got worse in the generation after Waterloo (1815) simply because of the growth of towns (see *graph 13*). To industrial waste was added that that gathers round any urban community, notably sewage. And since there were no early measures taken to deal with this situation, for such an urban growth had not occurred before, the urban death rate rose steeply. Within towns there was a definite variation, for the better areas had a lower rate than the poorer. In Manchester, the middle-class suburb of Broughton had in 1840 a death rate per 1,000 of 15·8; nearer to the town centre it was 28·6, and in the centre it was 35·2. This was typical of industrial cities and it demanded action on a large scale. The position was put succinctly in Edwin Chadwick's *Report on the Sanitary Condition of the Labouring Population* (1842). He contrasted rural Rutland with Manchester and other cities:

Average length of life:

	Rutland	Manchester	Bolton
Professional classes	52	38	34
Tradesmen	41	20	23
Mechanics & Labourers	38	17	18

	Bethnal Green	Leeds	Liverpool
Professional classes	48	44	35
Tradesmen	26	27	22
Mechanics & Labourers	16	19	15

The figures speak for themselves: it is incredible that the population continued to grow. In Engels's book on the working classes are many examples of living conditions that are inconceivable today, but were not uncommon in the 1840s:

'Immediately under the railway bridge there stands a court, the filth and horrors of which surpass all the others by far. . . . Everywhere before the doors refuse and offal . . . privies are so rare here that they are either filled up everyday or are too remote for most of the inhabitants to use them.'

The sudden pressure of people on the accom-modation available was the root cause of such conditions. Engels quoted a vicar of Bethnal Green, an area renowned for its slums:

'It is nothing unusual to find a man, his wife, four or five children, and, sometimes, both grandparents, all in a single room of ten to twelve square feet, where they eat, sleep and work. I believe that before the Bishop of London called attention to this most poverty-stricken parish, people at the West End knew as little of it as of the savages of Australia . . . I was rector near Huddersfield during the three years in which the mills were at their worst, but I have never seen such complete helplessness of the poor as since then in Bethnal Green. Not one father of a family in ten in the whole neighbourhood has other clothing than his working suit, and that is as bad and tattered as possible; many, indeed, have no other covering for the night than these rags, and no bed, save a sack of straw and shavings.'

The squalor of slums was worsened by the failure to lay proper drains. Often a gutter in the centre of an unpaved street sufficed. Privies were rare and as rarely emptied, so that many relieved themselves by the walls of houses or in the court-yards, whilst about the privies, excrement oozed. Families slept together in rooms beside walls and cellars covered by the filth. As late as 1883, the Rev. Mearns recorded visiting such rooms in *The Bitter Cry of Outcast London*:

'To get into them you have to penetrate courts reeking with poisonous and malodorous gases arising from the accumulations of sewage and refuse scattered in all directions and often flowing beneath your feet; courts, many of which the sun never penetrates, which are never visited by a breath of fresh air . . . you have to grope your way along dark and filthy passages swarming with vermin. Then, if you are not driven back by the intolerable stench, you may gain admittance. . . . Have you pitied the poor creatures who sleep under railway arches, in carts or casks, or under any shelter which they can find in the open air? You

will see that they are to be envied in comparison with those whose lot it is to seek refuge here.'

Death was a constant companion. There was no spare room for the coffin, and so it lay in a corner, often several days, while the living ate and slept beside it. Funerals were often costly things and families would cheerfully spend literally their last penny entertaining the mourners. Parents would often pay a little a week to a club that paid out small sums to meet such expenses—and sometimes families waited for a sickening child to die in order to pay a few debts. But the bodies had to be buried, and many of the existing town cemeteries and churchyards were so full that no new grave could be opened without revealing corpses in various stages of decomposition. No wonder grave diggers found it necessary to be drunk most of the time. Dr Lynch, giving evidence in 1842, said:

'We know the symptoms of the dead damp; it is a peculiar, indescribable smell, and any gentleman coming up Parliament Street may have remarked it. From whence did the stench come?—From the church yards!'

The burial ground in Russell Court, off Drury Lane, where the whole ground level had been raised several feet by constant burials, was 'a mass of corruption' which 'polluted the air the living had to breathe and poisoned the well water which in default of other they had to drink'.

The water supply was in the hands of private companies. It was becoming fashionable by 1810 for the wealthy to have water piped to their town houses (the number of wells shown on Ordnance Survey maps of the 1930s of villages will tell you how recently piped water for every home has been the case in the rural areas). Others had their water piped to a pump or stand-pipe, or drew it from a well. Drinking water was a valuable commodity in towns; consequently bathing was infrequent, and the consumption of water per person was very low. The poor used their available water for drinking, cooking and washing. Even when a stand-pipe served a series of tenements, the water would be flowing only occasionally. In 1844 it was reported:

'On the principal cleaning day, Sunday, the water is on for about five minutes, and it is on also for three days in the week for one half-hour, and so great is the rush to obtain a modicum before it is turned off, that perpetual quarrelling and disturbance is the result.'

Even when water was piped to houses there was no guarantee that the filter beds would ensure a reasonable purity. One Poplar householder, curious to discover why his water had stopped, 'took off the tap and to my astonishment found *an eel fourteen inches in length*. It was in a *putrid* state and the *stench* arising from it was most fearful. Since that time I have lost two children, who died of cholera, and my wife and other members of the family have also been suffering from the disease'.

The connection between impure water and disease was not generally recognised until the 1850s, and little care seems to have been taken to ensure purity. There was continual danger of *seepage*, impurities entering the water through the porous pipes used, or into wells, especially where they were near cesspools. The poor often drew their water from open streams used also as common sewers (the London rivers were not covered over until the later nineteenth century), so that it was necessary to let the sediment settle before drinking it. A good deal of the garbage and sewage found its way into the London rivers. When the water closet was introduced on a large scale, which itself required piped water-supplies, much of the effluent found its way into the Thames. The Thames is tidal, so the mess was carried back and forth up the open streams with the tide. Things got so bad that in the hot summer of 1858 there was what was known as the 'great stink', and Parliament had to debate what should be done. *The Times* reported (19 June 1858):

'Mr Mangles said that when he was a young man Thames salmon were celebrated. The salmon, wiser than members of Parliament, had avoided the pollution, and he was informed that cart-loads of fish were taken out of the Thames which had died in consequence of the state of the river.'

Cholera

One reason why contaminated water and accumulated filth was allowed to imperil lives was the medical profession itself. It was not at all certain how diseases were caught or passed on. Many doctors believed in the *atmospheric theory*, that diseases spread through 'bad air'. This view confused cause with effect: a bad smell is the result of chemical action partly caused by *germs* and *viruses* (tiny organisms, often too small to be seen under a normal microscope), and it is these *micro-organisms* that cause disease. However, in the 1850s medical research began to indicate that 'bad air' was not the cause of disease. Cholera, a deadly intestinal disease, broke out in 1854, and Dr John Snow was able to prove a connection between wells infected by sewage and the incidence of cholera. He plotted cholera cases occurring near Golden Square, London, and his map clearly showed the cases occurred near infected pumps, and not near pumps that were not infected. This was not enough for the medical profession, and many doctors showed a remarkable pig-headedness in rejecting the growing mass of evidence in favour of the micro-organism theory. At last, Louis Pasteur, a distinguished French chemist, and Dr Joseph Lister, famous for his antiseptic spray (1865), convinced the profession, but it was not until 1884 that the German chemist Koch discovered the cholera virus.

Cholera was a new disease in England. It appeared with frightful suddenness and struck with lightening speed. It took a frightful toll of the poor, though it was no respecter of persons, and there seemed to be no cure for it. The first visitation was in 1831 and the horror at the disease and the deaths shocked people into immediate action. In Leeds seventy cart-loads of sewage, the accumulation of thirty years, were cleared from local privies. But the outbreak died down quickly and authorities dropped back into neglect. In 1848–9 cholera returned, unaccountably striking different cities and not all

Dr Lister's anti-septic spray. In 1865 Lister had come to the conclusion that sepsis (wounds going poisonous) was caused by germs. To destroy them he used carbolic acid in a fine spray played upon the region of the operation. This antiseptic method resulted in a big drop in deaths from sepsis, but the spray was inconvenient and later discarded when superior antiseptic methods were introduced

big towns. It was worst in summer. In London the number of victims mounted: 246 in June; 1,952 in July; 4,251 in August; 6,644 in September. Again cholera returned in 1851, testifying to urban neglect, and it reappeared with less violence during the 1850s and 1860s.

Doctors showed commendable courage—many came to the affected towns to help and to study the disease. Each time cholera struck there was panic—in Scotland in 1831 the houses of cholera victims were burnt down and corpses often left unburied for fear of catching the disease by touching the body:

'A young robust fisherman . . . lay festering in a sand bank; the brawny blacksmith was decomposing in a mossy hole beside a thorn bush; half the inhabitants of the little fishing village of Inver were strewn in shallow furrows along the arid waste which surrounded their dwellings.'

Bearers refused to carry the coffins of cholera victims at shoulder height lest they breathe contamination. Not all towns sprang to action to remove possible causes of the disease and when, in 1853, the Scottish clergy recommended a day of prayer and fasting, the Home Secretary, Lord Palmerston, retorted that their time would be better spent cleaning up the towns. Perhaps he had in mind a scene like the following, taken from Henry Mayhew's *London Characters*.

'As we gazed in horror at the pool, we saw drains and sewers emptying their filthy contents into it, we saw a whole tier of doorless privies in the open road built over it. . . . And yet, as we stood gazing in horror at the fluvial sewer, we saw a child from one of the galleries opposite lower a tin can with a rope, to fill a bucket that stood beside her.

In each of the rude and rotten balconies, indeed, that hung over the stream, the self-same bucket was to be seen in which the inhabitants were wont to put the mucky liquid to stand, so that they might ... skim the fluid from the solid particles of filth and pollution which constituted the sediment.'

In 1854, Dr Snow had shown that cholera, an intestinal disease, was spread by contaminated water supply. The cholera epidemic of 1866 carried off 6,000 Londoners. That was a judgement upon those who were responsible. It was during his work among the dying poor in 1866 that Dr Barnardo decided to take up his great work for child care, founding the East End Mission for Destitute Children in 1867. But private charity was not enough. The problem was too vast. It needed the resources of the State, despite the current *laissez-faire* ideas.

Public health reformers

And yet we must try to keep a sense of proportion. Much of our evidence for social conditions comes from Reports on the condition of the very poor by reformers who were quite ready on occasion to stress the worst aspect of things in the hope of shocking public opinion into demanding immediate action. It is as well to remember that, despite the disgusting living conditions and the occasional horror of an epidemic, town populations continued to grow.

England was fortunate to have among her leading men a fearless administrator prepared to devote his outstanding abilities, tremendous energies and the whole of his time to the major social problems of his day. He was Edwin Chadwick, a Utilitarian, a man in the van of the fight (sometimes very bitter fight) for better conditions, for the removal of waste and the provision of better housing. Public health as a continuous Government requirement properly begins with Chadwick.

In 1836 the Government required the registration of births and deaths. This was important, because the *cause* of death had to be recorded and for the first time ever, it became possible to collect these *vital statistics* almost on a daily basis and so to recognise trends. The local registries were to send their entries to the office of the Registrar General where William Farr, Compiler of Abstracts, was able to pin-point public health black spots. He called it 'statistical nosology'. The figures he produced are an invaluable source of information.

In 1838 a serious outbreak of fever at Whitechapel led the Poor Law Commissioners to instruct Dr Southwood Smith of the London Fever Hospital, and Dr Kay Shuttleworth of Manchester, to make a Report. This was the first time fully qualified medical men, experienced in slum conditions, had been employed on such work. Their short report led Chadwick to compile his epoch-making *Report on the Sanitary Condition of the Labouring Population* (1842) showing that the annual death rate from typhus alone was double the number of allied casualties at Waterloo. He suggested a whole programme of public health reform. Disease, he argued (for he believed in the 'bad air' theory), was preventable by simple measures like supplying pure running water, and street cleansing, better sewage disposal (carrying the sewage in solution in pipes, for this was far cheaper than carting it away as had been the practice hitherto). The cost of the programme would be less to the country than the cost of poor law relief arising out of diseases. He argued further, that crime and a dissolute life sprang from bad social conditions, and thus reform would produce a more wholesome population.

The reformers were certain that once public opinion was informed of the bad conditions, legislation to produce effective measures would follow. They found that legislation more difficult to pass than they imagined, and even more difficult to enforce. Not only were the new town councils elected after 1835 concerned to keep local rates as low as possible, but there was an almost morbid fear of direction by the central government, lest the liberty of individual action be reduced. *The Times*, normally an advocate of moderate reform, asserted that the British would rather take their chance of catching cholera than be bullied into health. In addition, there was a host of private concerns, like water companies, private or denominational cemeteries, or contractors for the removal of waste, all of whom, in the dignified name of personal liberty, resisted reform in order to defend their vested interests. Then there were the slum landowners themselves, some being lords with considerable political influence. To proceed against such an array required political tact: Chadwick lacked tact. He was impatient of opposition and his vigorous denunciation of the vested interests that stood in the way of his public health reforms lost him public sympathy, so that he was eventually obliged to withdraw into private life in 1854, a much maligned and misunderstood figure. But, with the aid of Dr Southwood Smith, Lord Shaftesbury and Disraeli, the future prime minister, he had founded in 1839 the Health of Towns Association which brought together many reformers and led the fight for better conditions in the towns.

One of their greatest achievements was to secure (with the help of the 'great stink') the passing of an

Act in 1858 to give effect to the main drainage scheme, for London, of Joseph Bazalgette, the Engineer of the Metropolitan Board of Works. The scheme involved the covering of the rivers flowing into the Thames, and fitting valves to keep the tide from flowing back up them. Two great sewage systems, one north, one south of the Thames, were to carry sewage in great pipes and sewers across London to two outfall works further down river. Old brick sewers, often in danger of collapse, which had to be cleaned periodically, by sewer men, were gradually replaced by a self-flushing type of sewer pipe. This was made of glazed stoneware from which there was no seepage. It was developed at Doulton's pottery at Chelsea, and proved a very profitable business venture. Victorian civil engineers have had too little credit for solving the problem of large-scale urban sewage disposal.

Cholera helped the reformers by goading reluctant authorities into temporary action. It helped in passing the Baths and Wash-houses Act (1846) permitting local authorities to build wash-houses for the poor—their tenements boasted no bath rooms, after all. In 1848 came the Public Health Act, setting up a General Board of Health in London

Building the Camden Town sewer, 1862

with power to create local boards of health where 10 per cent of the population demanded it, and where the death rate was over 23 per 1,000. Chadwick was appointed Secretary to the Board.

Slackness and indifference, as well as powerful opposition obstructed the Board's work, and as the number of cholera victims rose in 1849, Chadwick bitterly remarked, 'self-satisfied bumbledum, in town and parish, incapable of grasping the implication of the crisis, cried out aloud against centralisation'. Left to themselves it proved all too easy for authorities who wished to do so to evade their responsibilities for public health. Chadwick's attempt to secure a single authority for London water supply was frustrated for fifty years. The Central Board of Health, attacked alike by local authorities and vested interests, was dissolved and Chadwick dismissed in 1854. This was a great blow to the reformers, but in 1866 the Sanitary Act compelled local authorities to take action to supply adequate water supply, and sewage and waste disposal services. Yet, after all the exposing of frightful conditions by the Health of Towns Association and other bodies, and all the demands for reform, a Royal Commission in 1869 still thought it necessary to say that among the things 'necessary for civilised life' were good water supplies and proper drainage, removal of nuisances, healthy houses, clean streets, inspection of food, and provision of adequate burial grounds. This shows the extent of public apathy, and for this the community at large was responsible: it will not do to blame only narrow-minded councils intent on keeping rates low. In 1871 the Local Government Board was created to supervise the work of local councils and to take over general responsibility for public health, and in 1875 Disraeli's Public Health Act codified the many regulations then existing into a single body of law and obliged the appointment of a Medical Officer of Health. (In fact, Liverpool had appointed Dr Duncan as early as 1847 and other cities had followed this example— Disraeli was merely directing remaining cities to 'get into line'.) But it was well into the twentieth century before adequate pure water supplies were

fully available and before a reasonable supply of wash-houses and water closets was available to the working class.

All these improvements should be seen not in isolation, but as part of the Victorian endeavour to come to terms with their rapidly changing world. Never before had two or three generations witnessed such Great Changes: it is a tribute to the Victorians that they were able to adapt themselves so quickly and to take necessary action to limit the worst abuses. Much, however, depended on local effort.

Reform of local government

To some extent, the frightful living conditions that developed in the towns was a result of the lack of proper local government authorities. This was partly because the towns, when they began to expand, did so with such rapidity that the existing parishes could not handle the problems that arose and no new system of town government was adopted quickly enough. Manchester and Birmingham were parishes although far larger than most borough corporations. The problem was simply that the Elizabethan system of local government was still the rule in nineteenth-century conditions that had altered the whole nature of local government problems. During the eighteenth century certain towns had obtained parliamentary permission to set up *Improvement Commissioners* who took upon themselves various duties, like water supply, sewage disposal, paving and lighting, and policing, and they were able to levy rates for their services.

The new and growing towns normally did not have a member of parliament until 1832 (see *page 158*), but once Parliament had been reformed, it was clear that reform of local government would follow. The first step was the Poor Law Amendment Act, 1834 (see *page 160*) for it began the complete transformation of local government, although it was not realised at the time. Hitherto the Poor Law had been the responsibility of parishes and local justices. The 1834 Act placed it firmly in the hands of locally elected Guardians directly responsible to the Commissioners at Somerset House in London. This combination of local election and central super-vision, provided the basis for the local government reforms of the century.

Next, it was the turn of the boroughs. In many cases existing boroughs had shrunk, or failed to grow, and most corporations were unusually corrupt and inefficient. Rarely did they take steps to deal with the rising social problems of the age. They were unrepresentative normally being only open to Anglicans, and often members of the corporation co-opted each other—and their powers were simply in many cases inadequate to deal with the new problems. The Royal Commission on Municipal Corporations (1835) commented:

'In conclusion, we report to Your Majesty that there prevails amongst the inhabitants of a great majority of the incorporated towns a general, and, in our opinion, a just, dissatisfaction with their Municipal Institutions; a distrust of self-elected Municipal Councils, whose powers are subject to no popular control, and whose acts and proceedings being secret, are unchecked by the influence of public opinion.'

It was not only neglect, but self-indulgence that bred this contempt, for the unreformed corporations held many private feasts on corporation funds—the ancient silver plate and goblets were put to good use. The Municipal Corporations Act, 1835, dissolved nearly 200 borough corporations and replaced them with councillors elected for a period of three years by ratepayers. In order to ensure continuity (and also to get the measure through the Tory House of Lords) the councillors were then able to elect aldermen for six years, normally chosen from elderly councillors or similar men of standing in the town. The councils were given powers to carry out public works like lighting and paving, and their accounts were to be open for inspection. Considerable opposition raged against the measure, especially from the old corporations themselves. It was vigorously led by Thomas Burbage, Town Clerk of Leicester from 1813-35. The new corporations, anxious to rid themselves of the self-indulgent attitudes of their predecessors, often sold the corporation plate and goblets for a song. The plate in some cases has been re-purchased at a very high price indeed!

The year 1835 should have been a great moment for the new towns, but the new corporations did not distinguish themselves as reformers. Reform cost money. Reform was most needed in the working-class areas, but the rate payers lived mostly in the better suburbs and were concerned to keep rates down: 'shopocracy' as the new local councils were called, was not renowned for its activity. But these authorities were required to undertake measures of public health.

Housing the poor

The Central Board of Health (see *page 108*) lasted from 1848 to 1854 and was then sacrificed to the prevalent feelings that central control should be at a minimum. Nowhere was this plainer than in the field of housing. This was left to private builders, but by the middle of the century local by-laws were beginning to impose some regulation upon building standards, if only to ensure the safety of the construction. Other by-laws in some towns laid down minimum standards for drainage and other services. In the 1860s some progressive councils gained powers of compulsory purchase (always a difficult thing in the nineteenth century) to rebuild the worst slums (Liverpool and Glasgow made some big advances in this field), and the Torrens Act (1868) granted this power to any council that could establish that the dwellings were insanitary. But it was a timid measure that did not force councils to act and did not permit slum areas to be cleared as a whole. The Artisans' Dwellings Act of 1875 was more important, for it permitted councils to deal with slum areas more extensively—but even then the re-building was in the hands of private builders and usually private landlords: there was little council housing before 1919. Joseph Chamberlain, the radical Mayor of Birmingham from 1873 to 1876, was particularly active in slum clearing: he drove Corporation Street through one of the worst slums and was able to say of his period as mayor

London's first Peabody Buildings

that Birmingham was 'parked, paved, assized, marketed, gas-and-watered and *improved*—all as the result of three years' active work'. But the cost was so gigantic that he was obliged to confess in 1884 'we cannot undertake to burden the ratepayers any more for the purpose; . . . we have done all this generation at any rate will be able to do'. Eighty years later there were still plenty of slums. Chamberlain had merely scratched the surface of the problem. It is important to grasp that not only can inactive authorities be blamed for leaving the slum problem to get worse, but the attitude of ordinary people is equally at fault, for it accepted slums almost with a spirit of indifference that the twentieth century finds difficult to understand.

Much private activity went on at local level to improve working class houses, such as the Peabody Trust that built blocks of flats after 1869. The Metropolitan Association for Improving the Dwelling of the Industrious Classes (1845), for which the

Prince Consort planned his artisans' dwellings, was also active. Yet Octavia Hill, at work in the 1870s had to admit that in thirty years a mere 26,000 people in London had been rehoused by private benevolence, and many of these were perfectly capable of housing themselves, for they were not the very poor.

Industrialists had occasionally built model villages, but Victorian England, saw, on a much larger scale, some remarkable pieces of town planning for working-class housing. Middlesbrough was begun in the 1830s as a piece of Quaker Victoriana on a grid plan of 600 acres of farmland—it was swamped by the development of the Cleveland iron trade after 1850. A similar case was Barrow-in-Furness, begun by the Dukes of Devonshire, but swamped by the development of the haematite ores. Saltaire, built in the 1860s on drained land, with houses of different design but each with its own water supply, was the brain-child of Sir Titus Salt. It had its own

Prince Albert's design for artisan housing, 1851

park, public library and social club—but no pub. Port Sunlight, built by W. H. Lever was also 'dry' and so was Bournville (1879), built by George Cadbury. But these industrial villages were small and fairly easy to control. It was the larger towns that presented the real problems. Facilities for leisure were rare until after the 1850s (apart from the London Royal Parks), but parks and recreation grounds began to appear later in the century— Wicksteed of Kettering made a national name by designing safe recreational equipment for children's parks, like swings and slides and roundabouts. Such things were a sign of rising prosperity and changing outlooks. Another sign of growing prosperity was the increase in traffic that choked the streets of the cities and created many new problems—the more so as there were still many streets used for driving livestock along, and the bulky carts were very heavy indeed, rumbling over the cobbles. London dealt with the traffic problem by cutting several long new through roads to the dockland area.

Rural local government

Changes in the government of towns preceded those for rural areas. Until 1888 the parish was the local unit of administration and the Church of England made some effort to adjust parishes so that they could perform their dual function of local government and local church regulation. The counties were run by the Lord Lieutenant and the Justices of the Peace meeting at Quarter Sessions. There was much confusion, waste and overlapping of duties and in 1888 a substantial change came with the Local Government Act. Administrative counties were established to be run by elected councillors and aldermen elected by the council. The administrative authority of the J.P. was ended, except as regards the control of the police force. Larger towns with over 50,000 people became self-governing county boroughs. These and the counties are called first tier authorities and they were responsible for the major duties of local government, in due course to absorb education (1902) and the Poor Law (1929). But although the administrative structure became more simple and direct, this was no guarantee of more effective management. (London was treated as exceptional and the London County Council, with twenty-eight metropolitan boroughs came into existence in 1899). Below the first tier a second tier authority was created by the Local Government Act of 1894 dividing the existing sanitary areas into urban and rural districts, with a third tier below again of the ancient parishes. The functions of the councils were strictly regulated, so that none might perform any action for which specific authority had not been granted. Some of these functions are *statutory* (obligatory) like public health, street lighting, fire-fighting etc., others are *permissive*, depending on the wishes of the council, like providing parks and museums. By the end of the century many local authorities were also providing services like water, gas, omnibuses etc.

Public services run by local authorities are often those services that it is not economic for private enterprise to supply. They are called *municipal utilities*. If they were not provided by the municipality, they would either not be provided at all, or be available only for the wealthy. During the century most authorities took over sewage disposal. Gas for heating and lighting, normally beginning as private enterprise, tended to be taken over by the larger towns by the early twentieth century. In some cases large authorities took over water supply (though it was 1903 before London had a single water authority). As with gas, this was necessary to ensure that adequate supplies were provided for the poorer areas of towns. In supplying what came to be regarded as the necessities of life, social policy, rather than the profit motive is the most satisfactory yardstick. Large authorities can supply these services very much more cheaply than private companies, because of the high initial costs involved. Thus, in the 1840s Manchester Corporation was already constructing reservoirs in the Pennines. Other cities were already beginning to follow this example, and a complex series of pumps and pipes and valves was laid throughout cities. Like gas and water, electricity was later often to become a municipal utility. What private companies could or would not do, in supplying the poor with necessary services, councils found themselves obliged by pressure of local opinion in many cases, to do for themselves. The principle of the municipal utility, ensuring a relatively cheap and adequate service in such matters as gas, water and transport, quite apart from public health, made the lives of the ordinary town dwellers of the 1880s far easier than anything their forebears had ever known.

9 · The life of the wealthy, and others, during the Great Changes

In the eighteenth century the aristocracy and landed gentry were recognised as the natural leaders of society. They dominated politics, and they continued to take a leading part in national politics and government throughout the period of the Great Changes, even into the twentieth century. But the nature of the aristocracy was changing. Men who made their money in trade, and later in industry, were created peers, especially in the nineteenth century, and it is a tribute to the good sense of the aristocracy that it accepted these new men without too much reluctance. England experienced profound changes, but it did not have a violent revolution as in France or Russia.

Country houses

Throughout the eighteenth and nineteenth centuries, the country seat of a great lord was the hub of social life for its immediate neighbourhood, perhaps even for the county. It supplied employment for the whole local community, either within the country seat or on the estate.

A country house was not always a sumptuous palace, but the prosperity of the eighteenth century meant that the gentry lived in fine and dignified houses. Often they were built by the local builders and craftsmen who copied the styles of fashionable architects. The simple classic designs and quiet dignity of eighteenth century taste were not difficult to copy. Books of designs were published. Chippendale, the foremost furniture designer of the age, published *The Gentleman and Cabinet Maker's Directory* in 1754. Two others were particularly famous; Thomas Sheraton who published *The Cabinet-Maker's and Upholsterer's Drawing-Book* in 1791, and Hepplewhite, whose sturdy chair designs were deservedly popular. The delicate, beautifully worked furniture that survives is a tribute to the craftsman's skill, and to their patrons,

Chippendale furniture—luxury combining elegance and simplicity

Victorian 'comfort' —fussy design, mass produced and redolent of the period

Chiswick Villa, Chiswick, London. This delightful house (wonderfully restored in the 1950s) was built by William Kent and Lord Burlington and exercised considerable influence over eighteenth-century architecture. It is often instanced as the building that launched the Palladian style in England

too, for they decided upon the designs. A century later 'Victorian taste' was characterised by comfort without refinement. Because of the huge sales possible, Victorian furniture was often made in small manufactures with simple machines, and it is sometimes maintained that it shows far less craftsmanship. This may simply be prejudice: Victorian furniture is now fetching high prices in antique shops.

In the eighteenth century it was fashionable to be an amateur, and lords and squires would often make their own plans for their houses and parks (you can see some of them at country houses or in local museums). The fashionable style was *Palladian*, based on classical models and derived from the work of an Italian architect, Andreas Palladio. Many important archeological 'finds' were excavated at

this time and these had a great influence on design and building. A number of prominent architects got their opportunity to produce very remarkable buildings which showed the influence of these classical examples. The Adam brothers were the most popular: they designed not only the building, but the furnishings, furniture and decorations too.

The great country houses built in the Palladian manner often had a massive central block dominated by a great hall, with two or four pavilions connected by corridors lying off the wings. The stables and coach-houses, home farm and vegetable gardens would often be quite separate from the house and some distance away. But at the height of this classical style there was also a fashion for building mock gothic ruins at vantage points 'to enliven the view', and in 1750, Horace Walpole, an important

Kedleston Hall, Derby. The Great House in the Palladian manner

art critic, built a 'gothick' villa at Strawberry Hill, Twickenham. People laughed at the medieval designs he copied, but it was the beginnings of the *gothic revival*, both in architecture and literature. Wyatt was particularly inspired, and he built the fabulous Fonthill Abbey in Wiltshire in the 1790s. By then the style had become more accepted and several Cambridge Colleges were enlarged using gothic designs.

New technical developments were incorporated —cast iron was used extensively in the Brighton Pavilion, the extravaganza built for the Prince Regent. In 1825 Knowle was heated by steam and Raby Castle had central heating in 1843. Stoney-hurst pioneered gas lighting and several 'castles' incorporated a miniature railway to transfer hot food quickly along draughty corridors between kitchen and dining room. It seemed a little unkind of *Punch* to complain in 1847, 'we shall be treated by posterity as people who live in the Middle Ages, for everything around us partakes of the medieval character'.

Parks

One of the glories of the English countryside is its fine parks. Many of them were laid out in the eighteenth century, sometimes enclosed from agricultural ground (whole villages were simply removed on occasion) sometimes enclosed from 'wastes'. The vistas from the squire's windows, over parkland all his own, would be 'improved' by planting avenues of elm or oak, perhaps with an obelisk at the end: a wood or a series of copses would add variety and supply cover for foxes and hares, and the best houses always had a lake or a stream meandering in the front. Streams would be diverted, lakes made, even hills were removed, 'shaped' or sometimes constructed.

William Kent made his name both as an architect and as a landscape gardener 'who taught the gentle stream to serpentine seemingly at its pleasure. The living landscape was chastened or polished, not transformed' (Horace Walpole).

A 'natural' atmosphere was maintained. The most

famous landscaper was 'Capability' Brown who began life as an ordinary estate gardener at Stowe, but became so fashionable that he designed 170 major parks, including Luton Hoo, Blenheim and Chatsworth. He had many imitators, and a great lord was always axious to employ an ingenious head gardener. Many new trees and shrubs were introduced at this time from all over the world, partly because of the fashion to 'improve on nature'. Captain Cook, for example, took Sir Joseph Banks, the distinguished botanist, with him on his voyages across the Pacific and Botany Bay (1774) was appropriately named; Captain Bligh of the *Bounty* was carrying botanical specimens when his crew mutinied. The fashion for landscaping continued into Victorian times; Humphrey Repton was a worthy successor to Brown. But perhaps the most famous 'gardener' was Joseph Paxton from Chatsworth, who was a gardener before he planned the Crystal Palace, from one of his greenhouse designs.

The great houses, nestling in their parks, were a solid tribute to landed wealth. People of quality would often visit them (not always by appointment) simply to admire the grounds, house, furniture and the collection of pictures and other art treasures that filled the public rooms—for they were something of museums even in their hey-day.

But for all this, even the great lords were human enough to remember their poor tenants. Dudley North, a great landowner in Suffolk, could write to his baliff:

'I am very sorry that James Hadman has had the misfortune to brake the small bone of one of his legs, pray let me know in yr. next how he does, and how he is taken care off, and weather he is very poor or not, and what family he has; Pray let me know how John French's knee does, and how he is taken care off.'

Country life

Great lords and ladies had time, money and opportunity for the social round. But the local squire, though he lived in a house and style that aped the aristocracy, was closer to his local community. He was a churchwarden, a Justice of the Peace, often the village banker, the trustee and executor for orphans, the settler of disputes: in a word he was the father of his village and the centre of its society. His wife had a constant round of visitors, and her family and servants to look after, as well as good works in the village to attend to, including perhaps taking Sunday School. She tended to be a good housewife keeping a keen eye on her servants and maintaining accounts and a recipe book that would often include herbal medicines as well.

There was a definite social bar between the squire and villagers: the vicar and doctor would be likely to be on terms of social equality, the schoolmaster probably not. Visits to neighbouring country houses were frequent (though it was rare for the squirearchy to move in aristocratic circles) and this social consciousness made it necessary for children to marry well—misalliances were a form of social plague. Marriages were normally arranged: the idea of marriage for love was probably a nineteenth-century romantic idea so far as this class of person was concerned. But there were few cases of marriage being forced positively against a person's will. The basic social point was well put by Marianne, a character in Jane Austen's *Sense and Sensibility*:

'£2,000 a year is a very moderate income. A family cannot well be maintained on a smaller. . . . A proper establishment of servants, a carriage, perhaps two, and hunters, cannot be supported on less.'

In 1790 there were some 25,000 families among the peerage and landed gentry: of these some 400 were 'greater gentry' with incomes of over £10,000; perhaps 5,000 had incomes of over £1,000; and some 20,000 managed on probably less than £1,000 a year.

There was sometimes little difference between the lesser gentry and prosperous farmers. As the farmers grew richer, their wives and daughters demanded fashionable clothes and furniture and visits to spas. The family farmhouse was enlarged and farm servants tended to be pushed into damp, unhealthy,

A Gillray cartoon of a farmer's daughter at the piano

cheap plaster and lath houses, for the practice of 'living-in' was becoming rarer, except in the North. A 'withdrawing' room was becoming a necessity, and daughters would often be brought up with ideas of social expectation in the hope of a favourable marriage.

Inequality was stamped at birth in the eighteenth century, and it was exaggerated by upbringing and education. The wealthy young man would complete a university course with the Grand Tour through Italy where he would visit art galleries and no doubt purchase copies of old masters (some Rome sculptors made a good living selling English lords copies of antique busts that were proudly shown in the lobbies of country houses back in England). A fashion for things Italian was fostered by this habit of the Grand Tour. As the Victorian Age came nearer wealthy parents took the family—Florence Nightingale gained her name from the city of her birth. As the age was aristocratic it produced many patrons of the arts, and it was very proper that Sir Joshua Reynolds should found the Royal Academy in 1768. The theatre was also in vogue in London and the provinces; the indefatigable Sarah Siddons, Colley Cibber and Charles Macklin were famous, whilst Sheridan's friend, David Garrick re-wrote *King Lear*, giving it a happy ending. Music had many devotees: musical evenings were frequent among amateurs, and the Philharmonic Society brought Haydn to London and commissioned major works from Beethoven.

Meticulous care in matters of dress and personal hygiene became important as the eighteenth century progressed. Lord Chesterfield advised his son:

'Washing yourself, and rubbing your body and limbs frequently with a flesh brush will conduce as much to health as to cleanliness. A particular

A dandy

attention to the cleanliness of your mouth, teeth, hands and nails is but common decency, in order not to offend people's eyes and noses.'

Dress became so fashionably exquisite for men that the dandy was in his element—Count d'Orsay boasted he never used powder since he never had the need; a specially favoured guest might be allowed to see him finish his toilette. But the fashion was short-lived, for the sober nineteenth century with its evangelicalism as well as its mass production and marketing techniques preferred dark and 'sensible' suits for males. Disraeli was already thought a trifle odd when he sported his brocade waistcoats and watch chains in the 1840s.

Wigs for men were passing out, although, for a brief moment, wigs for women became absurdly complex. But Victorians preferred a positively natural hairiness.

The fashionable world depended on the ministrations of a host of servants, among whom there was

an infinite range of different levels. A great house required a veritable army of servants—butler, housekeeper, cook, maids, coachman and grooms—and the wages bill might easily exceed £1,000 a year. The Duke of Kingston paid his Housesteward £100; his cook £40; his housekeeper £20, but his maids and grooms £4. There was food for them and a room: a servant's life in a prosperous house was not at all bad. It was in the poorer houses, in the houses of small employers and men on slender incomes, where a servant was required to perform many and varied jobs, that conditions might well be very bad. But in all households, servants worked hard for long hours and their efficiency could well improve the hygiene of an establishment. Beds, for example, were normally uncovered daily, not only to 'sweeten' them, but also to reveal the bugs and fleas which the domestics had to hunt down and kill. Many manuals upon the 'domestic arts' were published in the period 1790–1830, which suggests that in these years particularly there were many households seeking instruction in etiquette. Regency journals carried many advertisements for 'suitable places'—the 'servant problem' lay in the future. A common wage might be £8 a year, but this was eaten up by the cost of a uniform and there was

A prize fighter, eighteenth-century style

little left over for sickness, saving and old age—or even for amusements! In the suburbs a female servant might hope for 40s a year with full board and lodging and clothing. Those less 'fortunate' might be treated little better than slaves. There was a high turnover among the inferior domestics: some left for better jobs, many because they proved untrainable, or had simply become pregnant or ill (the 'master' could not be expected to keep an ill servant long, even if destitute), and some left to marry. Servants were better treated in the countryside: there was more community spirit there. It was to be seen, also, on the village green, where a great lord occasionally (though always as a very special favour) might play cricket with local craftsmen— but not normally with his labourers!

Prize fighting was popular: the contests were without gloves and lasted until one or other collapsed. It was brutal and bloody but attracted much support, especially from aristocrats, and Lord Queensbury devised rules for the sport. Horse-racing and hunting were also popular—the deer was hunted only in Scotland, but fox-hunting was growing and captured the popular imagination, with the Badminton, Pytchley and Quorn Hunts leading the fashion. Enclosure made hunting in the Midlands more exciting because of the jumps required. It also served to knit farmers and squirearchy together, and even the blacksmith might ride to hounds—but not, of course, the labourer! Vast sums were spent on game preservation and it is no wonder that the landed interest insisted on severe game laws (see *page 33*): too much can be made of the social integration to be found in rural England!

While the landed interest was enjoying itself hunting and at sport, Britain was engaged between 1793 and 1815 on the greatest war she had yet fought. It seemed that the titanic struggle could go on, with taxes rising and prices soaring, but the smooth tenor of country life was not disturbed. Jane Austen wrote in this period portraying very acutely the contemporary world of the lesser gentry: yet her novels scarcely mention the war. The Napoleonic Wars failed to touch the consciousness of the country as the Crimean War was to do, or to involve the people, as the struggles of our own century have done.

The LIBERTY of the SUBJECT.

The press gang

Press gangs

In war, Britain trusted in her Navy. But she had to have sailors. There was no great shortage of officers who, being gentlemen, led lives of relative pleasure and profit (though they had to acquire technical expertise). It was different for the men: they lived in overcrowded dank conditions and fed very badly. They were not always paid and were often cheated of some of the pittance that was their due. Harsh treatment was the rule and it was not unusual, when in port, for 300 lashes to be administered, each drawing blood. Marines were carried in case of mutiny, and it is incredible that mutiny (despite the rigorous punishment that it carried) did not occur more often. But conditions got so bad that in 1797, at the height of the Revolutionary War the fleets did mutiny. The Spithead mutiny was quickly ended by acknowledging the just claims of the men and by agreeing not to victimise anyone. The Nore mutiny was different. The self restraint of the sailors in refusing to molest officers who would willingly have had them shot, was remarkable. But the Nore mutineers blockaded the Thames and their ideas were very much influenced by the French Revolution: their leaders and some thirty others were hanged. It was no pleasant thing to be a common sailor of Nelson's navy, and it is not surprising that the Navy lacked recruits.

In time of war, this lack of man-power threatened to keep the navy in port. Merchantmen were commandeered for the war and sailors forcibly removed from other merchant vessels. But still there were not sufficient; this was why there was a *press gang*—a group of strong men armed with cudgels and sometimes swords and pistols, under an officer, toured the ports in search of 'recruits'. They were imprisoned until they could be officially enrolled in the crew of a naval vessel. Horrible punishments were meted out to those who attempted to escape. It was no wonder that riots and sometimes murder accompanied the visit of the press gang. There was no appeal once a commoner had been 'pressed', and this was ironic in a land that boasted of English liberties. Gentlemen, being well dressed, would not, of course, be 'pressed'—the liberties of

Englishmen were more the concern of gentlemen, whose liberties were rarely in danger, than of the poor, who lacked the money and connexions to defend themselves in court. But if there had been no press gang it is possible that there would have had to have been some sort of conscription: eighteenth century ideas preferred the poor to suffer rather than risk that!

Certificates were issued that 'protected' particular types of workers; for example, the Newcastle colliers carrying coal to London, freemen of the City, those with a parliamentary vote, and Atlantic fishermen and whalers. City apprentices were also exempted, although some masters literally sold their apprentices to the press gang. Those who forged 'protections' were severely punished.

Plenty of arguments were raised to defend the press gang system by those who had no need to fear it. It was useful, they said, in ridding ports of thieves, idlers and drunkards. In 1776, the Admiralty paid five shillings for 'each able-bodied landsman being received into His Majesty's service'. When an attempt was made in the High Court to challenge impressment, Lord Mansfield (the same judge who had disallowed slavery in Somerset's Case, see *page 19*) declared: 'The power of pressing is founded upon immemorial usage, allowed for ages.' Others spoke glibly of the few serving that the many might sleep secure. Sir Michael Foster, Recorder of Bristol, declared (1743):

'It is a maxim of law, and good policy, too, that all private mischiefs must be borne with patience for preventing a national calamity.'

Quite irrespective of the injustice of pressing men, it was not even effective, for it did not always get enough and those they captured were of very variable quality. In 1775 an admiral commented,

'I don't know where they come from, but whoever was the officer who received them, he ought to be ashamed, for I never saw such except in the condemned hole at Newgate. I was three hours and a half mustering this scabby crew, and I should have imagined that the scum of the earth had been picked up for this ship.'

They were not all English: at Trafalgar, Nelson's ship carried more foreigners than British.

Town life

By and large, despite the growing number of hospitals and other charitable foundations, the irresponsibility of aristocratic life in town contrasted surprisingly with the community of feeling in the countryside. This is partly explained by the fact that town houses were sometimes taken for the season only (especially in the spas, like Bath). London houses were of brick, built in terraces or the new fashionable squares. Steps led up to the front door across an area with steps leading down to the basement where the kitchen was, and the under-basement for storage. In the bigger houses storage space was also available under the well-laid pavements, which were often pierced with a grid to allow coal to be dumped into the cellar below. Oil lamps would be fixed to the railings and the bigger houses would have a winch for lowering goods into the storage area. The ground floor would be reception rooms with high ceilings with the dining room and library probably on the first floor. The family slept above that, and in the attics, shielded from sight by a balustrade, sometimes in very over-crowded conditions, the servants would sleep—they needed little accommodation, for they were kept at work all day.

A stable and coach house was also required for the really fashionable, and this produced the London mews between the fine terraced streets and behind the squares. Such additions could not be built in the middle class areas in the growing suburbs, but they frequently mirrored, on a smaller scale, the pattern of terraced house to be found in Westminster. Fortunes in real estate were made in this great expanse of buildings. The streets were cobbled in the better areas and teemed with carriages and horses, while the skill of the powerful sedan chair-men (by the end of the century almost replaced by hackney carriages) in weaving through the throng amazed foreign visitors:

'There are a great number of chariots and coaches belonging to noblemen and to gentlemen. These fine chariots, behind which stand two or three footmen attired in rich liveries . . . are a great hindrance to those who are not wealthy and go on foot, for the streets being generally very muddy, the passers-by get terribly bespattered and dirty. Pedestrians, it is true, would be far worse off were there not on either side of the street a sort of elevated footpath for their convenience.'

A season in London was a necessary part of the social round for the wealthy—it was also a means of arranging marriages. Self-indulgent pleasure typified the season, with parties, displays, riding in the parks, visits to the theatre, to Ranelagh and the Vauxhall pleasure gardens, and dancing at the Pantheon. All this was expensive but pleasant and innocent enough. Other pursuits were less innocent and pleasant—bull baiting and cock-fighting were common in the eighteenth century; public executions (which increased as the century advanced, despite the growing humanitarianism) drew great crowds; a visit to Bedlam of a Sunday to see the antics of the lunatics cruelly confined there, or to the Bridewell to see women prisoners whipped.

One of the most serious vices was gambling at dice or cards, that grew throughout the century and helped to establish the famous gaming clubs of Crockford's and White's. Charles James Fox, the delightfully human opponent of the Younger Pitt, would sometimes sit for twenty-four hours at play, losing at the rate of £500 an hour—he gambled away a fortune of £140,000 before he was twenty-five. A generation after his death, on the eve of the accession of Victoria, Disraeli gave an account of such gaming in *The Young Duke*:

'They played till dinner time without intermission; and although the Duke made some desperate efforts, and some successful ones, his losses were, nevertheless, trebled. . . . At first he had limited himself to ten thousand, after breakfast it was to have been twenty thousand; then thirty thousand was the ultimatum. . . . At midnight he had lost forty-eight thousand.'

They played on till 6 a.m. when the duke had lost £100,000. In the novel he discharges the debt with a simple cheque—in real life there sometimes were suicides and occasionally whole estates changed hands overnight. And after a gaming bout, drunk and in high spirits, these Regency Bucks, in the manner of the Mohocks before them (see *page 2*), would trip out to nail night watchmen in their boxes and roll them towards the river; to fight with the watch; to run swords through sedan-chair sides 'for fun'. But whereas children might be hanged for steal-ing a handkerchief, these young men, sometimes sons of government ministers and of bishops, did not ex-pect to be brought before the magistrate. They might be imprisoned for debt, but if such ill-luck befell them, they found pleasant times awaiting them in jail, if they were prepared to pay the jailor's prices. In *Sir Launcelot Greaves*, Smollett paints a picture of the King's Bench Prison:

'Except the entrance, where the turnkeys keep watch and ward, there is nothing in the place that looks like a jail, or bears the least colour of restraint. Hawkers of all sorts are admitted to call and vend their wares as in any open street of London. Here the voice of misery never complains.'

But times were changing in the last generation of the century. Duelling, once the prompt resort of gentlemen, was going out of fashion, and when the Duke of Wellington 'called out' Lord Winchelsea in 1829, he was thought a trifle old-fashioned. A more moral attitude was coming to dominate social relationships. The great unruly fairs at Southwark and Greenwich were closed by 1763. Organised vice was combated by the Disorderly Houses Act (1752) and the worst brothels had been suppressed by the 1790s, along with the less reputable 'tea gardens', which the magistrate Henry Fielding called

'certainly the most dreadful places in or about the metropolis . . . the resort of women, not only of the lower species of prostitution, but even of the middle classes; they were the resort as well of apprentices as of every sort of abandoned young man.'

Sexual morality remained loose among the aristocracy well into the nineteenth century—Gladstone commented that he had known six Prime Ministers, five of them adulterers—but there was already appearing in George III's reign a general disapproval of such behaviour, to such an extent that Asa Briggs has spoken of this generation as being 'Victorian before the Victorians'. Hannah More and Maria Edgeworth were producing before 1800 'improving tales' which might have been written especially for the Victorian nursery; and Dr Bowdler's famous edition of Shakespeare, so edited that a maiden might read it without so much as a blush, appeared in 1818. Even among the wealthy, social life was becoming what the Victorians called 'respectable'. But we must remember that there was still plenty of vice in Victorian England. Forty-two thousand bastards were recorded in the 1851 census and there were some 50,000 prostitutes known to the police. It is easy to gain a naïve impression of Victorian life from a glance merely at the drawing room.

The spas

The Georgian Age was one of great eating and drinking. Its doctors did not have extensive medical knowledge, and the indulgence of their patients led to the fashionable Georgian complaint of the gout, and the equally fashionable visit to a spa for a 'cure' drinking the medicinal waters. Several spas attracted high society as soon as the London season was over. Epsom and Tunbridge Wells were early favourites, but Bath was *the* spa of the eighteenth century, where Beau Nash, as 'Master of Ceremonies', had transformed a dirty, crowded, unsavoury town into the most fashionable spa with a well planned programme of entertainments and suitable accom-modation for public gatherings, in which his own list of rules was strictly kept. Visits by royalty ensured Bath's success and a great building pro-gramme was undertaken, principally by the Woods, who produced the Circus and Royal Crescent to give the town a European reputation.

But by the end of the century, Bath was no longer

predominant. The aristocracy went elsewhere, and Jane Austen's novels show that the middle class had taken over by 1800. There were many reasons for this decline: the Masters of Ceremonies who succeeded Nash were unable to maintain his strict code of social behaviour, especially as the population of the town shot up from 3,000 to over 30,000 and visitors from all walks of life attended. Retired officers (as the memorials in the Abbey show) settled in the town, changing the clientele, and improved transport (John Palmer's fast mail coaches were running in 1784, see *page 42*) encouraged frequent short visits rather than the long stays that had once been the rule. Perhaps the chief reason was that George III preferred Weymouth, and seaside holidays began to be the vogue. The claims that were made at the end of the eighteenth century for the medicinal effects of sea-bathing were remarkable, and several quacks made a good living simply by inducing wealthy patients to drink sea water as a cure for most ills. Scarborough, Margate, Southend, Bognor, Torquay became popular resorts at this time, and most of all one little Sussex fishing village became the new and fashionable town of Brighton, favoured by the Prince Regent. Bath, along with many other inland spas suffered a decline.

Another reason can be found in the developing change in public taste. The neo-classicism of the eighteenth century was already giving way to the gothic revival by 1800, aided by a revolution in taste known as the Romantic Revival. Sir Walter Scott's unashamedly commercial historical novels

Queen Victoria and her children

seemed to set a new pattern in literature, and the 'gothick' novels by 'Monk' Lewis and Mrs Radcliffe, which Jane Austen satirised in *Northanger Abbey*, showed that there was a reaction from the simple lines of eighteenth century taste. The Orders .of Chivalry, in which the Victorians delighted, Tennyson's *Idyls of the King*, even the famous Eglinton tournament of 1839, at which noble lords dressed as crusader knights and fought a mock (and disastrous) tournament, all showed a certain backward-looking spirit which was surprising in an England pulsing with change. Perhaps the romantic love of the past was really a piece of escapism from the stress of the present, a reaction from the Great Changes that to some critics seemed to be changing England from a rural paradise into an industrial slum. Wordsworth, Carlyle, Ruskin, and a host of lesser writers were in revolt against the Great Changes that were producing the commercial predominance of Britain as the 'workshop of the world'. George Eliot in *The Mill on the Floss* caught the current of what they feared:

'It's this steam, you see, that has made the difference; it drives on every wheel double pace, and the wheel of fortune along with 'un.'

Of course, the Great Changes brought untold wealth to the upper classes, and this may be one reason why, throughout the industrial nineteenth century, the aristocracy continued to dominate politics. Joseph Chamberlain could shock Queen Victoria in 1883 by castigating them as a class

'who toil not, neither do they spin; whose fortunes have originated by grants made in times gone by for services which courtiers rendered Kings, and have since grown and increased, while they slept, by levying an increasing share on all that other men have done by toil and labour to add to the general wealth of the country.'

The atmosphere of an industrial Britain, a Britain with a cooler sense of tradition, is apparent in these words. The more democratic society of the twentieth century respects 'persons of quality' less than previous ages: yet it was not until the 1960s

that it was thought possible for a Conservative government to exist without a Lord Salisbury on the Front Bench.

Along with a quietening of their manner of life, the nineteenth century saw a change in the spending habits of the wealthy. As a class they no longer spent so lavishly as in the previous century, or as they were to do in Edwardian days. The Queen and Prince Albert mirrored and to a great extent projected an image of a new earnestness and concentration on domesticity. The new earnestness was reflected in humanitarianism and social reform, and in the efforts to understand their changing world which lie behind some important novels of the 1840s. Disraeli's *Sybil*, illustrating 'the two nations, the Rich and the Poor'; Charles Kingsley's *Yeast*, showing the vulnerability of the weak, and the speech of town labourers 'like the speech of savages'; Mrs Gaskell's *Mary Barton*, showing how high principled men like John Barton could be ground down into criminal acts by the conditions of working class life—all these were novels with a vigorous social purpose. Perhaps it was the very pace and extent of the changes going on about them that made men who had grown up with the Great Changes hesitate and look on in confusion. But that they did so showed their sense of responsibility. There was about the men of the eighteenth century an atmosphere that suggested pronounced complacency, that their century was one of perfection: the nineteenth century man believed he was striving *towards* perfection that would be enjoyed by his descendants as a result of his own endeavours.

Prisons

If the eighteenth century had an air of complacency, it also showed a growing humanitarianism, in which the rich played their part. The founding of charity schools and hospitals was not the only evidence of concern for social conditions. The Society for Promoting Christian Knowledge (see *page 130*). was active in publicising the appalling conditions to be found in the country's prisons, and a committee under General James Oglethorpe (who founded Georgia as a haven for prisoners and prostitutes prepared to lead a new life) in 1729 reported that 'the more they proceeded in their enquiries, the more dismal and shocking was the scene of cruelty, barbarity and extortion which they disclosed'. Starvation was not uncommon and in some prisons, the inmates would fight for their food with the rats: vermin infested the straw on the floor, and some cells were more like pits,

'often damp and noisome, half a foot deep in water, or with an open sewer running through the centre of the floor. They had no chimneys, no fireplace, no barrack beds; the wretched inmates huddled together for warmth upon the heaps of filthy rags and bundles of rotten straw reeking with foul exhalations and fetid with all manner of indescribable nastiness.'

Prison fever and typhus were endemic in these conditions, and occasionally prisoners appearing in court infected the whole assembly. Drunkenness was the frequent condition of most prisoners and corruption was the norm. There was no attempt to separate different types of prisoner, so that lunatics, children and hardened criminals might well be contained in the same room, sometimes males and females together. Forms of torture survived and in some prisons floggings were common and disagreeable tasks like working the treadmill, picking oakum and beating hemp were the rule. But in some prisons, by paying enough one could live well and comfortably, though it might well cost twenty guineas a week at Newgate. Half the prisons were privately owned and none properly inspected, while the jailors normally received no payment, and made their living by imposing 'fines' and other payments on their charges.

When John Howard became High Sheriff of Bedfordshire in 1773, his discovery of the condition in the local jail made him into a keen prison reformer about whom gathered a number of prominent men. If these reformers achieved very little in practice, they did much to awaken public conscience and to encourage discussion as to the most appropriate methods of dealing with criminals—many of their ideas are the basis of penal practice today. Among

Howard's suggestions for reform in *The State of the Prisons in England and Wales* (1777), were the exclusion of alcohol, the classification of prisoners, who should be housed separately (Jonas Hanway wanted them to be kept in solitary confinement) and employed on useful tasks under honest jailors who should be paid. In 1779 a Penitentiary Houses Act provided for the construction of new prisons where the inmates were set tasks 'of the hardest and most servile kind, for which drudgery is chiefly required'. There was no question of being 'soft' to prisoners. Nothing of consequence was done for the moment to build new prisons: instead, as a 'temporary' measure, prisoners were confined in old hulks, often along the Essex marshes. The hulks were still in use in the 1850s. Since the Americans had rebelled, it was necessary to find another place for transported convicts, and in January 1788 the first batch arrived at Botany Bay, Australia, and a colony was founded under Captain Arthur Phillip.

Jeremy Bentham was another prison reformer, and his idea of a Panopticon attracted much attention: it was to be circular, 'an iron cage glazed, a glass lantern about the size of Ranelagh. The Prisoners in the cells occupying the circumference; the Officers, Governor (Chaplain, Surgeon etc.) the centre'. Eventually Bentham was allowed to plan and build a prison at Millbank in 1821; but by the 1820s, for all the agitation, there were not many improvements in prisons. Prisoners were still unclassified and there were still cases of prisoners being chained to the floor. Sir Robert Peel's Act of 1823 insisted that a 'reformatory régime' should be established in each prison, but the Justices were to be informed of the infliction of 'tyrannical punishments' (Peel's reputation as a prison reformer has been exaggerated). The act of 1824, establishing the principle of classification of prisoners, was simply not enforced. In 1835, however, two Inspectors of Prisons were appointed. Their reports made shocking reading and this may explain why forty-five prisons were built or commissioned in the 1840s. A more imaginative approach to penology was beginning to emerge, however, and the 1853 Penal Servitude Act allowed prisoners to be sentenced to hard labour for certain offences, but also introduced the Progressive System, by which, as a result of good behaviour during their sentence, prisoners gradually earned more privileges. Between 1865 and 1877 prisons came under the control of the Home Secretary, to be administered through an independent Prison Commission.

The condition of women prisoners was not much better than that of the men, but Elizabeth Fry in 1816 began regular visits to Newgate. That year, her brother-in-law Thomas Fowell Buxton had founded the Society for the Reformation of Prison Discipline. Mrs Fry was not frightened by what she saw, as many might have been:

'The women, seeing visitors, pressed to the bars, stretching out greedy hands, whining, begging for pence to spend in drink at the tap of the prison (to get drunk). Those in front were fought with by those behind; hands snatched them back by the hair, pinched them, punched them in the ribs with fists and elbows.'

She organised regular visits and began a school for the children and Bible reading for the adults. She brought food and clothing and work for the women to help them regain their self-respect, asking only in return 'a voluntary subordination to the rule of sobriety, cleanliness and decent conversation'. Her success in changing depraved prisoners into decently behaved women was remarkable.

Police

The concern for a better enforcement of law and order was an indication that society, especially propertied men, was becoming aware of solid changes. The biggest obstacle to the establishment of a police force was the long tradition of local responsibility for maintaining order, and the real fear of a police force as being secret agents of the Government—this is why we have no national police force today.

The local watches and constables in the towns were quite inadequate to deal with the increasingly well organised crime of the eighteenth century, even if they had been efficient, but they were frequently old men who could scarcely chase criminals and who generally kept out of trouble. In case of riots, the military was frequently called out after the reading

A public hanging, 1760

of the 1714 Riot Act calling on the rioters to disperse. In order to recover stolen goods and to try to bring some criminals to justice, quite excessive rewards were offered by private citizens, insurance companies and the Government, so that it became a profitable business to act as a receiver of stolen goods and to claim the rewards, or to be a common informer (indeed, the Government made extensive use of the common informer, invariably against the poor).

Concern at the growth of crimes resulted in the increasing severity of punishments during the century, so that by 1815 a formidable list of over 200 crimes carried the death penalty. The list included murder, treason, rape, sodomy, piracy, arson, theft of anything valued at more than a shilling, impersonating a Chelsea pensioner, damaging Westminster Bridge, appearing armed and disguised in a deer park and a host of other offences. Executions increased at an alarming rate: but there was no diminishing of crime. The severity seemed to promote crime instead of preventing it, for criminals would rather have been hung for a sheep than a lamb. There was much discussion of the severity of the penal code in Parliament, although little progress was made until Samuel Romilly put himself at the head of the movement for reform and became Solicitor General in 1806. Some of the severer statutes were repealed, including that making pickpocketing a hanging offence (repealed 1808), especially on the grounds that with a capital sentence it was frequently difficult to obtain a conviction. Progress was very slow and Romilly, distressed at the death of his wife, committed suicide in 1818. His successors in the movement, Sir James Mackintosh and Thomas Fowell Buxton, were behind the relaxing of the penal code when Peel was Home Secretary, between 1823 and 1827. But there were still fourteen crimes carrying the death penalty in 1840; and in 1833 a boy of nine had been executed for stealing twopence-worth of printer's colour.

Executions were in public and attracted a great deal of attention, and sometimes the crowd was so great that children were crushed in the throng.

Those who could sell a window (or even a roof) space overlooking the scene made good money. Dr Johnson argued:

'Executions are intended to draw spectators. If they do not draw spectators, they don't answer their purpose. The old method was most satisfactory to all parties, the public was gratified by a procession; the criminal was supported by it.'

Unfortunately, the behaviour of the crowds watching hangings, showed that they were not interested in seeing 'justice done'. Charles Dickens was a strong opponent of public executions. When the Mannings were executed in 1849, he wrote to a friend, 'The conduct of the people was so indescribably frightful, that I felt for some time afterwards as if I were living in a city of devils', but it was 1868 before public executions were ended.

It is generally agreed that it is not the severity of punishment so much as the likelihood of detection that deters criminals. In order to ensure detection, a police force of consequence is necessary.

Eighteenth-century magistrates were sometimes suspected of making money out of fines and some were called 'trading justices'. In 1748 Henry Fielding became a *stipendiary magistrate* (paid) at Bow Street and refused to make money from fines. He was concerned to capture criminals and formed a force of what came to be called the Bow Street Runners. His plan was continued by his blind half-brother, John Fielding, and by 1760 the Runners were well established. Regular horse patrols began in 1763 and 'beats' on foot in 1782. Reports of crimes and criminals were published from 1772 in *Quarterly Pursuits*. But, although the Government in 1787 was spending £15,000 on rewards for information 'leading to arrest', the Bow Street Runners received little backing, and their reputation declined rapidly after John's death. It is difficult to explain this, because London was well aware of the need for a police force, and several armed civilian associations were formed to protect citizens.

In 1795 constables were allowed 12s a week and a magistrate, Patrick Colquhoun wrote a pamphlet recommending an independent force be set up. But the idea was not acted on because of the fear that such a force might become a Government instrument of repression and imperil British liberties. However, Colquhoun's Marine Police (1798), for the purpose of checking pilfering from ships in the London docks, proved so successful that the Government made it into the Thames River Police in 1800 (it was absorbed into the River Police in 1839).

Serious disturbances between 1815 and 1820, both in London and in the provinces, convinced many people of the need for a regular police force. The Duke of Wellington told the Prime Minister in 1820:

'In my opinion, the Government ought, without the loss of a moment's time, to adopt measures to form either a police in London or military corps, which should be of a different description from the regular military force, or both.'

But it was 1829 before the Metropolitan Police Force was formed under the Home Secretary, Sir Robert Peel. It was kept deliberately small in order to satisfy those who feared it might become an instrument of tyranny. The policemen were paid and commanded by two Justices (later called Commissioners) whose headquarters were Scotland Yard. They were responsible for Westminster and some parishes in Middlesex, Surrey and Kent, but not the City of London itself. Under Richard Mayne, a barrister, and Col. Charles Rowan, the Force was organised on military lines, but their only weapon was a short wooden baton. Their pay was poor, considering many of them were former n.c.o.s in Wellington's army, and this may account for the frequent resignations in the early years (there were dismissals for corruption, too). One observer wrote to Peel:

'Three shillings a day for men capable of even *reading*, to say nothing of *understanding*, and *executing* the printed instructions seems wholly inadequate.'

At first they were resented and their work obstructed. When a policeman was stabbed to death in a baton charge on a meeting at Cold Bath Fields, 1833, a verdict of 'justifiable homicide' was returned. But by the end of the 1830s opinion was no longer hostile, and after 1835 the new corporations of towns began to ask for officers to be released to train their own forces. A Rural Police Act came in 1839, though few counties availed themselves of the opportunity to create local forces, but the Police Act (1856) made county forces compulsory and empowered the Home Secretary to inspect them and to make a grant to those forces found to be efficient. At first many of the local forces were too small and after the reform of County Councils in 1888, a Police Act (1890) provided for a single county force under the direction of a Joint Committee of County Councillors and Justices of the Peace. Only County Boroughs, the largest towns, were allowed to maintain separate forces. Each of these forces, apart from the Metropolitan Force, was independent of the Home Secretary, except that he had powers of inspection to ensure that they were efficient and conducted themselves properly.

10 · Religion during the Great Changes

When we look at periods in the past we must be careful not to be prejudiced by what people wrote at the time, or afterwards. Instead, we should look for evidence: in this way we will find out more accurately what conditions were like. Many people have judged the eighteenth century Church of England harshly, saying it was corrupt, lazy, indifferent. But a closer look at the evidence shows that much of the criticism has been exaggerated.

At the head of the Church were the bishops. These were appointed by the Crown on the advice of the leading minister, and as they had a vote in the House of Lords, they were accused of supporting the Government of the day because *preferment* (promotion of the clergy) was regarded as the reward for 'good service' in the House. Bishops might be promoted for 'good service', but they earned it often by hard work on committees, not simply by idly voting when required. Their salaries varied widely. In the 1760s, Bristol was the lowest at £450, whilst Canterbury had £7,000. Some bishops were indifferent to their duties in their bishopric (*diocese*), like Bishop Watson of Llandaff who preferred the life of a gentleman on his Westmorland estate. But some bishops were active in their diocese, despite the difficulties of travelling. To some extent the Church suffered because it was a career for gentlemen, and younger sons of lords and squires became priests because a local vicar's job would be pleasant and could lead to a bishopric.

The local squire frequently was able to choose the local vicar (the *incumbent* of the *living*), so long as the bishop approved his choice. Often he chose his younger son (who could not inherit the estate) and it was unusual for such men to be of advanced views. Their income came from the *glebe* (land rented or farmed, but it belonged to the Church and could not be sold), from tithes, and from fees for services. If a junior vicar or *curate* were employed, he would be paid a *stipend* which was sometimes

The vicar of the parish receiving his tithes

not enough to keep him and his family.

There were not enough clergy, and as some livings were too poor to support a priest, the practice of holding more than one living (*pluralism*) was common. Sometimes vicars employed curates to help them in their services in the different parishes, but frequently it became a matter of simply not holding services. Some of the vicars and curates were very badly paid, and cartoons of the period often showed the well-fed vicar and the poor, thin curate. But the status and the pay of the lower clergy improved during the century, and Queen Anne's Bounty was used to supplement livings with an income of less than £50. New rectories were built, more suited to the standing of a gentleman, and by the end of the century, more priests entered the ministry.

The Church was not demonstrative. It had a

positive horror of what it called 'Enthusiasm' ('a vain belief of private revelation; a vain confidence of divine favour or communication,' as Dr Johnson defined it in his *Dictionary*). The previous century had been one of religious extremes: the eighteenth century preferred calmness. Generally 'low' church services were preferred, with little ceremony, and the music provided by a small band and sometimes a choir. Pews occupied the nave of the church. These were often rented by local wealthy families— the poor sat or stood at the back in the draught from the door. Sermons had been popular in the previous century: they were continued in the eighteenth, although they were often the published sermons of popular preachers rather than the vicar's own work. These popular sermons stressed the importance of Christian charity and good works, but they were not very exciting. Indeed, Archbishop Secker admitted:

'We have, in fact, lost many of our people to Sectaries [the reformed religions founded in the previous century] by not preaching in a manner sufficiently evangelical.'

A growing sense of toleration also typified the Church, and after 1728 an annual Indemnity Act was passed, allowing *Dissenters* (but not Roman Catholics) to hold public office. Eventually the acts imposing restrictions on the Dissenters, the Test and Corporation Acts, were repealed (1828). Roman Catholics were allowed the same rights as other citizens by the granting of Roman Catholic Emancipation (1829). Jews were admitted into the House of Commons (1858) and members of denominations other than the Anglicans, were allowed into Oxford and Cambridge Universities (1871).

Eighteenth-century Anglican clergy may not have been very exciting men, but they did play an effective role in society, especially in the countryside. Dr Johnson observed:

'that it might be discerned whether or no there was a clergyman resident in the parish by the civil or savage manner of the people.'

Some vicars refrained from charging for baptism

and funeral services if the family were poor, others helped by paying doctors' bills, others by helping parishioners to settle disputes among themselves. Gradually we are learning more about the actual work of eighteenth-century clergy, rather than the stories told by their critics. The picture is less one of despised, over-worked and underpaid curates performing the tasks of absentee vicars who preferred hunting to preaching, than of 'conscientious and dutiful men trying to do their work, according to the standard of their day'.

One of their difficulties, particularly in the growing towns, was the administrative organisation of the Church itself. Convocation, the Assembly of the Church, did not meet during the century after 1717, and therefore the Church lacked some degree of cohesion. Again, the parish, ideal for rural society, bringing some degree of social harmony and, as the century progressed, usually a school as well, could not easily be altered. As new towns developed especially in the Pennines, there was often no priest available, or the church might be a considerable distance from the new houses, or the parish might be of enormous size and have several townships growing up rapidly within it. This simple administrative point often meant that the Church could not be as effective a missionary force as it might have been. Even so, there was considerable activity; and it is partly to be measured by the increasing number of charitable foundations, schools and hospitals and almshouses. The Society for Promoting Christian Knowledge (S.P.C.K., 1699) and the Society for the Reformation of Manners (1692) were both vigorous during the century, and at its close the great Anti-Slavery movement (see *page 19*) drew its leadership from within the Anglican communion. Furthermore, although Methodism was clearly a sign that the Church failed to satisfy, Wesley himself had been nurtured in the Church and always regarded himself a member of it.

The Methodists

The poor often lay outside of the Church, especially

in isolated areas. It would be a great mistake to suppose that Methodism was a religion of the poor, but it was among them that it had its first successes.

John Wesley was an Anglican priest and Methodism was his creation. Its immediate success owed much to his power and courage as a preacher and teacher, and its continued growth was partly due both to the fact that he was able personally to control the movement for fifty years, and to his outstanding powers of organisation. His early life showed how serious religious observance could be among young Anglicans—there was no slothfulness among the members of his 'Holy Club' whose strict practices and visiting of the sick and needy undermined the health of more than one of them. But he felt dissatisfied, and after several attempts to discover a more direct approach to God, he had a profound religious experience in 1738 that launched him upon his 'revivalist' campaign. He recorded the experience:

'In the evening I went very unwillingly to a society in Aldersgate Street where one was reading Luther's Preface to the Epistle to the Romans. About a quarter before nine, while he was describing the change God works in the heart through faith in Christ, I felt my heart strangely warmed. I felt I did trust in Christ, Christ alone, for salvation; and an assurance was given me, that He had taken away my sins, even mine, and saved me from the law of sin and death.'

At the moment when the Church was most strongly opposed to 'Enthusiasm' he began preaching in a direct and personal and very emotional way. Fashionable London rejected his 'vital' religion—indeed he had often to contend with mobs set upon him sometimes by the magistrates themselves.

He preached out of doors because he found the churches closed to him, and his sermons were often accompanied by violent scenes of hysteria, shriekings and sobbings. It was perhaps stories of such scenes that so offended the contemporary Church and made it distrustful of Wesley's message. But Wesley persisted: indeed, he was an indefatigable preacher, journeying an average of 4,000 miles a year preaching. He turned to isolated communities like the Kingswood miners, near Bristol, preaching that religion was not the preserve of the socially respectable. In his early years the numbers of conversions were great. John Nelson remembered the joy he experienced on his conversion:

'I was like a wandering bird, cast out of the nest till Mr John Wesley came to preach his first sermon in Moorfields. Oh, that was a blessed morning to my soul.'

Since so few ordained priests joined him he was obliged to make use of lay-preachers and when the problem arose of sending them to the American Colonies, he could find no bishop to consecrate them priests; so he did it himself. It was upon this matter of Church discipline that the Anglicans rejected his movement. He refused to recognise his rejection and prescribed attendance at monthly Communion for his followers; but inevitably, the movement identified itself as a separate unit.

Most revivalist movements die down: Wesley's survived because of the excellence of his organisation, which he controlled personally—'Pope John' was his nickname. As the movement grew, he created preaching circuits responsible for running their own affairs under a central council. Wesley controlled this council by the simple device of deciding who should attend it. His personal control was shown by the fact that it was only after his death that the movement began to break into divergent parts (often on the basis of social class); the Kilhamites (the New Connexion) left in 1797 and the Primitive Methodists, the most important breakaway, in 1811.

The backbone of Methodism came not from the very poor, but from the semi-skilled and skilled craftsmen and shopkeepers. It was a positive act of choice to become a Methodist, for it was not only a great religious experience, it was also an inspiration to a disciplined life with an accent upon hard work, thrift and charity (even by the very poor who themselves had insufficient to make life bearable). Their days were spent according to a self-devised time-table, so that each hour was used to best effect:

their very name, Methodist, emphasised the husbandry of time. Wesley himself rose at 4 a.m.:

'By *soaking* . . . so long between warm sheets, the flesh is, as it were, parboiled, and becomes soft and flabby. The nerves, in the meantime, are quite unstrung.'

Methodists were keen observers of the Sabbath and laid great stress on Bible reading (consequently they did much to help the spread of literacy). Soon they were not laughed at, but recognised as very reliable workmen. In 1787, Sir Robert Peel, father of the great Prime Minister, commented:

'I have left my works in Lancashire under the management of Methodists, and they serve me exceeding well.'

Their self discipline made them admirable factory labour: one did not need to fine Methodists for being late. It meant that they had a great self respect, too, and their morale was high: they learnt rapidly to organise their own community, with the chapel as the centre of their lives (it was often the only place for relaxation apart from the pub). This experience was to help them during the nineteenth century in the running of Friendly Societies, Co-operatives, trade unions and political associations; indeed, the early history of the Labour Party (see *page 218*) is far more concerned with Methodists than with Marx. Many early Labour leaders were Methodist lay-preachers.

But during Wesley's lifetime, and in the anxious days of the French Wars (1793–1815), Methodism turned its face from politics. Wesley himself was a High Tory and had no interest in altering the existing order of society; both he and the Calvinist Methodists under Whitefield rejected any idea of social or political radicalism—the Calvinist Methodists in Cornwall excommunicated those of their members who went on strike, joined a trade union, or supported Roman Catholic Emancipation. Self discipline, respect for authority and good behaviour, taught Methodists to accept their position in life and to seek their salvation in hard work: they were averse to politics at first. They were also, socially,

the potential leaders of a working class political movement, and it has been argued, especially by Halevy, that because these men rejected politics, Britain was saved from the threat of the French Revolution. In 1831, Gravener Henson of Nottingham wrote:

'The effect of this sect has been great upon the manners and opinions of the people, as they invariably inculcate the doctrine of passive submission to events as happening according to the fore-knowledge of the Deity.'

This interpretation has been attacked on the grounds that Methodism's main impact was in the isolated areas, away from politically conscious big towns. It seems that it was not so much Methodism, as the refusal of the British worker to be revolutionary, that saved us from the French Revolution. After the French Wars, although the Wesleyans seemed to avoid politics, the groups that broke away *were* politically active. When Lord Londonderry evicted coal miners on strike in 1844, two-thirds of them were Primitive Methodists.

The impact of Methodism was tremendous. By 1801 there were about 100,000 Methodists and perhaps as many as 600,000 'adherents'. Church attendance was badly affected in some rural parishes, especially as more and more cheap red-brick chapels were built for Methodist worship. But, for the most part, the people who became Methodists were those whom neither the established Church of England, nor the other dissenting Churches, had managed to attract. Throughout the early nineteenth century they grew at a rapid rate, but their principal centres remained those areas in which Wesley had had his great successes. They were strongest in Yorkshire, Wales, the Potteries and Cornwall. By 1851, however, a real social division had appeared. The Wesleyans were increasingly lower middle class, while the 'Primitives' were the poorer workers. However, Methodism helped the British working class not only to become adjusted to the new social conditions of the Great Changes, but also it taught them to behave with greater sobriety than their grandfathers would have thought possible.

The Evangelicals

Just as there was a developing humanitarianism during the eighteenth century, so there was a deepening of the religious experience among all denominations. Within the Anglican Church, especially among its wealthier members, there was the Evangelical revival that had perhaps more impact upon society in general than had the Methodists. The Evangelicals rejected the insolence, vulgarity and violence of the behaviour of many young men, and worked towards bettering the moral condition of the poor. Like the Methodists they laid stress on moral conduct, strict observance of the Sabbath, hard work and thrift. They can claim much of the credit for the developing public concern about conditions in the slums, and, of course, for the campaign against Slavery (Wilberforce, Lord Shaftesbury, Dr Barnardo were all Evangelicals). They were active against cruel sports (the R.S.P.C.A. was founded in 1824), and for prison reform, and their missionary zeal spread their Christian message across the globe. The Church Missionary Society was founded in 1799 (the Dissenters founded the British and Foreign Bible Society in 1804: there was tremendous rivalry between Christian sects), and both Evangelicals and Dissenters were active in education (see *page 141*).

It is difficult to isolate the founder of the movement; perhaps it was Henry Venn, a vicar at Huddersfield who moved to Cambridge and had a considerable influence on young men there. His son, John Venn, became rector of Clapham and gathered around him a number of wealthy men whose views and conduct earned them the nickname the 'Clapham Saints'. But their influence was felt throughout the Church of England, especially because they were wealthy and well connected, and they hoped that their social influence would help them to pass Bills to secure the reforms they sought. They were concerned to improve human conditions, not to upturn society—they were even further removed from social revolution than was Wesley. However, they awakened the politically powerful to the need for reform and greatly invigorated the Anglican Church, so that it could, with good heart, face the challenge of the Great Changes. But it was always a matter of reform 'from above' with them, and it is difficult to avoid the conclusion that they were rather patronising towards the poor. A good example of how this could take a practical form was in the Government provision of one million pounds in 1818 for the building of churches, increased by £500,000 in 1824; they were known as the 'Waterloo Churches' and it was hoped that providing churches for the poor would help to keep them in good order.

Perhaps the best example of this sort of thing is provided by Hannah More, the 'old Bishop in Petticoats' as William Cobbett called her. She was a philanthropist and educator whose writings were extremely influential, laying stress on self discipline and personal responsibility and on an earnest endeavour to fulfil that rôle in society 'to which God had been pleased to call you'. But she was also anxious to make the rich aware that charity and good taste were no substitute for Christianity. 'What Wesley had done for the poor, she was doing for the rich.'

Perhaps it was a combination of Methodism and Evangelicalism that created the peculiar social cement of nineteenth-century Britain and helped us avoid a revolution. When the Great Changes were at their height, self respect, sobriety, discipline became the key-note of society: for the wealthy a concern for the lot of the poor, for the rising poor that attitude of 'self-help' that Samuel Smiles was to immortalise. Victoria's court, so different from that of her uncles, the dissolute sons of George III, set a good example as well. But the working man, whose education the wealthy were concerned to extend (see Chapter XI), was expected to have a *deferential* attitude to his social superiors—he was expected to respect them and to defer to their wishes, and not to contemplate any radical social change. In Victorian England, 'The rich man in his castle, the poor man at his gate', was a very real expression of social attitudes.

Yet, for all the good example, it was clear that the great mass of the working classes were outside the Church of whatever denomination. The Religious Tract Society boasted of a huge circulation, but it was among those who went to services, not those who

stayed away. In 1849, Charles Kingsley published *Yeast*, a novel in which one character says:
'After all the expense, when they've built the church it's the tradesman and the gentry and the old folk that fill it, and the working men never come near it from one year's end to another.'

Perhaps only the Roman Catholics could claim any very steady progress among the very poor—and this was rather because of the Irish immigrants than from conversions, although Father Gentile who died of cholera in 1848, and his Institute of Charity, did useful work.

The Oxford Movement

It seems incredible to us that when the greatest challenge facing the Churches was this mass of working class families, who stolidly refrained from following the example of their 'social superiors' and refused to attend service, they should waste their energies on sectarian controversies. The Oxford Movement almost tore the Church of England apart, and was a controversy, at least on the surface, over organisation and church ceremonial. This is a warning against making too facile judgements in history: men do not always see what seems important to later generations, nor do they always concern themselves with the problems their successors recognise as the real ones. We should judge men first according to the standards of their day.

When the Whig government in 1833 attempted to modernise the organisation of the Anglican Church, John Keble preached a sermon entitled 'National Apostacy'. This touched off the Oxford Movement. His principal allies were John Henry Newman and Edward Pusey, and together they urged a return to what they called the traditional ritual of the Anglican Church, encouraging a greater sense of grace and beauty in church services with the use of vestments and greater ceremonial. Newman's *Tracts for the Times* began appearing in 1833 and were widely read. Great enthusiasm was aroused among both clergymen and congregations, and many of the young clergy followed the Movement, especially in the

Mr Punch asks, 'Which is Popery and which is Puseyism?'

wealthier parishes.

Statues and pictures, banners, processions, vestments and elaborate ritual certainly made for colourful services, but the movement also raised a great deal of hostility, the more so as it seemed that it was moving nearer and nearer practices common in the Roman Church. Now, although Roman Catholic Emancipation had been granted in 1829, there was still a great deal of latent hostility to Roman Catholicism. The suspicion that the Oxford Movement was leading Anglicans to Rome was deepened when *Tract 90* sought to stress the similarities between the Anglican and Roman Church. Macaulay said that a man might hold the worst doctrines of the Church of Rome and the best benefice in the Church of England. At local parish level deep cleavages were apparent within congregations, especially when a new vicar brought in ritual for the first time, and congregations were often divided bitterly. Many ordinary people suffered trials of conscience and some stayed away from service.

But those who gained publicity were those who actually joined the Roman Catholics, and among them were leading men of the Oxford Movement, including Manning (in 1851) and Newman, both of whom became cardinals. So great was the popular reaction to these conversions that Newman wrote, in beautiful prose, a self-justification, *Apologia pro Vita Sua* (1864-5).

Popular feeling against Rome was shown when the Pope determined to appoint bishops to a new division of Roman Catholic dioceses in Britain; this was condemned as the 'Papal Aggression' and the Ecclesiastical Titles Act was passed (1851) to prevent the Pope choosing the name of any existing Anglican bishopric. (It was repealed in 1871.) This was an extreme case, but the Oxford Movement did raise violent feelings between High and Low Church views—and one can still come across something of this feeling today, despite the moves towards Christian Unity. The Movement touched an important current of opinion, which helps to explain its importance. It also inspired parishioners to beautify their churches and build new ones. It helped to raise funds for restoring existing churches—for the Victorians were great restorers of medieval buildings. It was also partly to be explained as a reaction to the ugliness of the developing industrial towns: the visible symbol of Victorian England is the steam engine and the gothic-revival church.

Christian Socialism

The Christian Socialists differed from the Oxford Movement by laying emphasis upon the social need of responsibility for the welfare of the poor: 'Our Church must apply herself to the task of raising the poor into men; she cannot go on . . . treating them merely as poor', wrote one of their leaders. They should be 'mediators . . . between young England, the middle and upper classes, and the working people', and free Christianity from 'caste morality'.

After watching the Chartist meeting at Kennington Common in 1848 (see *page 164*) a group of young men determined to form a society of Christian Socialists to promote the reformation of society without revolution through 'self help'. Their leaders were F. D. Maurice, who wrote many pamphlets, Charles Kingsley, the novelist, and Thomas Hughes, author of *Tom Brown's Schooldays* and first Principal of the Working Men's College. Their writings influenced middle class opinion and helped spread ideas of social reform as well as a deeper sympathy for the condition of the working man. Among the objects for which they agitated were the establishment of limited liability (see *page 85*) and the expansion of the co-operative movement (see *page 166*), temperance, savings like the Post Office Saving Bank (1861) (see *page 85*), life insurance (like the Prudential, 1848), slum clearance and adult education.

'Our object has been to separate in what seemed to us the most effective way, that socialism, which Mr Southey and other eminent Conservatives believed to be the best solution to the practical difficulties of England, from Communism and Red Republicanism, or any anarchical opinion whatsoever.'

F. D. Maurice wrote this justification in 1851, it shows clearly what place they occupied. Their work was less patronising than that of some organisations, and they deserve to be better remembered.

'Heathen' England

It comes as a shock to realise that most Victorians did not go to church or chapel. In March 1851, a religious census was held that revealed from a calculation of those attending services, that large areas of the working-class sections of towns were 'heathen'. Men were profoundly shocked that in a self-consciously religious age, out of a population of nearly eighteen million, only 7,260,000 attended a service that day: 'a sadly formidable portion of the English people are habitual neglectors of the public ordinances of religion' commented the Report of the Census.

Attendance was lowest in London and the great towns. 'A church, Sir, so I've heard. I never was in a church', a London costermonger told Henry Mayhew when asked what building was St Paul's.

There were many reasons for the working class resistance to religion. The Churches, including the Methodists, had rarely touched the poor workers in the big towns. Payments and tithes caused much ill-feeling and misunderstanding. The Parish, suitable enough for rural England, was a singularly poor instrument of organisation for urban conditions, especially if the original church were not near the new centres of population. Certainly some churches were not much concerned for the poor. Social distinctions were common: pew rents meant that the middle class went prosperously to church, the few 'free seats' were not well placed; (some churches still display notices that the seats, today, are free, or that the repairs to the church had been paid for on condition that the seats were free). The lack of a good suit also kept many away. Some prosperous parishes would build a meaner church elsewhere for the workers. Many stayed away simply because the wealthier went, or because they were exhausted by their work or rendered indolent by their living conditions. There were also insufficient clergy and churches. Nevertheless, in addition to extensive missionary work abroad, great strides were made to provide new churches. Between 1801 and 1851, 2,529 Anglican churches were built at a cost of nine million pounds.

At the same time, many Christians were going through a great crisis of belief, for the Victorians were not smug and complacent. Scholars had cast doubt upon the validity of some of the books of the Bible, and scientific studies began to destroy faith in the story of Creation and the Flood. Both Sir Charles Lyell's *Principles of Geology* (1830-3) and Chambers's *Vestiges of the Natural History of Creation* (1844) showed that living things existed long before the time customarily thought of as the Creation, and that they appeared at different periods, not all being created at the same moment. Then, after accumulating a huge volume of evidence, Charles Darwin published *The Origin of Species* (1859) suggesting that living things were not created so much as developed out of existing species. Those species that failed to respond to the challenge of changing natural conditions died off, and those that

did respond successfully, frequently altered their actual form in order to survive. All this took longer than humans were able to conceive of, and it quite destroyed the hope of accepting the Book of Genesis as the literal story of the origin of life on earth. Darwin had no intention of attacking religion, and was horrified when popularisers of his ideas began to do so. The intelligentsia was divided between those who accepted Darwinism and rejected Genesis, like Professor T. H. Huxley, and those who followed Huxley's great opponent, Bishop Wilberforce, in rejecting Darwinism as atheistic. The Churches took a long time to recover from the blow that Darwin had inadvertently delivered.

In George Eliot's *Middlemarch*, one of the older characters says:

' "When I was young, Mr Lydgate, there was never any question about right or wrong. We knew our catechism, and that was enough; we learned our creed and our duty. Every respectable Church person held the same opinions. But now, if you speak out of the Prayer-Book itself, you are liable to be contradicted."

' "That makes rather a pleasant time of it for those who like to maintain their own point", said Lydgate.'

Towards the end of the century, all Churches came under a concentrated attack suffering a waning of support in the towns, and in the rural areas, too. They have not yet recovered.

The Salvation Army

But the contribution to the life of towns, especially in the working class areas, is not to be underestimated. The churches, chapels and church halls are solid reminders that the Victorians performed what they took to be their social duty on a scale far beyond that of previous generations. And at the same time there was a massive flow of funds and recruits into missionary endeavour overseas. This missionary work, which gained much publicity at the time, was not confined to the 'backward' areas of the world, it was also to be found in our own cities.

The Victorians did not neglect the working classes. Bible classes and social work among them occupied a large part of middle class life, and a number of 'settlements' were founded run by charitable trusts, university colleges or schools—Toynbee Hall (1884) is a good example. They did useful work relieving wretchedness and helping with adult education; but it was (and is) difficult to avoid a patronising attitude of 'good works' from 'social superiors'.

There was nothing patronising about the last great religious movement of the century—the Salvation Army. This was a 'revivalist' movement that sprang from the people, often from the classes that even the chapels had failed to touch. Catherine Booth, the wife of the founder, put her finger on the reason for the movement's success:

'You cannot reform man morally by his intellect; this is the mistake of most social reformers. You must reform man by his Soul.'

More was needed than sermons, education and better conditions. The Salvation Army achieved what the many denominations had failed to do: it spoke to the working man in his home in his own language and its conversions were many. It touched even the casual workers at the very bottom of the social pyramid.

William Booth was converted to a sense of salvation in 1846 as a Wesleyan in Nottingham. He became a revivalist preacher among the poor of such

A Salvation Army meeting is broken up by a mob

power that he found himself edged out of the Wesleyan Connexion, much as Wesley had been edged out of the Church of England. In 1865 he and his wife, from a tent in Whitechapel, launched a 'Christian Mission to the Heathen of Our Own Country'. The mission witnessed scenes of ecstasy as great as those of Wesley's day and grew into the Salvation Army, taking this name in 1880. Military dress and drill was popular then and there were a number of religious 'armies'. (The Volunteer Movement that formed a sort of army 'reserve' helped to set this pattern.) The famous brass bands played an important part in the Salvation meetings— and they drowned the noise of hostile crowds, for the movement raised much opposition. In 1882 the *War Cry*, its journal, reported a Liverpool meeting:

'Stones were thrown, a brickbat striking the head of Sergeant Fellowes, breaking his head, and causing the loss of a pint of blood. He was taken to the hospital, had his head bandaged, and came back leaping and praising God.'

Rarely did the Salvationists reply in kind to the mobs who provoked them, even when the Skeleton Army was formed (perhaps by brewers and publicans because the Salvationers were teetotallers) to break up their meetings. In the early days the police deliberately broke up the meetings, while in Whitechapel police refused to intervene as thugs attacked them. But by 1883 *War Cry* had a circulation of 350,000 weekly, with editions all over the world. And the organisation was closely controlled by General Booth himself (much as Wesley had done for the Methodists a century earlier).

Eighteen-ninety was a turning point. The direst poverty existing in our cities was being revealed in the press and in books. Booth produced *In Darkest England—And the Way Out*. It demanded extensive social reform as an aid to man's salvation—'Here is General Booth turning socialist', commented the *Methodist Times*. Certainly, the influence of Robert Owen could be seen in his suggestion of labour colonies for the unemployed and a colony farm near London, together with depots for food and shelter for the distressed. The book was a huge success at first, but interest in it died away.

The movement itself also ceased to expand at the same rate as in its early years. It did not convert the multitude as Booth had hoped, but it brought—and brings—relief to many. Indeed, it is a business undertaking of some consequence today. At the end of his life, General Booth was pleased to note that the churches which once had scorned him, were beginning to use some of his own methods.

But for all its success in the very areas that other Churches had failed to touch, it had to be admitted that the Salvation Army, even with its accent on social reform, could not hold the attention of the working man, and, like all other churches, it experienced a wasting away of support from about the 1890s. It seems as though modern urban society has yet to discover that form of religious observance which can maintain continued support from a wide stretch of social classes, such as appears to have been the condition of the Church in the seventeenth century.

11 · Education during the Great Changes

If you had been born in 1870 your chances of getting a reasonable schooling would have been quite different from those of a child born in 1770, for these hundred years saw the development of the provision of schools for most English children. In 1770 the type of education available depended on your social class and the money available. Girls then were lucky to be anything more than literate and trained housewives. The wealthy son might have a private tutor (governesses come in with the nineteenth century) or go to a public school at a very early age. Thereafter, he might go to the Inns of Court (London) or a University, or on a *Grand Tour* to absorb fashionable culture by travelling in Italy, France and Germany. Dissenters would go to the Scottish Universities or to Holland because religious tests excluded them from Oxford and Cambridge until 1871. These two English Universities were at a very low ebb indeed, for students and dons spent more time hunting, drinking, and gambling than studying, and the examinations they took were a farce, even at Cambridge, where they were taken seriously. George III caused a sensation by expecting Regius Professors to lecture. However, things were already on the mend by 1770. There were some good tutors, and although Classics and Hebrew were the

OXFORD TRANSPORTS or *Albanians doing Penance for Past offences.*

A cartoon of eighteenth-century university life

principal subjects, science was being introduced and professors of Botany and Chemistry were appointed. The Universities were reforming themselves, and religious observance among the dons (all of whom had to be in Holy Orders) was improving.

If you wanted to train for the professions, then you had to work through a period of training, rather like an apprentice, though at a different social level. The 'mercantile classes' had fee-paying local grammar schools and Academies run by Dissenters. These Academies, begun because the Universities were closed to Dissenters, were outstanding and were characterised by fresh and experimental methods of teaching, active co-operation with the boys in order to develop a sense of personal responsibility, and a curriculum well suited to the business world. It is not surprising they produced so many scientists and reformers. The Scottish schools were similarly outstanding and many young Scots came South to seek their fortune and give England the benefit of their abilities.

The Poor

Most children of the poor went to work, for this was a feature of the domestic system. Private charity supplied their needs so far as schooling was concerned. During the century, helped by the S.P.C.K., many charity schools were founded to supplement those begun in the previous century. By 1800 a school was felt to be a proper thing to find in each parish—and the charity schools were usually Anglican. Addison called them 'the glory of the age' and there was one in each county in 1727. They took girls as well as boys and taught the Anglican catechism and the '3 R's'—although the girls usually did needlework instead of arithmetic. Many of the teachers were of poor quality and what was lacking in education was supplied by an excessive concentration on piety, often with an accent on the gratitude due to social superiors. The charity schools were not to provide opportunities for advancement, as did the Scottish schools. Yet they were attacked for educating children above their proper station. When Hannah More opened a

school for poor miners' children in the Mendips, a farmer's wife stated:

'The poor were intended to be servants and slaves: it was pre-ordained that they should be ignorant.'

This attitude worried those concerned for the education of the poor. But Mrs Sarah Trimmer had the answer:

'The objection against giving learning to the poor, lest it raise them above their station, is completely obviated by making such learning as general as possible; for then it ceases to give pre-eminence, or to be a distinction, and must eventually qualify them all the better to fill their respective stations in society: and nothing could be thought of so well calculated to diffuse a moderate and useful share of learning among the lower orders of people, as these schools.' (*Reflections upon the Education of Children in Charity Schools* (1792)).

Attendance was voluntary, and if Charity Schools offered very little, at least they were better than nothing.

There were also Dame Schools, many of them very wretched and little more than an old woman paid for minding children during the day. But some were good—Dr Johnson attended one. It is estimated that in 1815 there might have been some 50,000 children at Dame's Schools.

Then there were Parochial Day Schools of Industry that concentrated on 'useful crafts', especially for girls, rather than on book learning. They could easily become profitable sources of child labour, but they were defended on the grounds that:

'by mixing labour with learning, they are particularly eligible for such children as are afterwards to be employed in manufactures, and other inferior offices in life, as well as for training those who are usually called *common servants.*'

We should not, however, be too hasty to condemn the people who ran these schools for the poor for they were not accustomed to the idea of equality of opportunity.

Sunday Schools

Supplementing the Charity Schools, and perhaps more concerned with social training than education, were the Sunday schools. They were originally for poor children and those working in textile factories and intended to keep them occupied during their one free day of the week—for most working-class children were working throughout the week, and their earnings were valuable to the family. Many thought the provision of some instruction merely on a Sunday perfectly adequate for the poor, and there was a similar concentration upon reading and piety with rather less writing and much less arithmetic than was to be found in the charity schools. Robert Raikes is generally credited with founding the movement, but one should not imagine that Sunday schools did not exist before he began one in Gloucester in 1780, for their origin lies in the previous century at least. His intention, an important one in adjusting to changing conditions, was to make 'idle, ungovernable, profligate and filthy "boys" more orderly, tractable and attentive to business'. In 1785 a Sunday School Union was founded and the movement became very popular. Raikes was insistent on his social purpose, and wrote in 1810:

'Pay special attention to instilling moral and religious truths into the minds of children, giving them views of their situation and sound practical rules for their conduct. Such matters are of much more consequence than making them good writers or accountants.'

Some of the schools opened evening classes and taught adults as well, but, as a Government report put it in 1833, although implanting 'feelings of religion' their educational task 'was imperfect without daily instruction also'.

However, there was an increasing awareness of the need to educate the poor, despite the fear that this might lead them to become acquainted with 'advanced' political ideas of equality. Dimly, contemporaries were realising that the old apprenticeship methods of training were no longer altogether appropriate: more self-discipline and training was required of quite low category workers by the new industrial processes and this meant that the poor needed 'social training' if not actual education in an academic sense. One can complain that too little was done, that there was no planning or system, but one cannot say that educators were idle, or did not respond to the challenge facing them. It is also worth remembering that the period of the Great Changes, when the whole pattern and manner of life of many people was altered, was not the easiest of times to decide what was the best pattern for the education of future workers. What experience was there to guide educators? There was none: they had to devise their own systems as they went along. Certainly the schools did much to discipline the children of the poor at the very time that people were beginning to distinguish between 'work', 'life' and 'leisure'. Much of this was achieved by imposing a training in self discipline. A Methodist girls' School of Industry at Pocklington, Yorkshire (1819) had among its rules:

'Every scholar must be in the school-room on Sundays, at nine o'clock in the morning, and at half-past one in the afternoon, or she shall lose her place the next Sunday, and walk last.'

No Saint Monday for these poor children!

Denominational schools

The Churches made the biggest contribution to educating the poor. In 1807 began the British and Foreign Schools Society, composed of Anglicans and Nonconformists, and this was followed in 1811 by the wholly Anglican, National Society. It was the latter Society that had the greatest success: by 1830 there were 3,670 schools and some 346,000 pupils. But a very small proportion of the poor attended the schools and they did not attend regularly: nor were they particularly well taught.

In order to overcome the difficulty of staffing the *Monitorial System* was used, for it had many advantages of a practical nature. Both denominational societies used the method, which is generally attributed to Joseph Lancaster (British and Foreign) and Andrew Bell (National). To some extent it intro-

Instruction by monitors, 1839

duced into the school room the mechanical atmosphere of the factory. The whole school would be accommodated in one big room in charge of a single teacher and the factual material of each lesson would be taught to a small group of senior boys (monitors) who would then teach groups of children. The whole class would then be tested orally. The practical advantages of the system were obvious—the more so as it economised on the use of teachers. A witness before the Committee on Education (1834) declared:

'I have heard it observed that it is the excellency of Dr Bell's system that 1,000 children may be under a process of mutual instruction, while the master merely supervises. The possibility of such a state of things is, I think, the great deficiency of that system.'

The consequence of using the monitor was that only the simplest and most mechanical learning could be attempted, and the children merely memorised without any necessary understanding at all. Proudly Joseph Lancaster boasted:

'I have successfully convinced a number of the boys in my leading institution of the beauty, usefulness and piety there is in ever speaking the truth; of the pernicious effects . . . not only as to lying, but swearing and various kinds of profaneness. These boys are bright examples and give the lead to the whole school.'

Lord Brougham called it the 'Steam Engine of the Moral World', even though it crushed out any enquiring spirit. It is incredible that it should have become so widely accepted, in the very schools to which the Government granted public money (see *page 147*), when in Switzerland, Pestalozzi was reforming education methods, and even in England, Maria Edgeworth was declaring in *Practical Education* (1801), 'Play . . . is only a change of occupation . . . instruction and amusements of children may be so managed as to coincide with each other.' But perhaps the societies were more concerned to instil deference and good behaviour than encourage a spirit of enquiry.

Mechanics' Institutes

All over the country groups of adults were meeting to learn to read, often using the Bible; but in some towns others were meeting to learn about the new machines that were transforming industry. George Birkbeck formed such a group in Glasgow in 1799 which became the Glasgow Mechanics' Institute in 1823. The same year Birkbeck founded the London Mechanics' Institute with the support of leading political figures and London artisans. Other Institutes appeared in the big towns and by 1851 some 600,000 members were claimed for 622 Institutes. Most of them confined themselves to teaching crafts and skills—the Manchester Institute declared that its purpose was to enable

'Mechanics and Artisans . . . to . . . possess a more thorough knowledge of their business, acquire a greater degree of skill in the practice of it, and be qualified to make improvements and even new inventions in the Arts which they respectively profess.'

But they were often obliged to teach the 'three R's', and they inspired a determination to learn that was reflected in their impressive libraries—The Birmingham Institute had over 3,000 volumes. The bigger Institutes had their own buildings, paid for by local subscriptions from members and interested manufacturers. The Leeds Institute cost £30,000 to build.

Brougham did much to encourage them, and education as a whole, through his Society for the Diffusion of Useful Knowledge, and despite opposition from those who feared that education of the poor would give them ideas 'above their station in life', the idea of education as an end in itself became popular. Samuel Smiles wrote of it 'raising the entire condition of the working man'.

There was much idealism and great dedication among a working class striving to 'improve' themselves. It was a pity that many of their efforts were frustrated because they lacked the time, the money, the leisure, and in some cases had not had the opportunity of attending a school as a child. By the 1850s, however, the fustian jackets were giving way to the black coats of clerks, and the Mechanics' Institutes were becoming more frequented by the 'middle and respectable classes'. The London Mechanics' Institute was to become Birkbeck College and other Institutes were to become Working Men's Colleges, all of which did great things for working class education, but it was a pity that the early attempt at technical education by the Mechanics' Institutes should have been lost. It was lost partly because there was no national system to organise it, but more particularly because many of those in need of technical education were semi-literate and unable to understand the books and courses on the scientific principles underlying their trades. This itself was a powerful argument for a national system of education. But the first genera-

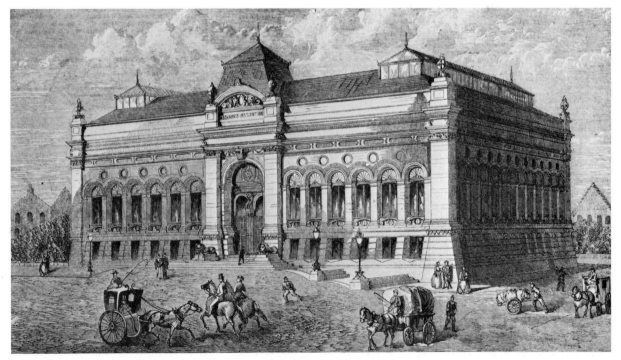

The Leeds Mechanics' Institute

tion of Victorians thought of academic education as a gentlemanly pursuit, whilst unorganised apprenticeships for the new skills which the industrial revolution brought, were thought adequate for the mechanical training of craftsmen. Below the artisan class, the common labourer remained virtually untouched by education until the end of the century.

Grammar schools

Grammar schools had been founded in a number of towns in Tudor times for the purpose of teaching poor boys, and occasionally girls. But by the late eighteenth century these were mostly in a very serious state of decay. Some had no money to provide for a proper master, because the *endowments* originally made to pay for the school were either too small or were no longer adequate because of the decline in the value of money (*inflation*). Other schools had a big income, but masters preferred to take very few pupils, whilst most parents still preferred to employ their children at home rather than lose good money by paying for them to go to school. At Buckingham during the French Wars, the school was

'of little note in any respect—none but the children of the lower classes having been educated here, from time immemorial. There are six boys only in the School.'

In Pockington the lower school room was used as a saw pit and barn and the master was an absentee.

Such examples could easily be multiplied, and it was rare to come across a really competent master. There were some good grammar schools, however, especially in the North, like Bradford Grammar under Benjamin Butler from 1728 to 1784 (a good master could transform a decrepit school into a respected institution in a few years). There were also experiments with the curriculum in these good schools, but normally it was restricted to Latin with a little Greek and less Hebrew, with very occasionally some English and a little arithmetic. When Leeds Grammar School tried to make its curriculum more appropriate for the needs of its pupils, Lord Eldon

declared it the law (1805) that grammar schools taught only Greek and Latin and Hebrew: not until the Grammar Schools Act of 1840 could many schools enlarge their curriculum.

About the turn of the century a number of private boarding schools were founded, but many were as bad, if not worse than the decayed grammar schools—Charles Dickens painted a startling picture of one of them, Dotherboys Hall, where Nicholas Nickleby taught.

At the same time the Evangelical movement (see *page 133*) was encouraging reform in education. Rowland Hill's school at Birmingham had a curriculum not unlike those to be found in schools today. By the middle of the century most grammar schools were efficient. One result of this reformation was the *Taunton Commission* that reported in 1867 along lines that were to influence developments in education for a hundred years. It recommended three types of school, an Upper School for those proceeding to the professions or to universities, a Middle School for those likely to become managers in the commercial world, and a Lower School for those likely to remain clerks (technical education did not appear). It was, of course, assumed that the boys attending the different types of school would be from appropriate social classes; they did not envisage a labourer's son attending an Upper School. The Report was a dead letter in that its recommendations were not immediately applied, but it did help the passing of the Endowed Schools Act (1869) releasing more charitable funds for educational purposes. Classics still continued to dominate the curriculum, but more 'modern' subjects, like languages and history and, more occasionally, science, were gradually introduced. This broadening of the curriculum was hastened by the reformed universities setting school examinations that could be taken as a certificate of educational standard and a qualification for jobs. The Cambridge Local Examination was the first of them in 1871 and from this pioneer move grew the national system of examinations of the present century now represented by the General Certificate of Education (G.C.E.).

Public schools

The grammar schools that took boarders, and the older foundations in some cases, became schools to which eighteenth-century aristocrats and wealthy men sent their sons—Eton, Winchester, Shrewsbury and Westminster were the most famous, and they became the leading 'public schools' of the following century. But they were fearsome places in the eighteenth century. Boys would sometimes go at a very tender age; conditions were bad, supervision, especially of dormitories, was minimal, bullying and brutality were commonplace.

'Their teaching had reduced itself to an endless covering of the minutiae of the grammar and versification of the classical tongue, and their discipline to a savage rule of the rod, interspersing an anarchy in which elder boys tyrannised over younger, and stronger over weaker, with all the unimaginative brutality of the natural boy.'

It was not unusual for a flogging to confine a boy to bed for days, and the system of 'fagging' was open to the grossest of abuses. Mutinies were not unknown and in 1818 troops had to be called to quell a riot at Winchester.

But industrialists who hoped to establish their families socially, looked to these schools as the means, for it provided their sons with the opportunity to rub shoulders with the aristocracy. It was not long before a number of schools were founded in order to cater for this new demand. They were boarding schools and were often sited in isolated places to reduce the distractions likely to arise—the railways made it possible for them to draw upon a very wide area.

As with the grammar schools, a good master could make the reputation of a school, like Samuel Butler at Shrewsbury between 1798 and 1836, who laid great stress on the development of self-reliance and discipline through his prefects, and, later, Thring at Uppingham from 1853 to 1887, who introduced music as an important activity and also built workshops for developing skills, as well as stressing games as the way to develop character and maintain healthy bodies (the first public school cricket match between Eton and Westminster was played in 1796). It was Thring who launched the Headmaster's Conference, to which all public schools belong today. So vigorous was the impact of the headmasters of some of the new or reformed public schools that the non-boarding grammar schools, by the end of the century, were trying to imitate them.

The best known and the greatest of these Victorian headmasters was Thomas Arnold (at Rugby from 1828 to 1842) whose principal aim was to produce leaders of society who were Christian gentlemen (hence his concentration on his Sixth Form as leaders of the school and on the chapel as the focal centre of the school). The Provost of Oriel College wrote in 1828:

'If Arnold were elected [headmaster of Rugby], he would change the face of education all through the public schools of England.'

The picture given in *Tom Brown's Schooldays* (1857) has tended to build up a portrait greater than life size. It is important to remember that Arnold was not an innovator, but a brilliant teacher who applied other men's ideas with a genius that was truly remarkable. He transformed life at Rugby by adapting rather than making a new start. Thus prefects continued to run the school, flogging was liberally administered, but bad influences were expelled. And the wealthy middle-class public continued to show their confidence in the new types of schools that grew up under the influence of Arnold, by sending their sons and paying for the buildings as well—though, as Professor Toynbee put it, they

'looked to the schools to provide a common platform enabling their sons to associate on equal terms with those of families who, if increasingly outdistanced in income, still diffused a faint aroma of social superiority.'

But, although Victorian public schools provided leaders of society and governors, their curriculum was not necessarily the best. In the 1860s Huxley complained that it was possible to go through the public schools and never hear that

'the earth goes round the sun; that England underwent a great revolution in 1688, and France another in 1789; that there once lived certain notable men called Chaucer, Shakespeare, Milton, Voltaire, Goethe, Schiller'.

When France and Germany were laying emphasis upon teaching technical subjects to fit children for a technical age, it is amazing that Britain, still the leading industrial nation, should have ignored the teaching of science and engineering in most schools. The Clarendon Commission on Public Schools (1864) put it simply:

'Yes: they see great statesmen and great financiers at the head of the Government rise out of a classical education, and they think this is the education their sons ought to have.'

They were not necessarily correct: the leading British nineteenth-century statesmen achieved their fame because of their social position and personal abilities, rather than their education in the classics. By the end of the century, science teaching was growing in schools, but by then the damage had been done. The social influence of the public school was (and is) out of all proportion to the numbers of their pupils, simply because the leaders of society sent their sons to them—and because they employed a number of excellent teachers.

Women's education

The education of girls was an upper class affair. Sometimes they were sent to boarding schools (like Becky Sharp in Thackeray's *Vanity Fair*.) Such girls led a sheltered life with servants to sustain them. Less wealthy girls had to be efficient housewives and had to learn to manage with fewer servants. But it occurred to few girls and fewer men that women ought to have the opportunity of a career of their own, beyond being good mothers and companions to their husbands. Surprisingly enough, considering her position, Queen Victoria was shocked at the idea of opening professions to women.

But as her reign progressed, a movement to emancipate women from the home and to give them greater equality with men, gradually gained strength. It began, perhaps, by making school teaching, apart from being a governess, a respectable career. It was much advanced by transforming nursing, under the eagle eye of one of the most domineering of women, Florence Nightingale. Gradually the universities were opened to women, and then the professions. Elizabeth Garrett Anderson became a doctor in 1865, but it was 1909 before the Royal College of Surgeons admitted women. Eventually the movement was to reach a climax in the suffragettes (see *page 183*).

Education for girls, normally, was more 'social training' than learning. The Taunton Commission (1867) noted:

'want of thoroughness and foundation, want of system; slovenliness and showy superficiality; inattention to rudiments; undue time given to accomplishments, and these not taught intelligently or in any scientific manner; want of organisation....'

But a quiet revolution was being worked. In 1848 the Christian Socialists helped King's College, London, to found Queen's College in Harley St., as a training college for girls. Miss Frances Buss and Miss Dorothea Beale were both students there. In 1849 Mrs John Reed established a girls' college for higher education in Bedford Square (it was to become Bedford College, London). George Eliot, whose real name was Mary Ann Evans, and who became a great novelist, was a pupil. In 1850, Miss Buss became Headmistress of the North London Collegiate School and, like Arnold at Rugby, established a pattern that was followed by many new girls' grammar schools, especially by those founded by the Girls' Public Day Schools Trust (1872) of which there were thirty-three with 7,000 girls by 1900. In 1858, Miss Beale established a similarly great tradition at the Cheltenham Ladies' College. It was now only a matter of time before the universities would admit women. By 1880 there were two ladies' colleges at Oxford and at Cambridge, but although girls would take the examinations, they were not admitted to degrees until 1920 at Oxford and 1946 at

A Ragged School

Cambridge. Why, is not easy to say. London University granted them this right in 1880.

All this, of course, concerned the daughters of the wealthy. Working-class girls, before the 1880s, might learn to read and write at Sunday or charitable day schools, but this instruction was only rudimentary. For the very poor something was done by the Ragged School Union, where very basic instruction, more of a 'social' than 'educational' nature, was given. The boys and girls were often orphans and distressed children, and came more for gifts of food and clothing than anything else. Lord Shaftesbury gave his support and so did Mary Carpenter, founder of the first reformatory for girls.

The growth of a national system

Before 1833 Parliament spent nothing on education. Men argued that it should be left to parents and that what the poor needed was merely to learn a trade. There was also a fear of 'national systems'. But since the beginning of the century pressure had been increasing for some measure of assistance to help provide some elementary learning for the poor. Schemes for a national system paid for from local rates proposed by Whitbread (1806), Brougham (1820) and Roebuck (1833) all failed, but in 1833 the Government consented to subsidise existing schools run by the British and Foreign and the National Societies. There was to be no national system yet!

The subsidy was a grant of £20,000 to be divided between the Societies. By 1837 a Report showed that the education received was of poor quality and 'that it extends (bad as it is) to but a small proportion of those who ought to receive it'. Clearly, the *laissez-faire* method of subsidising existing societies was not adequate, and in 1839 the subsidy was raised to £30,000 (by 1860 it had become more than £500,000). However, a Committee of the Privy Council was set up to administer the grant and *inspectors* were appointed to examine the work of schools. The Secretary to the Committee was Dr Kay-Shuttleworth. For ten years he worked tirelessly and with great tact to try to establish a truly national system of schooling for the poor. But he was not successful. The biggest obstacle was rivalry between the societies for they accused each other of trying to get all the children in their schools to follow their own denomination. This *sectarianism* often came near to wrecking some of the best schemes of the age. Kay-Shuttleworth's *Instructions to Inspectors* (1840) made the best of the situation by urging the encouragement of local effort in improving education:

'Promoters of schools [should be given] an opportunity of ascertaining, at the periodical visits of inspection, what improvement in the apparatus and internal arrangements of schools, in school management and discipline, and in the methods of teaching, have been sanctioned by the most extensive experience.'

But no great improvement in education would occur unless better trained teachers replaced the monitors. In 1840 many teachers were quite untrained but there was no agreement on the best method of training them. In that year Kay-Shuttleworth opened a private training college at Battersea based on experience gained at an experimental pupil-teacher school at Norwood. At first there were twenty-four working-class boys of thirteen who entered a seven-year apprenticeship. After three years they went to Battersea village school on teaching practice and for the last two years they worked as assistants to experienced teachers. Whilst at the College they also had to work several hours a day in the kitchen and gardens—this, Kay argued, improved their moral training; it also reduced running costs. Several colleges were founded on the model of Battersea, but none were as big, and in 1843 the College was handed over to the National Society. It had demonstrated a cheap and effective way of training teachers. In 1846 the idea of Queen's Scholarships to enable successful pupil-teachers to attend an approved training college was adopted and the Government laid down a suggested wage scale for fully qualified teachers, partly paid by the Government, partly by the school managers. A

pension scheme was also begun, and in 1854 practising teachers could earn the title of *registered teacher*. All this aid meant a considerable increase in Government subsidy. Incredibly enough people complained, especially Anglicans, on the grounds that the Government was treating all denominations alike!

Another type of school providing elementary education for working-class children was the factory school. Some employers, like Robert Owen, had run excellent schools for their workers' children. The Factory Act of 1833 required factory children to have two hours' schooling a day, which the factory inspectors were to enforce. It proved difficult to enforce this part of the Act, because mill owners often made no special arrangements for a schoolroom, sometimes using the boilerhouse, and a casual labourer as 'schoolmaster'. The children themselves were often too tired to derive benefit, and would simply not attend. An attempt to increase the hours of factory schooling, so making it more effective, was defeated in 1843 largely because the Nonconformists feared the schools would be dominated by Anglicans. Lord Shaftesbury bitterly complained of this sectarianism:

'the really suffering parties were the vast body of neglected children, who, as present appearances went, were now consigned to an eternity of ignorance.'

As more day school places became available, especially in the big towns, an attempt was made to combine working and teaching by the *half-time system*. Children of eight to thirteen were required to work half-time in the mill and attend school for half a day six days a week by the 1844 Factory Act. The system was never very effective, for the half-timers had to take their place in schools catering for full-time pupils as well. But the system lasted until the Education Act of 1918. An Inspector's report of 1844 gives an indication of the problems the half-time system introduced:

'They are dirty and labour-soiled, in ragged and scanty clothes, with heavy eyes and worn faces . . . I fancied, perhaps wrongly, that there was little notice taken of them in the business of the school . . . The master professed himself unable to include them in the various classes, without materially injuring the progress of the other children.'

In 1861 the Newcastle Report recommended a system that became known as *payment by results*. There had been complaints that some schools were too ambitious in their teaching of bright children at the expense of basic instruction for the dull children, as well as grumblings at the mounting costs. The Report suggested that grants should be paid upon the basis of the number of children who satisfied a direct test in elementary education, graded according to age. Inspectors were to conduct the examination, and this made them objects of distrust to school teachers, for the system was embodied in Robert Lowe's Revised Code of 1862. Certainly it reduced expenditure—temporarily—from £813,000 in 1861 to £637,000 in 1865, and certainly it raised the efficiency of the poorer schools. Prizes were given for good performance in the narrow formal test, and for regular school attendance, for this also affected the grant. But the Revised Code was universally condemned by educationalists because of its concentration upon the low standard of literacy required at the expense of intelligent children, and because it

A school built by the London School Board

confined the freedom of teaching in schools. But it is too easy to condemn. The code unquestionably raised the efficiency of many schools, and if it adversely affected teaching in some of the better schools, it probably did little to restrict the range of teaching in most of the schools. Perhaps, in terms of the 1860s its worst effect was to change the position of Inspector from a councillor and encourager of better teaching methods to that of an inquisitor. The system remained in force until 1897.

In 1867, the Second Reform Act (see *page 164*) gave the better off artisan in the towns the vote and it was felt necessary to 'educate our masters', as Robert Lowe put it. They were the majority of urban voters, yet less than half the children of the cities attended school. The case for elementary education for all the poor seemed obvious, and in 1869 the National Education League was formed in Birmingham with Joseph Chamberlain as President, demanding free, compulsory education on non-sectarian lines, financed from the rates. The league's activities certainly helped to pass the Forster Education Act (1870), providing for nation-wide elementary education (although it was neither free nor compulsory). Forster's purpose was not to increase educational opportunity, so much as to instil attitudes of good behaviour; he spoke of children as:

'growing up to probable crime, to still more probable misery, because badly taught or utterly untaught. Dare we then take on ourselves the responsibility of allowing this ignorance and this weakness to continue one year longer than we can help?'

The Act was a compromise from the beginning, but at least it set out to make a national system of elementary education a reality. It required an estimate to be made of the need for school places. (Derbyshire, for example, needed 9,000 places and required forty-two Boards by 1882—an indication of the lack of provision before the Act.) Those parishes not adequately provided for by the voluntary societies were allowed six months' grace to make suitable provision. If it was then not adequate, school districts were to be created to establish local

'Drill' in a Board school yard

School Boards, to be elected every three years by rate payers. The School Boards would provide and run adequate schools and they had wide powers to levy an education rate and to meet the school fees of poor children. They had power to enforce attendance, although few used it. The Department of Education could, and did, dismiss School Boards and appoint new ones if they were inefficient.

Sectarianism came near to destroying the Act, despite the compromise known as the Cowper-Temple clause, which sought to remove the danger of children being indoctrinated by a particular denomination. Under this clause the Board schools were prevented from teaching any 'catechism or religious formulary distinctive of any particular denomination', while the existing voluntary schools were to allow parents to withdraw children from lessons in religious instruction if they so chose. The storm of protest that this clause provoked came near to endangering Forster's public career and caused some elected School Boards to adopt obstructive tactics.

If you study the minutes of Church Councils and School Boards in the 1870s, you would discover that voters were clearly less interested in education than in keeping the rates low, getting hold of future young workers and instructing them in acceptable opinions. There were considerable efforts, especially among the Anglicans, to open new schools at considerable expense, in order to avoid the necessity to create a School Board under the Act (there were even cases of school fees for National schools being paid for poor children). When School Boards were formed there was sometimes active competition for pupils between the Board school and the local small private schools (some of which stopped all punishments lest the children leave for the Board school—so much for the stern Victorian schoolmaster!).

However, the School Boards in the big cities did some remarkable work, building schools where they had never before existed on a scale far superior to the voluntary schools. The teaching was often at first confined to very rudimentary matters—frequently it was a case of simply scrubbing the dirtier boys clean,

for washing facilities were not always available at home. Discipline had to be strict and vigorously enforced; games in the public schools involved some element of enjoyment, but 'drill' in the Board schools was very regimented. Even so, a new career was created by these schools, the career first of pupil and then elementary school teacher; many working-class men and women found this the only way to get any further education, and it was the way that a number of Labour politicians began the long journey to Westminster.

Earlier in the century few seriously advocated compulsory education for all—children's wages were too valuable a source of money for the family. By the 1870s opinion had changed (although there was still quite a degree of working-class opposition), but there were scarcely enough school places. However, in 1876, Sandon's Act provided for enforced attendance up to the age of ten and this was strengthened by Mundella's Act (1880) placing the responsibility for attendance on the parents and the School Board—even so there were many thousands of children for the next decade who avoided school. 'Fetching gin and no boots' was a frequent excuse that may well have meant the child was earning a few pennies at work. In 1899 the school leaving age was raised to twelve.

In 1891 elementary education became free, but there was still no legislative provision for secondary education within the State system; nor for technical education, despite the great success of the French and Germans in this field. Lyon Playfair had already pointed out this glaring deficiency to the Taunton Committee in 1867:

'France, Prussia, Austria, Belgium and Switzerland possess good systems of industrial education for the masters and managers of factories and workshops, and England possesses none.'

Despite the technical colleges that were growing up in the 1880s technical education remained a neglected field. In 1889 the Technical Instruction Act allowed money from the rates to be spent on technical education, but much of this tended to go towards the provision of courses in the pure sciences.

In fact, there was a rising demand for education beyond the elementary stage, for many of those who elected members to the School Boards were artisans who desired to see wider educational opportunities for poorer families. Children tended to stay on beyond thirteen in some schools, and in 1880 the Sheffield School Board opened a 'higher grade' school for older children. By 1894 there were sixty-three such schools. Secondary education, with more advanced classes in English, History, Languages and Pure Science as well as classes in metalwork and pre-apprentice technical classes, was possible under the Revised Code's payment-by-results system. The money for the classes came from various Government bodies, like the Science and Art Department, founded at South Kensington out of the profits of the Great Exhibition, as well as the rates. Strictly speaking, the School Boards had no legal powers either to provide secondary education or to pay for it out of the education rate, but many of the Boards in cities were actively extending the field of education available to children. In 1895 the Bryce Committee produced a Report that was to lay the foundation of future developments in secondary education. It recommended the creation of a Government department with a cabinet minister at its head to supervise education, the creation of local education authorities to provide the necessary schools, and the separation of elementary education from secondary. The Report had little immediate effect because the Education Bill prepared to give effect to it failed to pass the Commons. But a weak Board of Education, with vague and limited powers, was created in 1899.

The fact that some School Boards were producing schools that were beginning to rival the existing grammar schools was not lost upon Robert Morant (later Sir Robert), a senior civil servant. He encouraged Cockerton, the Government Auditor, to challenge the legality of using the rates to pay for secondary education. In 1901 the courts decided in the *Cockerton Judgment* that this was illegal, and so the Prime Minister, A. J. Balfour, secured the passing of the Education Act of 1902. This consoli-

dated the national system for elementary education and replaced the School Boards with what came to be called Local Education Authorities (L.E.As.), namely an education committee of the County Councils and of County Boroughs, with London treated as a separate unit. These committees were to be composed of elected councillors and others co-opted on to them for their special qualifications. They were permitted to provide for secondary education, but there was no obligation to do so and the Act was deliberately vaguely worded. The Act established the basis of the education system for the next generation, but it raised immense sectarian opposition from the Nonconformists who felt that it unfairly favoured the Anglican schools. Indeed, in some parts of the country, especially in Wales, many refused to pay the education rate and had their belongings forcibly sold to raise the sum they refused to give.

It must not be thought that the Act brought equality of opportunity; if anything, it prevented a number of bright children from among the poor rising up the education ladder, for they had a better chance in the former Higher Grade schools. The Regulations for Secondary Schools (1904) issued under the Act, required secondary schools to provide a four-year course including English, History, Geography, a foreign language, mathematics and science. The science and maths should occupy no more than a third of the time-table, however, because the intention was that secondary schools should not offer courses of a vocational type. Grammar schools were delighted with the Regulations, for they had no need to modify their curriculum at all! The opportunity of providing for high level technical education at school was lost for a generation. The trend towards lower fees which the School Boards had begun was reversed by fixing the minimum fee for grammar schools at £3 per year, quite beyond the means of the manual worker. In 1907 the *Free Place System* was introduced, allowing children to sit a scholarship that would provide for the payment of tuition fees. But other payments had to be met, like uniform and games equipment and books, so that even children who gained a scholarship might not be able to take it up. And there were not many 'free places'—47,000 in 1907, 60,000 in 1913. Secondary education well beyond the elementary stage was very far from available to all under the 1902 Education Act. But, although we can easily condemn the Act as a piece of legislation wholly favourable to the middle class, we should remember that few people in Edwardian days ever thought of equality of educational opportunity, or, for that matter, imagined that there was widespread academic talent among the working classes.

Universities

The nineteenth century saw a complete transformation of the university scene. Oxford and Cambridge shook off their lethargy and, although remaining the preserve of the rich where many students lived in regal splendour, became once again places of scholarship and religious fervour. There was much discussion about the form of 'liberal education' best suited to a gentleman, and this led to a revision of courses and examinations. Modern Languages, History and more sciences were introduced. Amid tremendous opposition, in 1871 the religious tests had been abolished and five years later the first tiny group of women students were sitting university examinations.

But changes of far greater importance were happening elsewhere. Because Dissenters were excluded from Oxford and Cambridge, educational reformers like Dr Birkbeck and Henry Brougham founded the non-sectarian University College in London (1828). Condemning it as 'that godless institution in Gower Street', the Anglicans established a rival King's College in 1831. Fortunately the two came together quickly, in 1836, to form the University of London as an organisation for examining candidates and conferring degrees. Later, other colleges were added and the practice of awarding external degrees to students unable to attend the University was begun. It was a pity that, after the Exhibition of 1864, a second University, with accent on the sciences and engineering, was not founded, although the City and Guild Institute, the Colleges of Music and of Arts, and the Imperial Institute and School of Mines were established in South Kensington.

Other universities followed the founding of London University, at first taking London external degrees but later awarding their own degrees. Durham, with its strong ecclesiastical connexions, came in 1837, then Owen's College, Manchester, opened 1851, gained University status in 1880. The following year Leeds University was founded, growing out of the medical school; and in 1901 Birmingham followed, also growing from the medical school, and the Mason Science College. Bristol gained a University College in 1876 and Reading in 1892. Nottingham was unusual in that its College (1881) was under municipal control. All these new universities were non-residential at first. They owed a great deal to local benefactors, especially industrialists, and they were characterised by offering more varied degree courses, with something of a concentration on science and the applied sciences. Their freer atmosphere was demonstrated by admitting women to their degrees at an early stage.

By the end of the century it had become an established fact that a university course should be available to all who could afford it: but a university course (or even secondary education of a fully academic type) was not yet thought of as the right of all those who were academically qualified for it.

12 . Working-class movements during the Great Changes

The demand for parliamentary reform

Parliament consists of the House of Lords, which in the eighteenth century was composed of hereditary peers and those men whom the king ennobled, and the House of Commons. The Commons was elected by all those who qualified to have a vote (the *franchise*). Each member of the House sat for a particular *constituency* and the country was divided into rural constituencies and borough constituencies. These constituencies had, in Tudor times, reflected the distribution of wealth and population; but by the middle of the eighteenth century it was already becoming clear that this was no longer the case, for tiny fishing villages in Cornwall were represented by two members, whilst growing towns had none. Manchester and Birmingham had to wait for the First Reform Act (1832) before they had a member of parliament. A *redistribution of seats*, taking members away from tiny towns and giving representation to growing boroughs, was already being demanded in 1770. The demand was to grow until it had to be satisfied. By the 1880s a fairer distribution of seats, reflecting the distribution of population had been achieved.

But there were two other serious faults in the election of the eighteenth-century House of Commons. The franchise was quite unsystematic. In the counties men owning a 40 shillings freehold had the vote. This was straight-forward; it meant that men of moderate means had the franchise, so that 'property' was represented (all M.Ps. had to be landowners until 1859). In the boroughs there was no set pattern at all. A small number of boroughs had a very *democratic* franchise but in most boroughs the vote went to men whose qualification varied widely and usually it meant that very few people in the town had a vote. This brought with it the third fault with the representative system. It was very corrupt. In the counties, at election times, there was a good deal of money poured out by candidates soliciting votes, but as there was a fairly large number of voters and most of them were men of property, this was not a serious abuse. In the boroughs it was, for votes were openly bought and sold and the extent of bribery and intimidation was considerable. Voting was 'open', for the voters were required to state their name and the candidate for whom they wished to vote at a public meeting upon the day of the election. Corruption was so extensive that on occasion the House of Commons declared an election void and called for a new election, or even *dis-franchised* boroughs for gross corruption.

In the 1760s and 1770s there was a growing feeling of opposition to the King's government that took the form of demanding reform of parliamentary representation. Much of this demand came from men of property who wanted to secure more control over the conduct of Government policy: they were not interested in *manhood suffrage* (one man one vote). But many pamphlets were published and some of them were very radical indeed. Major James Cartwright published *Take Your Choice* in 1776, demanding universal suffrage, annual parliaments (a general election each year) and secret voting by ballot. This was to become the programme of reformers who wanted a democratic system in which public opinion, as well as the opinion of 'men of property', should have full effect at election times. It is important to remember that there was not very great support for this democratic idea. Most informed opinion saw no reason to give the vote to men who were mere wage-earners, and lacked what they called 'a stake in the community'. The hope of convincing more people of the justice of manhood suffrage was dashed first by the Gordon

'The Election' by William Hogarth

Riots of 1780, when London was terrorised by riotous mobs, and then by the excesses of the 'democratic' French Revolutionaries (Jacobins) and the war that was fought between 1793 and 1815.

Corresponding societies

But Jacobin democratic ideas inspired many people, including a large number of the educated working class. Pitt, the leading minister, was frightened that these ideas would lead to the outbreak of a social revolution in this country, and so he embarked in the 1790s upon a repressive policy that was continued until the 1820s. Hopes of democratic reform were dashed for a generation. There were a number of popular movements to be repressed. The most important was The London Corresponding Society

of 1792, organised by a shoemaker, Thomas Hardy, among the London artisans. Its ideas were derived from the advanced social ideas of the Jacobins and its *Address to the People* demanded:
'Taxes diminished, the necessities of life more within the reach of the poor, youth better educated, prisons less crowded, old age better provided for.'

This was much too advanced for the Government which became nervous when the Society copied the organisation of the French revolutionaries by developing close contact with brother societies in other big towns like Manchester, Stockport, Sheffield, Leeds and Norwich. In Scotland, a Convention of a Society of the Friends of the People meeting at Edinburgh in 1793, prompted the judges to pass severe sentences on the organisers and one of them,

Thomas Muir, was transported for fourteen years' penal servitude to Botany Bay. Government spies and common informers presented exaggerated reports that gave the Government the impression that a revolution was being planned, and when Hardy organised a national convention of workers to meet in London as a direct challenge to the unrepresentative House of Commons, Pitt suspended *Habeas Corpus* (the act preventing imprisonment without trial) and arrested the leaders.

But the English courts refused to convict Hardy of high treason and so Pitt planned further measures. The opportunity came when the Corresponding Society organised a huge meeting at Copenhagen Fields, London, in 1795, to demand annual parliaments and universal suffrage. The meeting ended in a riot and Pitt brought in the Treasonable Practices and Seditious Meetings Act that destroyed the Society. Two years later there were serious mutinies in the Navy and an act against the taking of 'illegal oaths' was passed. These were years when people feared revolutionary activity among the poor; they were years of bad harvests, economic crises and serious inflation, too. In such conditions demands for more pay to meet rising prices were frequent, and workers began to act together (i.e. combine) to secure higher wages. A group of London master mill-wrights got Parliament to pass the *Combination Acts* (1799 and 1800) making combinations of workers illegal (those of employers were also declared illegal, but they were less easy to discover). The acts were not always enforced and they did not prevent workers going on strike or forming trade unions. But they were a restriction on workers' freedom and curtailed the healthy development of trade unionism. In 1824, largely as a result of the active pressure of Francis Place and Joseph Hume, M.P., they were repealed.

The Luddites

Between 1810 and 1812 there was a serious economic crisis and very high food prices. The demand for parliamentary reform revived in London and the provinces, but in the textile area of Yorkshire the demand was fused with well organised incidents of machine-breaking. In these years there was a serious threat of machine-breaking on an extensive scale in the East Midlands and the Pennines. It was said that 'General Ned Ludd' directed the machine-breakers from his headquarters in Sherwood Forest. In fact, Ludd did not exist, although we call the machine-breakers Luddites.

We cannot speak of a Luddite Movement because different areas had different aims and acted on different lines. Also the Luddites kept their affairs very secret, so that the Government learnt little about them—they tried using spies (*agents provocateurs*) to provoke workers to commit crimes and to try to discover more about the Luddites. The reports they received frightened them into supposing that a widespread revolutionary movement was being organised. So far as we can tell, although they were very well organised in particular localities, the Luddites did not attempt to form a national or even a regional movement. Theirs was not simply a movement demanding reform: it was a movement of industrial action. In some areas new machines were imperilling the livelihoods of skilled artisans, in others the protest was against unfair business methods, in others, again, it was a protest against poor pay, for at a time of steeply rising prices, Lancashire wages (1812) were half those of 1802. The machine breaking followed no definite pattern and was scattered about the particular areas affected. The Luddites clearly had the support of the local population, sometimes even of local employers, and rarely did they threaten life. The principal areas affected were the East Midlands, especially round Loughborough, South Yorkshire, Lancashire and Cheshire. The Government, lacking a police force, took them so seriously that a larger army than Wellington was permitted to have to fight the French in Spain was used to keep the Luddites down. The Luddites have attracted a great deal of attention, and have become something of a symbol of working-class resistance to employers and oppressive governments. They were very selective in the machines they broke, for there was no question of them simply destroying machinery for the sake of it. Machine-breaking was not uncommon during the previous century: the Luddites broke only particular machines belonging to particular employers. Unquestionably there was much class feeling in their attitude.

Machine breaking was a way of bringing pressure to bear on employers in the early stages of industrialism before trade unions were common. It was not necessarily labour-saving machinery that was attacked (in mining areas the winding gear was usually the first victim in order to immobilise the mine), nor was it worth while, unless things had gone so far that it was not possible to go on working for the money offered. This situation had come by 1811. The machine breakers were not men resisting technological innovation—in the East Midlands the frames broken were not new machines at all. And the Luddites had tremendous local support: on occasion whole villages refused to give information. In Nottinghamshire, where there were a great many Luddites, none was denounced and there must have been a good deal of intimidation. The Government were well advised to take a serious view of the situation; this was not the behaviour of men who were merely rioting because of hunger.

The Nottingham Luddites were most active in 1811. They were skilled frame knitters whose complaint was that some employers insisted on knitting broad-cloth that could then be cut into strips for hose and sold more cheaply than cloth woven on stocking frames. These 'cut-ups' were of low quality and brought the price of stocking-frame goods down heavily. The Luddites struck against these wide frames. In Lancashire and Cheshire, and occasionally in South Yorkshire, the Luddites struck against power looms. In other parts of Yorkshire it was shearing machines that were broken. In the North the Luddites were violent and more clearly political than in the Midlands, and the courts were severe against those whom they could convict; but it was probably the troops and better harvests that quietened the disorders, though they were to reappear with each bad harvest for the next few years. The Luddites showed two new things, first that a movement of consequence, even if it was very regional, had been formed by the working class,

and secondly, that the movement was in the provinces: London was no longer the principal centre of radicalism, it had moved to the industrial north.

The Luddites also left a deep-seated social bitterness against exploiting employers, for the class war was part of their inspiration. The Government made machine-breaking a capital offence and for the next ten years pursued their policy of repression, resisting every demand for reform lest it lead to revolution.

In 1849 Charlotte Brontë published *Shirley*, a novel in which an employer is attacked by the Luddites. Class hatred comes over very clearly:

'A crash—smash—shiver—stopped their whispers. A simultaneously hurled volley of stones had saluted the broad front of the mill, with all its windows; and now every pane of every lattice lay in scattered and pounded fragments. A yell followed this demonstration—a rioters' yell—a North of England—a Yorkshire—a West Riding—a West-Riding-clothing-district-of-Yorkshire rioters' yell... Caste stands up, wilful against Caste; and the indignant, wrong spirit of the Middle Rank (i.e. middle classes) bears down in zeal and scorn on the famished and furious mass of Operative class. It is difficult to be tolerant—difficult to be just—in such moments.'

Disturbances after the war

There was no planning of the change from war to peace in 1815, and serious unemployment resulted. High prices, aggravated by the indirect taxes essential after income tax was abolished in 1816 worsened the position for the poor. Distress was widespread in town and country. Machine breaking occurred, and in the Eastern Counties in 1816 there were violent disturbances, with men marching under the banner 'Bread or Blood'. The military was called out to silence them and the ring-leaders were transported. Elsewhere, coalminers, dragging their carts after them, toured the country in search of work and food.

A demand for reform so that 'something could be done' to improve conditions, grew rapidly and it was fanned by orators like Henry Hunt and journalists like William Cobbett, whose *Political Register* attacked the Government so sharply that Shropshire magistrates ordered two men to be flogged for distributing it. Mass meetings were held and that at Spa Fields, London, (1816) ended in a riot. The Government feared the disturbances and relied on spies and the military to keep order. In 1817 a great march of working men was planned from Manchester, (called the march of the 'Blanketeers' because they carried their blanket to wrap around them at night). It was turned back by the military. There was also a pathetic rising in South Derbyshire, inspired by a government spy. The Government suspended Habeas Corpus and passed the 'gagging acts' designed to prevent public meetings. One of the leading working class radicals, Samuel Bamford, wrote:

'It seemed as if the sense of freedom were gone down and a rayless expanse of oppression had finally closed over us.'

The climax came in 1819, one of the most troubled years of the century. Meetings were held in many Midland and Northern towns to support a great campaign for parliamentary reform, culminating in a monster meeting on St Peter's Fields, Manchester, to which thousands of men, women and children marched from the surrounding towns. The magistrates decided to arrest Henry Hunt who was to speak, and the local yeomanry entered the close-packed crowd to take him into custody. Believing them to be in difficulties, the cavalry were ordered to clear the meeting and in the resulting confusion, the soldiers charged with drawn swords upon the defenceless unarmed peaceful crowd: eleven people were killed and over 400 injured. The Government welcomed the news and praised the magistrates: the workers called it Peterloo in hollow mockery of Wellington's victory over the French at Waterloo, and it has remained a symbol of working-class resistance to oppression that was a rallying cry well into the present century. The class war had arrived with a vengeance: and Peterloo was in the industrial north. The Great Changes were producing new areas of political activity.

But no revolution followed Peterloo. Instead, the government passed the Six Acts (1819) increasing the powers of magistrates to convict political offenders, to search private homes for arms, and to prevent public meetings and unauthorised drilling of men; the penalties against sedition were increased and a heavy tax was put on newspapers and periodicals (a move directed against Cobbett's *Political Register*). A general strike at Glasgow was easily suppressed—eighteen men were transported and Andrew Hardie (ancestor of Keir Hardie, see *page 218*) and John Baird were hanged, drawn and quartered. Even the desperate attempt of Thistlewood and others to murder the cabinet, in the Cato St. conspiracy of 1820 was easily foiled by *agents provocateur*. There was to be no revolution. Instead, the 1820s were a period of relaxing tension, developing reform and growing prosperity—although there was a trade slump in 1826 and another, accompanied by bad harvests in 1829, which had its effect on the 'last rising of the rural poor' (see *page 34*). In that year the Tory Party split over Roman Catholic Emancipation and the Whigs, committed to parliamentary reform, won the election of 1830. A Reform Bill could no longer be delayed: out of a total population of twenty-four million, only 478,000 had the vote, and most of the growing new towns in the North were without Members of Parliament. The struggle for the Reform Bill lasted two years and the First Reform Act (1832) eventually passed only because of the threat of a creation of Whig peers to give a permanent Whig majority in the Lords, and because of fear of revolution if it were not passed. Monster meetings and stories of men training on the moors were common in the North and in Bristol and Nottingham there were serious riots. But the workers, who had done so much to get the measure through, gained no benefit. The electorate was scarcely doubled and remained 'men of property', for in the towns the £10 Householders got the vote and in the counties, the forty shilling Freeholders and various categories of leaseholders. There was a redistribution of seats in favour of the big towns in the North; but of what use was that to the worker who was unable to vote? There was no manhood suffrage, no end to bribery and corruption and no payment of members to allow working men to become M.Ps. Small wonder the workers spoke of the 'great Whig betrayal'.

Owenism and the trade unions

Among the writers at the beginning of the nineteenth century who were to have great influence on the ideas of the future, Robert Owen was particularly important: he has been called the 'father of British socialism'. He began as a self-made industrialist managing a Lancashire cotton mill at the age of twenty. In 1800 he took over David Dale's New Lanark mill near Glasgow and proved that he could make a fortune in textiles without exploiting his workers; instead he paid good wages and provided good working conditions and good housing. No children under ten were employed in his mills; they went to his school instead. Because he had made such a success in the business world, people listened to him with respect, and his views were surprisingly modern. He believed a person's character was formed by his environment. What was needed to improve society, therefore, was to provide good living and working conditions. He urged people to co-operate together for the general good, rather than to seek personal profit through competition and capitalism. Through co-operation, he argued, a new society could be built that would have no need of a poor law—and he made New Lanark an example of an ideal 'village of co-operation'. He published his ideas in *A New View of Society* (1813/14)—Cobbett disapproved and called his proposed village of co-operation 'Mr Owen's Parallelogram of Paupers'. Between 1815 and 1820 important thinkers were deeply impressed by Owen's ideas—David Ricardo may well have been influenced by them in developing his own labour theory of value (see *page 87*).

Owen helped to pass the 1819 factory act, but he was disappointed that his ideas were not more widely accepted, and he went to the U.S.A. to establish New Harmony, a community based on Owenite principles. It was not successful and he returned to Britain in the 1830s, to be influential in establishing a 'labour exchange' to try to give effect to his ideas on 'labour time'. His ideas on co-operation were very important for the development of the co-operative movement and of trade unionism. There is no simple explanation of the origins of trade unions. They seem to have grown up naturally among artisans at the beginning of the eighteenth century as informal groups of friends to help each other when in financial straits; to help those 'tramping' in search of work; and to combine for better wages and conditions. Employers and Parliament viewed such combinations with hostility and passed the Combination Acts (1799 and 1800). These were repealed in 1824, but there were so many strikes that restrictions on the activity of what had already come to be called *trade unions* were imposed in 1825. But at least trade unions were now legal.

Hitherto, they had been very local affairs, but by 1830 attempts were being made to form unions of all the workers in a particular trade. Inspired by the ideas of Robert Owen, John Doherty formed the Grand General Union of All Spinners in the United Kingdom (1829) and a National Association for the Protection of Labour (1830) that claimed a membership of over 100,000. His hope was that existing unions of skilled men would combine into huge single units that could negotiate with employers from a position of strength, if not actually dictate terms. The employers had little difficulty in destroying his plans. But after the 'betrayal' of 1832, workers were more prepared to turn to such big unions both as a means of protest and as a method of improving their conditions. Robert Owen provided the inspiration for these big trade unions. His idea was simply to organise a gigantic union that would be powerful enough to challenge both employers and Government by calling a general strike that would paralyse the country and oblige a surrender to the workers. Such 'direct action' appealed to disappointed workers.

In 1832 he had founded a labour exchange in Gray's Inn Road with branches in the provinces, where workers deposited the goods they had made (you see how British industry was still very much a matter of craftsmen working for themselves) for which the worker was paid in notes which could be exchanged for goods at the exchange. The idea was immediately successful, but lack of sound management made it a failure by 1834. In 1833 Owen founded the **Grand National Consolidated Trades Union**, the culmination of many active and extensive union movements. Employers reacted vigorously with lock-outs and dismissals. Many presented their employees with the 'document', a paper declaring they were not members of a union, which if they refused to sign would mean their dismissal. Within **the year the Grand National Consolidated Trades Union was in ruins.**

The Government certainly supported the employers but did not proceed directly against the Union. Instead, with the 'labourers' revolt' scarcely over, they attacked a small group of farm labourers at Tolpuddle in Dorset, who had formed a union in 1833. This was perfectly legal, and so the six labourers were tried under the forgotten statute of 1797, passed at the time of the naval mutinies, against the administring of 'illegal oaths'. The judge and jury were openly prejudiced and the labourers were sentenced to seven years' transportation. It was to no avail that their leader, George Loveless, a Methodist lay preacher, stated:

'My Lord, if we have violated any law it was not done intentionally. We have injured no man's reputation, character, person, or property. We were meeting together to preserve ourselves, our wives, and our children, from utter degradation and starvation.'

Public outcry at the trial and sentence was vigorous. It was noted, for example, that Freemasons administered 'illegal oaths' but were not proceeded against! Robert Owen headed a national campaign to secure a pardon, but Melbourne, the Home Secretary, refused to be moved and ordered the military and the newly-formed Metropolitan Police Force to suppress disturbances. In 1838 the 'Tolpuddle Martyrs' were pardoned and small farms were purchased for them from a public fund that had been launched on their behalf: they remained symbols of oppression of the working class, and a rallying cry to many in this country and abroad.

The Poor Law

The Poor Law Amendment Act was introduced in 1834. This measure swept away the remains of the Speenhamland System (see *page 32*) and replaced the parishes as agents of poor law relief with new, elected local Boards of Guardians, responsible to the Poor Law Commissioners (see *page 108*). Unions of parishes were formed to finance the building of workhouses for the poor. These were bitterly hated and soon called the Poor Law 'Bastilles', for they were built and administered by men who regarded poverty as a disgrace and who sought to keep the poor rate low. As soon as the workhouse was built it was to become a condition of receiving relief that a poor family should agree to be inmates. 'Out-door relief' was to end. In order to ensure that families did not idly apply for this 'in-door relief', conditions were to be worse than those endured by the poorest labourers outside—Chadwick called this the '*less eligibility*' principle,

'the condition of the recipient should not on the whole be more eligible than that of any labourer living on the fruits of his own industry.'

The workhouses (called 'Unions') became another symbol of working-class oppression, a symbol hated and feared long after conditions within them had become reasonably comfortable. Originally it had been intended to build different types of workhouses for the different types of poor, but the desire to cut costs meant that only one workhouse was built in a Union, and on entering it families were divided up, the women in one wing, the males in another. This was not merely for administrative convenience, it was done deliberately 'to prevent them breeding'. Within the two wings of the workhouse there was no further segregation: the deserving poor, the vagrants, the sick, the old, the mentally ill, the young, all were forced to live together sometimes in conditions of overcrowding, and always in conditions of considerable discomfort. Harsh and difficult work,

The attack on the Stockport Workhouse

sometimes almost impossible to perform within the time allowed, often work of a degrading character, was normal. Occasionally things were so bad that inmates fought for the scraps of putrid gristle and marrow on the bones they had to crush to make fertiliser, as at Andover in 1845. A workhouse dress was to be worn and silence observed at meal-times. 'By the workhouse system is meant having all relief through the workhouse, making this workhouse an uninviting place of wholesome restraint, preventing any of its inmates from going out or receiving visitors, without a written order to that effect from one of the overseers, disallowing beer and tobacco,

and finding them work according to their ability: thus making the parish fund the last resource of a pauper, and rendering the person who administers the relief the hardest taskmaster and the worst paymaster that the idle and dissolute can apply to.'

It is no wonder the Unions have entered working-class folklore, and the able-bodied poor were driven to almost any labour rather than be forced to enter the workhouse with all the social degradation that it implied. Oliver Twist cried lustily when he was born:

'If he could have known that he was an orphan, left

to the tender mercies of churchwardens and over-seers, perhaps he would have cried the louder.'

It is no wonder that desperate labourers attacked the new workhouses—the one at Hackingham Hall, Suffolk, was burnt down. Yet the Act seems to have been effective, if brutal, in much of the agricultural South, reducing the poor rate.

Real trouble began when the Poor Law Commissioners turned to the North. Urban poverty was quite a different problem from rural, and required a different answer. Industry had not yet learnt to spread out production so that a smooth flow of work was available; instead, work was often available only on a casual hourly or daily basis. A family could be employed for part of a week and out of work for the remainder. What was needed was short-term out-door relief to tide the family over these short periods of unemployment. As this was contrary to the Commissioners' intentions, their impact would have been disastrous in any case. Unfortunately, they moved North just when a severe trade slump was beginning that was to last from 1838 to 1842. Each big town had an army of unemployed and there was no work to be had. Isaac Hough, a Rochdale Guardian put the point directly:

'When a man is no unwilling idler and is thrown upon the streets from mere adverse circumstances, I say that, instead of applying the labour test, he has a right to go to that fund he assisted in creating.'

The commissioners expected a hostile reception but they were amazed at the vigour of the opposition. At Huddersfield they were turned out of the town and there were ugly scenes at Bradford and Tod-morden. Some towns simply refused to build workhouses but continued out-door relief. Tremendous local feeling was working up and Stephens, a prominent orator, declared that English society was divided into two classes—'the rich oppressor and the poor oppressed'.

It was out of the betrayal of 1832, the failure of Owenism, the impact of the New Poor Law and the trade slump that Chartism arose.

Chartism

The Chartist movement has often been dismissed in Stephens's phrase as a 'knife and fork question'; certainly it required a trade slump and extensive unemployment and distress to make it effective. Thomas Attwood complained:

'the people of England never came forward to advocate the abstract principles of major Cart-wright . . . but when their employment and wages were gone.'

But a movement affecting whole areas of the country and based on the radical programme of the 1770s was more than a matter of empty bellies. If eighteenth-century radicalism had been concerned with abstract principles, the nineteenth century had converted those principles into a movement of social protest. The Corresponding Societies in the 1790s had indicated this change and Chartism was its clearest expression. It was a demand partly *from first generation* factory workers, struggling to adjust themselves to new conditions, partly from surviving domestic workers facing competition from machines for better conditions in towns and factories. But it was more than this, it was a demand that the working class, hitherto ignored in politics, but upon whose labour the country depended, should have a say in the government of the country. The Great Changes were producing a new political force driving the country gradually towards democracy. Thomas Carlyle expressed something of the view in a pamphlet published in 1840, called *Chartism*:

'Chartism means the bitter discontent grown fierce and mad, the wrong condition therefore or the wrong disposition, of the Working Class of England. It is a new name for a thing which has had many names, which will yet have many. The matter of Chartism is weighty, deep-rooted, far-extending; did not begin yesterday; will by no means end this day or tomorrow.'

Three years later, in *Past and Present*, Carlyle went further:

'It is not to die, or even to die of hunger, that

A view of O'Connorville

makes a man wretched . . . But it is to live miserable we know not why; to work sore and yet get nothing; to be heart-worn, weary, yet isolated, unrelated, girt-in with a cold universal "Laissez-faire". This is and remains forever intolerable to all men whom God has made.'

Chartism began in London when William Lovett formed the London Working Men's Association in 1836. It produced a petition which Daniel O'Connell, the Irish leader, called the People's Charter (from which we get Chartism); there were six points, recalling the programme of 1776—universal manhood suffrage, annual parliaments, vote by ballot, equal electoral districts (constituencies were to have as equal a number of voters as possible), abolition of property qualifications for M.Ps., and payment of M.Ps.

The centre of the movement soon passed to the Midlands and industrial north where the effect of the trade slump was particularly felt by the hand-loom weavers, now suffering from *technological unemployment* (competition of mass-production machines) and the imposition of the new Poor Law. Chartism affected rural areas, but never to the same marked degree as the towns. There were two distinct situations that gave rise to the movement in a vigorous form; areas of declining industry, like the West Country textiles, and new towns dependent on a single industry, like Stockport, badly hit by the trade slump. This often meant that the great new towns were less affected than the mass of smaller towns surrounding them. In the industrial north, where much of the vigour of the movement appeared to best effect, the great mill towns exaggerated the differences between rich and poor—'the

two nations', as Disraeli called them. A series of gigantic meetings were held to gain support for the Charter: at Kersal Moor, near Manchester, before an assembly of 250,000, the banners that had been trampled at Peterloo were unfurled.

If the language of some Chartists was violent, the movement was dominated at first by Lovett, who believed in the 'moral force' of peaceful persuasion. A Convention was held at London in 1839, but the petition, signed by 1,250,000 people, was rejected. As a result, the violent men seized control, led by Feargus O'Connor, editor of the Leeds *Northern Star*. There was wild talk of insurrection and John Frost, expecting there to be a general rising, led an attack on Newport in Monmouthshire. He was easily defeated. Plans were laid for a 'sacred month' as the projected general strike was to be called.

The Chartists were fortunate that the Home Secretary was now Lord John Russell who refused to panic. He passed the Rural Constabulary Act in 1839 (although the response was disappointing) to strengthen the forces of law and order, and placed the North under the control of General Napier, a merciful, clever soldier who invited Chartist leaders to displays of artillery fire.

' "Physical force!" he wrote "Fools! We have the physical force, not they. They talk of their hundred men. Who is to move them when I am dancing round them with cavalry and pelting them with cannon-shot? . . . Poor men! How little they know of physical force".'

Government restraint and the really bad conditions probably prevented serious trouble. A second petition, signed by three million people was rejected in 1842. It was followed by what appears to have been a spontaneous protest in Lancashire and the West Midlands, a sort of general strike caused by strikers removing the plugs from the boilers of steam-engines and thus preventing them working— it was called the 'Plug Plot' and was not unlike the action that miners took against winding machinery to bring their demands to the notice of the management. But O'Connor, whose violent words were never matched by violent action, failed to utilise the strike and Chartism died down, especially as trade and employment improved in 1842.

In the next few years, O'Connor tried to organise a Land Scheme designed to settle unemployed workers on small holdings. In 1846 the first settlement, O'Connorville, near Watford, was opened. But the scheme got into financial difficulties and had to be wound up in 1849. By then active Chartism was dead.

Following the Irish potato famine, the 1847 harvest had been very bad, and a severe financial crisis, partly associated with railway speculation (see page 55), spread across the whole of Europe and North America. Revolutions broke out in most countries of Western Europe in 1848 and O'Connor prepared a monster petition with 5,500,000 signatures. The Government was worried. It took military preparations, placing London's defence in the hands of the Duke of Wellington who disposed artillery at vantage points. One hundred and seventy thousand special constables were enrolled (the future Emperor of the French among them) and the Chartists were refused permission to march from Kennington Common to Westminster. The gigantic petition was delivered in a horse wagon: it contained less than two million signatures, many of them frivolous, like 'Pug Nose' and 'Queen Victoria'. The movement, since it clearly was not going to launch into a revolution, collapsed in a wave of arrests and a burst of ridicule.

Chartism failed as a movement because it was badly led. There was a division between the 'moral' and 'physical force' men that fatally weakened their proceedings. The mass support they attracted dwindled as conditions improved—this was particularly evident in 1848, when there was a rapid return of prosperity after the summer. There was also tremendous local variation in the movement, for it was never a truly national unitary movement. It lacked strong middle-class support, which tended to support the Anti-Corn Law Leaque (see page 90). Since the Government rejected its petition, its only hope of success lay in revolution, but the English working man was not a revolutionary. As prosperity increased, symbolised by the Great Exhibition (see page 82), conditions improved. Working men found employment—many emigrated—and turned to peaceful trade unionism, turning their backs, for the moment, on active politics.

But if the movement was a failure, it remained an inspiration for later generations. Only one of its six points failed to become the law—annual parliaments, for this was unworkable. Universal adult manhood suffrage was gained by the reform acts of 1867, 1884 and 1918; secret ballot was granted in 1872 (see page 168); the abolition of property qualifications in 1859; payment of M.Ps. in 1911 and equal electoral districts by a commission that periodically adjusts the boundaries of constituencies. Old Chartists themselves were to be found in the Co-operative Movement and in the New Unionism of the 1880s and in the early organisations that were eventually to form the Labour Party.

New model trade unions

When Owen's trade union failed, the skilled artisans tended to turn away from politics and to form craft unions to protect themselves alone. They played little part in Chartism; indeed they were determined to be 'respectable' that is they were determined to conduct themselves in a manner as close as possible to the way of life of the middle classes—and this meant avoiding agitation among the working men. By the 1850s they had developed into the new model trade unions (Amalgamated Societies) of which the Amalgamated Society of Engineers (1851) was the first.

These new model unions were craft unions of skilled men (the 'aristocracy of labour' as they are sometimes called) often growing out of smaller societies that had joined together in an effort to unite all those skilled in a particular craft. They charged high union dues and were soon financially very strong. After the serious lock out of engineers in 1852 (when the strikers gained some assistance from the Christian Socialists), they tended to avoid the strike weapon if possible, for they had seen how a big strike depleted union funds. But they would strike in a good cause, and they would support with gifts and loans a brother union that was on strike—workers' solidarity was a growing feature in Victorian England. As they grew financially stronger they used their funds for friendly society benefits—payments for sickness and old age, for example. Robert Applegarth explained it like this:

'The benefits are as follows:- Donation benefit for 12 weeks, 10/- per week; and for another 12 weeks, 6/- per week . . . tool benefit to any amount of loss, or when a man has been a member for only six months, £5; sick benefit for 26 weeks, 12/- per week, and then 6/- per week so long as the illness continues; funeral benefit £12, or £3.10 when a six months' member dies; accident benefit, £100; superannuation benefit for life, if a member 25 years 8/- per week . . . The emigration benefit is £6, and there are benevolent grants, according to circumstances, in cases of distress.'

The new model unions were perfect examples of the self-help that Samuel Smiles preached. In their second ten years of life, the Engineers spent £450,000 in friendly society benefits, and only £26,000 on strike pay.

Because they were so wealthy they could afford local offices so that they had no longer to meet in pubs. Many had central offices in London and paid a general secretary. This meant strong direction of union policy on a national basis, and as the general secretaries were men of outstanding ability they were able to meet the leaders of industry without that feeling of intimidation so common among working men when discussing with employers. There was a remarkable group of general secretaries in the 1860s, men like Robert Applegarth of the Carpenters, William Allan of the Engineers, Edwin Coulson of the Bricklayers and Daniel Guile of the Ironfounders. They formed the London Trades Council (1860) and were known as the Junta because they did much to consolidate and direct trade union policy in the country.

Employers were disturbed by the growing strength of unionism, especially as they were unable to prevent its growth by obliging their employers to sign the 'document' as they had done in the 1830s. But in Sheffield in 1866 a series of outrages committed by a group of extremists in order to intimidate strike breakers (blacklegs) and non-union men, caused the Government to appoint a Royal Commission in 1867 to investigate trade unionism as a whole. It produced a hostile majority report, but an eloquent minority report written by the Christian Socialists Thomas Hughes and Frederic Harrison, with the help of Robert Applegarth, was more favourable to the unions. In 1867, also, a legal decision in the case of Hornby v. Close declared that trade unions could not have the protection of the law to recover funds stolen by a dishonest official. It was fortunate that 1867 was the year of the Second Reform Act, which gave the vote to the better-off worker of the towns (many were members of the new model unions). Gladstone won the election of 1868 and granted the unions full recognition and protection of their funds in 1871, but in order to pass this measure he had to forbid picketing of factories where there was a strike. This made it difficult to hold an effective strike, and after much lobbying, Disraeli granted unions the right to peaceful picketing in 1875. Trade unionism had become an accepted institution. In the dark days of 1866-7, when the whole future of unionism was in the balance and unionists found it very difficult to get the press to publish their views, Samuel Nicholson, President of the Manchester and Salford **Trades Council suggested forming a Trades Union** Congress both to publicise the trade union's case and to serve as something of a general forum of the trade union movement. The T.U.C. was founded in 1868.

The Co-operative movement

The co-operative movement is generally dated from 1844, when a group of workers, the 'Rochdale Pioneers', opened a co-operative store in Toad Lane, Rochdale, that proved a lasting success and launched one of the major social movements in commerce of the last two hundred years.

It was not the first society. Other co-operatives had been formed, some failing through lack of expertise. Nineteen of those founded before Queen Victoria came to the throne (1837) were still going in 1898. To a great extent, Robert Owen was the principal inspirer of the co-operative movement, which he regarded as the means of changing the profit motive in commerce to one of social policy. There are basically two types of co-operatives: factories, textile mills, collieries, farms, even an Industrial Bank (which failed in the 1870s) communally owned and worked; and, secondly, retail trading, buying in bulk and selling both to members and to the public at large.

The Rochdale Pioneers saved weekly until they could afford to open a small shop and purchase a few goods. They were laughed at, but they managed to stay in business. Furthermore, they attracted custom because they offered fair trading at honest prices (unlike the tommy shops, see *page 98*) and their goods were not adulterated as was common practice in other shops, where one might find 'toxic Prussian blue in tea, plaster of Paris in bread, red lead in pepper and mahogany sawdust in coffee'. Food adulteration had become extremely widespread by the 1820s—probably because of the growth of towns and the consumer's greater dependence on shop-purchased and processed foods. Adulteration proved so easy and profitable that many took advantage, whether it was manufacturers (Henry Mayhew describes the large trade in used tea-leaves which were then dried, treated with black-lead to 'face' them, and then sold as good tea) or small retailers— but it was always the poor who suffered, for the wealthy paid higher prices and got better quality. Bread and beer were the staple items of diet most frequently adulterated, often with substances that were harmful if taken in quantity. Indeed, it was not until free trade budgets and bulk supplies from overseas brought cheap food (see *page 177*), that the practice declined. The working class were so used to the taste of adulterated foodstuffs that some co-operative Societies found great difficulty in selling pure foods because they 'tasted different'— one society had to employ a lecturer to demonstrate what good and wholesome tea should look like.

The principle that the Rochdale Pioneers (and their successors) worked on was to cut out the middleman (who was often responsible for adulteration) and to trade on a cash basis, for this reduced the risk of 'bad debts' and prevented that 'degrading bond of indebtedness' that was often the case with other shop keepers whose customers had run up bills they could not pay off. Members of the society got a dividend (the *divvy*) on the amount they had purchased over a period, so that they were in effect buying below the market retail price. In 1857 George Holyoake published an account of the Rochdale Pioneers. Significantly enough, it was entitled '*Self Help by the People*'.

'Husbands who never knew what it was to be out of debt, and poor wives, who, during forty years, never had sixpence uncondemned in their pockets, now possess money sufficient to buy their cottages, and go every week into their own market with coins jingling in their pockets; and in that market there is no distrust, and no deception; there is no adulteration, and no second prices. The whole atmosphere is honest. Those who serve neither hurry, finesse, nor flatter. They have no interest in chicanery. They have but one duty to perform—that of giving fair measure, full weight, and a pure article. . . .'

In 1851 there were 130 Co-operative Societies of the Rochdale type: by the 1880s there were over a thousand stores with annual sales of over £13 million: a new chapter of working-class activity was being written. The necessary legal basis for their expansion was provided by the Industrial and Provident Societies Act (1852). As their success grew they found it increasingly difficult to deal with certain merchants who refused to supply them with goods. As a result, partly to ensure continued supplies and a proper quality, and partly to enjoy greater economies of scale by bulk-buying, the North of England Co-operative Wholesale Society was formed in 1863 (to be called the C.W.S. in 1872). The co-operatives probably had their biggest social effects in the industrial North and Midlands, although they were also important in the London area. They provided an opportunity for artisans and those in regular employment to gain considerable experience in running the affairs of their own community, for co-operative societies are run on democratic lines with members of the society voting to elect a management committee that takes the full responsibility of running the affairs of the Society. As societies grew in size and influence, they extended their interest beyond the narrowly commercial and, in association with other brother societies provided educational opportunities for sons of members. In due course they played a part in the origin of the Labour Party, and some members of the House of Commons today are backed by co-operative societies.

13 · Taking stock

For over a hundred years the Great Changes had been producing a new type of society in Britain. After the 1880s there was no slackening in the rate of change, but there was a different atmosphere. The twentieth century has been concerned to adjust itself to the conditions of the industrial age that had emerged. An old man in the 1880s might recall the difficult years after the French Wars, or the Chartist processions, the Great Exhibition or the building of railways. But he would also recall that his grandparents had been country folk and that he had become a town dweller. The urban sprawl and the increasingly regular, closely organised work at the factory bench would be what chiefly distinguished his world from that of his grandparents. He would still see dire poverty among the working class, but he would remember the still greater poverty of his youth. People were better housed and fed now, and poverty itself was coming to be regarded as a social evil and not merely the natural lot of the 'lower orders'. Here was a new attitude; a modern attitude. And there was a new attitude among the lower orders, too. They were becoming more self-conscious. They still paid respect to their social superiors, but they were increasingly demanding a greater share in national prosperity.

The new electorate and the collectivist state

The gradual wiping out of the worst aspects of poverty has been the greatest social change of the present century. It is an achievement that has come in response to popular demand.

The twentieth century has seen democracy established. The ideas of the Chartists did not die with their movement. After a series of riots in London and the North that frightened political opinion, a Second Reform Act was passed in 1867. This gave the vote to the better-off urban workers and it touched off a series of major reforms in the ministries of Gladstone and Disraeli during the 1870s and 1880s, culminating in the Third Reform Act of 1884–5 which gave the vote to the agricultural labourer. By then there were 5,700,000 voters, nearly half of them working class. Because of the complexities of the franchise, *manhood suffrage* (one man one vote) was still some way off: in 1911 only 59 per cent of the total adult male population had a vote. Manhood suffrage came in 1918. At the same time as the electorate grew, elections became fairer, partly because there were now too many voters to bribe, partly because politicians in general no longer used bribery, but chiefly because of Acts of Parliament. In 1872 the great abuse of open voting was ended by the Secret Ballot Act, and in 1883 a Corrupt Practices (Elections) Act laid down strict limits as to the amount of money that might be spent on elections.

Because of the large electorate that could not be 'influenced' easily, a very radical change occurred in the structure of political parties. In Britain (unlike Europe) we have a tradition of two main political parties, one forming the Government, the other the opposition or alternative government. In the eighteenth century the division between one party and the other was very difficult to draw, so that when the Whigs formed the Government, their Tory opponents would sometimes decide to join them for the sake of political office. Parties were really groups of politicians led by powerful men. In the early nineteenth century this pattern was continued although the divisions between the parties hardened. By 1867 two distinct parties had formed, the *Liberals* under Gladstone and the *Conservatives* under Disraeli. The Second Reform Act made it necessary for the parties to develop a strong professional organisation in order to be able to mount an electoral campaign that would get voters out to vote.

By 1880 both parties had developed a broadly

similar structure (later followed by the Labour Party) with a central office and local party organisations in the constituencies. It was the effort of voluntary constituency workers that ensured a candidate's success. To maintain the enthusiasm of constituency workers and to give them a part in helping to form party policy, a system of committees was developed. Party members could vote for representatives on the local constituency party executive committee. This could elect members to an area, and then a regional committee. Then there was the National Executive Committee that was responsible for holding the Party Conference once a year, at which any party member could speak. In this way quite ordinary people could exert an influence upon the discussions that helped the forming of party policy. It was quite a new idea, but it was already working well in the 1880s. And party leaders were responsive to the voice of the large (predominantly urban) electorate. For this reason the volume of legislation passed by Parliament has continued to increase every year. In the 1870s a deliberate policy of cheap food for the working man was adopted, and the powers of the State were greatly increased in the field of elementary education, factory regulation, public health and local government. Trade unions were given legal privileges and the wealthy prevented from purchasing commissions in the forces and places in the Civil Service. In 1880, the Employers' Liability Act for the first time placed the responsibility for industrial illnesses and accidents upon the employer. Clearly the powers of the State were being extended in a way that affected the lives of ordinary citizens. At the same time people were realising that an industrial state was a complex thing that cannot be left to 'run itself' but required considerable control by government departments and local government. This expansion of Government activity has been called the growth of the *collectivist state*. It was difficult to reconcile it with the earlier tradition of individualism. A. V. Dicey, a great lawyer, put it like this:

'Somewhere between 1868 and 1900 three changes took place which brought into prominence the authoritative side of Benthamite liberalism. Faith in *laissez-faire* suffered an eclipse: hence the principle of utility became an argument in favour, not of individual freedom, but of the absolutism of the State. Parliament, under the progress of democracy became the representative, not of the middle classes, but of the whole body of householders: Parliamentary sovereignty, therefore, came to mean, in the last resort, the unrestricted power of the wage-earner. English administrative mechanism was reformed and strengthened. The machinery was thus provided for the practical extension of the activity of the state.'

In the 1880s, the most prominent politician to advocate these ideas was Joseph Chamberlain, former mayor of Birmingham (see *page 109*) who dreamed of supplementing private efforts with the power of the State in order to establish a new society in which all citizens would enjoy a reasonable standard of living and security in old age. He put these ideas into an election manifesto in 1885; but they were too extreme for Gladstone, the Liberal leader, and so the manifesto was called the 'Unauthorised Programme'. But Chamberlain's ideas were those of the twentieth century. It was a sad day for the Liberal Party when Gladstone drove him out of it in 1886. Chamberlain eventually served with the Conservatives between 1895 and 1903; but his radical ideas broke that party, too, (see *page 225*). In politics it is not always the man with great ideas who succeeds; more often it is he who can mould public opinion gently but firmly. In a democracy the force of public opinion matters: this is another of the important things that the twentieth century has demonstrated. It is not enough to have brilliant and vigorous ideas. The point was put brilliantly in a private letter from Lord Salisbury written in 1907 to Lord Milner, a man as vigorous in his ideas as Chamberlain:

'My opinions are so halting, so limited beside yours. You see the great vision of a consolidated Empire full square against the world and a national policy which will use to the uttermost the resources of the State for the common good. And I see the Conservative Party. It is a party shackled by tradition; all the cautious people, all the timid, all the unimaginative belong to it. It stumbles slowly and painfully from precedent to precedent with its eyes fixed on the ground. Yet the Conservative Party is the Imperial Party. I must work with it—who indeed am just such an one myself—but *you* must work with it if you are to achieve even a part of your object.'

The 'Great Depression'

The generation born just after the Great Exhibition, when Britain was the 'workshop of the world', found themselves facing a quite different situation from that of their parents. For, by the 1880s Britain had to face new rivals and had to admit that her economic predominance was passing. People called the period between 1873 and 1896 the years of the 'Great Depression'. Yet when we look at the period, it seems strange to us that businessmen made so much fuss. With the exception of agriculture, there

seems no reason to think in dramatic terms of great depressions.

There were plenty of signs that the world economic position had altered and was no longer so favourable to us. Industrialists found that prices were dropping steeply and so their profit was reduced. For example:

	1874			*1883*			
	£	s	d	£	s	d	
steel rails	12	0	0	5	7	6	a ton
iron rails	9	18	0	5	0	0	a ton
pig iron	4	17	6	1	13	0	a ton

To off-set the effect of this price fall, a tremendous increase in sales was needed, but orders were more difficult to get because trade rivals had appeared. For this reason merchants began opening up new markets in the tropics and huge areas of land in Africa were claimed for rival empires to secure these markets. At home, output per man seems to have expanded much more slowly between 1873 and

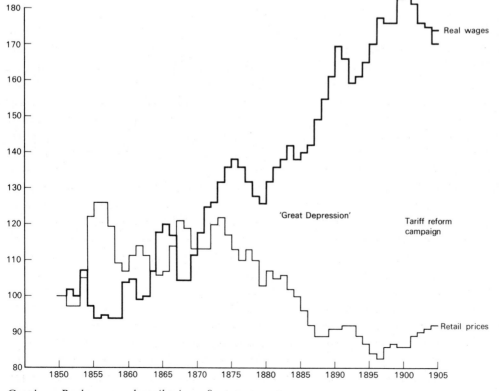

Graph 14 Real wages and retail prices, 1850-1905

'Bloody Sunday', 1887. A meeting of the unemployed in Trafalgar Square, London, was banned at the last minute by the Home Secretary. The police stopped the workers marching and riot took place. The police action was widely interpreted as a calculated attack on the working class by the wealthy

1913 than in the industries of our overseas competitors. Unemployment on a fairly extensive scale appeared in the 1880s (the 1888 *Oxford Dictionary* listed 'unemployment' for the first time). Many families emigrated. Others began to leave the big cities of the North and go to the South East and Midlands in search of better paid work. This was to become the feature of population movement in the twentieth century. Manufacturers began to form trade associations in order to restrict competition among themselves by deciding on prices and production rates. Clearly they had doubts about the future: indeed, the 'Great Depression' is best explained as a crisis of confidence among businessmen whilst they got used to the new world conditions.

But for all the fuss, there were plenty of signs of growing wealth. More servants were employed than ever before. The consumption of tea and sugar (a good gauge of working-class living standards) increased. Above all, the fall in prices meant cheap food, and thus *real wages* (what the money will actually buy, rather than the money wage received) rose rapidly (see *graph 14*). Workers were better off —provided they suffered no unemployment.

Foreign competition

It was in foreign trade that the new world conditions were most obvious. Our share of world trade declined, and, indeed, our exports stagnated in the 1880s (although they shot ahead at the end of the century). Other nations were taking an increasing share of world trade, notably U.S.A. and Germany. Both of these countries had outpaced us in population by the 1880s, both had a bigger home market to supply *from their own factories*, and both were developing profitable labour-saving machinery. In U.S.A., the railways being laid across the Continent developed her gigantic industrial and agricultural potential. In Germany, the development of *kartels* (an industrial organisation in which a central body controls prices and production rates), receiving far more active help from the big German banks and from government contracts than did British industry, led to a rapid development of heavy and manufacturing industries (see *graph 15*). German technical skill was also held to be superior to that available in this country, and this encouraged many to demand better provision for secondary and

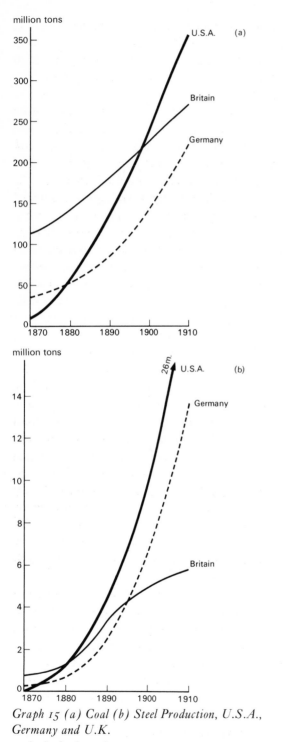

Graph 15 (a) Coal (b) Steel Production, U.S.A., Germany and U.K.

technical education.

Foreign competition on a big scale was a new experience for the Victorians, and there was a great deal of hysterical reaction. Germany (in actual fact one of our best customers, since we increased our trade with her by 100 per cent between 1896 and 1914) became feared in the popular mind as our chief rival. People complained that German kartels 'dumped' goods on the British market (dumping means exporting goods at a subsidised price so that they sell at an uneconomic price in the foreign country and make it difficult for home producers to compete). In 1896, E. E. Williams' pamphlet *Made in Germany* demonstrated the hysterical opposition to German-made goods:

'The toys, and the dolls, and the fairy books which your children maltreat in the nursery are made in Germany: nay, the material of your favourite (patriotic) newspaper had the same birthplace as like as not. Roam the house over, and the fatal mark will greet you at every turn, from the piano in your drawing room to the mug on your kitchen dresser. . . . Descend to your domestic depths, and you shall find your very drain-pipes German-made.'

Such fears were heightened because most countries ended any free trade policy and returned to protection, partly for revenue, partly to protect their own industries, partly to save their farmers from the effect of importing great quantities of cheap American wheat. The famous Cobden Treaty (1860) was not renewed in 1872, and the French and German tariffs of the 1870s hit our exports. But we did not change our free trade policy. Small manufacturers and farmers were the chief sufferers: they formed the Fair Trade League in the 1880s, to demand 'retaliatory tariffs' (imposing a tariff on imports from countries that put a tariff on our exports). The Government preferred cheap food to tariffs and refused, but it did require the country of origin to be stamped on all imported goods, so that housewives could knowingly 'buy British'. Complaints that our exports were out-priced by foreign tariffs while foreign goods entered Britain duty-free grew throughout the Great Depression, and culminated in Joseph Chamberlain's Tariff Reform campaign of 1903 (see *page 225*). Unfortunately for the advocates of tariffs, there was a pronounced revival of British trade in the last years of the century and this restored confidence in the policy of free trade by which we had grown so wealthy (when we had no serious rival). As a result, we remained free trade in a world that was fast adopting high protective tariffs, and we did not change the policy radically until 1932.

British failures

As more studies of the 'Great Depression' appear, it becomes increasingly difficult to see why the men of the time should call it 'Great'. It is true that they experienced an economic set-back, but not one that merited so dramatic a title. No single cause has been isolated. Some historians have pointed to the ease with which our rivals, leaning upon our experience and knowledge (and sometimes our financial backing) were able to open factories with new machinery, well planned for mass production. It was cheaper for them, but the British manufacturer had first to scrap his existing machinery if he wanted to re-equip his factory with the latest machines available, and so he was at a disadvantage. Others have blamed British management. In the last quarter of the century industrial progress was sluggish, and even the new machines that were installed were not fully utilised. Production costs in many industries were scarcely reduced. This was particularly true of the coal industry where the additional hazard of deeper mines and narrower seams was a factor. The price of coal affected the price of many other goods; thus the price of manufactured goods remained high. We also failed to develop new industries especially those based on scientific research (like chemicals). Indeed British manufacturers seem to have neglected basic research. The new 'growth' industries were chemicals and electricity. Both had been pioneered by us, but developed by our rivals; by 1913 Germany was supplying us with 90 per cent of our synthetic dye requirements and both Germany and U.S.A. dominated the electrical goods industry. The same was true of machine-tools, and of steel production, although the major processes used were British inventions. And at the same time as we failed to develop new industries, the old staple industries were beginning to reach the limit of their profitability.

To explain this sorry state of affairs, historians have often resorted to *sociological* reasons. For example, they argue that the incentive to adopt new ideas was lacking because industry was already successful. The heads of family firms did not need to know each part of the works, and they were frequently sent to public schools where they learnt no technical subjects at all. Family firms tended to be small (especially in Birmingham) and ill-equipped for expansion or to take advantage of a new process. Certainly there were few mergers of firms (like the kartels and combines of our rivals). Again, with managers and directors taught the classics rather than commerce, we quite failed to develop effective marketing organisations. Our banks failed to provide the guidance and drive towards investment in technological change that was such a feature of German banks. And there was a tendency to rest on past achievements and to resist new methods. We continued to use the Leblanc method of making soda for the chemical industry, although the more efficient German Solvay method was available from 1870. The makers of steam-engines continued to produce the best machines in the world, but failed to turn their hand to diesel engines. Engineers, trained in a craft tradition, failed to re-think their ideas so that they could produce factories properly planned for full mass production techniques. The workers themselves appear to have resisted new methods and techniques, especially when their jobs were threatened.

There is something in all these arguments. But they can be made about any industrial country at any time. If the 'boss's' son went to a public school, he returned to serve on the board, where his acquaintance with sons of bankers and financiers whom he met in his school-days would prove useful. He did not often return actually to manage the factory. And these years of depression were not without achievement. Our production of basic materials was increasing; and the spread of steam power and the replacement of iron with steel was at its height during the years 1873 to 1896. If

Lancashire in 1913 was much as it had been in 1873, Warwickshire and the Midlands had been transformed by the rise of light industries. In civil engineering, the Forth Bridge (1882–7) was a wonder of the world.

The picture of complacent stupor is unfair to British industrialists. That they talked so much of depression shows how concerned they were. Perhaps it was that they lacked confidence and that, at a time of falling prices and diminishing profits, the cost of converting existing methods and machinery was too high. The coal and iron industries were particularly good examples of this—indeed, the phosphoric ores of the East Midlands were not properly exploited until the 1930s.

Perhaps the simplest explanation of the lack of dynamic change comparable with that achieved by our rivals, was that the 'Great Depression' was not great enough to shake British industry into re-equipping old factories and pouring money into growth industries. Instead, we retreated from the threat of foreign competition by concentrating increasingly on our imperial trade and our trade with the 'under-developed' areas while our rivals developed new markets in Europe and America (markets where there was a demand for machinery and electrical goods).

Yet there was an increasing tendency for firms to join in trade associations for the purpose of deciding how much competition they would have and what their prices should be. As yet they were neither strong nor numerous, but they were an indication

A grocer's shop in the 1880s

of change and a sign for the future (see *page 247*). Another, especially evident in heavy engineering, was the development of larger and more economical units of production, like the giant shipping firm of Cammell-Laird and the Armstrong and Whitworth armaments and machine-tool factories. These bigger units enjoyed economies of scale and were able to concentrate greater reserves of capital for development. In some cases they were able to phase-out production at unprofitable works and to concentrate it in others, or to concentrate the production of certain goods in particular factories. This is what economists call *rationalisation*.

There was also, in these years of the so-called 'Great Depression', a revolution in the retail trade, for the specialised multiple grocery stores, Lipton's, Home and Colonial Stores; the chain shoe shops, like Freeman, Hardy and Willis; Hepworth the tailor; Boots the chemist (with 150 shops by 1900), all made their appearance at this time. These were a new type of store, bringing reliable trading at moderate prices, run by a highly efficient management that enjoyed economies of scale because of the many different shops. They also provided an effective market for goods from a wide range of industries. Only multiple stores, with their massive turn-over, could provide an effective market for Joseph Lyons' mechanical bakery. The use of packaged and standardised domestic goods, often with a brand name, was becoming common. There was no sign of complacency or unwillingness to experiment in this branch of industry and commerce.

The pattern of trade

During the nineteenth century our trade with the rest of the world increased significantly, but there was a profound change in the way this trade was distributed. From the 1830s onwards our export markets became more and more those of the under-developed world of the tropics. This is well illustrated by the pattern of our exports of cotton goods (see *graph 16*). We tended to draw much of our raw materials and a good deal of our food from these same areas, so that by the end of the century,

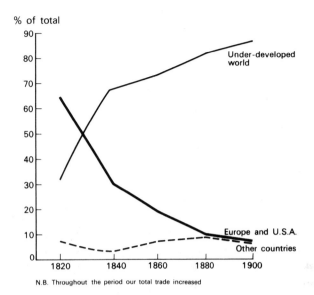

Graph 16 Export of cotton piece goods, 1820–1900

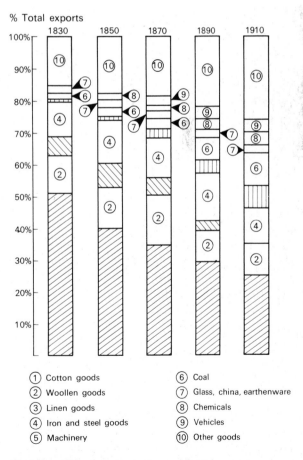

① Cotton goods
② Woollen goods
③ Linen goods
④ Iron and steel goods
⑤ Machinery
⑥ Coal
⑦ Glass, china, earthenware
⑧ Chemicals
⑨ Vehicles
⑩ Other goods

Graph 17 The changing pattern of British exports

especially as food and raw material prices were falling, we came to depend heavily on the tropics and our Empire for cheap imports to support our industry and work people. We exported manufactured goods to these markets, so that a pattern of trade developed not unlike that of the old mercantile system, with under-developed markets supplying our needs in return for our goods. When the depression of the 1880s came, (our first real international challenge since the days of Napoleon) we escaped not by modernising, but by exploiting the remaining possibility left to us—the tropics. The steam ship came just at the right moment, for it enabled us to expand our trade rapidly simply because it carried more goods more quickly.

But this could only be a short-term answer. It did us very well for the period up to the first world war (1914–18). Thereafter, when British capital and machinery had produced textile factories in Asia and India, the Lancashire cotton industry, that great pace-setter of the industrial revolution, was doomed, for factory-made Asian textiles were cheaper both abroad and in this country, than Lancashire goods. Fortunately, the second half of the century saw a great growth in the range of goods normally exported, so that as the market for one type of good failed, another took its place. This increase in the range of goods being exported is called *diversification* and is well illustrated by Graph 17.

Balance of trade and balance of payments

If a country is to trade without getting into financial difficulties, it must exchange for its imports at least an equivalent value in exports. This is called balancing *visible trade*, and a country would be very lucky to get a precise balance, especially if its trade were as varied and extensive as Britain's. It is a good thing to have more exports than imports, because then the country is earning money. But if imports exceed exports, then the country is losing money, for the imports have to be paid for, perhaps in gold, and if this happens regularly the country would go bankrupt very quickly. During the whole of the period that Britain was the 'workshop of the world',

and during the 'Great Depression', Britain had an unfavourable balance of visible trade (see *graph 18*). This was scarcely recognised at the time, partly because of our predominance as the major commercial nation of the world, partly because trade statistics were not published before 1903 and few people would have understood their significance in any case. What saved us from disaster was our gigantic *invisible earnings* (payments for shipping, for banking and insurance services, and income from foreign investments). Because of our invisible earnings, our *balance of payments* (the account showing how much we spend and how much we earn abroad) was always in credit during the century, and in the early years of the twentieth century, the period of Edwardian prosperity, we had a remarkably favourable balance.

Because of our invisible earnings there was no balance of payments problem before 1914. That year we had about £4,000 million in foreign investments, whilst U.S.A., Germany, France, Belgium and Holland together had just less than £5,000 million: clearly, we were the bankers of the world. Even so, there were fears expressed before 1914 that we were living on our capital. This was particularly evident when bad harvests added to low prices reduced the money available for purchasing our exports in the newly exploited markets of the tropics. The 1880s were a time of especial economic uncertainty for this reason, partly because some foreign governments defaulted, partly because of a temporary decline in exports that meant our cashing some of our foreign investments to balance our payments.

The crisis in agriculture

To a great extent, the 'Great Depression' was true of British agriculture. Here the cause was not complacency, for there had been rapid strides forward in the period of 'high farming' (see *page 36*): it was foreign competition, aided by developments in transport and technology.

U.S.A. was justly praised for its labour-saving machinery, and the McCormick reaper that had been exhibited at the Crystal Palace in 1851, made

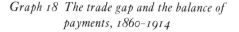

Graph 18 The trade gap and the balance of payments, 1860-1914

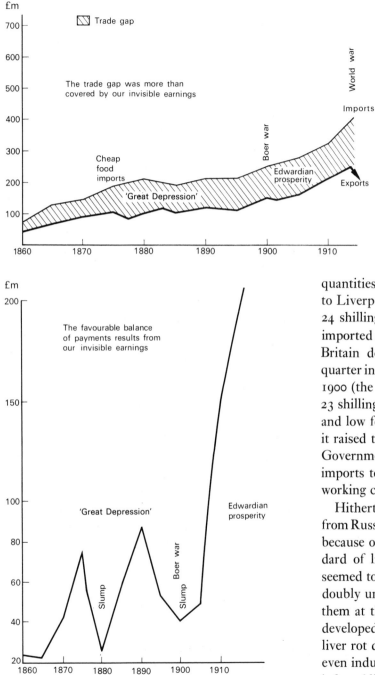

quantities. Freight charges for wheat from Chicago to Liverpool fell from 65 shillings a ton in 1868 to 24 shillings a ton in 1882 and the vast quantities imported into Europe brought the price of wheat in Britain down from an average of 55 shillings a quarter in the 1860s to 33 shillings between 1875 and 1900 (the lowest price for 150 years was in 1894 at 23 shillings). Naturally our food imports increased and low food costs benefited the working class, for it raised the real value of wages. Consequently, no Government dared impose restrictions on food imports to help British agriculture, lest it lose the working class vote.

Hitherto our grain imports had come mainly from Russia and Germany, but these were dwindling because of increasing population and a rising standard of living in these countries. American corn seemed to come at the right moment: farmers were doubly unfortunate, for a series of bad harvests hit them at this moment—wheat was mildewed, hops developed fungus and foot and mouth disease and liver rot decimated livestock (the Government was even induced to pay compensation for slaughtering infected livestock in 1877). The harvest of 1879 was one of the worst of the century. Thus at the very moment when it needed to be most competitive, British agriculture was in difficulties simply from the weather. Ironically, Disraeli, who had made his name attacking Peel for repealing the Corn Laws in

the extensive cultivation of the prairies possible. But it was only with the big development of railways after the Civil War and the growth of shipping (especially the iron steam ship) that the harvests of the Mid-West could reach Europe in significant

1846, was now Prime Minister, and he showed no disposition to restore Protection. As a result some types of farming had to bear all the strains of adjusting to our conditions without any form of Government assistance. The corn lands of the South and East suffered most (farm rents in Cambridgeshire dropped by 35 per cent between 1871 and 1896). Wheat output dropped from 22 per cent of the gross agricultural product in 1870 to 7 per cent in 1903. Oats and barley fell in price, but farmers continued to grow them for fodder and straw.

But the North and West, where grazing was predominant, remained prosperous (farm rents even rose in Lancashire). Low grain prices benefited stock breeders, and the rising real wages meant a rising demand for animal products. Technology threatened in the form of refrigeration (the first frozen meat and butter from Australia and the Argentine reached Liverpool in 1880), but the quality, then as now, meant that the frozen meat competed only with cheap meat. Stock breeders could concentrate on the quality, higher priced, market. Dairy farmers found an increasing market for milk (railways helped here, of course). But sheep farmers found that the price of wool dropped 60 per cent.

After 1896 there was a slow recovery in prices, but by then many farmers had adapted their techniques to the new situation. The speed with which they did this reflects great credit upon them and makes one think twice about stories of the inadequacies of British management. Mixed farming became popular; dairy farming and market gardening grew up near towns. Careful economies were made, cheaper and better fertilisers and feeding stuffs helped and there was a big increase in machinery, making the labour force, already shrinking during the period of high farming, diminish more. While the total population rose by some 40 per cent between 1871 and 1914, agricultural workers fell from 1,250,000 to about a million. This meant the end of Joseph Arch's farm workers' trade union (see *page 35*), and often enough the end of the traditional healthy rural community in many villages. Young men and girls left quickly for the towns, or emigrated. Small farms were productive and many great estates were models of good husbandry, but there were many more fields where the thistle appeared (especially as the acreage left to grass increased): this was a sign of lack of manpower.

Fearful of raising food prices the Government refused to act. Two Royal Commissions reported (that of 1893-7 was actually instructed to investigate 'the agricultural depression') and in 1889 the Ministry of Agriculture was established. Local authorities were encouraged to rent out allotments and small holdings for the Agricultural Holdings Act (1875) gave tenants greater security and compensation for improvements.

The logic of the situation was clear: a new balance had been established in the British economy, which the rising democracy was anxious to maintain, namely that Britain would produce the manufactured goods and other countries would supply her with over half her food more cheaply than if she had produced it herself. When the urban population first exceeded the rural in 1851, this situation was not yet possible. Technological and transport changes had produced it within thirty years. It was hard on some farmers and their labourers, but the urban workers benefited from the cheap food. It was effective so long as trade was not disrupted and Britain could easily pay her way in the world. In the first world war, the U-boat threat forced the Government to aid agriculture (see *page 238*) and after the war, with a deteriorating trade position, it became necessary to increase that aid.

The stability and prosperity of mid-Victorian England rested on our virtual monopoly of world industrial production and trade, and on the diplomatic predominance of Britain throughout the world. By the 1880s these bases were challenged and a new and very different age was dawning. In the next eighty years, even greater changes than those that had altered Britain in the previous century were to occur, but they were to change the whole pattern of the world at the same time as they altered the pattern of living in this country.

14 · The appearance of twentieth-century society

During the period of the Great Changes, society had to adjust itself rapidly to quite new ways of life. Since the 1880s there have been changes of a less dramatic nature, but of as fundamental a character. Society today is much more closely integrated than ever before. Sociologists call the easy movement between classes, *social mobility*, and this has become so much a feature of twentieth-century life that it is sometimes difficult nowadays to distinguish between social classes. To a great extent this mobility rests upon the Welfare State, which is a twentieth century phenomenon. The greatest period of social change was the 1940s and 1950s, during and after the Second World War (1939–45), but the whole period from the 1880s shows the rapid build-up of the factors that have produced our society of today.

After the so-called 'Great Depression' came the Edwardian period. This was a time of great prosperity and comfort, remembered by those who survived the First World War as even more prosperous than it may in fact have been, because of the rapid changes that followed the war. But the prosperity was only for the wealthy—and they flaunted their wealth in a provocative and extravagant fashion. The poor lived in a different world: a life of hard struggle, made harder by a rise in the cost of living that reduced the level of their real wages. They had better public health facilities than their parents and better medical care was available— infant mortality among the poor fell sharply. A measure was introduced for the feeding of needy schoolchildren and school medical inspections were started in 1906. There was less unemployment— but there was also more hostility to the rich. Indeed so disturbing did the class hatred become, that there were genuine fears of some sort of rebellion in the years just before the war. The decision of the House of Lords to throw out what had become known as the People's Budget in 1909 further heightened the tension, and so began a political crisis that came near to destroying the accustomed basis of British government. The years 1909–14 were years of constitutional crisis and deep underlying social discontent (see *page 219*).

Nevertheless, the wealthy enjoyed life to the full in those Edwardian years. They are well portrayed in John Galsworthy's *The Forsyte Saga*. They visited luxury hotels on the Continent, sailed in private steam yachts, occasionally hired a private train; in Scotland they shot scores of game birds and deer, and in 'Town' (London) they drank unbelievable quantities of the best wines and champagnes. What made their display of wealth and pleasure the more odious was the gulf that divided the rich and the poor. There was nothing new in this gulf: only it was now more recognised and less tolerated. Arnold Bennett put the poor man's dislike of the wealthy very neatly:

'Their assured curt voices, their carriage, their clothes, the similarity of their manners all show that they belong to a caste and that the caste has been successful in the struggle for life. It has been called the "middle class" but it ought to be called the upper class for nearly everything is below it. I go to the stores to Rumpelmeyers, to the Royal Academy and to the dozen clubs in Albermarle St. and Dover St. and I see again just the same crowd, well fed, well dressed, completely free from the cares which beset at least five-sixths of the English race. I do not belong to this class by birth. I was born slightly beneath it. But by the help of luck and strict attention to business I have gained the right of entrance to it.'

One of the best studies of this period is E. M. Forster's *Howard's End*, a novel in which the egoistic self-important attitude of a not especially wealthy Edwardian family is revealed by the efforts of two sisters with a social conscience, who did not regard the misfortunes of the poor either with mild curiosity or with lordly indifference.

The rift between rich and poor was revealed when 60 per cent of the troop volunteers for the Boer War were rejected as medically unfit. Seventeen years later, *after* the prosperity of the Edwardians, conscription was introduced in order to produce sufficient men to hold the line in France. Ten per cent of the young men were totally unfit for service—and standards had dropped since 1900 because of the need for manpower at the Front. Forty-one point five per cent (in London 48·5 per cent) showed 'marked disabilities' and only 33 per cent were declared fully fit for service.

'Ours was a country filled with a stoic mass of those destined to live all their lives on a bare and uncertain subsistence until old age threw them on to the scrapheap of the Poor Law, underfed, badly housed, badly clothed. By the standards of 1965, or even of 1939, the rise of the working-class standard to a modest human level had hardly began.' (Hobsbawm).

But, in this very period of flaunted wealth, genuine interest in social problems was growing. Several brilliant statistical studies of working-class conditions seeking to establish the causes of poverty appeared, and in the years between 1906 and 1911 in particular, the fight for better conditions for the poor to enjoy as a right, was begun (see *page 200*).

Emancipation of women

Yet, one of the most difficult things to account for in the years before 1914 was not the humanitarian desire to 'do something' about poverty, but the tremendous energy that was thrown into the fight for 'women's rights'. In part this was a reaction to the narrow and empty life of social entertainment to which middle-class women were condemned, and against which Florence Nightingale had rebelled. In part it was due to a rising tide of opinion demanding more equality between the sexes, which had begun with changes in education (see *page 146*) and nursing, and had passed on to the protection of a woman's private property against misuse by her husband in the Married Women's Property Act (1870). The typewriter, invented in 1867, the development of shorthand and the telephone (1876) introduced a completely new range of careers to women which gave them the opportunity to be independent.

Teaching, especially at elementary level, also

Ladies at work in the telephone exchange

provided this opportunity, and it is important to note that this, and the new secretarial openings were available for girls from the better working-class homes. Shops, millinery and factory work were not the only alternatives, now, to domestic service; and already, before the war, it was becoming progressively more difficult to get capable servants. In 1902 Mrs Peel wrote:

'The young working-girl of today prefers to become a Board School mistress, a post-office clerk, a typewritress, a shop-girl, or a worker in a factory—anything rather than enter domestic service.'

This was scarcely surprising, for pay and conditions were better, and a girl would have some leisure time—in service, she would be lucky to have a free day a month. It seems incredible that middle-class housewives should have been surprised if girls chose independence in preference to the partial slavery of domestic service. Here is a description of a maid's room in 1905:

'The room had a slanting roof and was whitewashed. The whitewash was dingy and had fallen off in places. There was a rusty grate, an old iron bedstead, and a hard bed covered with a faded coverlet. Some pieces of furniture, too much worn to be used downstairs had been sent up. Under the skylight in the roof, which showed nothing but an oblong piece of dull grey sky, there stood an old battered footstool.'

Where there was no alternative for girls, domestic service remained a means of earning a livelihood—many girls escaped from the mean lives of rural hamlets to take service in small households, where the housewife would cling to a servant as a sign of shabby gentility. Some might be lucky with a local family, but many must have suffered considerable exploitation. As more opportunities for work arose, it was no surprise that between the two world wars the domestic servant virtually ceased to exist except in the great houses. Instead, new labour-saving machines, products of a new technology, which had begun to appear in Edwardian households became plentiful—vacuum cleaners, polishers, refrigerators

WHAT WILL BECOME OF THE SERVANT-GALS?

Charming Lady (showing her house to benevolent old gentleman), 'THAT'S WHERE THE HOUSEMAID SLEEPS.'
Benevolent Old Gentleman. 'DEAR ME, YOU DON'T SAY SO! ISN'T IT VERY DAMP? I SEE THE WATER GLISTENING ON THE WALLS.'
Charming Lady. 'OH, IT'S NOT TOO DAMP FOR A SERVANT!'

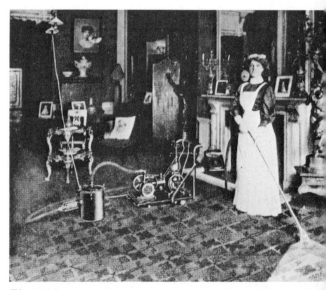

The early vacuum cleaner

and, later, washing machines. They took the drudgery out of domestic work, and as lower middle-class households purchased them, the housewife found it quite possible to continue her social round and keep up the house—a 'daily' would do the heavy work in a few hours each week (see *page 192*). The manufacture of the new machines also provided employ-

Women police, 1914

Women munition workers, 1916

ment in the suburbs of towns (often in the Home Counties) where light engineering factories were being built—there were many jobs for women on the light work of the assembly line.

But what caught the attention of contemporaries, was not this significant social change, but the demand that women should be entitled to vote at parliamentary elections. The demand was taken up by several organisations that are generally known as the 'suffragette movement', some parts of which went in for violent demonstrations.

It is difficult to see why women were refused the vote for so long, especially as they had been allowed to serve on local councils in 1907. But the 'suffragettes' had to be very courageous: they were often middle class ladies who faced social ostracism for demonstrating in public. Magistrates were hostile and physical violence from opponents was not unknown.

In 1903 Mrs Emmeline Pankhurst, widow of a local Labour leader, helped by Keir Hardie, leader of what was to be the Labour Party (see *page 216*) founded the Women's Social and Political Union and the shrill cry 'votes for women' became a frequent interruption at political meetings. Methods of peaceful persuasion failed to move the politicians, and so from 1909 onwards Christabel Pankhurst (Emmeline's daughter) led a campaign of violence, breaking windows, pouring acid onto golf greens, sometimes burning empty country houses and occasionally planting bombs. Mrs Pankhurst was in favour of reform, but she was no socialist—indeed, there was an open quarrel between her and her younger daughter Sylvia, who preached class war in the East End. Emmeline has deservedly attracted much praise for her courage and skill in organising her movement. Her career after the war was less spectacular, although, when she died in 1928, she was given an almost military-style funeral by former suffragettes, with 'General' Flora Drummond bellowing 'Women! Rally for the last time!'. Clearly, Emmeline inspired great devotion and in 1913, one of her closest followers, Emily Davison, hurled herself in front of the King's horse at the Derby and was killed. That year the Government brought

A carload of flappers arriving at the polls

in the 'Cat and Mouse' Act. Suffragettes sent to jail often went on hunger strikes. They were forcibly fed by liquid food being passed down a tube into the stomach. On occasion the food entered the lungs and caused pneumonia and at least one death. So the 'Cat and Mouse' Act permitted suffragettes on hunger strike to be released when they became very weak so that they might recover at home. Once recovered they could be recommitted to jail to complete their sentence. But neither the violent suffragettes, nor those (like the Pethwick-Lawrences) who sought the vote by peaceful means, were successful. Women got the vote because the nation recognised their importance in the community as a result of their war work (1914–18) on the land, in munition factories, as clerks, conductresses, relief workers, nurses and volunteers in auxiliary units with the forces. The 1918 Representation of the Peoples Act granted the vote to all adult males and also to women householders and wives of householders over thirty (known as 'the flapper vote'—it was thought to be influential in the results of elections in the 1920s). In 1928 a further act granted women the franchise on the same basis as men. (The age of voting was reduced to eighteen in 1969.) Women could also be returned to Parliament, and the first woman cabinet minister was Miss Bondfield in 1929. The Haldane Report (1918), which Beatrice Webb helped to write, contained a significant comment on Civil Service recruitment:

'The practical question whether women can be found suitable to perform duties comparable with those assigned to men in the Administrative (i.e. Senior) Class has to a large extent found an answer in the experience of the last four years, which has gone far to resolve any doubts upon the point. . . . We therefore think that it is no longer expedient in the public interest to exclude women on the ground of sex from situations usually entered by competition.'

What was recommended for the civil service was extended to other jobs and professions by the Sex Disqualification (Removal) Act (1919) admitting women to all employment on the same basis as men (except that often they had to leave if they married). They were soon making their presence felt on juries and on the magisterial bench as J.Ps (but the first woman King's Councillor (a senior barrister) was not appointed until 1949 and the first woman judge not until 1965). In 1923 the Matrimonial Causes Act extended to women the same conditions as applied to men over divorce proceedings, and the Guardianship of Infants Act (1925) made it possible for a wife to claim full custody of her children in the event of divorce or separation.

Yet, for all this equality by legislation, women have not come to rival men. Outside those branches of industry and commerce that are closely associated with women (fashion, especially), it is rare to find women in prominent positions. Few women have become cabinet ministers (women, as peeresses, were allowed in the House of Lords in 1958), and although 'equal pay for equal work' was admitted in the civil service and among teachers in the 1950s, there were large sections of industry where women were treated less well than men, although engaged on the same work. In 1969, however, there was something in the nature of a minor social revolution when, after several strikes by women workers, the T.U.C. declared it to be trade union policy to achieve equal pay. During the 1970s, women became increasingly vigorous in their demands for sex equality in domestic matters as well as in matters of employment and pay. The agitation took on an international flavour—1975 was known as 'International Women's Year', and there were numerous cases of women ceremonially burning their bras in public as a symbolic act against the subjection of women to the desires of males. By 1976 sex equality was supported by acts of parliament (see *page 297*).

Changes in towns

Towns grew fast during the Edwardian period and the development of municipal transport systems with horse buses and trams helped those who had to get to work early to live at some distance from their work. Living conditions were improved by the increasing number of water, gas and later electricity companies (often municipally controlled). But there was very little municipal housing for the poor, and private housing in Edwardian days was often built for sale, not for rent (as the slum dwellers of Birmingham whom Joseph Chamberlain rehoused, discovered to their cost). However, cheap lower middle class and artisan housing estates were built on the fringes of towns, served by public transport, so that the countryside around towns was rapidly consumed by suburbia. This was particularly the case round London, Birmingham and Manchester where what became known as 'conurbations' grew up. To some extent the new estates drew off population from the centre of towns, so that these actually began to decline (the City of London is a prime example of this). With cheap rail and underground transport, a new type of office worker appeared—the *commuter*, who might travel up to sixty miles a day, both ways, to work. The new building also brought more young people into the towns, and a very real drift from the countryside was apparent. Sentimentalists deplored the passing of old rural England, but the young men and women passed sufficient judgement on it when they chose the towns instead of remaining in the village. Several volumes of recollections of country life at the turn of the century have been published (Flora Thompson's *Larkrise to Candleford* is the best known), which give an unadorned picture of the narrow, brutal life of labourers and their poor living conditions. They had few recreations, their womenfolk scarcely any—and in some areas they knew that if their son did not go to work at the same farm they would be dismissed and evicted—for the 'tied cottage' remained a feature of rural life into the second half of the century, and the system was only finally abolished in 1976. It was not until the 1950s

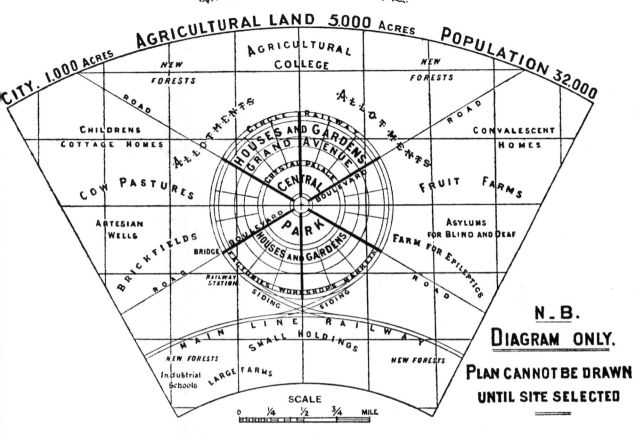

GARDEN CITY AND RURAL BELT

Howard's plan for a garden city. The plan is very basic, but shows many of the features adopted by twentieth-century planners—zoning into separate housing and industrial areas, well planned transport arrangements and a clear division between town and country

that the widespread use of the motor-car made it possible for people to live in villages and work in towns several miles away: but the recent growth in village population has not revived villages, rather it has converted older villages into suburbs of nearby towns.

As late nineteenth century towns sprawled outwards the lack of planned development became more obvious than before. Towns simply grew with no regard to amenities, the convenience of the occupants or the interests of others likely to be affected. The Government was aware of the problem, but the Housing and Town Planning Act (1909) lacked effective powers of enforcement. George Cadbury and the Lever Brothers both built new towns for their workers, planned as model estates, and the idea of combining the beauties of the

countryside with the conveniences of the town became popular and was a strong influence upon the thinking of twentieth century town planners. One of the most formative influences was Ebenezer Howard's *Tomorrow, a Peaceful Path in Reform* (1898), advocating 'Garden Cities' where the land would be communally owned and the town developed in zones, housing and factory areas separated, and a 'green belt' of preserved agricultural land surrounding the whole town. Letchworth was begun in 1903 and Welwyn Garden City in 1919, both based on Howard's principles. However, the idea was not widely followed, although the New Towns (see *page 267*) and the planning since the second world war owe much to Howard's pioneering efforts.

Parson's turbine

Gas and electricity

Sewage disposal by the end of the nineteenth century was under control and some effort was being made to provide public lavatories (and wash houses) to supplement the inadequate provision of amenities in the poorer parts of towns. Tremendous developments took place, too, in the provision of drinking water, which was sometimes piped many miles from reservoirs in the Welsh hills. By 1900 most artisan houses at least had a tap supplying water most of the day. The gas industry was well developed supplying fuel for street lighting, domestic lighting and power for domestic heating and cooking and for industry. There was tremendous variation in the quality of the gas supplied by the many different companies, many of which were too small either to extend their supply or to ensure a continuous flow of gas (this was a real problem in smaller towns). In the 1880s the industry suddenly faced a challenge from electric power. Faraday had established the principle of generating electric current in 1831 and F. H. Holmes had produced an efficient dynamo in 1857. At first the principal use for electricity was in public lighting, either lighthouses, or, with carbon arc-lamps for theatres and streets. In 1878, the arc-lamp demonstrated its superiority over gas by lighting a football match:

'The intense interest aroused by the application of the electric light to novel uses was strikingly apparent on Monday night in Sheffield, when 30,000 people gathered at Bramall Lane ground to witness a football match played under that light . . . the players being seen almost as clearly as at noon-day. The brilliancy of that light, however, dazzled the players, and sometimes caused strange blunders. The illuminating power was equal to 8,000 standard candles.'

The real challenge to gas came when a successful domestic electric bulb was developed in the 1880s jointly by the American Edison and the Englishman Swan. Dartford was the first large power station to be built (1889). Electric power was easier to install than gas piping and much more convenient for domestic use. By the 1940s it had replaced gas as the principal source of domestic and public lighting and had gone far to replacing it for heating and cooking, too. But what held back its more rapid development was the cost of producing enough electric power both for domestic and industrial uses. Some countries developed electric power quickly because of

An early London petrol bus, 1904

water power (hydro-electric power), but our power stations were largely dependent on coal usually driving turbines based on Parsons's design of 1884. Inadequate supply was a continual difficulty, as was the existence of different companies, for this meant not only that they produced current of different types but their fittings were often quite different, too, with the result that electrical domestic apparatus bought in one part of the country might be quite unusable in another unless costly adaptation was carried out. Even when a *National Grid* for the supply of electricity throughout the country was developed between the wars this problem was not overcome. Where the electricity was municipally produced, the principal streets were lit and power was provided for the electric tram, a completely new form of public transport.

Developments in transport

Horse drawn buses had become common since Shillibeer first introduced them from Paris in 1829, and horse-drawn trams appeared in the 1880s. These had two decks and seats that could face either way by swinging over the backs: they were drawn by horses along tram lines in the middle of cobbled streets, rather like the old wagon ways for coal in Northumbria. Steam trams, also, appeared, but the electric tram soon replaced them in the 1890s. Leeds was the first big city to electrify its trams in 1891. The electric power was either conducted along a central line or metal studs sunk between the wheel rails, or along overhead wires. It was not merely ease and cheapness of travel within the towns that the tram provided; often enough they gave an opportunity not available before for those living in the centre of towns to get into the countryside quickly and cheaply, for the terminus often was at the end of the town. But in Edwardian England there were many families in need of country air who could not even afford a couple of pence for the tram ride! Trams were very noisy and they were expensive to install, so that they tended to run on the principal streets and to the commercial centres rather than through the poorer residential areas of the town. They had, also, to follow the lines and it was not always easy to extend or change a route, and they tended to cause traffic congestion, even in Edwardian times. The petrol-driven omnibus, from about 1905 onwards, was both cheaper to run and could travel anywhere in town or out of it. By 1914 it was rapidly replacing the horse-drawn tram and by the 1950s it had replaced the electric tram. In rural areas, of course, the local 'bus added a new horizon to village social life; market towns were no longer places one visited

Village tranquillity disturbed (a Punch *cartoon of early motoring)*

MEMS. FOR MOTORISTS.

If you should halt at a Wayside Inn, keep an Eye on the Native Boy, or he will probably get into the Car, manage to set the Works going, and find himself kidnapped.

rarely and the local village no longer was quite so isolated a community; even so, this did not stop the young people leaving for the towns.

The first effective petrol engine was Daimler's of 1885 and the next year Karl Benz of Mannheim began selling petrol-driven 'horseless carriages'. English manufacturers were held back a little by the 1865 'Red Flag' Act requiring horseless carriages to travel at walking pace preceded by a man carrying a red flag. It was repealed in 1896 and the famous annual London to Brighton run of vintage cars commemorates the fact. Early motoring was a hazardous affair because of the frequency of breakdowns (*Punch* frequently contrasted the old and the new by a cartoon showing a horse pulling a car into a garage) and because the roads, suitable for horse traffic, were quite unsuitable for motors. Great clouds of dust were raised and the motorists needed all the protective clothing that they wore. However, private motoring remained a very rich man's pastime until the 1920s, and even in the 1940s it was unusual to find working men who could drive cars, unless it was part of their job. But it was the coming of the motor car that prompted County Councils to straighten roads and to put a new hard surface of tar-macadam down. It is due to private motoring (and to the farmer) despite the disapproval of villagers at the disturbance of the rural peace, that we have so developed a system of well-metalled roads even in remote areas.

Developments on the railways were not dramatic before the 1950s, except for the electrification of the Southern Lines (for these were furthest away from coal supplies). But in London the 'tubes' were constructed from the 1890s onwards, bringing hordes of commuters from outer suburbs and towns beyond into the City. After 1901 they were electrified, although steam trains still passed along the old Metropolitan Line until the early 1950s.

The most dramatic development in transport in this period, of course, was the appearance of the airship and the aeroplane but air travel made little direct impact upon the lives of ordinary people until the 1940s. Far less dramatic, but much more important for the people was the development of the 'safety' bicycle. There had been various designs for bicycles, including the famous penny farthing, but in 1885 J. K. Starley perfected one of modern design, with both wheels of nearly equal size and the rear one driven by a chain. The pneumatic tyre, developed by J. B. Dunlop in 1888 made bicycling (and motoring) comfortable and produced a whole new industry—the rubber industry—that, along with light engineering, often springing from cycle firms, helped to supply employment in the difficult years between the wars (many local garages began as cycle shops). Bicycling became one of the most popular pastimes of Edwardian England, and greatly helped the cause of female emancipation both in ladies' fashions and in providing opportunities for women to be released from the family and house for a few hours with their friends to go for a healthy ride. But it remained a pastime of the comfortably off because of the high cost of machines; it was only when prices began to fall as a result of the adoption of mass production methods that cycling became available for large sections of the community. In the 1920s the cycling clubs that had begun in the days before the war increased in number and whole bodies of cyclists pedalled along the newly laid 'tarmac'. Youth Hostels were opened in the 1930s for young hikers and others who joined in the popular and healthy walking and touring recreation of the time. Young cyclists, of course, often came home 'hanging on' behind a lorry (they travel too fast today for this to be a temptation) and pedestrians more familiar with the horse and cart had not yet got out of the way of calling a warning 'whip behind!' to the driver. The widespread adoption of shorts and sportswear for young women and men was probably another social effect of the bicycle.

Recreations

Youth movements were extremely popular in the first half of the century, although there was a decline in the 1930s. Baden-Powell is the obvious name here; he published *Scouting for Boys* in 1900, anxious to encourage healthy out-door activity because of the shock of realising that most of the working-class volunteers in the Boer War were either unfit, or only partially fit, for service. He was concerned also to invigorate youth in the sense of inspiring a movement for regeneration and if the Boy Scouts (1908) was not quite this sort of thing, he was at pains to stress service to the community as part of the scout's task. It rapidly became an international movement, with Baden-Powell as Chief Scout. In 1910 the Girl Guides was founded on similar lines and was as successful—it was also a sign that girls were no longer thought of merely as useful creatures to adorn the home. The Boys' Brigade (founded in Glasgow in 1883) was also very popular, but it suffered during the post-war period

An air-liner of the 1930s

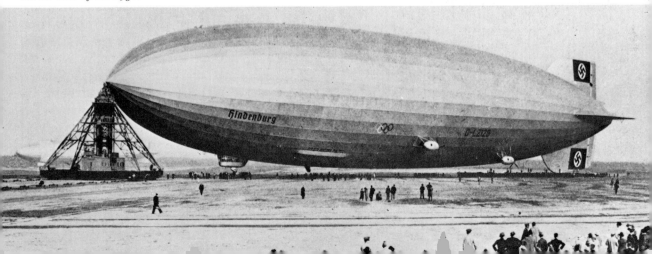

because its organisation was so obviously military. These youth societies did a great deal to bring the various classes together, especially in rural areas (but the scoutmaster was normally middle class); they were much less successful in the slum areas. Youth clubs in towns, often associated with churches or chapels, proved very popular between the wars, and there was a big extension of organised sport both by local authorities and by the National Playing Fields Association providing sports fields.

Sport, indeed, became big business. Horse racing had always attracted a great deal of money, but in the 1920s greyhound racing, using an electric 'hare', found a great following among the urban working classes. Tennis and golf became more and more popular as more facilities became available, but these tended to be sports of the better-off. It was football that caught the imagination of the workers and

Wembley Stadium on Cup Final day, 1936

gigantic stadiums were built to house great crowds of spectators watching their favourite club. It has even been suggested that if cricket helped to build the Empire, football helped to save us from class war. The first professional team was Notts County in 1862, and in the following year the Football Association was formed to supervise the conduct of the sport. The first cup-final was played at the Oval in 1872 before a crowd of 2,000. At the Crystal Palace in 1901, 110,820 spectators attended the cup final. The following year Edward VII agreed to be patron of the Football Association. London was invaded on cup-final days by working men from the North brought in by excursion train, men who wore their cloth caps, thick suits and heavy boots, who had watched their club grow from simply a group of local players and whose every Saturday afternoon had been spent supporting it. Rugby League in Lancashire and Yorkshire attracted similar support, but has never gained the national following of football (it is perhaps a pity that public schools play according to rugby union rules).

Gambling, always an English habit, spread alarmingly with racing, football pools, boxing and wrestling organised on professional lines, but somehow cricket, although the County Championship had begun in 1873 and W. G. Grace had become something of a national hero, failed to attract the gambler. Perhaps it was that the game lasted rather longer than a working man could afford to attend, perhaps, also, it was a 'gentleman's' game. The rising popularity of swimming and athletics sports (some companies provided their own tracks and sports grounds) gave a summer alternative to cricket. The first modern Olympiad was held at Athens in 1896 and the Olympic Games were to become almost a feature of international diplomacy.

Heavy drinking by the working man declined very rapidly after 1914. There were many reasons for this social change. The public health measures of local authorities had at least provided cheap pure drinking water. Then the rising standard of living, and perhaps the smaller number of children per family, made the working man's home a place for greater relaxation, especially if the house were of modern construction and had its own lavatory (nineteenth century pubs had lavatories when very few were available in the terraces around them). At the same time civic-mindedness had provided a greater number of public rooms than ever before, especially with the growth of public libraries. Temperance societies (in the 1830s they had been thought slightly mad) had had a tremendous impact and saved many families from the degradation of poverty produced by a drunkard wage earner. There were also more consumer goods and a greater range of food stuffs on which the working man might choose to spend his money, rather than on beer. Housing standards had improved and there were better facilities for the employment of his leisure hours, including, of course, a higher level of literacy, so that the working man had less incentive to escape from wretchedness into drunkenness. Also there were fewer pubs, as a result of various licensing acts, and the hours of opening, restricted severely during the first world war, remained restricted afterwards; the beer, weakened during the war, continued weaker, and the price rose. There was also less money available. Between the wars, the English working man was probably at his most sober.

If the workers were staying away from the pubs, the middle class and artisans in the towns were staying away from church and chapel. It was a tendency that had been growing since the 1880s, and it had many causes. Simple religious faith did not seem to have recovered from the blow it received at the hands of Huxley and other followers of Darwin. German biblical scholars further weakened acceptance of the scriptures and at the same time the growing acceptance of Marxist thought and the conclusions of sociological and anthropological studies, revealing that quite different pagan cultures had religious myths closely resembling those of Christianity, (Frazer's *Golden Bough* was published in 1890) dealt another intellectual blow to the Churches. Then, in 1913, Sigmund Freud's *Interpretation of Dreams* was translated into English and exercised a huge influence on intellectuals in the 1920s and 1930s. Freud's theories were not widely

understood for some time, but his ideas began as great an assault on accepted codes of behaviour and attitudes of mind as Darwin's views had launched. Irish immigration helped to check a decline among the Roman congregations, but by the 1940s even these were admitting to a falling off of observance. Two distinct attitudes arose out of this situation; first, an increased awareness among clergymen of the need for social justice in society (advocated especially by William Temple who became Archbishop of Canterbury) and secondly the Oecumenical movement for Church Reunion that began to make conspicuous strides only in the 1960s. The pattern of religious observance since the 1880s shows the Churches on the defensive even among the wealthy.

Ballroom dancing became a great vogue between the wars, and partners, sometimes man and wife (for the dance halls were where many young people met their future spouse), often entered competitions. But the traditional organised formal dance was giving way to a much more informal, much more demonstrative type of dancing. Rag-time and Jazz were coming in before 1914 and the tango, charleston fox-trot and quickstep followed rapidly.

Dress for both sexes was becoming much simpler and casual. Mass production and the growth of chain stores made clothes cheaper, too. Women's fashions were dominated by advertising and changed rapidly: to some extent this was accentuated in the 1920s by the appearance of what was called the 'Bright Young Things', young and wealthy men and women, whose hectic gaiety seemed a deliberate attempt to forget the suffering of the war years and the economic difficulties of the decade and to recapture the lost days of Edwardian opulence. There was plenty of money about in the years between the wars, but it was confined to a small number, some of whom were what Baldwin in 1918 called 'the hard faced men who had done well out of the war'. Among those with the money, week-end parties, either still on the grand Edwardian style or more intimate country cottage affairs, were in vogue. Yachting, hunting, shooting and fishing revived and bridge and whist became a favourite way of passing the evening. In the 1930s the middle

A fancy-dress party in 1925

class households would not have a domestic living in, but there would be a daily; in the kitchen there would be stainless steel cutlery, an electric iron, a washing machine, and the vacuum cleaner was in the hall cupboard. The car was in the garage outside and the gardener would call twice a week. For some, life was fairly easy and carefree.

But it was the poor who claimed most of the attention during those two generations before the second world war. It is a strange reversal in history, for before 1800 one scarcely hears of the poor. In the nineteenth century they appear in novels (often sentimentalised), and Royal Commission Reports reveal horrific living conditions (which may not have been general), but, for the most part it is the doings of the mighty that constitute history, even in the Edwardian Age when the 'condition of England' question was a burning issue. Yet, between the wars, the writings and the obvious memories are of

the sufferings of the poor. This underlines a feature of the twentieth century, the concern for social justice and the development of a more egalitarian society.

Temporary unemployment was normal in English working-class life, but the unemployment between the wars was extensive (see *page 206*) and, for some, permanent bitterness and resentment as well as a fatalistic acceptance of poverty and insecurity was the result:

'My husband never changes his dole money, but although he doesn't keep a halfpenny pocket money, still we can't manage. And we don't waste nothing. And there's no enjoyment comes out of our money— no pictures, no papers, no sports. Everything's patched and mended in our house. What's gone is past, but I wouldn't like to live a minute of my life over again. With all the struggling, you can't manage. All the struggling is just for food.'

Strikes and demonstrations underlined the discontent and there was some dangerous class feeling. Reports of victimisation of labour leaders by employers, the police and magistrates were not uncommon; in the 1930s, indeed, it seemed that the authorities were rather more tolerant of Fascist demonstrators than of Communists.

Next to unemployment, poor housing was a cause of discontent. The national average for over-crowded dwellings in the 1930s was 3·8 per cent but there were wide regional variations: infant mortality was 32 per thousand in the south, but in the north it was 134. ' "The thing that keeps me away from home", as a middle aged man, the father of two children and fond of them, said, " is the smell".' For the lucky ones who were rehoused there came a new problem: new houses meant higher rents and a bus fare to work—families economised on food to meet these payments, and malnutrition resulted. J. B. Priestley recorded his impressions in *English Journey* (1933):

'I saw again the older men, who, though they knew they were idle and useless through no fault of their own, felt defeated and somewhat tainted. Their self-respect was shredded away. Their very manhood was going. Even in England, which is no South Sea Island, there are places where a man feels he can do nothing cheerfully . . . but the maximum of unemployment today is in those districts that have a tradition of hard work, and of very little else. Life on the dole in South Devon, let us say, may be bad enough, but life on the dole on Tyneside is a great deal worse.'

This was England just over a generation ago. How far we have moved in terms of better conditions and social happiness can be gauged only by contrasting Priestley's picture with the England that you know and experience today.

Mass communication

An obviously new feature of twentieth-century life is the way in which public opinion can be moulded by the organs of mass communication. Newspapers and magazines, important since the eighteenth century as formulators of popular taste and opinions, have gained a great ascendancy today. Advertisements, skilfully devised, can have a tremendous impact, and between the wars radio broadcasting has greatly enlarged the scope for controlling the reactions of public opinion. But in the period 1880 to 1940 the national press has been the most important organ of communication for the general public, and the men who built up the popular press have all (understandably) aspired to great political influence.

In 1880 George Newnes launched *Tit Bits*, its style well suited to people who could read only a little—the products of the 1870 Act. Alfred Harmsworth launched the *Daily Mail* (1896) using much the same techniques, but adding racy reports of crimes. This was the popular press, 'Written by office boys for office boys', complained Lord Salisbury stuffily, but the readers were not all poor or ill-educated. In 1904, the *Daily Mirror*, a tabloid with more illustration than text, proved another huge success. In 1905 Harmsworth became Lord Northcliffe (his brother became Lord Rothermere in 1913) and in 1908 he purchased *The Times*. 'People like a good hate', Northcliffe used to say, and he ran his papers promoting one campaign after another with an eye to sales rather than to anything else. Lord Beaverbrook with the *Daily Express* for forty years quite unashamedly ran campaigns to 'get the people on his side'. He was not always successful, but he proved an invaluable ally to the Conservative Party. Large circulations meant higher advertising revenues and cheaper production costs, but they also meant concentrating the newspaper industry into a few hands, so that newspaper owners wielded a tremendous influence. In the 1930s every large paper indulged in a frantic race for a bigger circulation offering all sorts of prizes and competitions. In the struggle many local papers went out of business and the national dailies took their place.

Wireless telegraphy and the telephone made a great difference not only to the spreading of news, but also to businessmen. Electric telegraph had been used by the railways since 1843 and before 1900 London had been linked with most of the important capitals in the world by submarine cable, so that messages sent in morse could travel round the world in a matter of minutes. In 1876 Alexander Bell patented the telephone: it was now possible to talk to people miles away. So much chaos arose when private companies installed their own systems that the Government acquired control of the telephone system, operating it through the Post Office (an early example of nationalisation—except that Hull retains its municipal service today). The telephone created a whole new industry as well as career openings for women, and it greatly enlarged the life of people living in isolated places (if they could afford the telephone).

Wireless telegraphy is attributed to Marconi, although much of the theoretical work was done by Clark Maxwell and Hertz. By 1899, Marconi was transmitting messages across the Channel in all weathers and in 1901 he transmitted across the Atlantic. The invention revolutionised communications, especially at sea: it was how Dr Crippen was arrested for murder, when on his way to America in 1910.

In 1920, the Marconi Company experimented by broadcasting a concert by Dame Nellie Melba, the opera singer. Broadcasting had become a fact. But to exploit the invention required considerable finance, and the danger was that commercial interests would control broadcasting for purely commercial purposes. In consequence, despite the pressure for commercial radio, a Conservative Government in 1922 created the British Broadcasting Company with a monopoly of broadcasting. The first General Manager was John (created Lord in 1940) Reith whose strong guiding hand gave British broadcasting its special character combining education with entertainment. Great pressure for commercial radio continued, but in 1926 the British Broadcasting Corporation (B.B.C.) was established to prevent commercial broadcasting for a generation. Radio Luxemburg, however, soon appeared as a 'pirate' commercial station. The early receivers, called 'crystal sets', used headphones, but an effective loud speaker had been developed by 1924. A new force in communication that brought the spoken word into the home, had been created. However, one must not exaggerate its impact, for by 1927 only two and one-quarter million licences had been issued and radio remained something of a luxury until the 1940s. It came into its own during the war, for Sir Winston Churchill gave a series of broadcasts to the nation-at-arms that were epoch-making both as speeches and as examples of radio communication. Television was also at first very much of a luxury, although broadcasts from Alexandra Palace began in 1936. (The first outside T.V. broadcast was of the coronation procession of George VI.) Television was the product of many investigators, but the man most responsible, probably, was James Logie Baird who had relayed pictures on a cathode ray tube receiver in 1933 after years of experimenting. By the 1950s television had entered almost every home and largely displaced newspapers and radio as the principal means of mass communication. It has also displaced the cinema.

The English pioneers of moving pictures were John Rudge and William Friese Green whose experiments began in Bath. Their first 'movie' was of traffic at Hyde Park Corner in January 1889. It is remarkable that the commercial world simply ignored the event, but by the end of the century films

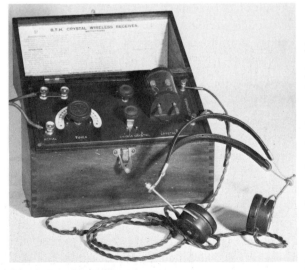

The early radio receiver

were being made in some quantity and the first half of the twentieth century was to see both the rise and fall of the cinema and the creation of a huge consumer goods industry in amateur photography.

By 1914, Hollywood, with natural advantages of scenery and climate, had established a predominant position in the film industry. But the quality of early films was so poor that they were called 'shakies'. There was no sound track and captions roughly indicated the dialogue, whilst a pianist played a frantic non-stop accompaniment to the film. Some of the early films were of high merit and artistery, but most had no lasting quality, for the industry was based on box-office success. In order to encourage British films, a Conservative government in 1927 passed the Cinematographic Films Act limiting the importation of Hollywood films. A government subsidy was given to the industry in the 1930s and some remarkable films were produced at the Pinewood Studios. 'Talkies' arrived in 1929 and many of the stars of silent days had to be replaced. Cinemas had now been built in every town and several were opened in the larger towns, showing several films a week. 'Going to the flicks' became as much a part of life as any form of mass entertainment, and, with its immediate impact on the mind, the cinema could have become a tremendous educative

force. But it remained purely an entertainment concern, a possible escape from the dreary present: 'queues stand in the rain to buy three hours of warmth, comfort and star-solace for lives spent in factories and counting houses or shopping in dismal little streets'. Colour films arrived in the 1930s and further extravagant developments, like '3 D' cinema in the late 1940s and the exceptionally wide screen in the 1950s. But no one, looking at the cinema queues in 1950 would have predicted that, within twenty years there would be towns without a cinema where once there had been several, and that those surviving would be half empty except when given over to a Bingo night. This is the measure of the impact of television and the extent of choice of entertainment available to the young of today.

Since the 1880s gigantic changes have occurred in England. The most obvious have been the growth of direct Government interference in the daily lives of individuals and the gradual removal of dire poverty. New inventions have enlarged the lives of all classes and created employment opportunities that present young people today with a range of career choices that have never been so easily available to any generation before. Living conditions have improved immeasurably and England has become a happier place.

'Going to the flicks', a queue outside a cinema

15 · The widening scope of government

The Edwardian crowd—children waiting for a free dinner

If you look at a photograph of a crowd of Edwardian working-class people, you will see that many were of stunted growth, and the children had peculiarly swollen faces and bowed legs, with pronounced signs of rickets (a disease almost unknown today because of our better dieting). Standards of living had been rising for the previous fifty years, but the poor were still very poor indeed. Their employment was not always regular, and a single accident, like the principal wage-earner being off with 'flu, could send a family into real need. Because wages were so low among the lower paid, even families who strove to 'keep above the water line' could scarcely manage to avoid getting into debt. There was a pattern of poverty among the labouring class: they tended to reach a peak of earnings between the ages of eighteen and twenty-five. They probably lived with their parents and helped support them. Then they married and whilst the wife worked they lived relatively well. But as children were born, even if they died in infancy, family earnings dropped because the wife stayed at home, whilst family costs rose. By the age of thirty a labourer's family was in poverty. He

could put little by for periods of illness and old age.

It is difficult for us to believe that such widespread poverty continued in the prosperous Edwardian age; but times were beginning to get harder, for prices were rising after 1900 and the wages of the poor bought less. Drunkenness was declining (this was always a vice among the poor: among the rich it was merely an affliction), but people were spending more on tobacco, especially as the factory-made cigarette was beginning to displace the self-rolled cigarette and pipe. Travel was cheap, but the poor could not afford it: lower-class housing was relatively cheap (especially as there was little internal plumbing—one tap in the kitchen and no hot water system) but the poor stood little chance of getting a mortgage.

Over-crowding was still the condition of the working class. In the countryside it was less obvious than in the towns, but it was there: in a Somerset two-roomed cottage (without plumbing) two girls and three boys slept in one room and the mother and three children slept in the other. The 'cottager' was badly off indeed. The idea of a bath being installed in a cottage struck society ladies as mildly funny;

A pawn shop in Edwardian England

House and Gardens in 1906 commented quite happily: 'It must be frankly admitted that the average cottager would have little use for it.' When the agricultural labourers' wage was 17s 6d a week (14s 6d in Oxfordshire) there was little left to spend after bread and bare necessities had been paid for.

Economic security was denied the urban poor as well. Housing, better than a generation before, was still of low quality and lacking in most amenities. Overcrowding was common, and the threat of eviction for failing to pay rent was a very real one indeed. Underfed children were commonly seen without shoes, although fewer than in the previous generation. The pawn-broker was essential to the housewife: father's suit (if he was lucky enough to have one) went into pawn on Tuesday for 3s, to be redeemed on Saturday for 3s 6d—a fantastic rate of interest, but the ready money was needed and the

practice was so common that people accepted it as normal. The tallyman was equally useful to the housewife: she bought domestic requirements from him on the 'never never' as they called it, for 'hire purchase' or 'extended repayment' were terms they neither understood, nor, had they known of them, would they have expected such schemes to apply to the likes of them. Poverty was normal, its suffering was less bitter to those who never anticipated anything better. If beer drinking was declining, however, there were still fights for the wage packet between anxious wives and reckless husbands—indeed, some wise wives would go to the foreman to get loans for the family's food, to be deducted from the wage packet at the end of the week, before the husband got the wages. A poor housewife could easily destroy a marriage, for one had to be very careful to 'make ends meet'. Extra expenditure meant hungry bellies: 'if there's anything extra to buy, such as a pair of boots for one of the children, me and the children goes without dinner', said one housewife, speaking for very many. It is easy to see why the working class should have resisted compulsory school attendance, for it withdrew from them the source of a little extra money from their children's earnings. If it cost 21s 8d to keep a family of five out of poverty, then labourers could never rise above poverty, for their wage was between 18 and 21 shillings. Poverty would only begin to be checked when the lower-paid worker was paid more.

Even so, there was a lower level of poverty still, as the novelist Jack London reported, sickened to see unemployed men fight for the scraps from hospital kitchens:

'The hospital scraps ... were heaped on a huge platter in an indescribable mess—pieces of bread, chunks of grease and fat pork, the burnt skin from the outside of roasted joints, bones, in short, all the leavings from the fingers and mouths of the sick ones suffering from all manner of diseases. Into this mess the men plunged their hands, pawing, turning over, examining, rejecting and scrambling for. It wasn't pretty. Pigs couldn't have done worse. But the poor devils were hungry.'

Was it any wonder that there was a massive difference in mortality between the wealthy and the poorer areas of towns, even though the mortality rate was dropping dramatically for the country as a whole? In the West End, the average length of life was 55 years in 1901. In the East End it was thirty years, and one in four died a pauper. The East End was a different world. It stood as a bitter indictment of the glitter of the Edwardian Age. A thirteen-year-old public school boy was on average five inches taller and eleven pounds heavier than a Board School boy. Eighteen per cent of children born in the West End, died before they were five: in the East End this mortality was 55 per cent. It was still customary to insure infants at a half-penny a week in order to have some ready money if one died.

School attendance officers had to track down truants who were earning a much needed few

shillings. Whatever the law said children worked in the smaller mines and factories—your grandparents might even remember actual cases. In Lancashire and the north there existed the 'half-time' system, (see page 148). Mornings, six to twelve, were at the mill, and school in the afternoon for one week and school followed by the afternoon shift in the mill the following week. By 1900 this system affected largely those in their last year at school and probably wasted it entirely—although it added a few shillings to the family budget and kept the education rate down, for there was no need to supply accommodation or teaching staff for half the top class. There were 'free places' at local grammar schools, which fortunate working-class children might take up and thus gradually rise in the social scale—but too often the financial sacrifice of covering the extra clothes needed could not be borne and so many places were not taken up—even when they were, academically promising youngsters had to leave early because their parents could not keep them indefinitely at school and often required them to leave as soon as they reached fourteen.

But if poverty was normal, it was harder to bear, both because of the growing gap between the poor and the wealthy, and because opportunities for rising above poverty were just beginning to appear. Private charity there was in plenty: but it merely touched the surface of a grave problem which needed the full power of the State to solve.

The writers

Several prominent writers threw emphasis on the social problem, (notably the plays of G. B. Shaw and the novels of Wells and Galsworthy), while the Fabians produced pamphlets, and official Reports were published. Some good sociological surveys appeared, like Chiozza Money's *Riches and Poverty* (1905) and Charles Masterman's *The Condition of England* (1910). The Rev. Andrew Mearns published in 1883, *The Bitter Cry of Outcast London*, which caused a great stir for it showed conditions in some quarters had not greatly improved since Chadwick's great Report of 1842 (see page 106), and other works showed that Mearns did not exaggerate. In 1890 General William Booth produced *In Darkest England—And the Way Out* (see *page 138*):

'The denizens of Darkest England, for whom I appeal, are (1) those who, having no capital of their own, would in a month be dead from sheer starvation were they exclusively dependent upon the money earned by their own work; and (2) those who by their utmost exertions are unable to attain the regulation allowance of food which the law prescribes as indispensable even for the worst criminals in our gaols. . . .
'I sorrowfully admit that it would be Utopian in our present social arrangements to dream of obtaining for every honest Englishman a gaol standard of all the necessaries of life.'

Perhaps the most effective work of all, although it could not have been widely read, was a series of volumes produced by a team of investigators (among whom was Beatrice Webb), led by Charles Booth, and published under the title of *The Life and Labour of the People in London* (1886–1903). Booth found that 30 per cent of Londoners lived in depressed conditions:

	Percentage of population
Middle and Upper classes	17·8
Comfortable working classes (including servants)	51·5
The Poor (18s to 21s wkly)	22·3
The Very Poor (under 18s)	8·4

Seventy per cent, therefore, lived in comfort, itself a tremendous advance over any other century; but 30 per cent earned less than enough to secure a proper livelihood. Low wages were the root cause. The evidence that Booth's clear sociological and statistical survey revealed made it impossible any longer to dismiss poverty as the reward of intemperance or idleness, or to suppose poverty was confined to a small proportion only of the population. Certainly, Booth showed that drunkenness and improvidence also were real causes of poverty, but only to a limited extent; more serious were temporary

unemployment and sickness, and low wages, which, he claimed, accounted for 68 per cent of London poverty (Chadwick had already hinted at this in his Poor Law Report of 1834).

London, a great metropolis, had problems peculiar to itself. But it came as a shock to discover that what was true of London was also true of local county towns: in 1899 Seebohm Rowntree produced his study of York, which he called *Poverty: A Study of Town Life*. He calculated a poverty line of seven shillings a week for a single male, or 37s 4d for a family of eight. In York 43·4 per cent of wage-earners fell below this line—27·8 per cent of the city population.

'Families regarded as living in poverty were grouped under two heads: (a) Families whose total earnings were insufficient to obtain the minimum necessaries for the maintenance of merely physical efficiency. Poverty falling under this head was described as "primary" poverty. (b) Families whose total earnings would have been sufficient for the maintenance of merely physical efficiency were it not that some portion of it was absorbed by other expenditure, either useful or wasteful. Poverty falling under this head was described as "secondary" poverty.'

A great radical historian, R. H. Tawney put the point fully:

'The problem of poverty is not primarily to assist individuals who are exceptionally unfortunate. It is to make the normal conditions under which masses of men work and live such that they may lead a healthy, independent and self-respecting life when they are *not* exceptionally unfortunate.'

But to achieve this ideal required the full powers of the State. And the Liberal Party, returned with a huge majority in 1906 (but conscious of a significant number of Labour Party M.P.s at its back), set itself the task of organising the relief of at least some of the poverty by developing the powers of the State. One of their leaders, Winston Churchill, spoke of 'drawing a line below which we will not allow persons to live and labour'. Between 1906 and 1914 many of the administrative lines upon which the

Welfare State of today was to develop were laid down, in particular there was a 'new horizon' in social legislation for the Liberals were prepared to go further than the Victorians by allowing the State to take an active part in organising people's actual lives. Many objected that the independence and vigour of individual citizens would be seriously undermined, for they feared the poor would become indolent if too much help was given them by the State. The Liberals persisted, however, and their measures raised a storm of protest that added to the political hysteria in the years before the war. Indeed, the politics of these years are so dramatic, that it is easy to exaggerate the work that the Liberals actually achieved. By 1914, they had improved on the work of their predecessors, enlarged the field of direct State aid, and pointed the way to the future. They had not produced a social revolution, as their opponents predicted. That social revolution had to wait until after the second world war. For the first forty years of the century, poverty was writ large in the land, and the extravagance of the few wealthy classes merely drew attention to it.

The Liberal social reforms had to be paid for, and one of their most impressive measures was the 'People's Budget' of 1909, devised by Lloyd George, Chancellor of the Exchequer, himself a man of humble upbringing. The wealthy were soon up in arms at his budget proposals, insisting that they were being mulcted to pay for relief of indolent poor, and the House of Lords threw out the Budget in 1909. This began a crisis that ended in the abrogation of the Lords' powers over finance by the Parliament Act of 1911, and adding to the hysteria. Yet the proposals were not very extreme: for all the fuss, there was virtually no *redistribution of income* (when money is withdrawn from one section of the community to be distributed amongst others). After paying his income tax, the bachelor of 1903 with £10,000 a year retained £9,375: in 1913 he retained £9,242. In 1960 he retained £4,642!

Regulating the conditions of the workers

A Conservative government in 1897 passed an Employers' Liability Act making the employer liable to pay compensation for any industrial injury received. This was an important declaration of principle but its trouble was that the worker himself had to prove his own case. This could often be difficult and costly. The measure was greatly strengthened by the Workmen's Compensation Act of 1906 (and a second in 1923), but the trouble was that as firms did not have to insure themselves against the risk of claims for industrial injury, small firms often chose to declare themselves bankrupt rather than meet a heavy claim, so the injured workman was left with nothing. The acts did, however, encourage the adoption of safer processes.

The Factory and Workshop Consolidation Act (1901) not only drew together the principal parts of Victorian factory acts, but tried to enforce safety regulations and to ensure that workers paid on piece-rates received fair treatment. It was supplemented by a whole series of regulations governing new processes, and by a Merchant Shipping Act in 1906. Conditions of employment in shops were regulated by a Shop Act in 1904 that forbade 'living in' (assistants having to live in the same building as the shop, often in bad conditions and frequently exploited) and allowed an early closing day. These

Shop workers protesting against 'living in'

regulations were strengthened by a further Act in 1911. It was not until 1937, however, that the definition of 'factory' was extended to almost any place of work. The Factory Act of 1937 was a strong measure, requiring a forty-eight hour week for women and young persons, with no work after 1 p.m. on Saturdays, or a half-day off in lieu. Working conditions were further regulated and medical supervision extended. The Factory Inspectorate (now including women) was increased to enforce the act.

There were also advances in regulating trades where workers were not able to defend themselves through trade unions. The 'sweated trades' were the worst offenders here. These were trades where much of the work was still done by hand and paid for on a piece-rate basis, often being carried out at home or in the house of a small master—much as in the days of the domestic system. Tailoring, with long hours

in small masters' houses that inspectors could not control, was the principal offender here. If an inspector came to the street, news was passed from house to house, and workers would be crowded into bedrooms which he had no power to enter. The small masters were themselves exploited by clothes merchants. They got orders for cheap clothing and distributed the necessary tasks into small jobs requiring little skill that could be done quickly. By dividing his labour force in this way he speeded production, but seriously hampered any chance of betterment his employees might have. But he made small profit himself: cloth shirts went for seven shillings a dozen complete. When serious massacres of Jews (pogroms) occurred in Tsarist Russia in the 1890s, the influx of Jewish refugees was rapidly absorbed into the sweated tailoring trades of East London (Whitechapel was particularly notorious for 'sweat shops') and the low standard of living that the

The sweated workshop

refugees had experienced enabled masters to reduce wages still further.

It was necessary to protect 'sweated workers' from exploitation. The method adopted was one already in use in some trades in the North and Midlands, namely, an arbitration committee composed of workers, masters and merchants which decided the rate to be paid for particular jobs. The Trade Boards Act (1909) established Trade Boards on this pattern for tailoring, and, later, lace making, box making, chain making and other trades. The Board of Trade was empowered to enforce the rate agreed upon, in the courts if necessary. This was a great step forward, but it was still confined to particular trades. The Act was amended in 1918 to cover all trades 'where no adequate machinery for the effective regulation of wages' existed. By 1922 some three million workers were covered by Trade Boards.

During the first world war plans were made to extend this idea. The Whitley Committee (1917–18) recommended a National Joint Industrial Council for each well organised industry, to represent management and labour, with district councils to settle special local matters. The trade unions shunned the idea since it was their principal function to do just this. However, *Whitley Councils* were formed for the less well organised trades, like pottery, road transport and building. There were sixty-four Whitley Councils by 1932.

Labour exchanges

Another example of State action directly affecting individual lives were labour exchanges established for the purpose of advertising vacancies to the unemployed, unlike Owen's Exchange of 1832 (see *page 159*). William Beveridge, later to have great influence on social policy after the second world war, published *Unemployment, a Problem of Industry* (1909), and this, together with German experience, persuaded Winston Churchill to begin labour exchanges in 1909. Hitherto, an unemployed man had little help in finding work. He had to tramp from factory to workshop in search of 'Hands Wanted' notices, walking round his neighbourhood and often

An early Labour Exchange

missing a job simply because he happened not to be there at the moment. Trade unions had helped by keeping a register of vacancies, but the registers were not extensive and not always up to date. The idea of the labour exchanges was to have a local office at which workers could call to get information of vacancies supplied by local employers. Eventually a national system of offices was built up, which made it possible to pass news of particular vacancies for skilled men around the country. Also, as they gained experience, the managers of local offices could interview young men and help them in their choice of career. At first, however, there was virtually no information about different industrial processes available (an odd situation for the former 'workshop of the world'!) and quite unsuitable jobs were sometimes offered. It took a little while for the effect of this to wear off and for workers to have confidence in the offices. But the exchanges grew in reputation and influence. Today they continue their work as an integral part of the Welfare State, and through the Youth Employment Service offer advice to school leavers on careers and further education courses, as well as arranging careers conferences and short experience courses.

Care of children

The twentieth century has laid increasing emphasis upon the welfare of children and has been prepared to interfere with family relationships to ensure proper treatment for a child. In 1901 the infant death rate was 151 per 1,000, and one of the causes was insufficient care of babies. Infant Welfare Centres, offering advice, a little rudimentary medical attention, and distributing free milk to poor and needy mothers, appeared first at St. Helens in 1899. By 1906 there were a dozen of them, and the Liberal government gave financial assistance to local authorities to open more. Manchester pioneered the idea of 'health visitors' to help and advise young mothers (for few working-class families could afford to call in the doctor except in cases of extreme emergency). Midwives were still poorly trained and difficult deliveries frequently resulted in permanent damage to mother and child, if not in their death. At St. Pancras, a 'school for mothers' opened. Wherever such 'schools', health visitors or welfare centres existed, infant mortality fell. By 1912 the national figure was 95 per 1,000 (it is below 20 today).

A school medical inspection, 1912

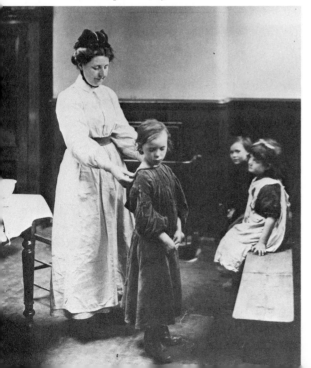

In 1906 a special Education Act permitted local authorities to provide meals for school children desperately in need, free of charge. It was a small beginning to the school meals service that today supplies subsidised meals for many school children. The following year the school medical inspection service began, vigorously pressed by Sir George Newman, the Chief Medical Officer of the Board of Education from 1907 to 1935, who also encouraged the establishment of treatment centres to follow-up medical inspection with necessary treatment. In this way the grosser illnesses could be diagnosed earlier and checked—and advice on bodily cleanliness also given. In working-class areas, where medical attendance was a rarity, these quick school inspections made a great contribution to better health.

Then, in 1908, the 'Children's Charter' (Children's Act) was passed, providing a series of regulations to protect children from harmful influences. This is the act that prohibits you from pubs and purchasing cigarettes for your own use, and from sending those under 14 to prison. The Borstal system, which was to last for sixty years and in its time to be acknowledged as one of the most advanced methods of dealing with young offenders, was introduced in 1909, so that young persons would not mix with hardened criminals. Juvenile and Probationary Courts were also established, for the causes of juvenile crime are frequently quite different from adult crime and call for different treatment. The Children and Young Persons Act (1933) extended protection against cruelty to children, and the use of juvenile courts was extended.

Social security

Perhaps the biggest social change of this century has come in the field of social security. Instead of leaving to the individual the task of providing for his family, the State has today assumed responsibility for the individual's welfare, from the cradle to the grave. This is the meaning of the Welfare State. But it appeared in this fully developed form only after the second world war.

A landmark on the road to the Welfare State was

the Royal Commission Report on the Poor Law (1909). It revealed how many old people died in destitution in the Poor Law hospitals, and how, despite improvements in recent years, conditions in the workhouses were still so very bad that the poor retained a deep-seated dread of the workhouse. Infants were often removed from their mothers to be left with the aged or the feeble-minded (about 33 per cent of infants died each year in the workhouses) and young and old, healthy and ill, all mixed with the frankly insane. George Lansbury told of a visit to the Poplar workhouse:

'I inspected the supper of oatmeal porridge. On this occasion the food was served up with pieces of black stuff floating around. On examination we discovered it to be rat and mice manure. I called for the Chief Officer, who immediately argued against me, saying the porridge was good and wholesome. "Very good, madam!" said I, taking up a basinful and a spoon, "here you are, eat one mouthful and I will acknowledge I am wrong." '

The days of the Andover scandal were over (see *page 161*), but there was still a long way to go. The 1909 Commission found

'idiots who are physically offensive and mischievous, or so noisy as to create a disturbance by day and by night with their howls, living in ordinary wards. . . . We have seen imbeciles annoying the same, and the same tormenting the imbeciles. We have seen half-witted women nursing the sick, feeble-minded women in charge of the babies, and imbecile old men put to look after boys out of school-hours.'

Lack of money and staff lay at the root of these troubles. So did the old idea that the poor were indolent and ought to be made to work. Some authorities gave out-door relief to the unemployed, provided they consented to the 'labour test' (usually stone-breaking in a labour yard). Poplar workhouse, in the middle of London's casual dock labour, earned a reputation for especial severity with the 'labour test'. It was to be a different story when George Lansbury became mayor of Poplar! In 1905 the Unemployed Workman's Act per-

mitted local authorities to raise money through the rates to help the unemployed—the Liberals in 1906 supplemented this with a Treasury grant. Clearly, the idea that unemployment resulted from casual labour and the state of the economy, was being recognised. It was in 1905 that the Poplar Board of Poor Law Guardians demanded that the relief of unemployment should come from national, not local sources, since the poorer boroughs had to carry the heaviest burdens and were least able to do so.

In their Minority Report for the Poor Law Commission of 1909, the Webbs wanted to break up the Old Poor Law because it was no longer relevant to modern conditions. Poverty, they argued, arose from many causes of which low wages, sickness, the casual nature of employment and trade depressions were among the most important. These were beyond the control of any worker, and 'the enforced idleness and prolonged privation characteristic of unemployment' meant first a loss of production to the nation and secondly 'degradation and deterioration of character and physique' for the worker. There were many different types of unemployment, all requiring different treatment; and they concluded:

'That, in our judgment, no successful dealing with the problem is possible unless provision is simultaneously made in ways suited to their several needs and deserts for all the various sections of the Unemployed by one and the same Authority.'

But if the ideas of the Webbs were to be those that inspired reform of the Poor Law in the future, there was no immediate action on their Report.

Old-age pensions

Low wages and the usual set-backs of periodic unemployment without any payments, and occasional sickness, meant that very, very few of the working class could make any really effective provision for their old age: they simply relied on their children. The idea of old-age pensions was widely supported by the beginning of the twentieth century, and in 1908 Asquith introduced a Bill. It did not provide pensions as of right, but proposed a noncontributory pension of 5 shillings a week (7s 6d for married couples) to those over seventy, whose income was less than £31 10s a year. The pension came into force in 1909. Over three-fifths of the over-seventies qualified for pensions: there were great variations in the numbers of pensioners in various towns. In Bournemouth there were 267 per 1,000 of the population, in Bermondsey 778, in Northamptonshire 801. But at the same time, there was a huge drop in the numbers of elderly paupers. Those on out-door relief fell from 168,096 in 1906 to 8,563 in 1913, at a time when prices were rising. Clearly, in one sense, pensions were paying for themselves, as well as granting easier conditions of life to the aged!

National Insurance Scheme, 1911

It was German experience and the advice of William Beveridge again that led Lloyd George to produce a National Insurance Scheme in 1911 that would combine insurance against sickness and unemployment and so help to overcome a contributory cause of poverty. It was to be paid for by compulsory contributions from the worker, the employer and the State—a three-sided arrangement that has been adopted throughout the world as the normal pattern for social security funds.

The sickness insurance scheme provided for weekly sickness benefit payments over a limited period, a maternity benefit, and medical treatment, including medicines, through a registered doctor who would put the worker on his 'panel'. Instead of creating a Government department to administer the funds, Lloyd George chose to work through existing Friendly Societies which had applied to be 'approved'. This was a mistake, for some were badly run and could only supply the bare minimum the law required, while others could afford to pay additional benefits and help with specialist treatment, or a period in a convalescent home. In 1916 the Ministry of Labour was created to supervise and run the whole scheme.

All manual and non-manual workers earning less than £160 a year, were included in the scheme, membership of which was compulsory. Contributions were deducted before wages were paid.

In order to obtain unemployment benefit, a worker had first to register with a labour exchange (called employment exchange in 1917) and be prepared to accept any suitable job offered him. If he refused a job he could not draw benefit. But the unemployment insurance was available *only* for about 2,250,000 workers confined to building construction, shipbuilding and engineering. This part of the 1911 scheme was far from comprehensive and was never intended to guarantee a minimum subsistence level to workers, but simply to provide a temporary assistance while a man found other work. All got the same benefit, whether bachelor or family man. The 1911 scheme was not conceived on the same basis as the Welfare State of today.

'War Socialism': 1914–18

One of the most significant achievements of the first world war was so to familiarise the British with the facts of direct government control that nineteenth-century ideas of *laissez-faire*, although they did not disappear by any means, lost a great deal of their force. As the war progressed and it became obvious that we were fighting for survival, the coalition government took many steps to enlarge the sphere of government, steps that were not dismantled after the war. But the government only did this from necessity. Nevertheless, it represented a very significant change in attitude, taken in the stress of total war—a change from which there was to be no turning back.

Serious food shortages were obvious in 1916 because of the success of the German U-boats in the Atlantic. To meet the situation, the government adopted a series of measures that were known as 'war socialism'. Import licensing, control of home production, especially agriculture (see *page 238*) and finally a primitive form of food rationing had to be introduced. In 1917 five new Departments of State were established for shipping, labour, food, national service and food-production. Businessmen headed the new ministries. But there was no over-spill plan: 'like the country at large, the government entered war socialism backwards, and were surprised at what

No. G 677501 MINISTRY OF FOOD.
SUGAR
REGISTRATION CARD.

I desire to purchase my supplies of Sugar for my household from:—

A. *Retailer's Name* J. Lyons & Co Ld

   Address Cadbury Hall

I hereby declare that no other Sugar Registration Card has been signed on behalf of my household.

B. *Signature* Arthur Griffiths

   Address 70 Burbage Road. S.E. 24

   Date 22nd Sept 1917.

5. No. of persons.................... Initials....A.G....

District ....

This part to be kept by the Retailer.

MINISTRY OF FOOD.

No. G 677501 SUGAR
REGISTRATION CARD.

C. *Name* Griffiths Arthur

   Address 70 Burbage Road
   S.E. 24

Retailer with whom the Householder has registered:—

D. *Signature of Retailer* J. Lyons & Co Ld

   Address Cadbury Hall

5. No. of persons.................... Initials....A.G....

District ....

S.2.

This part to be kept by the Householder.

A ration book and coupons, 1918

they had done'. Considerable powers of requisitioning were granted (though they were rarely used) and even food rationing was in effect voluntary, since it was left largely in the hands of retailers. A much stricter form of rationing was introduced in 1918 simply because the situation had deteriorated. There were ration books and coupons, and subsidies were made to stabilise bread prices. There was also an attempt to control prices generally in order to stabilise the cost of living that rocketed during the war. These measures were never adopted as a system, but were, like conscription (perhaps the greatest invasion of individual liberty by the State), emergency measures for the war period. But they created a new attitude with regard to government control that survived the war.

This was important, because the years between the two world wars were troubled years where trade, finance and employment were unsettled. Economists and governments the world over had not yet learned to handle national economies, indeed, the study of economics in the 1920s was still to some extent in its infancy. The period has been called the 'economic doldrums' (see *page 225*). Although over the period as a whole prices fell, so that real wages rose, it was dominated by a quite new feature in the British economy: long-term unemployment, especially in the hitherto prosperous North, without the chance of a job however hard one tried. Between 1921 and 1939 there were never less than a million unemployed and in 1932, the worst year, it reached 2,750,000 (22·4 per cent of all workers).

In these conditions, the unemployment scheme was enlarged. In 1920 it was extended to nearly all workers (agricultural workers were included in 1936), and since unemployment lasted for such long periods, 'extended benefits' had to be allowed, continuing the payments after the official entitlement had been exhausted. These extended payments of unemployment benefit to those 'genuinely seeking work' were nicknamed '*the dole*' (1921). They were to continue until the second world war, and they made it impossible for the insurance scheme to be self-financing. In 1922 the government passed two acts that were a milestone on the road to social security. The Unemployment Insurance Act, and the Dependents Allowances Act acknowledging that a man with a family to support needed more 'dole' than a bachelor, converted what had begun as self-financing insurance scheme into an undertaking by the government to meet the expenses of unemployment out of taxation. Without intending it, the government had assumed the position of guaranteeing something like a minimum income to its citizens.

But this had to be paid for, so that, despite government economies, the level of taxation remained high. Rising costs also led in 1925 to Neville Chamberlain's Contributory Old Age Pensions Act. The 1908 pension had been increased after the war to 10 shillings (1919): the 1925 Act allowed 10 shillings a week for widows and 7s 6d for orphans and provided the 10 shillings old-age pension at sixty-five for the worker and his wife. But pensions were now made contributory through the National Insurance Scheme, and weekly contributions by both employer and employee were increased to cover the new charges.

The men who were responsible for the new measures of social security in the 1920s were not idealists but hard-headed businessmen and politicians. Their measures were far from generous and did little more than prevent those already on the fringe of poverty from sinking into destitution, yet they deserve more credit than they have been given for seizing their responsibilities and passing measures of relief. They were not the men to devise the Welfare State as we know it, but at least they did not impede its development.

Provision of cheap housing

Since the mid-nineteenth century there had been

A slum family at home, 1920

by-laws regulating building standards, and permissive acts, like the Artisans Dwellings Act (1875), had authorised slum-clearance. Yet 'jerry-building' remained a feature of cheap housing (indeed, it is with us still). Slums often remained untouched until the 1920s and 1930s, except for the laying of water-pipes and sewers—the 'pail system' was common in Lancashire throughout Edwardian days, and the water closet remained a luxury for working-class housing until the 1930s. Few working men could buy their homes; families lived in rented accommodation, often one or two rooms. Rents were high—a couple might pay 2s 6d a week simply to sleep on the floor.

The medical officers of the Poor Law Unions and social investigators like Charles Booth were continually pointing to the ill effects of over-crowding and insanitary conditions. But little was done, beyond the work of individuals like Octavia Hill or the Peabody Trust. The 1885 and 1890 Housing of the Working Classes Acts, and the Housing and Town Planning Act of 1909, all lacked proper powers of enforcement. Acts urging local authorities to build working-class housing for rent and to inspect that built by the private builder were not enough. For all the population increase, there was little municipal housing before 1914 and the private builder conspicuously failed to provide housing at prices the worker could afford. The builder was not entirely to blame, for the worker could not afford to pay an economic price. So workers continued to crowd into slums, with the obvious well-known consequences of ill-health, poor hygiene, poverty and violence.

The change came after the war. Before it, there was a serious housing shortage: during it building almost stopped and existing slum property deteriorated rapidly. After the war there was a very serious housing problem. There was a great deal of enthusiasm to rebuild a better Britain and the glib slogan 'Homes fit for Heroes' was widely repeated. Commissions of Enquiry in the last year of the war had revealed something of the extent of the problem. In 1918 at least 600,000 new houses were needed, not to mention the redevelopment of existing slum property. The private builder could not supply this need, and certainly not at rents the 'heroes' could afford. So the Government (a Conservative one) forced local authorities to build for themselves.

Dr Addison was the Minister of Health responsible for the Housing and Town Planning (Addison) Act of 1919. It required local authorities to conduct surveys of housing needs periodically and submit plans to meet the most pressing needs to the minister. Once their plans were approved, the Government undertook to help finance local authorities build working-class housing. Subsidised rents (often those fixed during the war) were to be charged and the minister could insist on the council providing certain amenities—like a bath, for example, which many councillors thought superfluous for the workers, because, never having had them before, some council house tenants kept their coal in them. A subsidy was to be provided for working-class houses built by private enterprise, so long as they satisfied specified standards. The Addison Act began a quite new chapter in housing: the Government was taking direct responsibility for properly housing the working-class.

The economic crises (see *page 226*) cut expendi-

ture on the scheme in 1921, but the principle of the Act was not reversed. In 1924 the first Labour government passed the Wheatley Act granting a subsidy of £9 a year for forty years on all new council houses built and let at controlled rents (£360 was the average cost of a good council house in 1924). As a result, about half a million council houses were built by 1933, when the subsidy was withdrawn. Slum clearance was pushed ahead by direct government subsidies under the 1930 Greenwood Act and under acts passed in 1935 and 1936.

There was plenty of better class housing available by the 1930s and the growth of Building Societies made house purchase easier for the lower middle-class worker—mortgage repayments were low; it was the cheap housing that was lacking. George Orwell put the need forcibly:

'the mere difficulty of getting hold of a house . . . means that people will put up with anything—any hole and corner slum, any misery of bugs and rotting floors and cracking walls.'

Yet, although one can complain of slow progress, when one remembers the economic uncertainty of

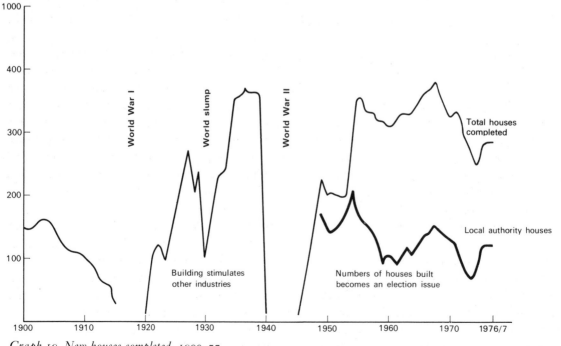

Graph 19 New houses completed, 1900–77

Ribbon development in the 1930s

the period between the wars there was quite an achievement, for a million local authority and three million private enterprise houses were built in those twenty years (see *graph 19*). The building boom certainly helped national recovery, for its effect spilled over into a host of other industries, and it stimulated employment.

But the boom also created a planning problem for the future. Many local building firms were too small to build an estate and therefore they built single houses beside existing roads, for it was cheaper and existing sewage, gas, water and electricity pipes and services were often already available. This unrestricted *ribbon development* created problems of traffic congestion and put considerable difficulties in the way of future planned urban development. There was also little or no supervision of the plans of houses so that architectural blunders kept pace with the uncontrolled sprawl along main roads, leaving patches of agricultural land, often difficult of access, behind the single rows of houses. Look about you in market towns where there was some building in the 1930s which has not been swallowed up by later development. But the private builder was not the only offender, for some alarming errors were made by local authorities in re-housing. They tended to build sequences of identical houses that sprawled in an obvious plan producing a characterless area of housing that must have caused a great deal of social and psychological strain to the rehoused slum dwellers who had been brought up in tightly packed communities. Nevertheless, the achievement between the wars in public and private building was very creditable in the circumstances.

Destruction of the Old Poor Law

Among the committees set up towards the end of the war to plan a better Britain was one under Sir Donald Maclean which reported that the Old Poor Law should be replaced. But in 1919, when he created the Ministry of Health to supervise hospitals, public health pensions and health insurance, Lloyd George did not replace the Poor Law Guardians. These now had to face unprecedented problems as the economic doldrums of the 1920s advanced. The dole relieved the pressure from them a little, but there were still many more people than before seeking relief. The poor rate rocketed and Boards of Guardians had to borrow large sums from the Treasury in order to keep going at all.

Long-term unemployment was the biggest problem, the more so as it affected particular localities (often those with low rateable values) especially in the old industrial areas, like South Wales and the North-East where men 'with pocketed hands and lowered faces stood about in open places' and shivered in 'unlit rooms'. In these areas, least able to afford it, the poor rate kept on rising. It was this that eventually caused the end of the Old Poor Law.

The unemployed in the 1930s, 'hoping for something to turn up'

The issue was forced in 1920 by George Lansbury, who, as mayor of the London borough of Poplar, refused to apply the workhouse test of 'less eligibility' (see *page 160*) or to economise on relief expenditure. He demanded that Poplar, with its high poor rate and low rateable value should be subsidised by wealthier London boroughs that had a low poor rate and a high rateable value. Other poor boroughs copied Lansbury's extravagance—West Ham was £2 million in debt by 1925. The Government retaliated through Neville Chamberlain's Board of Guardians (Default) Act, 1926, allowing the dismissal of Boards if they incurred excessive debts, and the West Ham Board was promptly dismissed.

But it took Chamberlain three more years to convince his colleagues that the Old Poor Law would have to go. Chamberlain's reputation has suffered because of the policy of 'appeasement' with which he was associated in the later 1930s, and he has received too little credit for his excellent work in the reform of local government. In this field his achievement probably exceeds that of his father, Joseph Chamberlain. His Local Government Act of 1929 was a comprehensive measure which went far to carrying out the principal recommendations of the 1909 Poor Law Report. It abolished 642 Boards of Guardians and transferred the responsibility of looking after the destitute to the sixty-two counties and eighty-three county boroughs. In this way he hoped to create in each local area a single authority for health matters. The local authorities were to appoint Public Assistance Committees to supervise the administration of the Poor Law, but also to re-classify the former institutions as local authority hospitals, maternity and child-welfare centres, homes for the blind, and asylums (as the 1909 Report suggested). The unemployed, as opposed to the destitute, were to be covered by National Insurance.

This attempt to bring order out of chaos was spoilt by the world slump of 1929–31. The National (Conservative) Government in 1931 reduced National Insurance benefits and increased contributions. At the same time the Public Assistance Committees were required to oblige all applying for 'extended benefits' to submit to a *means test*. Details of a family's total income had to be revealed and the dole reduced by a proportionate amount, and some fathers had their dole stopped because their children had regular jobs and lived at home: the means test penalised the thrifty and undermined family solidarity. The Committees did their job so well that whilst unemployment rose in 1932, expenditure fell from £110 to £104 millions. Today, any suggestion of a 'means test' is avoided if at all possible because of the bitter memories that still survive of how the test was administered in the '30s. There are many novels that tell of the feeling of hostility and degradation which the means test aroused; among them is Walter Greenwood's *Love on the Dole*. Harry had gone to the local Public Assistance Office to see why his dole had stopped. The man in front of him had come for the same reason:

' "You've a couple of sons living with you who are working, haven't you?" "Aye," the man answered, "One's earnin' twenty-five bob an t'other a couple o' quid, when they work a full week. An' th' eldest . . ." "In view of this fact," the manager interrupted, "The Public Assistance Committee have ruled your household's aggregate income sufficient for your needs; therefore your claim for transitional benefit (*dole*) is disallowed." He turned from the man to glance interrogatively at Harry.

The man flushed: "The swine," he shouted, "Th' eldest lad's gettin' wed . . . 'as 'e t' keep me an' th' old woman?" raising his fist, "Ah'll . . ." But the attendant policeman collared him and propelled him outside, roughly, ignoring his loud protestations.

Harry learnt that, in the opinion of the Public Assistance Committee his father's dole and Sally's wages were sufficient to keep him. No more dole would be forthcoming.'

In 1934 Chamberlain transferred the cost of maintaining the unemployed from local to national funds and set up the Unemployment Assistance Board to pay those who qualified for the dole. The Board ran 'assistance' through local offices throughout the country (it became the Assistance Board in 1940 and with this the poor law died). It imposed new rates of assistance lower than those fixed by the local authorities and it applied a rigid means test that often required families to sell off dear posses-

sions at ridiculously low prices. Their bitter anger and hopelessness was revealed in George Orwell's *The Road to Wigan Pier* (1937) which noted how people accepted their situation

'without going spiritually to pieces. A working man does not disintegrate under the strain of poverty as a middle-class person does . . . they realise that losing your job does not mean that you cease to be a human being. . . . Life is still fairly normal, more normal than one really has the right to expect. . . . The people are in effect living a reduced version of their former lives. Instead of raging against their destiny they have made things tolerable by lowering their standards. . . . They have neither turned revolutionary nor lost their self-respect; merely they have kept their tempers and settled down to make the best of things on a fish-and-chip standard.'

Seebohm Rowntree, who had in 1899 investigated urban poverty in York, made a second investigation there in 1936. He found low wages still the principal cause of poverty, but unemployment was almost as great a cause. The aged, too, lived in penury, for they had had no chance to save during their working life, and their pensions in 1936 were insufficient. In 1899, nine per cent were living in 'primary poverty': in 1936 there were still four per cent, despite determined efforts by the corporation to rehouse slum dwellers, and quite good educational opportunities.

'If, instead of looking backwards we look forward, then we see how far the standard of living of many workers falls short of any standard which could be regarded as satisfactory', Rowntree commented.

Rowntree's second survey was not an optimistic one. He did a third in 1950, and found that poverty, as he defined it, had been virtually eliminated, except among the aged. But this was after the second world war, and by that time a quite new attitude had become common, namely that it was the duty of the State to provide opportunities and rewards for all its citizens. This change is as great as any of the social changes of the last two hundred years.

It is getting progressively more difficult to realise the insecurity and misery under which the poor lived only forty years ago. But it is worth pointing the contrast in living standards between today and yesterday, by quoting from C. F. Garbutt's *In the Heart of South London* (1930):

'On the ground floor of the house in south London there lived two families. In the front room were the father and mother with six boys and girls. . . . Two of these slept in their parents' bed, the other four as best they could on mattresses on the ground. The rest of this floor was occupied by a family of ten; the parents and two children slept in one room, three in the kitchen, and the other three in a small box room most of which was occupied by furniture and a perambulator. The whole house was in a bad state of repair and infested by rats. . . . Measles broke out among the children, one of them died from pneumonia following it; two were removed to the hospital suffering from the same complaint, and one of these also died. A crowning touch of horror was added to the tragedy when the undertaker entering the room with the coffin killed a rat which was trying to get at the dead body of the child.'

This could easily have come from Chadwick's great Report on the *Sanitary Condition of the Labouring Population* (1842)—in fact it was written nearly a century later. Today, a case such as Garbutt describes—not so very unusual for the 1930s— would provoke a national outcry. Here is the measure of our material progress in living standards during the generation since the second world war. But it is important to grasp the fact that it *is* only since 1945; for the speed of social change in the last three decades has been so great that we are in real danger of forgetting what things could be like for our parents. Theirs seems to be a different world.

16 · The 'Humbler Orders' become Governors

A man born in 1880, the son of a coal miner or a farm labourer (or, for that matter, of a junior bank clerk) might, if he emigrated, become a prominent politician in one of the new Dominions or in U.S.A. If he stayed at home he might make a local name in local politics, or perhaps rise to a high position in a trade union. But it would not have occurred to him that he might satisfy legitimate ambitions in national politics by becoming a cabinet minister. That was for others; sons of wealthy fathers, who enjoyed the advantages of leisure, of better education, of familiarity with the world of governors, a world of which he in his cottage, lit by a solitary candle, had but the dimmest notion. He would have accepted this as perfectly natural, for there had never been a time when sons of miners, merely because they grew up able men, should become cabinet ministers. Yet, before his fortieth year he would see a Labour Party working man in the cabinet—Arthur Henderson joined Lloyd George's war-time cabinet in 1916. And within a decade, Ramsay MacDonald had become the first Labour Prime Minister in 1924. Given good fortune and determination, an able working man now could rise to the heights of national politics. This, in itself, was a social revolution: it also meant that a great mass of administrative talent, formerly untapped, could now be at the disposal of the community.

The new unionism of the 1880s

Already the new model unions, or Amalgamated Societies, (see *page 164*) had demonstrated that their general secretaries were men of tremendous ability; but, as yet, these unions took little part in politics. Things changed fundamentally in the 1880s. A 'new unionism' appeared organising the semi-skilled and labourers who had, before Joseph Arch's efforts for farm labourers, proved too difficult to organise. A new chapter was begun in trade-union

Manhandling cargoes in the London docks in the 1880s

history. There were several reasons why the new unionism should emerge at this time. Technical changes were throwing a great deal of emphasis upon the less mechanised processes simply because of the increase of power and of speed in industry. The docks provide a good example: the iron ship (see *page 60*) meant more cargo as well as bigger docks, and this meant a greater concentration of dockers to clear and re-load the holds so that costly time lying in port should not be wasted. The bulk of cargoes were man-handled, so that the docker became a key link in a chain of work. Another good

example was the gas stokers who worked shifts of up
to twelve hours periodically topping up retorts. It
was not highly skilled work, once one got used to it,
but until one did a single unskilled stoker in a gang
would immediately affect the level of gas pressure
when demand was high—especially in the big gas
works. The stoker had become something of a
specialist.

'So far does adaptation go that the men working
beside him, whose business is to wheel barrow-
loads . . . to the furnace door, can wheel barrows all
day, but could not carry on the furnace operations.'

As the consumption of gas in London rose during
the 1880s by some 20 per cent great demands were
made on the skill, and the muscles, of the stokers—
hence their great bargaining power. Better real
wages giving a greater sense of independence, and
leadership from their own men and from some
Marxists, also helped the new unionism. Elementary education may also have been a factor.

These new unions differed from the Amalgamated
Societies in several ways. They were general unions
of unskilled labourers within an industry—and the
older unions of skilled men often resented their
growing power (this was to be a source of inter-union
disputes and labour troubles for the future). They
charged very low subscriptions (their members were
poorly paid), but as they had many members they
were soon financially strong. Their policy was to
concentrate less upon Friendly Society benefits than
on direct industrial action to raise wages, reduce
working hours and improve conditions—unlike the
skilled unions, their strongest card was the threat of
strike action, which had been made much more
effective by the legalising of peaceful picketing in
1875—although employers, at the risk of violence,
frequently resorted to 'black-leg' labour to break
strikes.

They were not restricted to industrial action, for
they demanded the direct intervention of Parliament
to oblige employers to provide better pay and
conditions. Consequently they had an interest in
politics quite foreign to the tradition of the new
model skilled unions. The new unionism changed

Blacklegs leaving a factory, through a picket

the whole atmosphere of the Labour movement and
helped prepare the ground for the emergence of a
Labour Party. Perhaps the most remarkable achievement of the new unionism was that it organised
within a very few years the great mass of unskilled
workers whom hitherto it had been thought impossible to organise, either because they lacked the
money and ability to see the advantages of combination, or because the nature of their employment
tended to be casual. Their success was due to a few
powerful leaders whose tremendous moral authority
deserves to be better remembered.

In 1888 the London match-girl workers of Bryant
and May formed a union and struck for more pay and
better conditions. Their grievances were very real,
for their wages were pitifully low (eight shillings a
week for an adult, four shillings for a girl) and subject
to fines. The work could be dangerous because of the
sulphur which was not only highly inflammable, but
gave off poisonous fumes. Much of the work was also
done on a domestic basis where there was ample
opportunity for exploitation. Herbert Burrows and
Annie Bessant described their condition in an article
White Slavery in London, and called for a boycott of
Bryant and May matches. The firm threatened legal
action and obliged their girls to sign a document
declaring they were well treated. One girl was
dismissed because she refused to sign it, and 1,400

The London match girls, 1888

Ben Tillett addressing a dockers' meeting

struck in protest. Annie Bessant raised subscriptions and made public opinion fully aware of the plight of the girls: their appearance in the West End caused a sensation because of the state of their clothes and their generally unhealthy appearance. Finally arbitrators settled the strike, and the firm was compelled to end levying fines, pay better wages and recognise the Match-girls' Union. The following year Will

Thorn, with the help of Marx's daughter, formed the Gas Workers' and General Labourers' Union in London and won an eight-hour day for stokers simply by demanding it—the threat of a strike stopping gas supplies was enough. The power of the new unionism, simply because of the place occupied in the production chain by its members, was being recognised. Inspired by these victories, Ben Tillett,

Dockers waiting to be picked for gangs

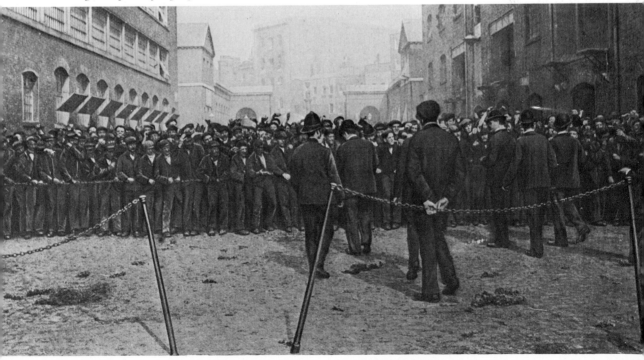

who had formed a General Labourers' Union among the London dockers in 1887, called out his men at the West India Dock and began the great London dock strike of 1889, for nearly all dockland came out in support of the West India men. Tillett was helped by labour leaders like John Burns and Tom Mann.

The dockers had very special grievances. It was not only that they were working under greater pressure because of the increasing volume of trade and the growing size of ships, the long hours and the low pay (fivepence an hour); it was that for most dockers the work was 'casual'. They would collect at the dock gates and struggle to be picked for a gang. The lucky ones got hard work and a little cash. The rest went hungry. If they were luckier next day they had to 'pay themselves off' in order to get food to be able to go on working. So a vicious circle was created. Now the dockers demanded a minimum employment of four hours at sixpence an hour: their slogan was 'The Dockers' Tanner'.

Public opinion was soon heavily behind the dockers—the more so as gigantic meetings of dockers and big demonstrations went off peacefully, although dockers were normally known as violent men. Ben Tillett controlled the crowds with a wave of his straw hat. In the docks, the food began to go bad, yet the owners refused to move, expecting the strikers to be compelled to surrender very soon. But public subscriptions helped the strike fund to the tune of £49,000 and the Brisbane dockers telegraphed £30,000 from Australia in support. Ships diverted from London found that dockers elsewhere, even in continental ports, refused to handle the cargo. A new solidarity was being shown that pointed the way to the course of the next century.

Eventually, public opinion, with the mediation of Cardinal Manning, forced the employers to pay the 'dockers' tanner':

'The rate per hour to be raised ... on and after Nov. 4th to 6d per hour and 8d per hour overtime. Men called in not to be discharged with less than 2s for the day.'

This success inspired a rapid growth of new unionism—even among black-coated workers (1890

saw the foundation of the National Union of Teachers and the National Union of Clerks). In 1889 the Miners' Federation of Great Britain was formed. The new unions were led by men who were often keen socialists with an eagerness to interfere in politics. In four years, between 1888 and 1892, trade union membership rose from 750,000 to $1\frac{1}{2}$ million, and at the Trades Union Congress, the new unionism annually clashed with the older craft unions. But many of the new unions were financially weak. Furthermore, employers were themselves getting together in order to try to defeat the unions—indeed, it was like a counter-attack by the owners.

The rise of the Labour Party

One of the most important thinkers of the nineteenth century was Karl Marx who spent most of his life in London. But few realised how important his work was during his lifetime and he was extremely poor, being kept for the most part by his friend and collaborator, Engels. He was so little known during his life that *The Times* eventually reported his death in the course of printing a report from a foreign correspondent. But by 1880 his work was already attracting attention and a small band of intellectuals who called themselves Marxists had appeared. In *Capital* (1867) Marx argued that the economic structure of modern industry was such that it would lead to its own destruction. It herded workers into factories where they became well aware of their exploitation and where they could combine for their own defence. But because trade and production was not well regulated, over-production would lead to periodic slumps and in the resulting unemployment and suffering the worker would recognise that his interests were best served by uniting to resist the exploitation to which he was exposed and eventually to take over into his own hands the control of all the forces of production, transport and exchange, in order to organise them so that they served humanity and the cause of co-operation. In this way a classless, ideal, communist state would be created. Marx's followers were revolutionary and his slogan, taken from the *Communist Manifesto* of 1848 was: 'The

Proletarians have nothing to lose but their chains. They have the world to win. Workers of the world unite.' His ideas have had a gigantic influence on the twentieth century and there are several large Marxist parties in various European countries; but in this country his influence outside of a small number of intellectuals has been small. The English working man is no revolutionary. But he ought to acknowledge that some of his leaders were inspired by reading Marx. Others were inspired by the American, Henry George, whose *Progress and Poverty* (1879) advocated the nationalisation of land.

In 1881, Henry Hyndman, a wealthy old Etonian, influenced by Marx, formed the Democratic Federation, with a programme recalling the Chartists (see *page 162*) and also demanding universal free education, State-aided housing and the eight-hour day, together with nationalisation of land, railways and the mines. He was joined by a romantic figure, William Morris, a man in revolt against the squalor of industrial life, and the movement was renamed the Social Democratic Federation (S.D.F.). But Morris and his friends left within a year to form the Socialist League (1884). Both movements failed to attract much support, for they were too concerned with theory, whereas politics to the English working man was a 'knife and fork question'.

The Fabians

There were several groups of intellectuals in the 1880s concerned for social reform. One of these called themselves the Fellowship of the New Life. But they were not as idealistic as their original name suggested. They, too, thought of politics in 'knife and fork' terms, and they saw that if they were to achieve their aims they had to influence opinion among leading politicians of the day. So they changed their name to the Fabians, after the Roman general who continually pursued Hannibal's troops without giving them battle. Their slogan was 'the inevitability of gradualness' for they hoped by persistent persuasion to wear down resistance to change in matters of social policy. The leading members were Sidney and Beatrice Webb (whose personal fortune

and acquaintance with public figures proved invaluable), Graham Wallace and Sidney Olivier. Writers like H. G. Wells and G. B. Shaw also helped. Their ideas were mildly socialist, although they were not Marxists, and they hoped by lectures, articles, serving on local councils (especially the L.C.C.) and even Royal Commissions, to spread their collectivist ideas of social reform.

They played an important part in the development of the Labour Party, but their reputation has been greatly exaggerated. They claimed to have

'destroyed the influence of Marxism [i.e. revolutionary socialism] in Britain, to have inspired the Labour Party, to have announced and indeed laid the foundations of the Welfare State, or more modestly, of municipal reform and the London County Council' (now the G.L.C.).

On examination these claims turn out to be ill-founded. But they were good self-advertisers and did much educative work, especially among young Labour supporters. Of the 1945 Labour government, the Prime Minister and nine of his cabinet colleagues were Fabians. However, they were more the sign that a new era was dawning, than the creators of a new age.

The Labour movement was not a matter of middle-class intellectuals providing a leadership and guidance of which the working class was incapable by its own unaided efforts. The movement was a deeply felt demand for greater social justice and it drew its strength not from the discussion at London tea parties, but from the earnestness of ordinary people struggling to live decent lives and 'improve' their minds among the wretched conditions of life and work in nineteenth-century industrial England. Some of its leaders were from the middle class, but the ordinary local officials, the party workers upon whom any big national organisation depends, were ordinary working men and women inspired by ideals of social justice, seeking a readjustment of the relationship between the classes in order to provide every member of the community with a full life. There was (and is) great idealism in the Labour movement: to many it was an expression of a way of life, something almost religious. Indeed, lay preachers played so prominent a part in the early days of the movement that people have spoken of there being more Methodism than Marxism in the Labour movement. Philip Snowden, a cabinet minister in the 1924 Labour government, born the son of a weaver, showed something of this in his *An Autobiography* (1934):

'Working men who had toiled all day at arduous work went out at nights into the streets to preach in their simple way the new gospel of emancipation. Men who had never before attempted public speaking were given courage and the gift of effective oratory by the new passion for social justice which consumed them. The movement was something new in politics. It was politics inspired by idealism and religious fervour.'

A touching glimpse of this deep-seated fervour and devotion to the actual and spiritual welfare of ordinary people was given in the letter of resignation by Mr Ray Gunter, Minister of Labour in 1968, when he spoke of the need to get back to the way ordinary people felt and thought.

Working-class M.P.s did sit in the House after 1874, but they had Liberal support and were known as 'Lib-Labs'. It was not until the 1890s that genuine Labour members were returned, and by that time the Labour movement was beginning to make itself felt both in the new unionism and in political demonstrations—like 'Bloody Sunday', 1887. A Scottish Parliamentary Labour Party had been founded in 1888 with Keir Hardie as Secretary. He was elected to the House in 1892, turning up in a cloth cap, check suit and preceded by a brass band. The Independent Labour Party (I.L.P.) was founded in 1893 with Keir Hardie as Chairman and Tom Mann as Secretary, but it had little success in electing M.P.s and the T.U.C. held aloof.

However, a special conference in 1900 decided to form the Labour Representation Committee with Ramsay MacDonald as Secretary. What was needed was trade union support and this came fully in 1901. For a couple of decades employers' associations had been trying to destroy trade unionism (the engineer-

ing employers were the most active). The Taff Vale Case (1901) appeared to be the peak of the attack. The Taff Vale Railway Company successfully sued the Amalgamated Society of Railway Servants for losses resulting from a local strike and the Union was fined £23,000. This judgement completely reversed what everyone had supposed had been the law since 1875, and it meant that the very right to strike was in danger because unions might be heavily fined for losses occurring as a result. The only way to reverse this judgement was by Act of Parliament and this brought the Unions to support the L.R.C. A 'political levy' was paid to L.R.C. funds out of union dues in order to help the return of Labour candidates and to pay for them after their election. The Tariff Reform Campaign (1903) with its threat of a 'tax on food' (see *page 225*) greatly helped the movement and by-election successes followed. Anxious to work with the new party, the Liberal Chief Whip, in very great secrecy, met MacDonald in Leicester Isolation Hospital in 1903 and agreed that if Labour would not oppose Liberals in some constituencies, the Liberals would leave other constituencies to Labour at the next election. The 1906 election resulted in a landslide Liberal victory, but twenty-nine L.R.C. members were returned, who now adopted the name of Labour Party and proceeded to influence much of the successful legislation between 1906 and 1914, notably the 1906 Trade Disputes Act that reversed the Taff Vale Judgment.

But in 1909 another blow was struck against Labour by the Osborne Judgement, which declared it illegal to use trade union funds for political purposes. This struck at party funds and at the existence of Labour members in the House, for most of them had no private income. Once again the only hope was to reverse the judgement by legislation. This was done in two stages; in 1911 M.P.s were paid a salary of £400 (a sum calculated as adequate for a gentleman), and by the Trade Union Act of 1913 Unions were permitted to engage in political activity provided a majority voted in favour. Union funds for political purposes were to be kept in a separate account and each member of the

Union had the right to 'contract out' of paying the 'political levy' by signing a declaration to this effect.

Under Ramsay MacDonald's care the Labour Party in these years had been building up a solid political machine in the constituencies. By 1914 it had become a formidable force, so that when the Liberal Party disintegrated during the war into the followers of Asquith and those of Lloyd George, the Labour Party emerged in 1918 as the largest Opposition party, displacing the Liberals as the alternative government. But despite the 1918 Constitution that Sidney Webb drafted, it was not a socialist party in the Marxist sense, and when it came to power in 1924 and 1929-31 its policy was far from revolutionary. It was very wise in steering clear of Marxism, for revolutionary movements have never carried much support in England. Even so, Labour has never received wholehearted support from the working class, for about half the workers solidly vote Conservative, either because they feel it is 'safe' to entrust the country to men who naturally move in government and managerial circles, or because of a deep-seated 'deference' to social superiors, which has been a very significant factor in English politics for the last century.

The great strike movement

The new unionism of the 1880s was clearly connected with political activity. One group of extremists, influenced by Marxism, and to some extent the Owenite tradition of 'direct action' (see *page 159*), thought in terms of calling out all the essential workers of a country in a general strike. This would hold the country to ransom and oblige the Government either to surrender to all their demands, or simply to give power into the hands of the unions. In this way they would secure workers' control of industry. This was a revolutionary idea and its supporters were called *syndicalists*. They had considerable support in U.S.A., France and Italy, and among some trade unionists in this country. But the general strike is a weapon that no Government can allow to be used, if it is to remain in control: it is compelled to defeat it, or be defeated itself.

There were a series of massive strikes in the 1890s, especially in the coalfields, but these were 'prosperity' strikes (those in which the strikers feel confident of improving their wages and conditions because of the prosperity of the industry). However, in the years 1910 to 1914 the cost of living was rising and a wave of strikes occurred that so disturbed the nation that people began to wonder whether our democracy would survive. For they were not ordinary strikes; they had a political side to them,

Police charge in the Old Kent Road, 1912

and were influenced by syndicalist ideas. This was also the time of the constitutional crisis, of the Conservative Party's open resistance to Home Rule in Ulster ('if they can sabotage the Constitution for their own ends, why can't we?' was the reaction of many workers), and of the violent suffragette campaign (see *page 183*).

Since 1900 there had been attempts to form a single national union for each major industry by amalgamating existing unions, like the Miners' Federation of Great Britain. In 1910 Tom Mann and Ben Tillett formed the National Transport Workers' Federation and in 1913 the National Union of Railwaymen was established. As James Connolly the Irish Labour leader put it, the aim was

'to build up an industrial republic inside the shell of the political State, in order that when that industrial republic is fully organised it may crack the shell of the political State and step into its place in the scheme of the universe.'

This was splendid revolutionary stuff, but it was dangerous to follow in practice. Troops had already been called out to control miners and transport workers (Tom Mann was imprisoned for calling on the troops to disobey orders if asked to act against strikers). In 1914 the three biggest unions, the miners, the transport workers and the railwaymen (the Triple Alliance, as they were called) agreed to

call out their members in the September. Only the outbreak of war in August prevented the outbreak of a general strike which, in the conditions then prevailing, might have led to violent revolution.

But if the war stopped a general strike, it did not stop local strikes: indeed, in spite of increasing government control of industry and compulsory arbitration for industrial disputes, there was a rising tide of strikes low in comparison with peace-time, but surprising during a war. In 1915, 2 million days were lost; in 1916, $2\frac{1}{2}$ million; 1917, $5\frac{1}{2}$ million: this was the background to the Whitley Councils Scheme (see *page 202*).

After the war, despite an early short-lived burst of prosperity, strikes and riots were common—there was even a police strike in 1919. During the war, extensive government controls had helped industry keep pace with national requirements; the railways and the mines had been, in effect, nationalised and wages had been regulated to meet the very sharply rising cost of living (in 1919 it was 115 per cent above that of 1914) (see *graph 20*). Naïvely, workers expected this extensive regulation would continue into the peace to ensure at least a smooth change to new conditions. But this was not the Government's intention: the politicians sought a speedy 'return to normalcy'. The railways, consolidated into four big companies were handed back to private enterprise. In 1919 a Commission under Lord Sankey reported

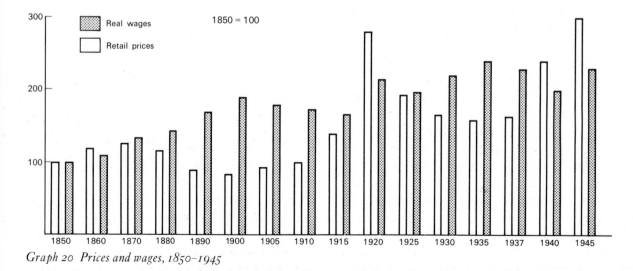

Graph 20 Prices and wages, 1850–1945

that the coal mines should be properly nationalised:

'the present system of ownership and working in the coal industry stands condemned, and some other system must be substituted for it, either nationalisation or a method of unification by national purchase and/or joint control.'

But, with lost markets and increased production costs, the Government was not anxious to accept the idea, and the mines were returned to the owners who now had to face a very difficult situation (and it is easy to forget that it was a situation out of which there seemed no obvious way other than nationalisation). In 1921 the coal owners determined to cut wages severely in an effort to bring down costs. The miners struck for a living wage and called upon the Triple Alliance of 1914 to come out in sympathy. At the last moment the railwaymen held back and the miners fought on alone: the day the Triple Alliance failed to act was called 'Black Friday'. The miners' struggle was a hopeless one, despite £86,000 raised by the *Daily Herald*, and they were compelled to accept the wage cuts.

There was much more than a demand for a living wage in the strikes of the early '20s. They reflected the growing sense of uneasiness at the economic position of the country, the loss of old markets and the disruption of international finance after the war (see *page 225*). In order to regain strength in foreign markets, employers sought to reduce costs and regarded wages as the first target for economies. The workers had not only to accept a rising cost of living with low and sometimes reduced wages, they had to face unemployment, not the temporary unemployment of Victorian England, but permanent unemployment because there was no work to be had (see *graph 21*). If people had guessed that there would be over a million, sometimes over two million unemployed throughout the '20s and '30s there might well have been revolution, for the Government, willing to extend unemployment benefits (see *page 206*), was not prepared to take responsibility for providing employment. There was a great fear of Russian Communism spreading to Britain and overthrowing society. In every major strike,

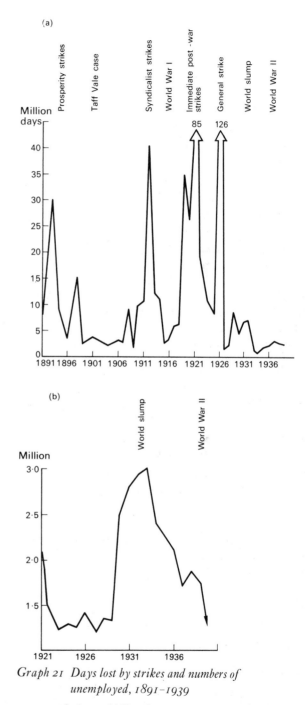

Graph 21 Days lost by strikes and numbers of unemployed, 1891–1939

many of the middle class were prepared to see a political conspiracy. More strongly than before, there was a determination among them that the workers should be shown 'who were the masters', and kept firmly in their place. The Government used troops extensively and encouraged the formation of a Middle Class Defence League as one enthusiast put it 'to get the workers back to their kennels. Back to cheap labour. Back to discipline'. Many middle-class supporters were spoiling for a fight: it is difficult today to capture the aggressive class feeling—indeed, it is remarkable that the workers remained so placidly good humoured. As in Chartist days, they were not revolutionary; they were simply underfed, underpaid, unemployed.

But by 1921 Government plans to deal with a possible general strike were laid. Under the 1920 Emergency Powers Act wide powers to control transport, food, fuel and power supplies could be taken immediately a 'state of emergency' had been declared. When the first Labour government took office in 1924, dependent on Liberal support, it did nothing to dismantle these powers. A general strike, such as had been threatened in 1914 and in 1921, after all, was a direct challenge which no Government could ignore.

But the Labour government did not last out the year, and the Conservatives under Baldwin took control. In order to attract foreign investment to London, Winston Churchill, now Chancellor of the Exchequer, in 1925 returned to the 'gold standard' (i.e. restored the value of the pound to its 1914 level). Money flowed into the London money market. But the price of our exports was raised too, and coal was almost impossible to sell. The mine owners decided on a further wage cut and the miners, their position in no way improved since their defeat in 1921, called on the Triple Alliance to help them by striking. Faced with this threat, Baldwin paid the mine owners a subsidy for a year on condition that there would be neither strike nor wage cuts, and appointed the Samuel Commission to investigate the problems of the coal industry. Recalling 1921, the press called this 'Red Friday'.

Baldwin probably appointed the Commission in order to complete his plans, for an Organisation for the Maintenance of Supplies was organised before the end of the year, for the purpose of recruiting middle-class volunteers to help the Government maintain essential supplies and services should there

be a general strike. In 1926, the Commission reported in favour of major reforms in the administration of the mines, but also of a wage cut. Both sides rejected the proposals, and Arthur Cook, a miners' leader, declared 'Not a penny off the pay, not a minute on the day'. Negotiations between T.U.C. and Government made no progress and the miners were locked out. The Government declared a state of emergency and broke off negotiations on 3 May. Their plans were well laid, the General Strike had begun. The T.U.C. had no plans at all. Indeed, Ernest Bevin (to be acclaimed between 1945 and 1950 as a most able Foreign Secretary) complained, 'We are not declaring war on the people: war has been declared on us by the Government.'

There was a very widespread support for the strike among ordinary folk, who had nothing direct to gain from it. It was literally a nine days' wonder. Whatever the wealthy feared (and perhaps some of them hoped for it, because they controlled the troops) there was no breath of revolution. However, they enrolled as special constables and many undergraduates and the sons of wealthy parents turned up to run buses or drive trains. They enjoyed themselves, and so apparently, did many strikers. Rarely was there any violence, although there was sufficient provocation, both from *The British Gazette* which Winston Churchill edited, printing inflammatory articles, and from the troop movements and the concentration of tanks and artillery in the London area. But the T.U.C. was not provoking a revolution, and to the evident surprise of many strikers, they called off the strike on 12 May, returning on no conditions at all. The miners, once again feeling betrayed, fought on alone, to be almost literally starved back to work for less pay in the November.

Baldwin had promised the strike leaders that he would use his influence to prevent victimisation of strikers, and his leadership at this point deserves high praise. There was remarkably little victimisation (although the Railway Companies were in the habit of sometimes re-engaging engine-drivers, and other highly skilled men who had been strike leaders, on very low grade work). Flushed with a sense of victory, the Government cut unemployment bene-

A volunteer bus driver during the General Strike

fits and passed a Trade Disputes Act and a Trade Union Act in 1927, that made 'sympathetic strikes' (and therefore general strikes) illegal, prevented civil service unions from being affiliated to the T.U.C., and required all trade unionists to sign a declaration if they wished to pay the 'political levy' (this was a calculated blow at Labour Party funds and reversed the 1913 Trade Union Act by substituting 'contracting in' for 'contracting out'). The Acts were repealed in 1946.

The General Strike had failed: there could no longer be any serious fear of a 'red revolution' in this country. Unemployment continued and trade union membership declined. Although no one realised it at the time, 1926 was the end of an era. There were to be many strikes in the future—even a naval mutiny in 1931—but there was never again to be a direct confrontation between capital and labour.

In 1929 a second Labour government was re-turned, like its predecessor, dependent on Liberal votes. But it had no answer to the economic problems of the age and was swept away by the world slump that coincided with its period of office. In 1931 the party split—an insight into the conduct of British political life was provided by the fact that the Labour Prime Minister, Ramsay MacDonald, remained as Prime Minister of a National (Conservative) government until 1935. Most of the members returned for Labour in 1929 were defeated in 1931; but now this party, firmly grounded upon the working class, had become accepted as a party of alternative governors to the traditional rulers of England.

This itself represents something in the nature of a social revolution. And during the 1930s the party attracted many intellectuals determined to produce a plan that would guarantee employment and good living standards to all citizens.

17 · The changing nature of Britain's trade

By the beginning of our present century our trade had settled into a pattern: on the one hand we were coming to depend more and more upon the easier tropical areas (often within the Empire) for our sales, and on the other we were importing goods to a far greater value than we were exporting. This imbalance on visible trade (see *page 176*) was already £25 million in 1850: by 1900 it had risen to £160 million. At the time this trade gap was no problem because our invisible earnings were more than enough to cover it, so that we never had to face a balance of payments crisis. In any case, the Edwardians were very successful in increasing our exports and especially our foreign investments, so that in 1913 our balance of payments position was very healthy. It would cease to be if those investments failed and our balance of trade worsened. As it was, because trade statistics were only collected and published on an extensive basis from 1903, it took bankers some time to realise that the world's foremost trading power had been conducting its business upon a basis that could become very unsound indeed. They understood this after the First World War.

Tariff Reform

What worried the Edwardians was the appearance of trade rivals who raised tariff walls against others while they continued to enjoy the benefit of free trade in the British markets. There were two reasons why we did not retaliate: our manufactures depended on imported raw materials (see *graph 22*) and a tariff would increase costs, and, secondly, the price of food would rise and this would be disastrous at an election. So, while the rest of the world went for protection, we continued to offer them the benefits of the free trade policy that made us wealthy two generations before.

But people protested when their interests were affected. The agriculturalists had been calling for a tariff since the 1880s and they were joined by the small manufacturer who faced foreign competition at home and abroad. Birmingham was particularly affected. The small manufacturers were fortunate in finding Joseph Chamberlain as their spokesman. Not only was he prepared to re-impose tariffs, he was inspired by a vision of the Empire, as a massive economic unit of free trade countries bound together by a common tariff against the rest of the world. He

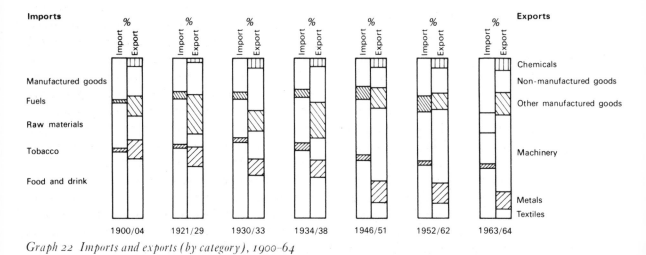

Graph 22 Imports and exports (by category), 1900–64

wanted to make the Empire a self-contained free trade area:

'We must draw closer our ties of sentiment . . . and interest. If, by adherence to economic pedantry and old shibboleths, we are to lose opportunities of closer union which are offered us by our colonies . . . if we do not take every chance in our power to keep British trade in British hands, I am certain that we shall deserve the disasters that will infallibly come upon us . . . The days are for great Empires and not for little states.'

In a great speech at Birmingham in May 1903 he launched his *Tariff Reform* campaign. His principal idea was Colonial Preference—a tariff on imports, remitted wholly or in part for colonial goods. It was Chamberlain's last campaign and it roused tremendous enthusiasm among the younger Conservatives. It also raised bitter opposition, especially from bankers, and the party was badly split. It united the Liberals in defence of free trade and of cheap food—for a tariff would raise the price of food, and the Liberals made great play with an election poster contrasting the 'free trade loaf' with a tiny 'tariff reform loaf'. The party split and the fear of higher food prices took its toll of Conservatives in the 1906 General Election, and Britain remained a free trade country. A generation later, Chamberlain's son, in very different circumstances, was to introduce protection as a policy. It is impossible to say whether our economic fortunes would have been better served by abandoning free trade earlier: in 1929, U.S.A., the most protectionist country in the world, suffered an economic collapse greater than our own.

The steps to protection

The First World War forced the first change in trade policy—at the hands of the Liberals, advocates of free trade. We had found ourselves short of shipping space and needed all we could get for essential goods, while at the same time we needed to save valuable currency to pay for these supplies. And so in 1915 the McKenna Duties were introduced, imposing a duty of $33\frac{1}{3}$ per cent on all imported luxury goods (cars, bicycles, clocks, musical instruments and film). The duties were repealed in 1924. Immediately after the war ended (1918) there was a brief trade boom. But by 1920 we found ourselves struggling with a quite new situation—one that affected the whole western world. It has been called the 'economic doldrums'; trade shrank and countries found that their economies were in a parlous state. People had hoped that they could return 'to the normalcy' of the pre-war conditions simply by dismantling as many of the emergency war-time controls as quickly as they could; but instead, they were faced with a developing crisis of which none had experience and for which no-one had an effective answer.

We had made big loans to our war-time allies which had been either repudiated (by Soviet Russia) or not repaid, simply because of the disrupted state of world finance and trade. And we owed a big war debt to the U.S.A. Our *invisible earnings* were greatly reduced because we had had to sell off (liquidate) some fifteen per cent of our foreign investments, and although these had been restored by 1929, our income from foreign investments was lowered in these vital post-war years. World trade contracted and our earnings from shipping, banking and insurance also fell. We were face to face with our problem of the *balance of payments* (see *page 176*).

Our exports suffered, too, and they continued to decline from 1921-45. World prices of raw materials fell so that our markets in the tropics could not buy more goods from us. They were also now protected by tariffs assisting new industries that competed with our own exports and even our own home market. This had an immediate effect upon the old staple industries, notably cotton, coal and shipbuilding. Widespread and relatively permanent unemployment resulted and the industrial North became a 'depressed area' from which people moved if they could to find work in the new light industries of the Midlands and the London area. The coal industry caught public attention first because after the short post-war boom, loss of European markets, shorter orders at home (factories were on short time and needed less coal), and rising costs forced the owners

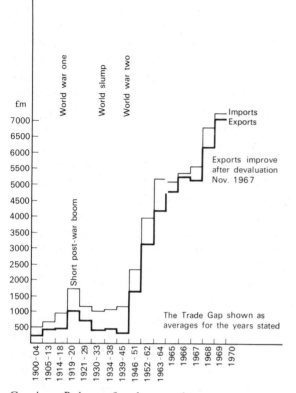

Graph 23 Balance of trade, 1900-64

into a policy of wage cuts that produced a series of extensive strikes (see *page 221*). Soon, competition from electricity and oil as sources of power added to the difficulties.

Between the wars, unemployment proved a frightful waste. Not only was it bad for morale (especially in the areas of the old staple industries that were now in decline), but it meant that, wherever unemployment was long-term, there could be little hope of effectively stimulating the home market, simply because people lacked the ready money to buy consumer goods. As unemployment grew and the 'dole' appeared, a powerful committee of bankers and businessmen under Sir Eric Geddes advised rigid economy in government spending in an effort to 'save money'. The 'Geddes axe' was responsible for cuts in social services, war pensions, education and civil service staff. At the time it was thought sound practice by the Government: in fact it reduced both employment and the

purchasing power of the poor. What was needed was more money in circulation, not less, so that the home market could expand—but this proved too advanced an idea for the 1920s (see *page 228*).

But if our exports did not rise, our imports did. The *trade gap*, present since Victorian times, now assumed alarming proportions (see *graph 23*) because there were fewer invisible earnings to safeguard the balance of payments. Partly to encourage international bankers to make use of the London money market, partly as a prestige measure and as an effort to raise business confidence, the Government in 1925 returned to the gold standard we had abandoned during the war (when notes had replaced sovereigns and half-sovereigns). This had the effect of raising our prices abroad and exporters suffered immediately. They fell back on short-time working and reduced wages in an effort to remain competitive. The General Strike arose out of this situation.

Looked at from the vantage point of fifty years of economic crises, the return to a gold standard was a profound error (the pound remained overvalued until the devaluation of 1931). But at the time few economists condemned it. John Maynard Keynes was the principal one to oppose it, but his views were not then understood. It was not the return to a gold standard that was wrong, but to a standard at pre-war prices. The resulting rise in our export prices delayed our recovery seriously by making our exports more expensive—although foreign money did flow into the London market.

What drove Britain to protection was the world slump of 1929-31, following the 'Wall Street crash' of 1929. It was the worst trade slump the world had yet experienced and, coming after the uncertainties of the 1920s, it took most of the next decade to recover from it. Starting in the U.S.A., the crisis was so severe that it seemed to many at the time that the whole capitalist world was about to collapse. In Germany, high unemployment helped Hitler to power. In the U.S.A. Roosevelt's 'New Deal' programme—frankly 'collectivist' in flavour—helped recovery: but in this country there was no such imaginative application of new ideas. In fact, the crisis in Britain, thought so tremendous at the time, was less severe than in other countries. The downward slide of world prices in the 1920s had resulted in less export orders because our overseas markets were receiving less money for their own exports and so could not afford to buy our goods; therefore industry suffered. Trade was also sharply affected by the withdrawal of American lending abroad that had done much in the twenties to sustain international trade. The economy, already seriously weakened through shrinking markets and lack of capital investment (especially in the old staple industries), crumbled. Had the idea of hire-purchase (paying for goods over an extended period by so much a week) been more developed, and had there been more money among lower income groups, the crisis might not have cut so deeply. As it was, there was a complete collapse of confidence, as much in industry as in the City. The deepening crisis destroyed the second Labour Government (1931) and replaced it with a National (Conservative) one. The balance of payments problem had come into the open and a withdrawal of funds by foreign bankers drove the National government in effect to devalue the pound by 30 per cent by going off the gold standard. This was a complete reversal of the policy of 1925 and was, in fact, the very thing the new Government had been formed to prevent. Its hand had been forced by a monetary crisis that few understood and none of the leading politicians (or bankers) knew how to control. More in desperation than anything else, the Government was led to sweep away free trade and turn to protection, and at the same time to raise taxation and to cut social services at the expense of the unemployed. The real tragedy was not the death of free trade (it was surprising it had lasted so long in such adverse circumstances), but that the politicians, bereft of ideas, sought no more constructive solution, whilst national resources wasted and human dignity wore thin before the relentless pressure of the means test.

After devaluation came three measures to bring in protection. First, the *Import Duties Act* (1932) imposed a duty of 10 per cent on most imports, including raw materials and food. It also created the Import Duties Advisory Committee under Sir George May, to advise on tariff policy—it became a major instrument of government policy, getting duties raised to $33\frac{1}{3}$ per cent and more (50 per cent in the case of imported steel) and encouraging industrial reorganisation to promote efficiency.

The return to general protection gave an opportunity to introduce Joseph Chamberlain's idea of imperial preference. An Imperial Economic Conference held at Ottawa (1932) agreed to allow raw materials from the Empire into Britain at a low or at no tariff, and to accept British goods in return at a low tariff (generally they achieved this by raising tariffs higher against other countries). Greeted by some politicians as an expression of imperial solidarity, the *Ottawa Agreements* cannot be said to have enhanced relations between the Dominions: they were too clearly concerned to defend their own particular interests. The agreements led to a significant development—the imposition of *quotas*, specifying the quantities of foreign trade in food and raw materials: the Government had begun to control the current and direction of trade. Bilateral trade agreements were made with several countries and the Export Credits Guarantee Department of the Board of Trade helped exporters with finance and trade information.

The third measure, more important than the Ottawa agreements, and yet little remembered, was the creation of the *Exchange Equalisation Account* (1932). The idea came from German experience in rationing out the amount of foreign currency available to pay for essential imports. A fund was created to be a sheet anchor against speculation against the pound in the foreign exchange market. It was administered (under the general direction of the Treasury) by officials of the Bank of England who acted swiftly and secretly with a knowledge of the money market—in effect, it was a significant move towards the nationalisation of the Bank that took place in 1946. Despite hostility from bankers, the Account proved an effective instrument for curbing 'flights against the pound' whenever foreign bankers withdrew their money from the London market.

Neville Chamberlain put the purposes of the Account very clearly in a speech in 1933:

'. . . to smooth out the variations in exchange caused by three sets of phenomena—firstly, the seasonal fluctuations; secondly, the operations of speculators, which increase those seasonal fluctuations and other fluctuations, too; and, thirdly, the special flight of capital from other countries for the sake of finding a safer place to stop in for a time.'

We must, however, keep our view of the whole picture. While the period between the wars was one of economic disruption and there was much distress, there was both wealth and comfort, too. Indeed, there were two Britains: that of the depressed areas of the declining industries (see *page 249*), and the brighter, growth areas, typified by towns like Croydon or Dagenham concentrating on new light industries like electrical goods and chemical products. Since world prices were falling, food prices fell, too, and this meant a genuine rise in *real wages* from which all benefited. For those in full employment, especially those in 'safe' jobs, like bank clerks, insurance agents, garage proprietors, life was far from unpleasant. Some of them found the period one of relative ease; the lower middle-class father purchased his house (through cheap mortgages), a vacuum cleaner, perhaps a car. The sales of *consumer goods* (domestic goods and furniture, for example), helped by hire purchase and advertising (both expanding in the '30s), revived many light industries. Nevertheless, the problems of poverty and a too slow economic growth are rightly remembered as the dominant feature of the time.

Although bankers, businessmen and politicians deserve a heavy burden of blame for this situation, it is too easy to blame them entirely. Few had any positive suggestion as to how the economic difficulties might be solved. But the economy *did* survive! Also the Government hit upon the idea of varying *Bank Rate* (the rate at which the Bank of England discounts Bills of Exchange, which in turn controls the rate of interest banks charge for overdrafts and loans). A low Bank Rate means cheap loans and this normally stimulates industrial expansion. Bank rate

remained low until the 1950s: but the policy of '*cheap money*' (low interest rates) was not of itself enough to keep the economy buoyant. The need to achieve a satisfactory balance of payments, especially through increased exports, and the problems arising from the use of sterling as an international currency (until 1977 *see page 306*), have added to our difficulties.

The new economics

What was needed was State action to increase national productivity and prosperity. The principal exponent of this view was a brilliant Cambridge economist, John Maynard Keynes. He argued that the Government, by controlling interest rates and the flow of money, and through the provision of public works on roads, etc., should take up a central position in the economy. His views were distrusted at the time, but they have dominated economic theory and practice since 1940.

Keynes had already earned a reputation through his outspoken publications like *The Economic Consequences of the Peace (1919)* and *The Economic Consequences of Mr Churchill* (1925), but his rejection of the Victorian idea that the economy had to be left to right itself by some strange 'natural mechanism', (the ideal of *laissez-faire* economics), terrified cautious bankers and politicians. In 1936 he published his famous *General Theory of Employment, Interest and Money*. It was not so epoch-making a book as Adam Smith's *Wealth of Nations* but it deeply influenced government policy after 1940 (although actual Keynesian policies have rarely been adopted). He argued that the 'economic doldrums' were not an abnormally severe temporary slump that would right itself according to the cyclical theory of trade (see *page 84*). On the contrary, the domestic market was depressed because there was a lack of money to stimulate the demand for goods. The answer was to encourage industry directly by 'cheap money' and the central direction of economic policy, and to reduce wasteful unemployment by beginning public works, which would not only stimulate construction and industry generally, but

'All behind you, Winston' (A Low cartoon)

by putting money into workers' pockets would expand the home market.

'I conceive that a somewhat comprehensive socialisation of investment will prove the only means of securing an approximation to full employment; though this need not exclude all manner of compromises and of devices by which public authority will co-operate with private initiative.'

Keynes was no socialist: he sought a 'mixed economy' where the Government would use its powers in a positive and dynamic way to ensure that private industry was able to function at its most effective level. During the war (1939–45), Keynes himself was brought into the Treasury and many young economists, whose thinking had been much

influenced by him, rose to positions of importance. Their impact was seen in government policy after the war. The climate of opinion, too, had completely changed. This time there was to be no return to crude 'economic liberalism' and no speedy dismantling of the emergency powers the Government had taken during the war.

The Second World War

Modern industry is highly complex, for it is divided into many different units, each depending on others. This is well illustrated by the motor industry: a strike in a small components factory may put thousands of car workers out of work until supplies become available again. During war-time, this dovetailing of industry has to be particularly effective if the productive chain is not to be broken. By 1940, Britain realised she was close to invasion and defeat. She was lucky to be able to save a good deal of her army from the beaches of Dunkirk, and, under the firm leadership of Winston Churchill, a coalition Government set about organising the country's war effort in a vigorous way. The experience of Lloyd George in the First World War helped, but there was nothing half-hearted or uncertain about the planning in the Second World War. Detailed controls were imposed—rationing, strict quotas of imports, control of foreign exchange, close allocation of raw materials, etc. Three broad ideas can be seen to emerge from the detail: the determination to have 'fair shares for all' (expressed in the Beveridge Report, see *page 260*); the acceptance of a policy of *full employment*; and the recognition that neither of these would be achieved without extensive Government influence, if not control.

Air-raids, conscription and the control of civilian labour made the 1939–45 war a people's war in a real sense. This hastened the change in the political climate that was to produce the great changes after the war (see *page 261*). But first, the war had to be paid for—the 1914–18 war had cost enough, but the second world war left us seriously in debt with much-reduced foreign investments to fall back on. In 1939 we had capital assets overseas of £3,000 million and gold reserves of £450 million: in 1945 we had £1,800 million capital assets abroad and reserves of £300 million, and our external debt had been increased by £3,000 million. Our export markets were either war-damaged or had been lost to competitors, notably U.S.A., especially in Latin America. As a trading nation our balance of payments position was crucial. In 1938, the deficit in our visible trade was £300 million: in 1946 it was doubled and our invisible earnings halved. A balance of payments deficit of £700 millions was forecast for 1946. For a generation now, we have been living with this problem, which may not even be solved by the arrival of North Sea oil in bulk from the end of the 1970s.

The economic crises after the war

The immediate problem was met by Keynes (now Lord Keynes) in 1945 visiting the United States and eventually accepting a loan of $3,750,000. The *International Monetary Fund* (created in 1944 at a conference at Bretton Woods, California, to make emergency loans to members of the I.M.F.) provided a safety-net for currencies getting into balance of payments difficulties. (We were to lean heavily on the Fund in the next twenty years.) The atmosphere of international co-operation was furthered by the *General Agreement on Tariffs and Trade* (G.A.T.T., 1947) which attempted to reconcile differences between trading states rather than have trade disrupted by protective policies. But one of the conditions of the American loan was that Britain should allow *free convertibility* (the pound should be freely bought and sold for foreign exchange) between pounds and dollars. The result, in 1947, was an immediate 'flight from the pound' by foreign investors who promptly turned their pounds into dollars, which they rightly regarded as safer. Convertibility had to be suspended and a series of severe emergency measures taken to save the economy.

The Government gave priority to industries producing for export. A national campaign on the line of 'Export or Die' began to bring home to the public the nature of the economic problem facing them. As a result of the post-war difficulties, administrators and general public alike have learnt more about the working of the economic system than many businessmen knew in the days before the war. A highly commendable increase in our exports resulted. But it was not enough.

The 1947 balance of payments crisis was only the foretaste of what was to come. A second major crisis forced a devaluation of 30 per cent in 1949. It was a drastic measure to help save our export drive, but much of the advantages of cheaper export prices were whittled away partly because the Korean War (1951–3) increased world commodity prices, and partly because both Government and industry failed to be sufficiently vigorous. With tiresome

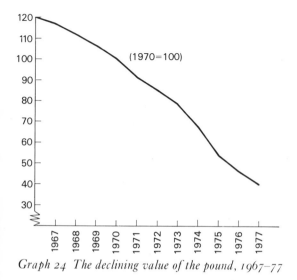

Graph 24 The declining value of the pound, 1967–77

employment levels as outside its control. Keynes had attacked this view in 1936 and Beveridge urged a high level of employment in his Report (1942). The 1944 White Paper committed all parties to a complete rejection of the traditional role of Government and to accept 'as one of their primary aims and responsibilities the maintenance of a high and stable level of employment.' It outlined plans as to how this was to be achieved through the co-operation of Government, banks and industry. Expenditure by the Government and local authorities would be used to maintain employment whenever private industry was declining, thus tending to smooth out variations caused by the trade cycle. (In the 1970s this policy of full employment has come under increasing pressure (see *page 301*)). But a warning was added:

'The level of employment and the standard of living which we can maintain in this country do not depend only upon conditions at home. We must continue to import from abroad a large proportion of our food-stuffs and raw materials, and to a greater extent than ever before we shall have to pay for them by the export of our goods and services. For as the result of two world wars we have had to sacrifice by far the greater part of the foreign investments which we built up over many years when we were the leading creditor country of the world. It will not, therefore, be enough to maintain the volume of our pre-war exports; we shall have to expand them greatly.'

But an old problem in an exaggerated form was added to the balance of payments; the problem of *inflation* (falling value of money due to rising prices) (see *graph 24*). Since 1945 the whole Western world has had to struggle with an 'inflationary spiral'—rising prices provoking wage demands that lead to price increases when the increased wages are passed on to the consumer, and this, in turn, leads on to further wage demands.

Because of the favourable terms of trade in the later '50s the principal cause of recurrent crises was that costs were rising more steeply than productivity, and for the first time wages played a very big part in extra costs. To check this the Conservative

regularity, through the '50s and '60s balance of payments crises recurred, each more serious than the last, further eroding British credit. But after the Korean War raw material prices fell and there was an understandable wish to expand the number and variety of goods available on the domestic market. A great wave of consumer spending resulted, helped by the rapid rise of many hire-purchase firms offering loans at high rates, but easy repayment instalments. This resulted in huge sales of household and other goods that expanded the home market and maintained high employment levels. But it imposed severe strain on our balance of payments, for the increased import of raw materials necessary was not matched by a similar increase in exports.

With a high level of employment went a high level of wages and this gave the impression of general prosperity. But many industries failed to take the opportunity of modernising and the shortage of skilled labour led employers to offer higher wages to staff rather than risk being short-handed. A policy of high employment levels was now generally adopted. In 1944, the wartime coalition Government published a White Paper on *Employment Policy* demonstrating a new outlook and declaring a policy of full employment after the war. Hitherto it had been Government practice to regard fluctuations in government from 1951 used Bank Rate, raising and lowering it in order either to expand or to restrict demand through control of interest rates. This in theory, controlled production levels and the level of investment in industrial expansion, as well as controlling consumption by increasing the cost of hire-purchase. But Bank Rate proved too blunt a weapon, for its effects were slow in appearing and tended to last longer than was originally intended. It did not check the inflationary spiral and by 1960 industrialists were complaining of a 'stop-go' policy that prevented them making effective long-term plans for capital investment. By the '60s the terms of trade were less favourable than in the '50s, and another grave crisis loomed: in 1961 there was even talk of devaluation.

However, both political parties had set their faces against devaluation. Instead the Conservative Chancellor, Mr Selwyn Lloyd, drew £536 millions from the I.M.F. and imposed a 'pay pause' for eighteen months and suggested that pay increases thereafter should be restricted to 2½ per cent. In 1962 the *National Economic Development Council* (Neddy) was established to help both Government and industry in planning to improve economic performance. It was followed in 1963 by a National Incomes Commission (Nicky) that was not a success. Optimistically, the Government launched an expansionist policy in 1963, although imports were 6 per cent up on 1961 levels, and exports only 2 per cent. The result was an even worse balance of payments crisis than that of 1960 which broke just after the 1964 general election that Labour won with a perilously narrow majority. Emergency measures were taken and a significant feature was the speed with which foreign central bankers leapt to defend the pound by granting a $3,000 million credit, for the situation was worse than at any time since the war.

Perhaps the safest thing the Government could have done was to devalue immediately in an effort to correct the adverse balance of £400 million it had inherited (and it has since been criticised for devaluing too little and too late), but it lacked a firm majority and in any case it chose to maintain sterling at its existing rate. Instead of devaluing, it used the same weapons as previous Chancellors had used

since 1961. The immediate crisis seemed to be over, and, influenced by the success of the French *Commissariat du Plan*, it put its trust in a *National Plan* (1965) to achieve controlled growth, and an incomes policy to check inflation by holding back wage demands and restricting wage increases. The Government intended to control the operation of the Plan through a new Department of Economic Affairs (created in 1964) and in December 1966 it established the Industrial Reorganisation Corporation to foster efficiency and profitability in British industry. By consultation with management and trade unions it sought to promote new ventures. Another means of making industry more efficient was the Selective Employment Tax (SET), devised by Professor Kaldor for the purpose of encouraging mobility of labour and introduced in 1966.

But the balance of payments could not return to equilibrium until 1967 at the earliest, and the pound remained under severe pressure. A serious seamen's strike and a docker's strike, together with the impact of foreign crises, especially in the Middle East, produced a further flight from the pound. After an extended series of negotiations with foreign bankers, who were faced by a situation recalling the collapse of 1929–31, and who feared that the international monetary market was disintegrating, the pound was devalued by 14·3 per cent in November 1967. It was admitted as a major defeat for sterling; seemingly the inevitable consequence of living beyond our means. Other currencies followed the pound, but the dollar held firm, and it seemed that a repetition of the 1931 crisis had been avoided. Whilst ensuring that the needy did not suffer, the Government cut expenditure on the social services and on defence and launched a renewed incomes policy, backed by 'Clause Four' giving the Government power to enforce the restriction of wage increases to 2½ per cent provided they also were linked with increased productivity.

For six months the Government was bitterly unpopular, but there were some signs of recovery by the summer, and in September 1968, the Basle *Facility Agreement* was signed in order to strengthen sterling which was again under severe pressure.

European Economic Community (1957) – the original members

Countries that joined the Community in 1972

Countries preparing applications for membership (1978)

EFTA countries (1977)

Countries with a 'Special agreement' with the Community

COMECON (1949) countries

Norway joined E.E.C. in 1972 but withdrew after a referendum.

Many former French colonies have a 'special relationship' with the E.E.C., as have some New Commonwealth countries.

East Germany has a 'special relationship' with the E.E.C. that distinguishes it from other COMECON countries.

Yugoslavia and Albania are communist countries outside the COMECON area.
Cuba and Mongolia are also members of COMECON

Map 6 The European Economic Community and COMECON

The Agreement allowed Britain to draw other currencies from the Bank of International Settlements to a total of $2,000 million in order to maintain her sterling balances. The Agreement meant that sterling would gradually cease to be an international reserve currency for other countries' trade, which had often in the past resulted in a drain on our reserves. The new arrangements contributed to

world monetary stability, but that stability was to be disturbed in the next decade by soaring inflation aggravated by a huge increase in oil prices (see *page 306*).

But the advantages of devaluation were painfully slow to appear and imports continued at a high level, although exports increased commendably. Further emergency measures had to be taken in

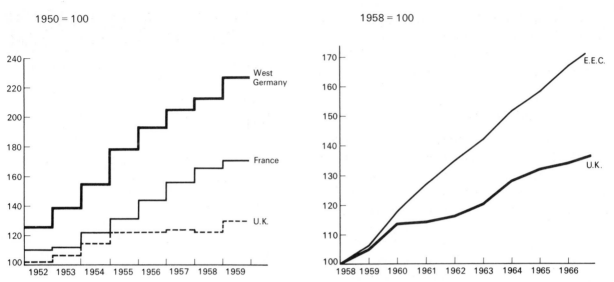

Graph 25 Growth rate of Common Market Countries contrasted with that of Great Britain, 1952–66

November 1968. It seemed that it was not enough for the Government to concern itself with the balance of payments and the securing of international credit: it must also remedy the major structural defects in the industrial system. This extensive responsibility was apparent in *The Task Ahead* (1969), a Government planning document outlining plans for the early 1970s. It argued that to gain the advantages of devaluation there had to be a major shift of resources from home consumption to exports so that a substantial balance of payments surplus could be built up. Investment had to be increased—our competitors devoted a higher pro-

portion of resources to investments than we did— and in the '60s the increase in investment had been in the public sector (Government and nationalised industries), while in the private sector, investment had lagged. A modest growth rate was forecast, and the hope was extended that, with co-operation between Government, industry and trade unions, the 1970s would see a return of secure prosperity and a strong balance of payments, helped by our gradual withdrawal from the rôle of a world banker. But the 1970s have been disturbed years (see *page 304*): we have not escaped from the succession of economic crises, and the world slump and inflation-

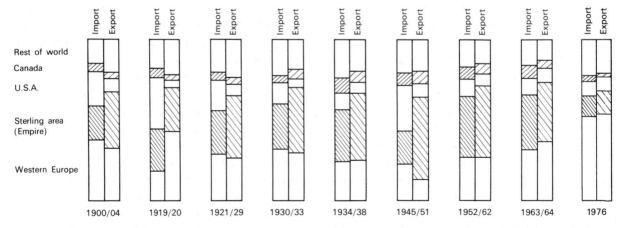

Graph 26 Comparison of imports and exports by region, 1900–76. (Note how 'Empire' trade has diminished in the last ten years and how Western European trade has become increasingly important)

ary spiral that followed the increases in the cost of oil brought us once more to the brink of catastrophe in 1976. But by that time we had joined our forces with Europe, and no longer stood alone.

The Common Market

Since the Second World War (1939–45) Britain has had slowly but surely to recognise that she is no longer a great power and that the basis of her wealth is precarious. Part of the reason for this has been the emergence of the two 'super-powers' Communist Russia (later to be joined by Communist China) and her opponent the U.S.A. For some years after the war there was real fear of another world conflict—it was called the period of the 'cold war'. Western Europe has sought in co-operation a means of defence against Russia and this has led to a union of certain states which is called the European Economic Community (E.E.C.) or the Common Market. But there is much more than fear of Russia in the E.E.C.

There was the feeling of idealism that blossomed during the war, particularly among the Resistance Movements against Nazi Germany—some of them in 1944 called for a Federal Union as a means of ending the nationalist ambitions that had engendered so much hatred and led to two world wars. It was a feeling that had been expressed as early as 1927 by Ernest Bevin, speaking at the Trades Union Congress. After the war the economic situation made some degree of co-operation essential if the economies of Western Europe were to survive. In June 1947 the U.S.A. decided that the economic crisis in Europe was so great that immediate economic aid was necessary. She offered this to both Communist and Western nations. The Communists rejected it and formed their own economic union which is called COMECON today. The West accepted what was called the *Marshall Plan* (named after the U.S. Secretary of State) which was to provide economic aid until 1952. To assist in co-ordinating European economic and financial policies, in 1948 the Organisation for European Economic Co-operation (O.E.E.C.) was formed. Marshall Aid probably

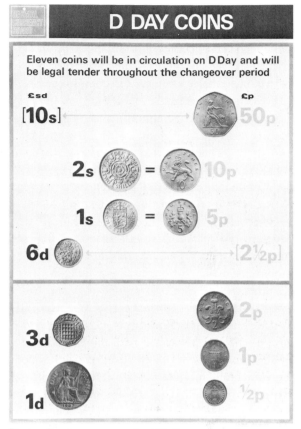

Decimalisation poster, 1969. 'D' Day was 31 August 1971

saved Western Europe from economic collapse. But Europe was anxious to save herself, and in 1950, encouraged by the success of the French economic plan, M. Robert Schuman the French Foreign Minister, put forward a plan to save the coal and steel industries of France, West Germany and Benelux (Belgium, the Netherlands and Luxemburg). It was accepted in 1951 as the European Coal and Steel Community (E.C.S.C.) that took over the running, production and marketing of the coal and steel industries of France, West Germany, Benelux and Italy (a group of six nations that now was referred to as the Six). But it was more than an industrial arrangement: the organisation had a structure that could expand into a much closer union, and it had a court to enforce its decisions. Clearly, a much bigger union was envisaged, for the preamble to the treaty called on the Six to 'substitute for historic rivalries a fusion of their essential interests; to establish, by creating an economic community, the foundations of a broad and independent community among peoples long divided by bloody conflicts, and to lay the basis of institutions capable of giving direction to their firm future common destiny.'

It was from this community that the Common Market was to arise. Britain had the opportunity to join but declined, perhaps supposing that the E.C.S.C. would fail. She argued that her links with her Commonwealth were too strong to permit her to be drawn into Europe (even Winston Churchill, who had called for a 'United States of Europe', did not think of Britain joining in!). Britain was importing much of her food cheaply and this was an important reason for maintaining links with the Commonwealth. She also argued that she had a 'special relationship' with the U.S.A. particularly over defence against Russian attack. In December 1954 we became associated with the E.C.S.C., but by this time plans were well advanced for developing the community into the Common Market. A conference was called at Messina in 1955 (Britain sent junior representatives only) and it adopted the idea of forming a European Common Market, intended to integrate the industrial and agricultural policies of the Six and, in due course, to create a genuine political union. The British idea of forming a free trade area of all O.E.E.C. members was rejected. In March 1957 the Treaty of Rome was signed (to come into force on 1 January 1958) creating the *European Economic Community*: the six member states were to reduce their tariffs between themselves, but they were to establish a Common External Tariff (C.E.F.) against the rest of the world. For the moment the Community was a union of economic policy; it was soon to stretch beyond into social and political life. Britain formed a European Free Trade Area (E.F.T.A., 1959)—there were seven members, and journalists wrote of Europe being at 'sixes and sevens'—but it was a very loose association with no concentrated policy. It failed, although it did reduce tariffs in line with those of the Six. But throughout the '50s, Britain was experiencing what seemed, in contrast to the drab years of

rationing after the war, a decade of prosperity with a consumer spending boom that was typified by Mr Macmillan's slogan for the 1959 election, 'You've never had it so good'.

However, by 1961 the situation had changed. The apparent prosperity that had made Britain into an 'affluent society' was under severe strain because of our balance of payments position, whilst the Six were enjoying an industrial expansion that makes it remarkable that we should have been so complacent in 1959 (see *graph 25*). Not only was Britain's economic performance poor in comparison, but the tariff reductions between the Six were proceeding at a rapid rate and Britain now faced the prospect of exclusion from one of the fastest growing markets in the world because of the Common Market external tariff, as well as competition in world markets from our Common Market rivals. In 1961, forgetful of E.F.T.A., and clearly from no position of strength, Mr Macmillan surprised his party and country by applying for membership of the Community. The negotiations were handled by Mr Heath.

There were special problems in the way of our entry into the Common Market, quite apart from the relative weakness of the British economy. The pound was an international currency likely to suffer from speculation; our special relationships with U.S.A. and our former Empire were embarrassments (our trade was declining in both these markets and that with Europe was expanding, see *graph 26*). British public opinion was clearly divided on the issue, and there was much force in the French contention that we were not prepared to sink our individuality in the Community as the spirit of the Treaty of Rome required. In 1963 the French vetoed our application at the start of the crisis that was to lead to devaluation (see *page 232*). In 1967, however, the Labour government, now convinced of the need to enter Europe, made a second application. It was again vetoed by France, but only at the cost of considerable strain within the Community, and special talks were begun between the Netherlands and Britain. Devaluation clearly made a difference to our position and may have strengthened our case for entry.

" But first, all passengers will vote on whether we step ashore or continue our luxury cruise."

In the summer of 1968 France experienced a wave of strikes and unrest, associated with student demonstrations in both universities and schools. The Fifth French Republic was severely weakened, both politically and economically, and in February 1969, despite the huge gold and foreign currency reserves, there was serious talk of a devaluation of the franc. In 1969, President de Gaulle resigned, and a major obstacle to our entry into the Common Market was removed. France still objected that Britain did not seriously intend to become thoroughly a part of Europe, but she had lost a good deal of prestige and support among other members of the Community, who had come to fear that France intended to dominate the Community herself. In August 1969, the franc was devalued and a vigorous policy of state control of the economy adopted to restore prosperity to France. At the same time our own economic position was greatly improving. With our opponent in such difficulties, and a new friendly disposed West German Chancellor, Herr Brandt, elected in November, a different attitude to Britain's application for membership emerged. In November 1969, further discussions for British entry began, the French this time no longer vetoing the talks.

In 1970, the Community accepted the French plan for agriculture which favoured the continuance of small farms enjoying the benefit of guaranteed prices—for which the consumer paid heavily through high food prices. This seemed to remove a further barrier to our entry—although it raised the problem of steeply rising food prices, which would prove an added burden on our balance of payments, should we join the Community.

By 1971 opinion in Britain was moving steadily towards the idea that joining Europe was inevitable —it seemed to be typified by the adoption of a decimal coinage coming into operation in 1971. Difficulties over the balance of payments persisted, and it was clear that we were dropping behind our European rivals. Our rate of economic growth continued to be sluggish while that of the E.E.C. was rapid with a strong balance of payments and a rising standard of living, coupled with a social policy that in some ways outshone our own—for example a superior pensions system. The advantages to be gained from free access to an expanding market of nearly 300 million people were obvious, and it would give the chance for industry to meet the challenge of technological change, especially in the fields of aerospace, computers and electronic equipment. If Britain stood out of Europe, her future might be at risk—her links with the Commonwealth had been eroded during the '60s (Commonwealth countries were, after all, pursuing their own interests—compare the position in the 1930s (see *page 227*)).

Problems of high food prices and the size of the British contribution to the Community Budget remained, but in June 1972 a Treaty of Accession was signed, and Britain, along with Eire and Denmark, officially joined the E.E.C. on 1 January 1973—the Six had become the Nine, (see *map 6*). The Labour Party was divided on the issue, and in any case argued that the conditions of entry were too harsh and disadvantageous to us: it promised to re-negotiate the terms and to hold a referendum so that the people might express their will directly on the issue (particularly as it was becoming clearer that joining the Community meant that a country lost some of its control over its own policies). After Labour won the election in February 1974 highly complex negotiations took place which resulted in decidedly more favourable terms being secured. In 1975, a referendum (hitherto an unknown thing in Britain) was held and resulted in a two-to-one majority for remaining a member of the Community on the revised terms. It was clear that opinion was convinced that the consequences of leaving the community would be too damaging—but it was also clear that the advantages which supporters had claimed for membership were slow in appearing. This was partly because of the world slump in the mid-'70s, aggravated by the big rise in oil prices after 1973 (see *page 306*), and partly because Britain's industrial growth remained slow whilst her rate of inflation leapt ahead at an alarming rate.

The problem of agriculture

At the time of the Great Depression, agriculture received neither aid nor protection from the Government (see *page 177*). It suffered badly. Today it is prosperous because of government policies of aid through guaranteed prices and subsidies. This complete change of policy came first during the first world war. By 1917, the German U-boats' success in sinking merchant shipping had reduced food imports to a dangerously low level, and forced us to look once more to our own agriculture to produce the bulk of our food. The Corn Protection Act (1917) guaranteed farmers a higher price for corn and farm labourers better wages. By 1918 we were producing 80 per cent of our food requirements and a vast acreage had been brought under the plough. But after the war, much of this corn land reverted to grass and we were supplying only 39 per cent of our own food needs in 1929. But we were using much more efficient methods. More machines were introduced, and the farm labour force fell (this also broke down the community feeling among farm labourers —the tractor-driver works alone; formerly, the labourers worked as a team with horses of which they were justly proud). Dairying, market gardening and fruit farming increased, but, in general, farming shared in the industrial depression, especially between 1929 and 1933.

Government assistance saved the situation. A new industry was fostered after 1921 by grants for the extraction of sugar from sugar beet, and in 1935 the British Sugar Corporation was established to control the industry. In 1929, farm buildings were de-rated (farmers paid no local rates on their farm buildings), and with the return to protection in 1932 (see *page 227*), imports of meat and tinned milk and some cereals were restricted if they did not come from the Empire. The Agricultural Marketing Acts (1931 and 1933) created elected marketing boards empowered to fix prices and determine amounts to be produced (in order to maintain efficient production), for potatoes, hops, bacon pigs and milk. Government subsidies were extended to wheat (1932) and meat (1934), and the cost of State agricultural support rose from £45 million in 1934 to £100 million in 1939.

British farming was saved and its strength and efficiency was proved in the Second World War (1939–45). In April 1939 (four months before the outbreak of war, but in time for ploughing), a grant of £2 an acre was made for grassland ploughed that season. Executive committees were established to offer farmers technical advice. County Agricultural War Committees controlled crop production and by 1943, $7\frac{1}{4}$ million acres had been ploughed, including 'wastes', grassland and ornamental parks. Mechanisation was encouraged and the labour force increased both by the Women's Land Army (women from all walks of life volunteered for this essential war work) and school children who were let off school for harvesting and potato-picking. Householders were encouraged to grow their own vegetables and local authorities created many plots of allotments. Costs rose steeply, but farmers' incomes rose too, and many were able to pay off much of the debt that had accumulated during the period between the wars.

After the war, State support continued with the Agriculture Act (1947) providing for an annual price review and guaranteed prices and production by agreement between the Ministry of Agriculture and the farmers. By 1957 the cost of State aid to agriculture was £239·2 million. Milk production and grain crops doubled and cattle increased by 25 per cent. At the same time, the farm cart horse rapidly disappeared to be replaced by tractors, even on the smaller farms, and combine harvesters and other big machines became a commonplace (thirty years before they would have drawn an admiring crowd in rural areas). Farming has become very scientific, demanding sophisticated fertilisers and foodstuffs. 'Broiler houses' for chicken have worked a social revolution both by producing chicken as one of the cheapest meats available and introducing a whole range of new-style eating houses offering cheap luncheons to city workers. Veal, produced in similar conditions, is also cheap. There have been protests against such 'factory' methods of treating livestock and the Ministry of Agriculture keeps a close watch over conditions on 'broiler' farms.

But the cost to the tax-payer of maintaining a profitable farming industry is very high, and there is a limit to the subsidy farmers can reasonably expect. The price review for 1969 aimed at expanding meat production rather than the heavy concentration upon corn-growing of recent years (although grain acreage was to be extended). It aroused vigorous opposition from farmers, but the principle upon which the Government granted aid, was that production should be efficient and that there should be a proper concentration on the types of crop most

Shire cart-horses, now largely replaced by tractors

needed. The cost to the tax-payer could be offset to some extent by important savings in our import bill, and the Government proposals hoped to save some £160 million by 1972/3 on the cost of imported food-stuffs.

Their calculations were proved false by the movement of world prices. One hundred and fifty years ago Britain had little need to consider the cost of cereals on the world markets. Today, the situation is very different. The size of the harvest in the USA, or a serious drought in the USSR, may well affect the price of bread in the shops within a few months. We are not isolated producers of food, and we must take account of world movements of prices and supplies in a way that our Victorian predecessors would not have understood.

In addition, of course, our joining the Common Market (from 1973) has worked a significant change in government farming policy. We had followed a policy of cheap food, with the farmer supported by subsidies and guaranteed prices. When we joined the E.E.C. we had to accept the Common Agricultural Policy (C.A.P.) in which farmers are guaranteed a relatively high price for produce which is determined periodically in Brussels. It is a policy designed to protect the farmer (especially the small, less efficient farmer), by ensuring that his produce is purchased—even if it has to be purchased by the European Commission itself in order to be stored for future sale. It has been contended that the C.A.P. helps the small peasant, particularly in France, at the expense of more efficient farmers elsewhere, and the consumer, who pays high food prices. (During 1973 C.A.P. was calculated to have cost £1·63 for every Briton, whilst every Frenchman gained £7·86.) It has certainly caused a glut of beef and butter and even of wine which has been stored and not released, in order to maintain prices (in 1973 there were many complaints about the 'butter mountain'). In fact because world prices have risen sharply since 1973, the British farmer has not done as well as he contemplated from the C.A.P. policy, and the consumer has done rather less badly than was feared. In particular, the consumer has benefited from the use of the *green pound*, the name given to a theoretical currency used by the Commission to establish the price of agricultural produce at a fixed point (since the pound sterling varies daily in value). Because sterling has *depreciated* (declined) so much in the 1970s, the use of the green pound has meant that during the winter of 1976–7 the Community was subsidising the British food bill to the cost of £1·5 million daily. Understandably, we resisted attempts to devalue the green pound, for our *inflationary spiral* would be aggravated by the rise in food prices necessary to bring our prices into line with those of other member countries. The British farmer got a lower price for his produce than other community farmers, but it cost the housewife less than would otherwise have been the case. By 1977 it was clear that the C.A.P. was under attack and would have to be reformed. However, for 1978, Britain agreed to a small devaluation of the green pound much to our farmers' delight.

Although British farming has been made better and more prosperous than ever before through Government aid, agriculture has declined in relative

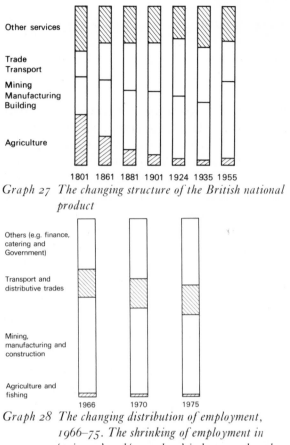

Graph 27 *The changing structure of the British national product*

Graph 28 *The changing distribution of employment, 1966–75. The shrinking of employment in 'primary' and 'secondary' industry to less than half of the total represents a significant change in the nature of British industry*

importance in the national economy (see *graph 27*). Also, the tendency is for the rather small-scale farmer to have his farm absorbed by his larger neighbour. On the other hand, although the farmer is now prosperous, the farm labourer, who has now become something of a specialist in the use of quite advanced agricultural machinery, has not benefited from this prosperity in anything like the same degree. His life is easier today, especially with improvements in rural life through better housing, amenities, transport and educational opportunities, but he still remains among the lower-paid workers, and, if only because of the nature of his work, his accommodation has often been in a 'tied cottage', going with the job. This has reduced his independence. Efforts to end the tied cottage system in England were finally successful in 1976.

18 · The managerial revolution

By the 1880s, the tremendous growth in industrial capacity that the Victorians had achieved, was beginning to slacken in pace. There were many reasons for this—the appearance of rival industries in other countries that affected our markets and enjoyed the benefit of our pioneering experience; the limits of improvement by the technology then available in the staple industries was being reached —coal-mining was coming to the end of the easy, profitable seams; the development of new industries in which competitors made greater strides; and, in a sense, British industry, although it was not losing its vigour, was beginning to change. Firms began to specialise upon particular processes and this made the organisation of industry very complex, for it had to be closely interwoven so that all the processes could be brought together. Firms tended to grow in size—a tendency that was to transform twentieth-century industry into small firms or very large firms indeed. Increasingly, a paid manager took over the day-to-day running of businesses: he was often no more than a well-paid employee, but on his expertise depended the success or failure of his company. The growth of limited liability companies (see *page 86*) helped the development, for it made expansion easier and specialists in finance, administration, sales etc. could be elected to the board of directors. But the managing director, or the manager of a particular firm, were the key men on whom everything depended—and by the end of the century they were often quite unrelated to the family who had built up the business, and, indeed, might have no especial background in that particular industry. It was their organisational flair and their industrial sense that mattered. This growing dependence upon a new class of professional industrial managers was going to transform British industry: it has been called the managerial revolution.

But management in late Victorian and Edwardian England failed in an important respect: it

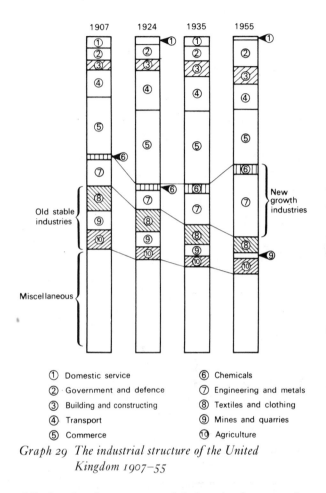

| | 1907 | 1924 | 1935 | 1955 |

Old stable industries

New growth industries

Miscellaneous

① Domestic service   ⑥ Chemicals
② Government and defence   ⑦ Engineering and metals
③ Building and constructing   ⑧ Textiles and clothing
④ Transport   ⑨ Mines and quarries
⑤ Commerce   ⑩ Agriculture

Graph 29 The industrial structure of the United Kingdom 1907–55

failed to develop new growth industries fast enough, and instead relied on the old staple industries that were still profitable. Although there was no lack of British inventiveness, the pace-setters of the future were developed in other countries far faster than in Britain.

The old staple industries

The rise in prosperity of textiles during the Edwardian era did not encourage the adoption of new machinery, so that the industry was ill-equipped to face competition from new producers and artificial fibres in the 1920s. Here was a failure of management. The story was the same in the coal-fields, where an ample labour supply discouraged the adoption of labour-saving equipment, and the price of the failure to modernise was paid in the labour troubles of the 1920s. Germany and U.S.A. left us far behind in steel production (shipbuilders even imported steel because our own was so expensive) and the price of this slow development was paid in 1916 when we could not produce enough steel for shells to supply the Somme offensive.

These staples were ill-equipped to meet the competition and slump conditions of the inter-war years. Once they were the leaders of the Industrial Revolution: by the 1920s they had become 'depressed areas' associated with serious unemployment. New industries displaced them, industries that had been largely developed in other countries before the war (see *graph 29*).

The new industries

The chemical industry was to be a pace-setter of the twentieth century, but we lagged sadly behind Ger-

many. In the 1920s the amalgamation of smaller firms into larger units made for greater efficiency, but the major development in chemicals was in *man-made fibres* like rayon (a French discovery of the 1890s) produced in Britain by Courtaulds and British Celanese, or nylon (1927), or terylene (1940) and the more sophisticated plastics derived from crude oil by the development of polymer-technology in the 1950s.

Electricity as a source of power was remarkably slow to develop—we relied on Germany for our magnetos until 1914. In 1919 Electricity Commissioners were appointed by the Government to try to get voluntary co-ordination of supplies and a common standard for electrical fixtures from small producers. Their failure was answered by the creation of the Central Electricity Board (1926) to concentrate production on efficient power stations, standardise voltage supplies and construct a National Grid across the country from which industry and domestic users could draw their power. This revolutionised the location of industry for it allowed light engineering works to be sited in the suburbs of towns or even in the countryside, no longer de-

A National Grid substation with overhead electric cables

pendent on coal and water power. As a result the London area expanded at a phenomenal rate.

The motor-car, followed by the aeroplane, has made one of the most significant contributions to industry, the economy and social life. Again, both were developed in other countries. It was some time before we had equipped factories for producing cars in quantity, and this was certainly a failure to grasp the possibilities of new engineering developments. Far-sighted engineers produced outstanding machines, but it was mass production that was to make the motor-car industry a pace-setter. One of the foremost of these engineers, whose ability as an inventor and production engineer rivalled that of Daimler and of Ford, was the Englishman, F. W. Lanchester. His career illustrated both the difficulties of pioneering a new industry and the lack of enterprise in British mechanical engineering at the end of the century. He wrote:

'The difficulties of management were very great, partly owing to the fact that no ancillary trades had then developed and we had to do *everything* ourselves, chassis, magnets, wheels, body-work, etc., everything except tyres; moreover, for many pur-

poses I had personally to train my labour. Especially did this relate to the making of interchangeable body-work. Those who have entered the field in the last twenty-five years have no conception of what the organisation of even a small motor vehicle factory meant in those early days.'

Yet, by 1907, motors and cycles accounted for $12\frac{1}{2}$ per cent of engineering production—more than the whole electrical industry. Lanchester produced a small well-planned factory, a model of integrated production—but it was a long throw from Henry Ford's Detroit works. It was not until the mid-twenties that the British car industry turned to mass-production techniques, and then almost in desperation because the expensive cars they were producing were not selling.

Such a record speaks ill of a nation that was once the 'workshop of the world'. Fortunately, the record was quite different after the second world war, for production expanded in both new and established fields at such a rate that people have spoken of a *second industrial revolution*. The petro-chemical industry, giving a whole new range of fertilisers, insecticides and a new plastics industry, and motor

An aerial view of Calder Hall power station

An I.C.L. computer

and aero-engineering have been the pace setters, but there have been important developments in new techniques. *Automation*, an extension of electrical engineering by which whole processes, sometimes of considerable complexity, can be performed mechanically and controlled to a degree of accuracy beyond human judgement by a handful of men, has appeared especially in the car industry and in steel mills and, on a limited scale, in the tinned food and allied industries—but progress here has not been so great as in U.S.A. or in the U.S.S.R. Atomic energy, developed during the war from the early work of scientists like Rutherford, has been developed for peaceful purposes under a public corporation, the Atomic Energy Authority (1954). A system of strategically placed nuclear power stations (Calder Hall (1956) was the first in the world) feed electricity into the National Grid. Atomic energy has immense potentiality for the future, but as yet it has proved more expensive than generating electrical power by conventional means; it has also serious problems of disposal of radio-active waste, and also of production, for reactors *can* get out of control. However, in 1978, despite the

A radar installation. Radar, developed by Watkins Watt in the 1930s, is able to track the position of objects, moving or stationary, over a wide area. It was the development of the radar network before the war that made it possible for us to win the Battle of Britain in 1940. Radar is also useful for navigation in rivers, harbours and straits, and in fog.

North Sea Gas pipeline installation

protests of environmentalists, the Government decided to use a 'fast-breeder' reactor that would ultimately reduce the cost of producing electricity and also use up radio-active waste.

Since the 1960s *computers* have played an increasing part in industry, commerce and administration. These are complex electronic machines capable of making advanced calculations at incredible speeds and, through their 'memory' (impressions on magnetic tape), are capable of supplying a vast range of data within a matter of seconds. Applied to automative techniques they can simplify and speed up factory production and the capacity of the more sophisticated computers to reach answers to problems of management by selecting the relevant factors is bound to have tremendous impact on the conduct

of business and Government, simply because it accelerates the speed of decision-making. U.S.A. dominates the computer market (it is an essential adjunct of the space projects), but Britain has been able to maintain her own computer industry because the Government has persuaded the rival firms concerned to pool their resources. In the 1970s the computer has become a familiar thing in business. Many firms and government departments carry much of their records and their accounting information on the discs of electronic tape used by computers and stored in what is called a *memory* (or *data bank*). Indeed, the *data processing* industry (converting information into a language code suitable for a computer to store in its memory and to produce immediately it receives the correct instruction) has become so extensive that fears have been expressed about the liberty of the citizen. So much information about individuals, often of a personal or a financial nature, is now recorded in data memory banks that restrictions upon its use have to be rigorously maintained. A finance firm can sometimes check up on the *credit worthiness* (can he pay his weekly contributions?) of a client by tapping a memory bank. Again, the secret files of research into new processes by huge industrial concerns can be simply stolen and sold to a rival by someone with access to the memory bank. A report in 1978 suggested that the security of the state might be imperilled by hostile action by computer operators with access to Government computers. At the same time fears were expressed for future employment prospects because of the rapid growth of *micro-electronic* techniques, especially the production of microprocessors (tiny integrated circuits on silicon chips that can carry the power of a computer) that bring automation into planning and administrative offices, displacing skilled staff.

Important developments in the field of telecommunication and of radio have also taken place. The radio and television industry has supplied a whole range of specialist employment, and worked a social revolution in the home. Radio communication by satellite has become a commonplace, and most ships and aircraft navigate in confined spaces by radar. Short-wave radio also helps in crime-detection and control.

In the last generation, Britain has shown herself worthy of the traditions established by the great entrepreneurs of the eighteenth century—a single instance of this is the speed with which North Sea Gas has been tapped and supplied to domestic and industrial users: this has necessitated whole pipelines being laid and the modification of nearly all domestic gas fittings—a gigantic undertaking completed so quickly that the public has scarcely realised its significance.

But modern industry can create a serious problem of pollution. This is not new by any means, but it has become a growing menace to health, both because of the growth of industry itself and of the dangerous chemical and other side-effects that industrial waste can have. Fear of radiation from atomic explosions increased the problem: by 1964 the mean ratio of radioactive strontium-90 in milk in the U.K. had risen to a dangerous level of 28·0. Restrictions upon nuclear tests in the atmosphere brought the ratio down to 2·8 by the mid-'70s. But a new awareness of the dangers of pollution resulting from exhaust fumes, industrial processes and from the dumping of waste products, made Governments anxious to control the problem, which was demonstrated by the severe 'smogs' in London in the early '50s (especially in 1952). A Clean Air Act (1956) regulated the release of smoke and fumes from factories and required the burning of smokeless coals in designated areas. As a result, the atmosphere of industrial cities that was once synonymous with grey skies has been greatly improved and it has been possible to clean public buildings without fear of them growing grimy with soot and smoke stains within a few months. Sheffield provides an excellent example of the difference that the Clean Air Act has made to the environment. Over the country as a whole the level of sulphur-dioxide concentrations was halved between 1961 and 1974. Measures to clear rivers have led, for example, to the return of some species of fish to the Thames and there has been a considerable reduction in the number of seriously polluted rivers in the country. Britain has

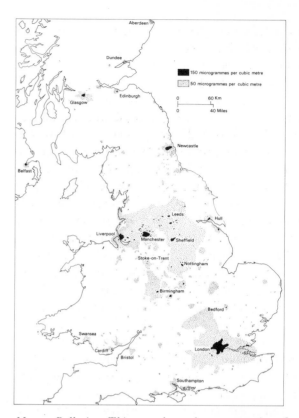

Map 7 Pollution. This map shows the concentration of sulphur dioxide in the air in 1972/3. Urban and heavy industrial areas are badly affected

made significant progress in checking this threat from the growing size of industry, although the level of carbon gases and other precipitates from the exhaust of cars and lorries remains a serious problem.

Changes in the structure of industry, 1880s–1970s

A tradition of vigorous competition between firms has survived from *laissez-faire* days; but in some cases it is merely a facade, for in some industries, it was common for firms to agree on just how much competition there should be. The *appearance* of competition was preserved, but it was so regulated as to have the effect of carving up the market so that firms might be certain of their sales at a price they would determine. Competition can be wasteful and disadvantageous to the public, either because the quality suffers or because the service that the public expects is cut to the barest minimum. It can lead to dangerous situations—for example, in the 1960s a number of motor insurance companies offered insurance at rates below what was economic in an effort to gain custom by 'cut-throat' means: several bankruptcies followed, and those who had insured with these firms had quickly to look elsewhere. But it is probably true to say that without the spur of competition or active public criticism, firms tend to become set in their ways and not well-fitted to play effective roles in a dynamic economy. Some old-established firms have shown an excellent capacity to change with the times, of course, like the Birmingham Small Arms Company (B.S.A.) founded in 1861 to produce small fire-arms with interchangeable parts, which began manufacturing bicycles in the 1880s (until 1957), motors in 1908 (until 1960) and machine tools from 1918.

In the 1880s associations of employers appeared and by 1914 agreements covering prices and production policies were strong among firms manufacturing soap, salt, explosives, tobacco, whisky and cement. The practice of requiring retailers to charge a set price to the public (*resale price maintenance*, R.P.M.) had appeared. Manufacturers were copying the example of the German kartels and American trusts. The first world war hastened the process of combining to restrict competition and to enjoy the benefits of some degree of control of markets and prices, and a Government Report (1918) complained:

'There is at the present time in every important branch of industry in the U.K. an increasing tendency to form Trade Associations and Combinations, having for their purpose the restriction of competition and the control of prices.'

During the war, the Government, with extreme reluctance, was compelled to take an active part in organising industry. The coal mines and railways were in effect nationalised and extensive control exercised throughout the economy. The controls were relaxed quickly after the war and industries restored into private hands. But the effect of central direction could not be effaced: in 1923 the 130

railway companies of 1914 were reduced to the 'big four' (L.N.E.R., L.M.S., G.W.R., S.R.) and the Government became an important customer; the Forestry Commission remained as a public utility; even the commercial banks, especially between 1917 and 1920, were being consolidated into the 'big five'. Combinations of employers (operating through trade associations) became widespread in the '20s because of the economic situation, both to restrict competition and to promote efficiency through *rationalisation*, and as firms grew bigger, the job of the manager became more specialised and tended to be broken down into particular functions to be shared by specialists like the accountant, works manager and personnel officer.

Cartels (groups of firms controlled by a central agency that determines policy and prices) appeared in both cotton and coal in the 1920s in an attempt to rationalise production within these old staple industries. The Lancashire Cotton Corporation was formed in 1929 (backed by the Bankers' Industrial Development Corporation) to help readjust the industry to worsening conditions. It was followed by a merger in ancillary textile processes under J. and P. Coates and the English Sewing Cotton Company, and in man-made fibres Courtaulds and British Celanese dominated. The electrical industry had been concentrated effectively into three companies by 1939. A similar pattern developed in the motor industry where amalgamations reduced an industry of eighty-eight firms producing some 90,000 vehicles in 1922 to one of twenty-two firms in 1937 producing 300,000 vehicles, of which six companies held seventy-five per cent of the market. In 1926 four old-established chemical firms merged to make Imperial Chemical Industries (I.C.I.). The process was accelerated by the economic slump of 1929-31, and under Government pressure the British Iron and Steel Federation (1934) and the National Shipbuilders' Security were formed. Rationalisation was pressed in the 1930s as a means of achieving efficiency, but as it was not always done with an eye to social effects, some areas of old-established industry suffered, like Mossend (Scotland), and Dowlais, (Wales). The National

Ship-builders' Security closed the yards at Jarrow, a town almost totally dependent on ship-building, and provoked the famous march of men whose livelihood had been snatched from them—their M.P., Ellen Wilkinson, wrote a book about it called *The Town that was Murdered*. Modernising and reorganising industry is no easy thing—as was shown by the problems of the Coal Board in the closing of pits in the 1960s, and by those of British Steel in rationalising its steel making plants in the 1970s.

Between the wars areas dependent on one major industry faced prolonged unemployment: things were much easier in the diversified industries of the Midlands and the London area. But even the growth industries adopted restrictive practices. The practice of 'branding' goods (marketing goods under a well-known name) made it easier to impose R.P.M. which manufacturers began to enforce in the courts. In 1937 the House of Lords decided it was lawful for the Motor Trade Association both to fine and 'blacklist' a garage owner for selling a car below the 'list price' (the price at which manufacturers required goods to be sold). Trade associations seemed to be able to enforce their wishes easily. Since they tended to pay more attention to devising and enforcing restrictive practices than to reducing costs, this was not always in the public interest. After the second world war, R.P.M. was greatly extended.

Many new small firms have grown up, especially in the new growth industries, since 1945, but there has also been a strong tendency for larger firms to amalgamate, especially in the motor trade, in order to enjoy *economies of scale* and effective marketing, as well as some degree of *vertical integration*. The Government has also emerged as the largest single employer of labour, and those huge public corporations, the nationalised industries have been developed.

The Government and industry

The first world war forced the Government to take an active part in organising industry and the 'economic doldrums' afterwards, meant that this expansion of Government activity could not be simply ended.

Indeed, the Government gave continual leads and direct assistance to industry throughout the inter-war years. Rationalisation schemes were encouraged, and a grant of £9½ million for the building of the Queen Mary was made (1934) on condition that the Cunard and White Star companies amalgamated. In 1936 central selling arrangements were established for coal, and mine owners' royalties were compulsorily purchased in 1938. The Spindles Act (1936) assisted the cotton industry in replacing old machinery and a Cotton Board (1940) was established to fix prices. Local government received subsidies for house building, and industry was de-rated in 1929, paying low rates, or no rates at all until 1964. The return to protection (1932) (see *page 227*) sheltered industry from much foreign competition. But all this Government assistance was piece-meal, 'uninformed by any set of general principles'. The idea of the public corporation, influenced by the success of the Port of London Authority (1908) in which a public body, representing the interests of firms within the London docks, ran the port centrally, was extended to the British Broadcasting Corporation (1926) and the Central Electricity Board (1926) and London Transport (1933). But, although the schemes worked out here were to influence the planning of the nationalised industries after 1945, the inter-war governments had no intention of extending the principle generally.

However, a fundamental change in attitude, in contrast to the *laissez-faire* views of the nineteenth century, was gradually emerging. More people were coming to accept the idea of a 'mixed' economy in which traditional private enterprise and the new type of public enterprise, would go hand in hand. When the Labour Party went in for a policy of *nationalisation* (public ownership and control) of major industries between 1945 and 1951, it was not being revolutionary. The idea of a 'mixed' economy had gained support in all political parties. Perhaps its most obvious sign was the launching of P.E.P. (Political and Economic Planning) in 1931. P.E.P. was responsible for producing some major detailed economic studies during the following twenty years. Three leading men in the organisation were Gerald

Barry, a socialist, Sir Basil Blackett, a Conservative and a director of the Bank of England, and Israel M. Sieff, of Marks and Spencer the remarkably successful multiple store firm.

Keynes, of course, advocated a mixed economy (see *page 228*) and Harold Macmillan as a young conservative M.P. (he was to be Prime Minister, 1957-63) put the case directly in two books, *The Middle Way* (1938) and *Reconstruction* (1933):

'Throughout the whole of the post war period there had been growing an uneasy consciousness of something radically wrong with the economic system; and this uneasiness had overshadowed political controversy both within and between all the political parties for many years. One of the consequences of the [1931] crisis was to confirm these suspicions and liberate men's minds from a continued subservience to the economic orthodoxy of the pre-war world.'

'Planning is forced upon us . . . not for idealistic reasons but because the old mechanism which served us when markets were expanding naturally and spontaneously is no longer adequate when the tendency is in the opposite direction.'

The ideas implied by these two quotations were too radical for the politicians of the 1930s. But some measures were taken, notably the Depressed Areas Act (1935), to counteract the unemployment produced by the decline of the old staple industries in areas like south Scotland, Tyneside, West Cumberland and South Wales (unemployment was often over 50 per cent in these areas as compared with 6 per cent for Birmingham with its many new light industries). A commissioner was appointed to revive trade in these depressed areas by inviting industry to build new factories—the Ebbw Vale Steel Works was one result—and the Government granted £2 million. In 1937 local authorities were allowed to build industrial trading estates to provide factories at favourable rates. This was not very dramatic and did not stop the areas continuing to become derelict, but it was at least a start and marked a significant departure in Government policy. Industrial reconstruction was too important to be left merely to businessmen.

In 1937 the *Barlow Committee* had been appointed to investigate the consequences of large concentrations of industry for the country as a whole. It reported in 1940, acknowledging that the depressed areas would continue to lose both population and industry unless the Government itself took active steps to stop the exodus. However, it warned that the factors affecting the location of industry were infinitely complex and that a Government department might be no wiser than industry itself in selecting particular sites for factories. After the war, the Distribution of Industry Acts (1945 and 1950) and the Town and Country Planning Act (1947) made some effort to implement the Barlow proposals by giving some direction to the location of industry, but the flow of population from the 'Development Areas' (as they were now called) continued, and continues still.

During the second world war extensive controls were imposed by the coalition government and the economy became completely controlled. Rationing, price control, direction of labour and the direct control of industry with each factory having a production schedule to maintain, became the norm—the name 'British Railways' dated from 1941. Plans for reconstruction were also being laid, and in 1944 a famous White Paper committed all parties to a policy of full employment (see *page 231*). Active co-operation of the T.U.C. and the Federation of British Industries (F.B.I., today called C.B.I.) was secured, and the experience gained during the war, and the realisation that the success of Britain's industrial future depended on the co-operation of labour and management together with the Government, meant that the days when management and men faced each other in two hostile ranks were passing.

Most of the war-time controls were retained until the early 1950s and the post-war Labour government (1945-51) pursued a policy of the nationalisation of basic industries. Today we accept nationalisation as a normal feature of the industrial world, and it is difficult to re-capture the bitter acrimony that typified the debate over nationalisation in the later

1940s. To Labour supporters it was more than a question of industrial efficiency, it was an expression of social justice; it represented an escape from the long tradition of exploitation in the coalmines and on the railways (easy enough to minimise today, but vital to an understanding of the psychology of working men of the time). In fact, the organisation of the nationalised industries (B.O.A.C., 1939, and B.E.A., 1946; the Bank of England, 1946; and coal, 1947, gas and electricity, 1948), did not greatly differ from that of any of the large cartels that had grown up during the inter-war period except that they had a minister in parliament who was responsible for very broad general policy decisions. There was to be no nonsense about workers' control: the running of the industries was left to professional managers. It was really an extension of the public utility idea that had been popular between the wars: also the industries nationalised were those essential to the smooth running of the economy which were heavily under-capitalised and in such very serious need of reconstruction that they could only have survived with Government aid.

Under Lord Woolton, the Conservatives ran what was almost a crusade against nationalisation, but when they were returned in 1951 they showed no marked desire to de-nationalise. Steel, nationalised in 1951, was largely returned to parent companies, but Richard Thomas and Baldwin remained under Government control and a Steel Board provided for central direction of the industry. Road transport, mainly nationalised in 1948, was partially de-nationalised in 1953. The other nationalised corporations have remained, and nationalisation ceased to be a major issue—when steel was re-nationalised in 1966 it caused scarcely a stir. In 1972 it seemed quite natural for a Conservative Government, by the Industry Act, to assume powers of directing and controlling the siting of factories—particularly for the benefit of the Assisted Areas (as the old 'depressed' areas were now called). However, in 1976 nationalisation returned to the political arena when the Labour Government forced through proposals to nationalise the ailing ship building industry along with aircraft manufacture. Both of these industries rely to a large extent on Government contracts and ship building requires considerable rationalisation and modernisation if it is to compete in an increasingly competitive world market. There was strong opposition, both in the House of Commons and the Lords which prevented the nationalisation of the ship repairing industry. But today Government and industry are closely interwoven.

The real significance of the transfer of so much heavy industry to public ownership is economic rather than political. The Government, its expenditure constituting about 40 per cent of the Gross National Product (GNP) is now the largest employer of labour in the country as well as a huge consumer on its own account. Nearly half the capital investment of the country is financed by Government controlled enterprises—the *public sector*. Today, the Welfare State with its extensive services in health, welfare, housing and education, requires the Government to take a principal part in the running of the economy. Industry today demands that governments provide conditions of reasonable economic security—it also expects to use sources of power like gas and electricity, transport services, like the railways and the fast roads and motorways without paying a full economic price simply because the Government, and not a private company, is responsible for them. We have moved a very long way away from the *laissez-faire* ideas of the Victorians!

This does not mean that we no longer worry about the spur of competition. Not only do we compete for markets abroad, but at home all sections of industry and commerce are keen for efficiency. One of the most obvious signs of this has been the major change in shopping habits, called the *retail revolution*, itself a triumph of managerial skill. Since the 1950s, assisted by the growth of consumer spending, there has been a considerable change in the retail trade. Many one-man shops and small concerns have closed because they cannot meet the competition from the big retailers who have expanded their *multiple stores* (e.g. Marks and Spencer, Sainsbury, International). These stores concentrate on a specific range of goods of a definite quality, and they offer cheap prices because they can pass on to the customer some of their economies of scale. Their success is measured not only in the size of their new stores, but in the fact that they are household names. In addition, many shops have developed self-service techniques, especially in tinned food shops where *supermarkets* have become popular. In consequence the 'High Street' of many towns has had a change of character, and the traditional family grocer, unless he supplies speciality goods or a scattered semi-rural area, has found it hard to survive. He still offers the chance of a friendly chat to the housewife, and it is apparent that the local corner shop will survive simply because of its friendliness and its convenient location and opening hours. But many of our city centres have new shopping centres, often reserved for pedestrians as *precincts*, where the large multiple stores attract a great many shoppers. Small specialist shops also appear to survive well in these big shopping centres—many of which are remarkable examples of town planning. In the mid-1970s there appeared a new type of shop—the *hypermarket*. This is a huge shopping area where the full range of household goods, large and small, may be purchased. It would be sited close to a busy motorway intersection not too far from several large towns, the idea being that housewives will drive to the hypermarket in order to do a whole week's shopping at prices that are often less than supermarkets in the towns. They can leave their car in the car park and sometimes there is a creche for babies and small children. There are also restaurants and cinemas so that a full day can happily be spent at these hypermarkets. Supermarkets have developed means of encouraging shoppers to buy goods, sometimes by offering tinned foods very cheaply in order to attract the shopper inside (this is called using a *loss leader*). They have been helped in this by the attack on restrictive trading practices, in particular resale price maintenance.

In 1948 a Monopolies and Restrictive Practices Act set up a Monopolies Commission to decide which monopoly practices were in the public interest. It was ineffective and by 1956 it was generally agreed that a strong measure was needed because parts of British industry were honeycombed with restrictive practices, whilst maintaining a public facade of free competition. The Restrictive Trade Practices Act (1956) outlawed the 'collective enforcement' of R.P.M. (a producer could not require all shops to sell his goods at a set price, although individual agreements between manufacturer and retailer were allowed). This ended the power of trade associations to control prices. The Act set up a Restrictive Practices Court to try cases of restrictive agreements brought before it. Those in the public interest were registered (some 2,000 had been by 1959). It was a vigorous act and certainly stirred industry, but by 1959 there were already some signs that industrialists were beginning to find ways round the measure. In 1964, in the teeth of bitter opposition from the small shopkeeper, Mr Heath passed a further measure restricting R.P.M., and today the 'list price' on many goods is no more than a guide to the shopkeeper—and

A hypermarket. Note its huge size, the cheap site in the countryside and the crowds. The chaos of congested traffic shows one of the problems connected with hypermarkets

shopper! The careful housewife will 'shop around' to find the lowest prices. Furthermore, the consumer has come to demand greater protection against 'shoddy' goods or unfair or misleading advertisements. So much money is spent on advertising that the advertising industry has its own 'watch dog' to prevent misleading advertisements appearing. The magazine *Which?*, produced by the Consumers' Association, keeps a close eye on quality and value for money, and in 1973 the Fair Trading Act appointed both a Director General of Fair Trading (Mr. Gordon Borrie) who is empowered to prosecute offenders, and a Consumer Protection Advisory Committee to look after the interests of the consumer. In 1974, a Secretary of State for Prices and Consumer Protection was appointed as a minister of Cabinet rank and in 1977 a reconstituted Price Commission, under Charles Williams, a former merchant banker, instituted a series of investigations that resulted in firms 'pegging' prices and the mini-

ster ordering a reduction in tea prices (1978). It is hoped to achieve a greater efficiency and more responsible pricing policy through the Commission.

Trade unions since 1927

After the General Strike (see *page 222*) a new relationship gradually emerged between Trade Unions and the Government. Lord Citrine, General Secretary of the T.U.C. from 1926 to 1946, put it into words:
'The principal lesson I had learned was that the trade union movement must exert its influence in an ever-widening sphere and not be contained within the traditional walls of trade union policy'.

During the Second World War that new relationship was cemented, and the T.U.C. took its place after the war as an important body with which the Government normally discusses problems well beyond the field of labour relations. In a phrase, since the Second World War, the trade union movement has entered the citadel of political power and is consulted by whichever party is in power over matters of economic policy. George Woodcock, who retired as General Secretary in 1969, put the point clearly at the centenary celebrations (1968), 'the T.U.C. contains some of the best economists in the country'. And the measure of their 'respectability' was the Queen herself attending their centenary dinner as guest of honour.

In the 1920s the trade union movement suffered a serious decline in membership (see *graph 30*), but since the late '20s membership has continued to grow, especially in significantly new areas, like the 'white collar' workers. However, the movement has not kept pace with the growth of the working population, nor have many women joined.

But the number of unions has declined owing to amalgamations, and this makes for greater efficiency and more powerful unions.

The movement was faced with a serious problem of adjustment to the conditions of full employment and relative prosperity of the post-war years: it has to change from the rôle of fighting for better con-

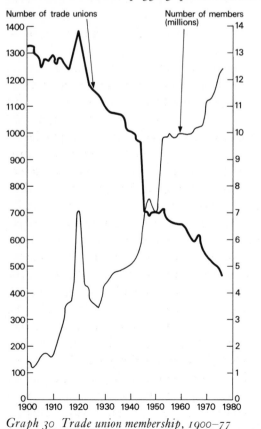

Graph 30 Trade union membership, 1900–77

ditions to that of smoothing the course of change and efficiency in industry. A serious problem, often arising from technological change, is inter-union rivalry (especially among the small craft unions) and '*demarcation disputes*' (disagreements over which craftsman should do a particular job—a 'who does what' dispute). This is often seen in the shipyards and on the railways, where the interests of A.S.L.E.F. members seem to be in danger of being swamped by the less skilled members of the larger N.U.R. *Pay differentials* (higher rates of pay for skilled work) between skilled and labouring men are shrinking, and this also causes friction between the craft unions and the general unions. In the docks there is also the problem of 'poaching' members from one union to another that has led to strikes. '*Wild cat*' strikes have caused a great deal of industrial unrest: these are spontaneous strikes, generally over very minor matters, which are not '*official*' in that the unions concerned have not called out the workers: the strikers are called out by their *shop stewards* (local union men, elected by the local members, over whom the union has no dictatorial control). This particular problem of industrial indiscipline is especially serious in the car industry. In the later '60s, the tendency has been for official strikes to decline and unofficial strikes to increase. This has led to much heart-searching, and the T.U.C. has investigated means of controlling unofficial strike action. Legislation to make unofficial strikes illegal has been suggested, but such interference with the right to strike has not gained very wide acceptance. Fines for unofficial strikers, again, might be difficult to enforce.

Trade unions themselves have at times become too authoritarian. Many unions seek the right to oblige all workers in particular works to be union members (the *closed shop*). This may involve the freedom of choice of particular workmen who do not desire to become trade union members (although, as their trade union colleagues will point out, they desire to share in all the advantages that the unions manage to gain for their members!) The issue was at the centre of an important but complex case, *Rookes v. Barnard* (1964). Rookes, a B.O.A.C. draughtsman,

had resigned from his union which had then persuaded his employer to dismiss him. The House of Lords eventually upheld Rookes's claim of £7,500 against the union for operating a closed shop against him and thus preventing him from working. This decision seemed to call in question the protection which unions were thought to enjoy under the Trade Disputes Act, 1906; this protection was continued in 1965. The whole problem of employers' associations and trade unions, and their relations with each other, the Government and the public, was investigated by the *Donovan Committee* (1968) which recommended some structural changes in the trade union movement, and greater central authority by the T.U.C.

Today, the Unions are recognised as an important body upon whose advice and assistance governments can lean. But they are under some strain because they are having to reorganise their movement in order to make it more up-to-date and more reflective of the changing structure of industry, and to change the attitude of their members, many of whom remember the days of very difficult labour relations before the war, from one of antagonism to the 'bosses' to one of co-operation with management and industry for the good of the country. In this they are not always helped by management, nor the attitude of their own more extreme rank and file.

The new rôle—so different from what many trade unionists and ordinary workers expect—comes under the greatest strain in time of economic crisis, for then the T.U.C. is often obliged to back a policy of wage restraint which to the man in the street seems exactly what 'the bosses' want to increase their profits. As more people become more aware of the inter-relationship of interests between the Government, management and unions in running the economy, it becomes less difficult to carry the trade union movement in agreeing to measures that are unpopular at the moment (like wage restraint) in order that greater prosperity might ultimately be achieved. The strain put upon the union movement, however, was apparent in the 1960s and rose to breaking point in the 1970s. It is not merely whether a factory is profitable that has to be considered, but the whole range of economic performance; and in Britain's case, even as a member of the European Common Market, our balance of payments is a crucial factor. The rate of inflation is closely linked to the value of the pound sterling: up to the 1950s wages probably played a relatively minor part in the 'creeping' inflation experienced since the war, but by the 1960s wages were beginning to add to the pace of inflation. Prices rose; real wages fell; workers, reasonably enough, demanded wage rises to keep up, and backed these wage demands with strikes. A wage increase was passed on to the consumer in the form of higher prices, rather than absorbed by the industry in terms of higher productivity. And so the wage rise no longer met the increased prices: a further wage rise was demanded. This adds to what is called an *inflationary spiral*, and although it is never quite so simple as this (many other factors are involved) wage demands have begun to exercise a vital influence on the pace of inflation. For this reason successive Governments have turned to some form of *incomes policy*.

In the crisis of 1961 (see *page 232*) the Chancellor of the Exchequer, Selwyn Lloyd, took emergency measures to vary the rate of certain taxes without reference to Parliament so that a crisis could be dealt with immediately. It was followed by a pay pause as well as the creation of the N.E.D.C. in 1962 (see *page 232*). It was not easy for the T.U.C. to carry its members into giving support to the new policy of co-operation. It might have been easier under the Wilson Government which launched the National Plan (see *page 232*) and created a National Board for Prices and Incomes (it was chaired by a former Conservative minister, Aubrey Jones) to ensure that wages get their fair share of the national cake. The devaluation crisis of 1967 put tremendous strain on the trade union movement. However, in 1969, the Government produced an important White Paper, *In Place of Strife*, proposing the establishment of a Commission on Industrial Relations (C.I.R.) under the chairmanship of George Woodcock, formerly General Secretary of the T.U.C., (it was formed in January 1969). Other proposals of the White Paper were that the right to belong to a trade union should be made a part of all contracts of employment; the C.I.R. should assist the T.U.C. to resolve inter-union disputes and help in modernising the trade union movement; an Industrial Relations Board should hear complaints by individuals against arbitrary action by trade unions; the Government should have the power to enforce a ballot of members involved, if strike action were proposed, and to impose a 'conciliation pause' of twenty-eight days for unofficial or hasty strikes in order to allow for adequate negotiation. But the economic situation of 1969 required the Government to insist upon a restriction of wage demands and the confining of wage claims to a set minimum. There was a wide-spread fear among union leaders that their traditional right to strike might be confined or impaired if legislation to enforce wage-restraint became a normal feature. They also feared that the whole area of industrial relations would be taken out of their hands by the creation of an Industrial Relations Commission which the Government proposed to establish. T.U.C. opposition led the Government to drop the proposal in the summer of 1969. Their successors, however, faced by further economic crises and determined to introduce some form of directed incomes policy, disbanded the National Board for Prices and Incomes (1971) and introduced the Industrial Relations Act (1971) in the teeth of hostile resistance from the trade union movement. The failure of their attempt to control industrial relations by Act of Parliament (see *page 299*) demonstrated both the difficulty of establishing the proper basis of co-operation between Government, management and unions, and the potential power of the union movement.

19 · The common man and the Welfare State

The roots of the Welfare State lie in Victorian England. But it is one thing to provide relief for the needy; the Poor Law had done this since Elizabethan times. It is quite another to regard the State as having the duty to supply for all its citizens, rich or poor, a full range of services designed to provide for their needs from the cradle to the grave. This is the meaning of the Welfare State. Social security and a range of opportunity is available for all; it is no longer the preserve of those with wealth. A tremendous change in attitude has taken place. This change can be dated from the period of the second world war.

War socialism, 1939-45

In the last years of the first world war, Lloyd George had introduced 'war socialism', but his measures were not altogether vigorous and most of them were relaxed after the war. But the second world war was different. From the beginning it was realised that it would be a 'people's war', fought with conscripted troops using weapons produced in factories where their wives worked.

A measure of conscription was introduced in April 1939, and was extended for both the armed forces and essential war work when the war was

The Home Guard and A.R.P. Warden, 1940

declared in September. Gas masks and identity cards were issued to civilians, a Home Guard was organised, air-raid precautions taken (actually from 1937 onwards) and in 1941 a National Fire Service was established. The British allowed themselves to be organised as never before because of the very real threat of invasion in 1940: it remained something of a habit after the war and helped people to accept the necessary central organisation involved in a complex modern industrial society.

Taxation shot up. A totally new scheme of income tax was introduced (1940) that was to remain the basis of income tax today. It was called *Pay As You Earn* (P.A.Y.E.) and was a triumph of accountancy techniques. A wage earner's total allowances for tax purposes are deducted from his annual wage and he is taxed upon the remainder on a sliding scale. The tax is deducted weekly or monthly by the employer according to a *code number* which the tax office issues. The sliding scale ensures that the rich pay more than the poor (this is called *progressive taxation*). The system is highly efficient and cuts down

the cost of tax collection: in itself it is a revolution in Government methods.

Profiteering, one of the vices of the first world war, was much less in the second, because of the rigid controls, and rationing that came in January 1940, for foodstuffs like sugar, butter and bacon, and was soon extended to most basic foodstuffs. Soap, clothing and footware were to be had *only* if one had *clothing coupons* for them and then the goods had to be of a 'utility' quality to ensure fairness and to

Utility Mark

The Utility Mark — The government guarantee of quality

Meadow Dairy was a chain of grocery shops. This leaflet gives some tips on using the meat ration. Notice that you could get your ration only from the shop with which you were registered

BOARD OF TRADE   Leaflet UFD/#

UTILITY FURNITURE

What the furniture is like

Supplies of utility furniture are limited by the shortage of materials and other productive resources needed make it, and for the present at any rate, there will be none to spare for display in the shops. The whole range of utility models can however be seen in a well illustrated catalogue which gives prices and general specifications, and exhibitions are being held from time to time in various centres. The arrangements will be announced in the local Press. The shopkeeper from whom you order the furniture will be able to show you a copy of the catalogue or you can buy one on ordering from any bookseller or newsagent, price 9d., or by post direct from H.M. Stationery Office, price 10d. net, at the following addresses:—

York House, Kingsway, London, W.C.2.
120, George Street, Edinburgh, 2.
39/41, King Street, Manchester, 2.
1, St. Andrews Crescent, Cardiff.
80, Chichester Street, Belfast.

Where to buy

You may order utility furniture from any furniture retailer in the area specified on your buying permit. The permit is only valid in the area shown on it. In order to save transport, you should choose a shop near to the address at which you will be using the furniture. The prices given in the catalogue include delivery up to a distance of 15 miles, but for greater distances the retailer may charge for delivery. You need not buy all the furniture at the same time from the same shop, and if you wish you may order it by post.

How to use Buying Permits

First read carefully the instructions on the permit. Remember that it is illegal to sell permits or units or to give them to anyone else. This

permit is issued to you personally, for your personal use to meet the special need you have described in your application form. There is very little furniture available and so it has to be kept for people with special needs. It is on trust— on trust for people who are bombed out and for the new homes of the newly married. So the permit is a privilege—it allows you a share of these goods because of your special need, and if that need does not arise—if you do not set up house after all—you must return the permit to the Assistance Board and not spend it on yourself or buy furniture and give it away to your friends or relatives.

Before you can use the units, that is before the retailer may accept them, you must see that the permit contains your name and address and National Registration Number, or Service Number and Rank. The whole permit must be produced when you order the furniture, and you must allow the retailer to detach from the permit the units needed for your order; you must not deposit units with a retailer until you have placed an order. It is illegal for the retailer to accept loose units, or to accept units without taking an order. If you order the furniture by post you must send the whole permit : the retailer will send back the units he does not require. The unit numbered 1 is valid only if it is attached to the panel bearing your name, Identity Card number, etc. You must, therefore, surrender the panel with unit 1 attached when you make your last purchase.

Validity of Utility Furniture Buying Permits

The permit is valid only for a period of 3 months from the date shown on the front, so you must order your furniture within that time : after that time it will be illegal for a retailer to accept an order from you. If you have not placed your orders by then you must return the permit to the Assistance Board.

What you may buy with Utility Furniture Units

With your units you may buy any of the items of utility furniture in the list below. The only other types of utility furniture being produced are

> Take great care of your buying permit—it is the property of the Board of Trade and they do not undertake to replace lost permits

The Utility scheme ensured quality and standards and was a great agent for equality, for everyone, rich and poor, was treated alike.

THIS WILL INTEREST YOU!

TO ALL CUSTOMERS REGISTERED WITH THE 'MEADOW'

Making Meat Rations Go Further

Meat rationing is going to call for very careful planning on your part. We are trying to help you by-

KEEPING OUR BACON PRICES AS LOW AS POSSIBLE

If you make full use of the family's Bacon Coupons you can supplement their meat ration and give them more variety too.

BOILING JOINTS available WITHOUT COUPONS
Limited Supply

TO ALL CUSTOMERS, WHETHER REGISTERED OR NOT

You are invited to participate in the Meadow

GOLDTIPS GIFT SCHEME

(One of the few Gift Schemes still running)

FREE GIFTS of all kinds can be obtained in exchange for Goldtips Coupons.

Goldtips Tea	per ¼ lb.	8ᴰ
Goldtips Cocoa	per ¼ lb.	4½ᴰ
Goldtips Cheese Spread	per box	6ᴰ

Ask the branch manager for full particulars and

START SAVING NOW

Have you read the astonishing facts overleaf?

Clothing Coupons, 1940

conserve vital raw materials for the war effort. The 'utility' scheme extended to furniture, textiles and other household goods. It succeeded in producing goods of an established quality made to a high standard of design—the simple style of the 1940s in dress and furniture owed much to the utility scheme. Iron railings, and occasionally some fine wrought iron gate-ways were cut down and melted to help the supply of steel. Advertising campaigns encouraged people to grow their own food in gardens, allotments and in public parks converted for the purpose. Lord Woolton at the Ministry of Food made rationing fair for all: nursing mothers and young children received allocations of cod-liver oil, orange juice and milk. But there was continual trouble from *black-marketeers* who sold food and goods (sometimes stolen) at a price, without asking for coupons. Every country had the same problem; some Governments shot their black-marketeers, ours fined or imprisoned them. Meanwhile, Government advertising was extensive both to maintain public morale and encourage careful practices which helped the war-effort. Slogans were widely used,

like 'Make do and mend' or '100 fires a day are helping Hitler', or this rhyme:

> 'Those who have the will to win
> Cook potatoes in their skin,
> For they know the sight of peelings
> Deeply hurts Lord Woolton's feelings.'

The rationing scheme, especially food rationing, represented a minor social revolution of tremendous significance for the post-war period. Simply, it was direct Government control of prices and of the quantities permitted, and it was the same for everyone: the two main features of post-war Britain were present here—Government intervention on a new scale and a move towards equality. Since public morale at home needed to be maintained at a high level (air-raids and then the 'doodle-bug' rockets made the war as much a civilian as a service matter) food rationing aimed at raising the living standards of the poor. Many were better fed on a more balanced diet during the war than ever before: indeed all the data available suggests that the diet of the urban working-class family in the war years differed little from that of the middle-class family. This 'levelling-up' effect had its influence on families for the future in producing healthier babies and children and raising standards generally. It succeeded as an English compromise, combining Government control and the willing co-operation of housewives and retailers. Price fixing also meant fixing profit margins (these may have been fixed a little on the high side to ensure co-operation)—the food price index rose only twenty per cent between 1939 and 1944. That year the food subsidies necessary to keep prices low and stable amounted to £152 million—a great contribution of out-door relief, as it were, to the entire population; but the poor benefited most, for between the wars they had often been poorly fed, while now they had an adequate diet.

Food rationing had been well planned for—it grew out of the Food (Defence Plans) Department (1936), which became the new Ministry of Food in 1939, with 19 divisional food officers to supervise the work of 1,250 local food executive officers. The scientific adviser was Professor Drummond, a man of considerable experience in the study of the dietary inadequacy of the food of the poor. Rationing would change this inadequacy, with the aid of food technology, helped by advertising in the press and on the radio (for people tend to be very conservative over food), and also by good wages and high employment. The British were probably the best fed people on the continent. De-hydrated milk and eggs, and vegetables, as well as new types of tinned meat (like Spam and Mor) that were sent from the U.S.A. under Lend-Lease Agreements after 1944, made quite a difference to our diet. Extra milk for school children, a scheme begun before the war, was extended, and for the workers, canteens to supply cheap, well-balanced meals were required in all factories employing over 250 people; there were 11,500 canteens by 1943. British Restaurants selling subsidised meals were opened in big towns for the general public—there were 2,115 by 1943, selling 615,000 meals daily.

Anderson shelters (they were named after a prominent civil servant)

The evacuation

There had been air-raids in the first world war, but it was clear that they would play a vital part in the second, inevitably striking at the civilian population, both to destroy morale and disrupt factory working—for in 'total war' everyone is a soldier. Although some cities suffered very badly, notably the East End of London, Cardiff, Southampton, Plymouth, Hull, Coventry and Sheffield, public morale remained high. Public shelters had been provided, these being supplemented by 'Anderson' shelters in the back gardens, and the London tube stations were used. Quite a large number also simply travelled out of cities in the evenings, returning in the morning after the raid—they called it 'trekking'. In addition the Government arranged the transfer of as many children as possible from the danger areas of docklands and railway marshalling yards and factory areas—substantially working class areas. In September 1939 about one and a quarter million people, mostly children, were evacuated to rural areas and this continued until 1941 when about three million had been moved.

The first wave of evacuation was a tribute to organising skill and the evacuees settled down to shared homes and schools in unfamiliar surroundings. But the evacuation brought home in an unpleasantly forceful way the bad housing and living conditions of the poor. It revealed that all the private charity and all the local and central government action had scarcely scratched the surface of the problem of urban poverty: it also says a great deal for the state of public opinion that the condition of the first evacuees gave rise to horror. The evacuation brought the poor to the people. In 1941, referring to the way the 'blitz' and the 'Dunkirk spirit' had broken down class barriers, Lord Woolton said, 'There had been a moral as well as an economic revolution in our society.'

Many evacuees were in a wretched physical state, many infected with fleas, vermin and head lice whose eggs ('nits') formed crustations on the scalp. The school medical service had done much to eradicate head lice from country children: it was

London evacuees leaving by train

still a scourge of the slums a generation after medical inspections had begun. Ringworm, impetigo, scabies and other skin complaints, resulting from bad feeding and bad hygiene, were common. Regular wholesome food was not a feature of slum life: 'fry-ups', pickles and sweets were more normal. It took some children (not all of them poor) a while to accustom themselves to a more balanced diet. Inadequate clothing and footwear was another headache. Many of the children did not possess underclothing or nightwear and some lacked proper shoes. Low wages had meant that the poor could not even afford much of the cheap clothing that had been available for a hundred years.

Understandably, there was an immediate wave of public resentment, but this rapidly gave way to a determination to solve the problem at its roots—this is where the post-war Welfare State comes from. In the darkest days of the war, whilst air raids destroyed our cities, plans were being laid for reconstruction and for providing greater social justice in the New Britain. It was no longer to be simply a matter of 'doing something' for the poor.

The Welfare State takes shape

Control of prices did not prevent a very steep rise in the cost of living, and this, together with the need to provide for war widows and orphans and victims of the 'blitz' led in 1940 to an extension of the work of the *Assistance Board* (formerly the Unemployment Assistance Board) and to supplementary pensions. Social services were now readily available for all, not merely the poor. In July 1940 a National Milk Scheme provided subsidised milk for expectant and nursing mothers and children under five. Thus a simple measure, paid for out of general taxation, provided for the improved health of the next generation. Welfare centres and food offices supplied cod-liver oil, black currant and rose hip syrups (for Vitamin C) free to expectant mothers, because of the shortage of fresh fruits, and dried milk and concentrated orange juice was imported from U.S.A. The school meal service was transformed (1940) into a social service supplying subsidised meals to all children regardless of their parents' income (many mothers of all classes were working in factories and on other essential jobs and could not be home to provide lunches). These services were continued after the war for some years. In 1941 free milk was supplied to all schoolchildren (in 1968 it was stopped for secondary school children). To guard against epidemics as a result of the 'blitz' an extensive *immunisation* programme was undertaken so that diphtheria, which took a terrible toll of life in Europe, ceased to be a 'killer' disease. Immunisation is now a normal part of the Health Service. So is mass radiography (begun in the 1940s) which does much to detect early cases of tuberculosis (which is no longer so widespread as before the war). In 1941 the Ministry of Health passed judgement on the cottage and municipal hospital services as a whole, by announcing a scheme for a comprehensive health service after the war. All these measures were to become part of the Welfare State: plans were being made and immediate action taken to meet immediate needs.

Beveridge Report, 1942

Perhaps the most important social document of the war was the Beveridge Report on the existing schemes of national insurance. It was produced in December 1942, as the Report of a committee under Sir William (later Lord) Beveridge. It recommended a comprehensive system to replace the existing administrative chaos in the social services. The Report was an immediate 'best-seller' and seemed to put the seal upon the new attitude to the social services, namely that it was the duty of the State to provide for all a minimum income, standard of health, education and housing.

'The aim of the Plan for Social Security,' declared the Report, 'is to abolish want by ensuring that every citizen willing to serve according to his powers has at all time an income sufficient to meet his responsibilities . . . want was a needless scandal due to not taking the trouble to prevent it . . .

'The first principle is that any proposals for the future should not be restricted by consideration of sectional interests . . . Now, when the war is abolishing landmarks of every kind, is the opportunity for using experience in a clear field. A revolutionary moment in the world's history is a time for revolutions, not for patching . . .'

'Social insurance fully developed may provide income security; it is an attack on Want. But Want is only one of the five giants on the road of reconstruction and in some ways the easiest to attack. The others are Disease, Ignorance, Squalor and Idleness . . .'

'Social security must be achieved by co-operation between the State and the individual . . . The State in organising security should not stifle incentive, opportunity, responsibility; in establishing a national minimum, it should leave room and encouragement for voluntary action by each individual to provide more than that minimum for himself and his family.'

Beveridge's scheme was for a comprehensive compulsory insurance system guaranteeing a minimum income during periods of sickness, unemployment and old age, and also special grants when heavy expenditure was likely, through maternity and funeral benefits. The scheme would be contributory —'all insured persons, rich or poor, will pay the same contributions for the same security.' He also stressed the importance of maintaining full employment and recommended the setting up of a national health service and of family allowances. After much discussion, in 1944 a new Ministry of National Insurance was established to plan the methods by which Beveridge's proposals might be implemented.

Social legislation after the war

In the General Election of 1945, Labour won a huge majority. This was as much a rejection of the Conservatives who had dominated politics in the interwar period, as a token of confidence in Labour. The electorate was not disappointed. Tremendous difficulties, perhaps greater than those faced by any other British government, stood in the way of national reconstruction. There was a huge foreign debt, and our trading position and economy was precarious. Our industry was badly in need of reconstruction after the war, and we continued to have heavy military commitments that absorbed a great deal of national revenue. Yet in the years between 1945 and 1951, Labour established the Welfare State. To say that the principal measures had been agreed by all parties during the war, does not detract from Labour's massive achievement. It is one thing, in the stress of war, 'when the war is abolishing landmarks of every kind', and the essential task in hand is to maintain national morale for victory, to pass measures of social security and plan for the future. It is quite another thing, when the peace has come, and the willingness to make immediate sacrifices is less strong, (and when faced by a serious economic situation), to press ahead and establish that Welfare State that had been talked about. The 1920s saw the 'Geddes axe' and the Means Test: the 1940s saw the *Appointed Day* (5 July 1948) when the Welfare State was formally established. That is the contrast between the two post-war periods.

Already, before the election, the *Family Allowances Act, 1945*, had been passed. This was designed to meet the expenses involved in bringing up a family, for the heaviest expenditure falls when the children are infants. (To some extent, too, it was hoped to encourage a higher birth rate.) The Act provided for a weekly allowance out of general

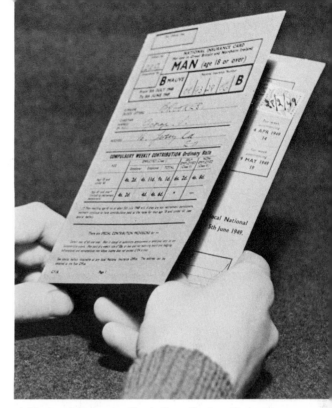

A National Insurance Card. Contributions (by employer and employee) were recorded by cancelling a stamp stuck on a card for each week.

taxation for each child *after* the first, as long as the child was at school. All families could draw this allowance, but the richer ones paid a good deal of it back through their income tax. The allowance has continued to rise with the cost of living.

In 1946, the *Industrial Injuries Act* replaced the old Workmen's Compensation scheme, by providing a compulsory insurance system to meet the risk of industrial injuries, financed by contributions from the worker, the employer and the State, so that there was now no fear of an injured worker receiving no compensation because funds were not available.

In 1946, also, a major step towards implementing the Beveridge proposals came with the *National Insurance Act*. It set up a compulsory comprehensive insurance scheme, no longer confined to particular classes, but covering everyone over school-leaving age who has not yet reached retirement age. Contributors are divided into three classes, the employed (whether highly paid managers or unskilled labourers), the self-employed (professional people and those in business on their own account) and non-employed (all the rest). The only exceptions are married women who are not working (these are covered by their husband's insurance), and the self-employed and non-employed with incomes less than £208 a year. The benefits cover unemployment and sickness pay, maternity and funeral grants, and pensions for men over sixty-five and women over sixty. The contributions were to come from payments by the State, the employee and the employer, and both rates and benefits were to be reviewed every five years. But inflation has necessitated more frequent revisions than had been anticipated. *Graduated Pensions* were introduced in 1961, whereby those employees not belonging to a private pension scheme (the majority) paid an extra contribution for a higher pension (the higher the earnings, the higher the contributions and the subsequent pension). In 1966 the same principle was applied to widows' pensions and to sickness and unemployment benefits (this is called *wage related short-term benefits*).

The *National Assistance Act* (1948) buried what remained of the Poor Law by making payments to those in need out of general taxation through the *National Assistance Board* (renamed Ministry of Social Security in 1966, when it absorbed the Ministry of Pensions and National Insurance, too). The difficulties of places like Poplar (see *page 210*) were thus ended and in place of grudging local officialdom, people were actually encouraged to apply for help—even so, people are still reluctant to come forward, either because of ignorance of the scheme, or from a sense of false pride. Inflation has depleted pensions (which have frequently been raised to meet the rising cost of living) and increased the number of people on national assistance.

The *National Health Service Act* (1946) established a 'free' comprehensive health service

'designed to secure the improvement in the physical and mental health of the people of England and Wales and the prevention, diagnosis and treatment of illness'.

It was the responsibility of Aneurin Bevan, Minister of Health, 1945-50. It grew out of war-time experience, for hospital facilities in the country as a whole had been demonstrated as fatuously inade-quate in almost every respect by a special survey carried out as early as 1938. The supply and distribution of doctors showed little or no regard for public need: Kensington having seven times more doctors per person than northern cities where the need was greater. Government, local authorities, public opinion and the doctors themselves were responsible for this situation. Great efforts were made during the war to remedy the situation. A scheme for a 'free' National Health Service, financed by national taxation, was produced in 1944, and this was enlarged to form the post-war scheme, embracing the full range of medical treatment and the services of dentists and opticians (rising costs obliged charges for some services in 1951 and these were later increased). Before 1948 few workers' families could afford what have been called the 'fringe' medicines—spectacles, regular dental treatment or ordinary chiropody. Now these are available to all, although a small charge is made for some services. Hospitals (except for teaching hospitals) were taken over by the Ministry of Health and placed in the hands of fifteen Regional Hospital Boards. Local authorities were to provide ambulance services, health visitors and a midwifery service and make provision for vaccination and immunisation. A national system of general practitioners, able to lean on hospitals and specialist services as never before, was organised to try to achieve an even distribution of doctors over the country, especially where they were most needed.

The opposition of the medical profession, led by the British Medical Association with the 'Radio Doctor', now Lord Hill, playing a prominent part, came near to wrecking the scheme. They were not so much worried by the idea of a state medical service, as by the fear of becoming salaried civil servants rather than professional men. However, good sense prevailed and a compromise was reached—for whereas the National Health Service could not work without doctors, few doctors were likely to make a fat living from private patients when the old 'panel' system ended. Discontent with conditions and pay have disturbed the Service ever since, and a crisis was reached in 1964 when threats of withdrawal were made by many doctors. A compromise was reached, but a further crisis broke at the time of the 1970 election. The problem of doctors' pay and their professional standing remains an intractable one. During the '70s, nurses and technicians in hospitals demanded the ending of the 'pay-beds' system by which wealthy patients could often get treatment more quickly than under the National Health regulations. Despite vigorous opposition from doctors, the 'pay-bed' system is being gradually phased out.

1951: the Festival of Britain

The Great Exhibition of 1851 (see *page 81*) had been the symbol of the prosperity of Britain as the 'workshop of the world'; it had demonstrated Britain's wealth and had been (for idealists) a great declaration of the moral force of Free Trade views, particularly in its international aspect as a sign of the removal of economic friction between nations. The centenary of the Exhibition was celebrated by a Festival of Britain designed to show that Britain had engineers and architects of verve, even if there was not much money to share amongst them in 1951. There were a number of exhibitions and celebrations all over the country, including the opening of the Battersea Pleasure Gardens, but the culminating exhibition was constructed on a cleared space of the South Bank of the Thames, by Waterloo Bridge. The site itself was significant, for the South Bank was then very 'down-at-heel'—this was to be a sign for the future, a 'tonic to the nation' amidst the austerity that had followed the war and appeared to have robbed us of the joys of victory. As a symbol of British ingenuity it achieved great heights—the present Festival Hall is the enduring legacy on the site itself. Many scoffed at the whole idea, complaining that it was a waste of money when the country had not recovered from the sterling crisis of 1947—but eight million people visited it. The architectural features seemed very modern at the time, but really they reflected brilliant European ideas of the 1930s, rather than the ideas of the young rising architects. Perhaps because of this, the major

rebuilding of our city centres in the 1950s and 1960s was in the hands of architects who reacted against these ideas and produced buildings of stark and brutal massiveness that earned rapid condemnation.

1851 had reflected the beginning of an era; 1951 seemed to reflect the closing of one. The age of the Welfare State was to develop on radically different lines from the way its planners had expected. The 1950s developed into a consumer boom; a reaction to the austerity of those post-war years of continued rationing and shortages. The 1960s were known as the 'swinging '60s' when the race to get consumer goods seemed to dominate people's lives, and the freedom of expression and manner in which the young indulged seemed important. In contrast, the '70s have brought a humbling recognition of the precarious nature of the apparent prosperity of the previous decade, and they have been called the 'sour '70s'. But in 1951, all this lay in the future. The Festival of Britain was welcomed as the hoped-for opening of an era; there was still much idealism in that post-war generation.

Housing

A serious housing problem existed because not only had building ceased during the war, but bombing had destroyed a great deal of the poorer housing in cities. There were many homeless, and while wartime controls were continued in order to ensure a fair spread throughout the economy of scarce materials, emergency plans were brought forward for the construction of 'pre-fabs' (factory-made mass produced units ready to be assembled to make a basic dwelling), which were expected to last about ten years (though they are still in use today). Housing was so scarce that 'squatters' took over empty buildings in desperation. Faced with so massive a problem, the Minister of Health, Aneurin Bevan, decided to concentrate on the public sector, encouraging local authorities to provide good quality council houses, subsidised and available for renting. More houses were built than in any other European country during the five years after the war. Private building was held back to conserve scarce materials

Prefabs, built in 1946. Intended to last ten years, they are still in use today—a tribute to their design and durability

for cheaper houses in the public sector. By 1956 a quarter of the population lived in publicly owned housing. That year the subsidy was withdrawn except for new towns and slum clearance schemes: private building leapt ahead for building materials were no longer scarce (see *graph 19*). The cost of housing had risen amazingly, partly because of rising raw material and labour costs, but also because of the higher standard of housing and fittings demanded by the rising standard of living. The demand for houses increased also because people now wanted to have their own house as soon as they got married and began a family: sociological surveys show that it is becoming increasingly rare to find family houses occupied for choice by several generations, as had always been the case in the past. Building Societies throve in the housing boom, often advancing as much as 90 per cent of the purchase price as a mortgage for a new house. Since 1952 it has been possible for tenants of Council houses to purchase their own houses, but this has not resulted in a great drive to purchase council houses.

In 1951 housing became the responsibility of the new Ministry of Housing and Local Government, and housing became something of a national campaign—300,000 a year were erected in the 1950s. The first need was to tackle the bomb-damaged areas of towns. Ideally, cities needed to be planned on a comprehensive basis, so that all the rebuilding would eventually fit into a new re-planned city—even if it took years to complete. Many cities produced master plans, some of them of high standard, particularly those with which Professor Abercrombie was associated (for example Coventry or Sheffield). But, in the nature of things, with little money and materials in short supply a good deal of the rebuilding was done in a piece-meal way. After the bomb-damaged areas, the surviving slums were next on the list (many of these had suffered bombing because they were near factories and railway-sidings). Major rehousing schemes dispersed slum-dwellers to new estates, some on the outskirts of towns, some built as 'inner-city' estates. Rehousing slum-dwellers was inevitably done by the local authority (the private developer was not interested in this part of the market). Some remarkable estates

The Roehampton Estate (L.C.C.—now G.L.C.). This was one of the first big council estates to be built after the war. The landscaping of the tower blocks and the different types of terraced housing help to give variety

were built, often combining 'high-rise' (tower-block) flats with well designed and imaginatively laid out terraces of houses—the L.C.C. estate at Roehampton or the Sheffield Gleadless Estate earned international acclaim. Many new ideas were introduced into the estates, like creating a focal point to help the growth of a community spirit by concentrating shops and facilities for social and recreational activities in one site; for councils acknowledged a responsibility for the social well-being of the community. Some estates were planned as 'neighbourhood areas' giving a greater sense of identity, many of them using *Radburn* principles (traffic is directed round the estate, not through it, and houses are grouped in bunches, often without intervening fences, with footpaths leading to shops and other amenities often crossing roads by foot bridges or sub-ways).

But the nineteenth-century city had left many problems for planners. Cities had tended to expand so that there were successive circles of different types of development radiating from the centre. Slums tended to be near the centre. Beyond them were

areas of what had been middle-class housing at the turn of the century; but as transport improved, the middle class moved out to suburbs, leaving their terraces to be converted, willy-nilly, into bed-sitters and small flats. Conditions in these areas had got so bad by the 1950s that they were known as 'twi-light zones' or 'grey areas' and were considered ripe for redevelopment. Anxious to gain possession, either to re-let at a higher rent or to rebuild, some landlords subjected tenants to harassment—a new word, *Rachmanism*, was coined in the 1960s, after a London landlord who used this approach. The result was the Rent Act (1964) that gave greater security of tenure to those in rented accommodation. But the problem of the 'grey areas' remains a pressing one, the more so as the very poor and often also immigrants from the New Commonwealth (chiefly the West Indies, India and Pakistan) drift into them, adding to the social problems involved.

Governments have been deeply concerned with the problem of these 'grey areas' and the need for 'urban renewal' lest serious social problems develop.

Gleadless Valley Estate, Sheffield. The planning of this estate has earned international praise. Note the variety of housing designs and the landscaping among the trees of the valley. There is little vandalism on this estate—unlike Hyde Park (see page 270), the scale is more human

There is often a good deal of vandalism in these areas. But some of the property is well built, and in the 1970s the idea of preserving towns by converting and repairing property, rather than by redeveloping it, has become popular. Priority, even over New Towns and development areas, was given to these 'grey areas' in an effort to arrest urban decay and provide better social and educational facilities. In 1977 a minister declared publicly that 'the decaying inner cities are Britain's own domestic third world'. In April 1977 the Government announced a scheme for a partnership between local and central authorities, backed by £100 million over two years, to bring a coherent approach to the declining 'inner areas' of Liverpool, Salford, Manchester, Birmingham, Lambeth and the London dockland.

In the '60s and '70s, the centres of many big cities were transformed. Three factors hastened this—the continued exodus of people, the increasing concentration of commercial offices and big shops in city centres, and the huge increase in road vehicles that has produced serious congestion in all towns. The centres of big cities have tended to be rebuilt on quite new lines, often dividing traffic from pedestrians by constructing special roadways and creating *pedestrian precincts* (a traffic-free area, often created out of an old street or square). Some cities have built dramatic centres, sometimes having different levels for shops, offices and public buildings libraries and theatres. Small gardens are often provided particularly for the benefit of office workers during their lunch-break. The City of London, with its remarkable Barbican scheme, is exceptional in seeking to bring back a residential population into the centre—but the costs involved mean that only the better-off can afford the rents.

Cities tend to sprawl, consuming agricultural land, raising land prices and adding to urban problems. This was already a problem in the 1930s. Anxious to check 'urban sprawl' and avoid 'ribbon development' (see *page 209*) the Barlow Commission (1940) recommended establishing around towns a *Green Belt*: an area of open land on which building would generally be forbidden. London and about a score of large towns have established Green Belts. This action does not solve the problem of urban growth, particularly as many private developers seek land near to open country for middle-class estates. There has been a tendency to leap-frog the Green Belt and build estates in villages and small towns close enough for commuters to drive in each day—thus creating 'dormitory towns' that tend to destroy the character of the original village or small town.

New Towns

As part of the reconstruction programme after the war the New Towns Act (1946) provided for the planned development of selected new towns each controlled by its own corporation. Originally the idea was to create a complete new town, balanced in terms of social class (there should be appropriate numbers of upper, middle and working class people), providing for all the main urban and employment needs. In practice the balanced community has not been achieved. However, there have been some remarkable examples of town planning and the New Towns are a marked improvement upon the 'grey areas' from which many of the early New Town dwellers came.

But people were not always happy in them—particularly the young wives who complained to their doctors of various nervous disorders. It became fashionable to talk of 'New Town blues'. The problem was largely a social one. The young couples were generally used to the close-knit society of

The Barbican (City of London) is a remarkable piece of town planning on a large scale. The height can be gauged by the underground trains

working-class life where uncles, aunts and cousins lived in the same street and 'mum' lived almost next door. In New Towns accommodation was spacious —and a long way from the rest of the family. Young wives felt lonely and isloated. They knew few people and there was often a lack of employment for them. Time hung heavily. This was one of the main reasons for the discontent—the simple shock of moving to a quite new environment. As families made friends (often through their children) and built up their own network of social relationships, there were fewer complaints—although the problem is never likely to be entirely solved.

Most of the original New Towns were grouped around London and had an old village as a nucleus. In the '60s more New Towns were created in the Midlands and near conurbations (see *Map 8*), sometimes absorbing older towns, sometimes built on extensive areas of derelict industrial land, as in the case of Telford in Shropshire. Some are planned as big cities in themselves, like Northampton or Milton Keynes, Chorley or Warrington, all of which were intended to reach a population of over 250,000 people.

Some of our older market towns that could provide few opportunities for their young people feared that they might decline as more and more people drifted off to seek better prospects elsewhere. One way of checking this was to attract new industry and to encourage people to come into the town. The Town Development Act (1952) enabled towns to seek Government aid to help build new housing estates

Runcorn New Town's central shopping area. Some new towns have made a big feature of the shopping precincts, transforming them into pleasant social areas

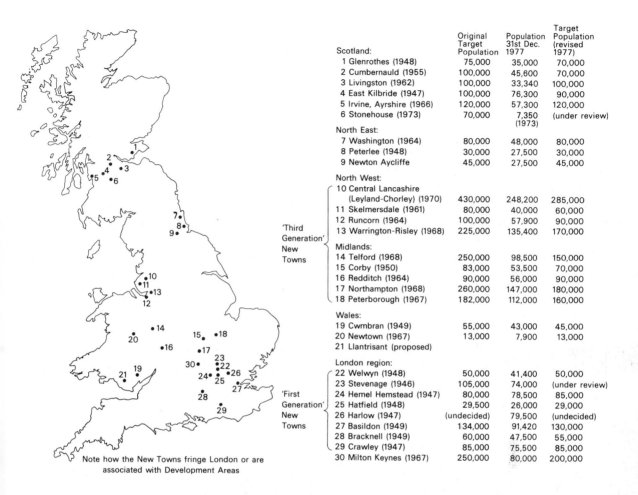

	Original Target Population	Population 31st Dec. 1977	Target Population (revised 1977)
Scotland:			
1 Glenrothes (1948)	75,000	35,000	70,000
2 Cumbernauld (1955)	100,000	45,600	70,000
3 Livingston (1962)	100,000	33,340	100,000
4 East Kilbride (1947)	100,000	76,300	90,000
5 Irvine, Ayrshire (1966)	120,000	57,300	120,000
6 Stonehouse (1973)	70,000	7,350 (1973)	(under review)
North East:			
7 Washington (1964)	80,000	48,000	80,000
8 Peterlee (1948)	30,000	27,500	30,000
9 Newton Aycliffe	45,000	27,500	45,000
North West:			
10 Central Lancashire (Leyland-Chorley) (1970)	430,000	248,200	285,000
11 Skelmersdale (1961)	80,000	40,000	60,000
12 Runcorn (1964)	100,000	57,900	90,000
13 Warrington-Risley (1968)	225,000	135,400	170,000
Midlands:			
14 Telford (1968)	250,000	98,500	150,000
15 Corby (1950)	83,000	53,500	70,000
16 Redditch (1964)	90,000	56,000	90,000
17 Northampton (1968)	260,000	147,000	180,000
18 Peterborough (1967)	182,000	112,000	160,000
Wales:			
19 Cwmbran (1949)	55,000	43,000	45,000
20 Newtown (1967)	13,000	7,900	13,000
21 Llantrisant (proposed)			
London region:			
22 Welwyn (1948)	50,000	41,400	50,000
23 Stevenage (1946)	105,000	74,000	(under review)
24 Hemel Hemstead (1947)	80,000	78,500	85,000
25 Hatfield (1948)	29,500	26,000	29,000
26 Harlow (1947)	(undecided)	79,500	(undecided)
27 Basildon (1949)	134,000	91,420	130,000
28 Bracknell (1949)	60,000	47,500	55,000
29 Crawley (1947)	85,000	75,500	85,000
30 Milton Keynes (1967)	250,000	80,000	200,000

'Third Generation' New Towns

'First Generation' New Towns

Note how the New Towns fringe London or are associated with Development Areas

Map 8 New Towns

to attract people from cities and to build factory accommodation to attract employment. By arrangement with a particular city they could become 'over-spill' towns. Aylesbury, Swindon, Thetford (Norfolk), Ashford (Kent), are examples of this. As a result, the character of the old market town has been quite changed, but the decline has been checked and the problem of excess population in big cities has been alleviated at the same time.

But the 1970s saw a change in attitude to planning. It was partly due to high costs; partly due to the social problems experienced in new estates and partly due to the ugliness of many of the new buildings. In 1977 there was a conference entitled 'Save Our Cities', and many councils are examining whether it is not cheaper and perhaps more satisfying to restore and renovate reasonable property in 'grey areas' rather than to redevelop it. It might be cheaper; it would preserve some good examples of town planning of eighty years ago; and it would help add variety to cities. This change in emphasis has already begun in London and other big cities.

Another factor making planners hesitate in devising radical new schemes for cities is the growing resentment among the people living in the new 'high-rise' blocks—a resentment that goes far beyond

'New Town blues'. It takes two principal forms. First, there is a rising tide of vandalism, not only in city centres, which are often fairly deserted at night, but also on the new estates themselves. This is a problem that planners, social workers and police have not been able to solve and it does not appear to be associated with the shock of moving to a new environment. New Towns in Lancashire, especially those near Liverpool, have attracted a good deal of press comment because of violence and vandalism. Secondly, people are now rejecting the idea of high-rise flats. These were the planners' answer of the '50s; but living in them presents many problems, especially to those with young children. There is a sense of isolation with mothers feeling cut off and continually fearful for their children's safety—on balconies, stairs and in the lifts (if they are working). The strain of living in multi-storey flats affects young children too. By the '70s many councils had decided not to build any more and most do not offer accommodation in them to families with young children, but reserve them for single people, newly married couples and the retired. Families with young children are often transferred to other accommodation—even in Sheffield's Hyde Park flats which attracted international acclaim in the 1960s and were provided with wide walkways at different levels in order to overcome the sense of isolation. The lower levels of population expected at the end of the century (see *page 295*) led the Government in 1977

Hyde Park flats, Sheffield. These dramatic cliffs of flats dominate the centre of Sheffield. They are designed as self-contained units with bridges at various levels between the blocks

to revise the target populations of some of the New Towns (see *Map 8*). The New Town Corporations were also encouraged to take more of the socially disadvantaged population from the 'inner-city' areas.

Education in the twentieth century

The 1902 Balfour Education Act (see *page 152*) opened a new chapter in English education by providing for secondary education and placing State schools in the control of local authorities. But the Act did not establish an educational revolution, for few children went on to proper secondary education, and there were not many 'free places' at local grammar schools (where fees were not abolished until 1946). Even in the late 1920s the full-time education of about 80 per cent of children did not go beyond the top class of the elementary school. Some of the larger Education Authorities had helped the non-grammar school children by opening *Central Schools* to provide courses leading to careers in commerce and industry. The children would attend full time for at least a year, and then continue with part-time classes when they began to earn their living. The L.C.C. took the lead in establishing this type of school and had opened thirty-one of them by 1912. *Junior Technical Schools*, for boys from 13–15 or 16, to give training in manual skills and prepare for apprenticeships (especially in engineering, since apprentices for engineering had to be 16) were also established. The Ordinary National and Higher National Certificate awards, established after 1918 suited these schools very well, and they did useful work for technical education.

Plans laid in the first world war and incorporated in the *Fisher Act* (1918), raised the school leaving age to 14 and provided for 'continuation schools' where those aged 14–16 might attend if only on a part-time basis. But the scheme was killed by the 'Geddes axe', and the wastage of academic talent among the poor continued. In 1923, 72 per cent of secondary school age children (11–14) were at schools that boasted of no 'advanced instruction' (they simply repeated the elementary course), and only about 10 per cent secured 'free places' to grammar schools.

The first Labour government (1924) appointed the *Hadow Committee* that reported in 1926 in favour of 'secondary education for all' between the ages of 11 and 15 either at grammar schools or at schools with a broad curriculum of studies modelled on the Central Schools. Those with a technical bent might at 13 be transferred to Junior Technical Schools. The economic crisis of 1929–31 delayed this proposal, but great progress had been made by 1938, especially by the larger urban authorities. In 1938 the *Spens Report* recommended that there be three types of secondary school; the grammar, to supply a Sixth Form from which would come university undergraduates and those destined for the professions, the technical high school ('secondary schools with a scientific and engineering outlook') and modern schools. It also hoped that there would be a 'parity of esteem' between the three types (i.e. each was to be considered as good as the others) and suggested that all three might be combined in the same school (here was the future *comprehensive school* in embryo). But the second world war prevented any immediate progress on this Report.

Public schools survived the financial difficulties of the inter-war years. Their teaching methods remained very formal and their curriculum and organisation remained very largely what it had been in Arnold's day. Flogging by masters and prefects was normal and frequent, and games continued to hold a major part of the time-table. It was not until after the war that an *Industrial Fund* contributed by old boys and industrial firms helped to provide adequate laboratories for them. Bryanston, among others, pioneered new teaching methods, and Gordonstoun, probably because of the personality of Dr Kurt Hahn, broke new ground in 'character training' activities, which he did not confine to the rugby field. But, for the most part, the public schools were not places of inspiration between the wars.

The war changed things. The *Fleming Report* (1945) recommended absorbing state-aided scholars into public schools in order to broaden their social basis. The idea was generally welcomed and has often been repeated since, but few schools made the experiment and fewer local authorities were prepared to pay additional sums for individual children to enjoy what the mass of their charges could not have. It was in the State schools that an educational revolution was worked through the great *Butler Act* (1944), piloted through Parliament as a non-party measure by R. A. (now Lord) Butler. It made secondary education freely available to all. Nursery schools were to be provided (as this was not compulsory distressingly few were opened) and for children aged from five to fifteen, local authorities had to provide education suited to the 'age, aptitude and ability' of children (special provision being made for the physically and mentally handicapped). During the war great success had been achieved with intelligence tests on adults, and it was thought that an objective test given at 'eleven-plus' could effectively predict whether a child was suited to academic studies or to more technically biased courses. There was to be a big expansion of 'day-release' arrangements for technical and commercial training and the school-leaving age was to be raised eventually to sixteen.

The sectarian disputes of 1870 and 1902 (see *page 151*) were skilfully avoided (in any case, sectarian fervour was less intense) and a new atmosphere of achievement inspired the education system, especially those schools in new buildings. Standards rose

rapidly in many schools. In 1951 the old School Certificate was replaced by the O and A Level General Certificate of Education (G.C.E.) and the appearance of a new type of examination (1965), often with assessment based on school work rather than on a terminal examination, the Certificate of Secondary Education (C.S.E.), provided inspiration for the less academic. Although the public schools attracted a far wider social class because of the rising prosperity of the 1950s and 1960s, they could no longer be regarded as normally superior to the state schools. Proposals for integrating the two systems were often discussed, but rarely with much serious intent of achieving integration.

The increased birth rate after the war caused acute shortage of space and necessitated a vigorous expansion in primary school building, to be continued into secondary schools in the '50s as the 'bulge' grew up. But by the 1950s increasing doubts were being expressed about the effectiveness of the eleven-plus selection. Transfer arrangements did exist for children who proved outstanding as 'late developers' to go 'up' to the grammar schools; but it was exceedingly rare for a child to go 'down'. The 'modern' schools rapidly became noted for taking working-class children, and it became clear as more and more sociological evidence was published, that the eleven-plus did not so much predict ability as measure what had been taught, so that children from

Tulse Hill Comprehensive School

less favoured homes and environments, especially from primary schools where staff were continually changing, were at a permanent disadvantage. The educational division, intended to divide children according to their potential abilities, was fast becoming a class division.

Some local authorities experimented with different types of school organisation to avoid selection procedure at eleven. Leicestershire, Croydon and the West Riding tried imaginative schemes, involving some degree of selection at a later stage, and the L.C.C. went in for large comprehensive schools serving the needs of a set area and providing a full range of courses appropriate to the abilities of different pupils, quite beyond the wildest dreams of smaller schools. Violent opposition was experienced, especially from middle-class parents, who feared that standards would drop and the brighter children suffer, and who also distrusted a too obvious mixing of social class. By the 1960s, however, most of the education authorities in the country were disposing of the eleven-plus selection procedures and experimenting with various types of comprehensive schools and sixth-form colleges. In the '70s the authorities were required to prepare plans for comprehensive secondary schools (and the Direct Grant selective grammar schools were to be phased out of the local authority sector over a seven-year period from September 1976). All the political parties accepted the comprehensive idea in principle (although not necessarily the complete removal of selective schools), but there was considerable controversy, especially over whether standards would be affected, particularly as many of the new urban comprehensive schools were large and suffered from a very high rate of truancy. One pressure group was particularly effective, producing several *Black Papers* largely in favour of traditional methods. By 1975 they had gained a considerable following, the more so as proposals for amalgamating the G.C.E. O level and C.S.E. into a 'common sixteen-plus' were far advanced, and as further proposals to replace A level with a more broadly-based examination at a slightly lower level were being discussed and some suspected that standards might fall. Figures pur-

porting to show an alarming drop in the success rate at A level for several educational authorities were produced—but they were for years not directly affected by any move to comprehensive schools. It is not possible to gauge standards on bald figures alone, for they take no account of either the explosion in knowledge or the more taxing questions with which candidates today are faced. However, there remains a widespread belief that standards are dropping everywhere. Industry has been loud in its complaints that school leavers can neither spell nor do simple arithmetic. Complaints have been levelled at the new 'child-centred' methods of teaching that became popular in the '60s, and this reached a climax in 1975 when the staff of William Tyndale School (an Inner London school) were suspended after parents had voiced dissatisfaction with their methods.

At the same time there was a distinct switch in Government policy as regards allocating funds. Education received less money. In 1976, partly to meet the economies required because of the serious economic situation (see *page 306*), but largely to meet the shrinking need for teachers in the future because of the falling birth rate, a major restructuring of some branches of education, notably teacher training, began. In order to sound out opinion over a wide area the Secretary of State held a number of regional conferences in 1977 as part of a 'Great Debate' on the future of education. There was much talk of greater parent participation in education, and the *Taylor Report* (1978) advocated greater powers for school governors. (In some schools children were elected as pupil governors.)

But, for all the hostile criticism, there have been notable contributions to education during the '60s and '70s, particularly through the Schools Council, a teacher-dominated body, that has produced a great many research and discussion pamphlets and launched a number of new courses in science, the humanities, maths and other fields. Two Royal Commissions have been particularly important: the *Plowden Report* (1966) *Half Our Future*, on the appropriate courses for less able children who from 1972 were required to stay on until sixteen; and the *Bullock Report* (1975), calling for concentration upon reading and literacy skills at all levels of ability and in all subjects.

The 1950s saw a great development in technical education in order to produce technologists and scientists required by new industrial processes. There was much justifiable criticism of the curriculum of schools, for it was out of date and failed to provide pupils with a well balanced education. There was much talk of 'the two cultures' (arts and sciences) and the *Crowther Report* (1959) called for more 'literacy' from scientists and more 'numeracy' for artists. In the 1960s there was a great increase in Liberal Studies courses, both in schools and in technical colleges, for there was a need not only for engineers capable of managing machines, but of managing men and businesses too. Great changes in apprenticeship schemes and in industrial training (by the Industrial Training Act (1964) the State has assumed responsibility for industrial training) were paralleled by the award of new technical qualifications, some at degree level (Dip. Tech. and the C.N.A.A. awards), some slightly lower (H.N.D.), and by changes in the university world that meant a quite fundamental reorganisation.

In 1889 a grant of £5,000 was distributed between the new civic ('red-brick') universities (Birmingham, Manchester, Leeds, Sheffield and Nottingham) and this grant was increased up to 1919. In that year the University Grants Committee was established to represent the interests of the universities and Government jointly and to decide on the allocation of the grant. In 1920, the grant was £800,000: in 1965 it had grown to £89 million. In addition to this massive growth, students receive individual grants from local authorities, so that our universities today are largely financed from public funds. Much of this investment in further education is for the development of pure and applied science. The need to improve technical education had been urged for a hundred years (see *page 151*) but little had been achieved. The first world war brought a striking transformation in the exploitation of science and technology. In December 1916 the *Department of Scientific and Industrial Research* (D.S.I.R.) was established in order to promote scientific and in-

dustrial research. A Medical Research Committee set up in 1913 came to life during the war and did valuable work on preventive and curative medicine as well as virtually beginning British applied psychology: in April 1920 it was renamed the *Medical Research Council*.

Unfortunately these early beginnings languished between the wars. However, a new attitude was abroad in the 1940s recognising that the future depended on a well-trained generation. A big expansion of university places occurred, first by expanding existing universities and then by building new ones at which different types of courses were available. Keele (1949) was the first. In the 1960s a whole series of new universities were opened—Sussex (Brighton), Essex, York, Warwick (Coventry), Lancaster, Canterbury, East Anglia, and Strathclyde and Stirling in Scotland. In order to ensure that those who qualified could attend courses of full-time study, *student grants* were raised so that every student now should be able to keep himself at the university, even if his family were too poor to help him financially. At the same time, encouraged by the *Robbins Report* (1963) on Higher Education, those cinderellas of further education, the technical colleges, were transformed. In 1956 the largest had been reorganised into ten Colleges of Advanced Technology (C.A.T.s) taking work of degree and post-degree level. In addition, there were twenty-five Regional Colleges taking advanced work for full- and part-time students, and area and local colleges, concentrating on less advanced work and providing classes for day release pupils. In the 1960s the C.A.T.s became universities in their own right, and proposals for the 1970s involve the development of Polytechnics combining most branches of further education (including Colleges of Art and Design). It is expected that the full-time student population will number 400,000 in the 1980s (see *graph 31*). There has been a similar growth in teacher-training establishments, now called Colleges of Education. Some of these specialise in training particular types of teachers (for example, for infant or nursery classes). Others have a full range of training courses, and some also provide for an extra

The University of East Anglia

fourth-year course leading to a new degree of Bachelor of Education (B.Ed.). But the predictions of population growth made in the '50s, have had to be corrected in the '70s. There will be fewer school children and the heavy investment in teacher training can no longer be justified. Many Colleges of Education were closed down in 1976 and 1977 and others had to amalgamate and to diversify their courses to take students other than intending teachers. Even the B.Ed. was in jeopardy.

This massive growth in student places led to a great deal of criticism from people who feared that academic standards would be undermined. They argued that 'more means worse'. As yet there is no great evidence to support this view. But the great cost of further education, together with a wish to help those who did not, or at the time could not, study for a degree, has led to the launching of an *Open University*. In 1963 a University of the Air was proposed to provide an alternative to full time courses, particularly for mature people who had not had the opportunity for university education in their youth and for those who wanted to add to their qualifications. The Open University got its charter in 1969 and opened in 1971. It was planned

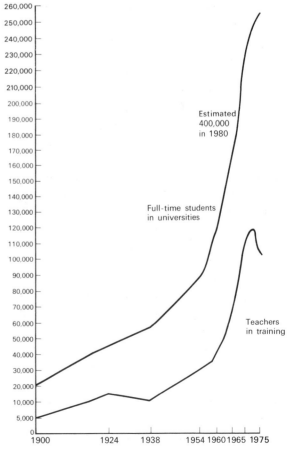

Graph 31 Numbers of full-time students, 1900–75

in partnership with the B.B.C. education service, so that television and radio broadcasts have become a regular part of its courses. The academic staff are centred at Milton Keynes and they are supported by regional tutors and part-time councillors. Students tend to be predominantly teachers and professional people, and housewives. Most come from the London area. Degrees are obtained through a 'credits' system of completing successfully certain courses. In 1971 there were 19,581 registered students, but the figure had dropped to 12,231 in 1976.

In 1976 a great drive began to deal with the problem of adult illiteracy. Modern society requires a far higher standard of literacy for the average adult than ever before (a U.N.E.S.C.O. survey suggested a reading age of thirteen was necessary). Many adults, shy of admitting their need, suffer from inadequate skills of reading and writing. The B.B.C. had nearly 110,000 adults seeking help through its Adult Literacy Campaign in 1976.

Changes in local government since the war

In the fields of social policy, housing and education, governments have had conspicuous achievements since the war. Local government has also had to readjust to new conditions. Two principal problems had to be faced: firstly, that there was a chaotic mixture of authorities which reduced efficiency, raised expenses and prevented the adoption of major schemes at local level. Secondly, the major authorities (London apart) were often too small effec-

The sign used in the Adult Literacy Campaign, 1975.

tively to provide their principal services.

The need for drastic revision was clearly demonstrated during the 'blitz' when some authorities were quite unprepared and unable to deal with the emergency themselves. One pamphleteer wrote:

'It was more than bricks and mortar that collapsed in West Ham on 7 and 8 September 1940; it was a local order of society which was found hopelessly wanting, as weak and badly constructed as the single-brick walls that fell at the blast.'

The Government had foreseen this situation, for a series of regional offices already existed before the war began (the first was officially opened at Leeds in November 1937) and a year later a list of Civil Commissioners had been drawn up, who would assume powers to govern and defend the region of the country committed to their charge should an emergency, like invasion, occur. Area Boards (January 1940) consisting of employers and trade unionists and civil servants, were created to deal with local problems of productivity, and the strong feeling in favour of central direction that emerged as part of the war effort, created the right atmosphere for cutting through a mass of local vested interests and creating a local government system better fitted to the contemporary world. Unfortunately, for a generation after the war no Government dared to reform the whole structure, although dissatisfaction with local government delays, failures and inadequacies have frequently been the subject of general comment.

However, in 1964 the L.C.C. was transferred into the much larger Greater London Council (G.L.C.) with boundaries more appropriate to the present London conurbation than the old boundaries of the 1880s. Also many of the more general services are now administered jointly by neighbouring authorities, thus the Fire Service and the Police have seen several significant amalgamations of local units that have helped efficiency. In 1969 the Government accepted in principle the proposals of the *Radcliffe-Maud Report*, although they provoked considerable resistance from the existing authorities, particularly over the staff changes involved. The Report recommended that England should be divided into

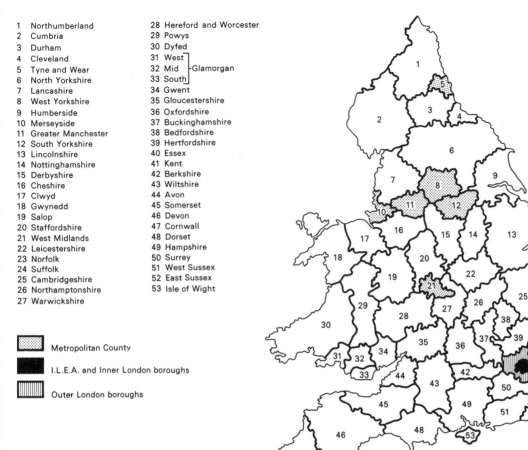

1 Northumberland	28 Hereford and Worcester
2 Cumbria	29 Powys
3 Durham	30 Dyfed
4 Cleveland	31 West
5 Tyne and Wear	32 Mid ⎤Glamorgan
6 North Yorkshire	33 South ⎦
7 Lancashire	34 Gwent
8 West Yorkshire	35 Gloucestershire
9 Humberside	36 Oxfordshire
10 Merseyside	37 Buckinghamshire
11 Greater Manchester	38 Bedfordshire
12 South Yorkshire	39 Hertfordshire
13 Lincolnshire	40 Essex
14 Nottinghamshire	41 Kent
15 Derbyshire	42 Berkshire
16 Cheshire	43 Wiltshire
17 Clwyd	44 Avon
18 Gwynedd	45 Somerset
19 Salop	46 Devon
20 Staffordshire	47 Cornwall
21 West Midlands	48 Dorset
22 Leicestershire	49 Hampshire
23 Norfolk	50 Surrey
24 Suffolk	51 West Sussex
25 Cambridgeshire	52 East Sussex
26 Northamptonshire	53 Isle of Wight
27 Warwickshire	

Metropolitan County

I.L.E.A. and Inner London boroughs

Outer London boroughs

Map 9 The new local government authorities (1974)

sixty-one new local government areas grouped into eight regions or provinces (London excepted). However, a rather different division of authorities was agreed upon in the 1972 Act that came into effect on the 1 April 1974 (see *map 9*). This Act divided England into thirty-nine counties and thirty-six metropolitan districts, the latter being grouped into six metropolitan counties. These 75 areas replaced the former 1,210 authorities in the hope that they would have 'greater vitality and efficiency' with far greater financial resources than the former authorities. Nevertheless, there remained a good deal of feeling that the new authorities were not matching some of the achievements of the old. Problems of finance at a time of economic difficulty stood in the way of many schemes for improvement and in 1976, hopes of

substantial subsidies from the central government were dashed and staff cuts had to be made. If the new authorities are to stand on their own feet, it has been argued, they should finance their own schemes.

This brings out one of the most significant problems in government that has emerged since the war. Central government today takes so great a part in the daily life of each of its citizens, that there are grave dangers of diminishing a citizen's basic freedom. To meet this danger, the *Franks Committee* (1955) recommended that very strict regulations be applied to the conduct of central government in its relations with individuals, and that the private citizen should have very precise powers of appeal, if a Government department took a decision that seemed to injure his interests. To assist the citizen in dealing with such complaints, a Parliamentary Commissioner for Administration, popularly known by the Swedish name, *Ombudsman*, has been appointed (1964). Complaints that are worth following up are passed on to him by M.P.s. The Ombudsman then establishes whether or not there has been maladministration leading to injustice. The number of cases referred to him is increasing. In 1970 there were 645 of which 59 involved some injustice. By 1976 the number of cases had risen to 815 of which 139 involved injustice. This increase both demonstrates the need for this office and the growing complexities of administration in a modern society. In 1973 the 'Parliamentary Ombudsman' was also made Health Service Commissioner and there has been a big increase (from 361 to 582 in 1976) in complaints in this sphere. Because of the increase it has been suggested that the public should have direct access to the Ombudsman. (Commissioners for Local Administration were appointed in 1974.)

The Civil Service itself has also been very greatly changed since the war in order to make it sufficiently flexible and strong for its new rôle of assuming responsibility for the daily lives of citizens. In the 1960s very significant organisational changes occurred in the structure of civil service departments, notably in the Treasury, which was reconstructed to fit it for its rôle of economic guardian of national prosperity. And in 1968, the Government accepted the proposals of the *Fulton Committee* recommending a fundamental change in the whole staffing structure of the civil service, so that a single, unitary structure replaced the old division between Administrative, Executive and Clerical classes. The Committee also recommended far more consultation with interested parties in the process of decision making. Clearly, the 1960s and 1970s have seen some major organisational reforms and proposals, designed to fit Britain for the highly complex and closely organised world of tomorrow.

Mass media and the consumer society

Helped by high wages and the expansion of hire purchase finance (the hire purchase debt had risen from £934 million in 1961 to £1,386 million in 1965) the last twenty years have seen a boom in consumer spending giving a new *affluence* to the life-style of most people. This has serious effects on our balance of payments and periodically restrictions have to be imposed on the availability of credit: but it also helps to ensure full employment and to maintain an increasing standard of living.

An essential feature in any developed society is the advertising industry that helps to inform the public and to persuade it to purchase goods and services. As such, advertising is a necessary link in the marketing chain. It has greatly benefited from the enormous expansion in the means of mass communication. Of these the greatest has been television that replaced the cinema to a great extent in the early 1960s (see *page 194*). In 1955 there were $4\frac{1}{2}$ million television licences; in 1976 there were 18 million, over half for colour sets, and the whole skyline of towns has been altered by the aerials. When, in 1954 Independent Television (I.T.V.) was allowed to compete with the B.B.C., advertisers made full use of the powerful medium, directing much of its appeal to the young adults who enjoyed high wages without family responsibilities and thus represented a massive consumer market. Entertainment has been the major concern of I.T.V. programmes, but in the later 1960s they began to lose their audience to the B.B.C. Many 'pop' groups and singers probably owe much of their reputation to the opportunities offered by I.T.V. Rivalry between the two organisations has been intense, particularly whenever there has been a chance of either extending the hours of broadcasting or opening another television channel. In the early '60s there were a number of 'pirate' radio stations that broadcast advertisements and record programmes, but these were largely stopped and the B.B.C. was allowed not only to open a second channel but also to start local radio stations broadcasting local news and programmes. During the '70s informed opinion has become concerned at the standard of broadcasts and production, even of the B.B.C. In 1977, the *Annan Committee* in, 'The Future of Broadcasting', proposed that there should be a new authority to run a fourth television channel (which annoyed both the B.B.C. and I.T.V.) and a local broadcasting authority to take over all local radio services after 1979. The Committee also proposed the creation of a broadcasting complaints commission.

Watching television has become a national pastime, and this has certainly affected the audience for sound broadcasting—the B.B.C. has had to make severe economies in its radio programmes. A great deal of complaint has been voiced against the bad effects of television—it is common to blame it for most of the ills of society, and educationalists have been particularly vigorous in their denunciations. However, the cultural level of programmes may be better than critics tend to suggest. Certainly, there is a huge demand for classics, even so big a work as *War and Peace*, if they are serialised on television. That there is more interest in serious music today than ever before may be more the result of radio than television, but literature and plays have benefited greatly from 'the box'.

Rising costs have caused many theatres to close, but there have appeared a number of good English dramatists (helped by T.V. showings) who have given a new vitality to our theatre—John Osborne's

Look Back in Anger (1956) was the first of a series of fine plays by young writers. A new school of writers known as the 'angry young men' appeared in the '50s. Much of their work attacked what seemed to be the 'double standards' of middle-class morality and there was a quite new concentration on working-class life and attitudes as the basis for literature and drama. Television greatly helped this new approach. But no really major writer emerged and this school seems to have been merely a passing phase. Social and political criticism, so active in the '50s, has seemed curiously quiet in the '70s. The national press, although often showing a more sophisticated level of political discussion and criticism of the arts than was common in the 1940s, has adopted a more casual approach in order to retain its readership. However, by the mid-'70s most of the great daily newspapers were losing circulation. The local press had shrunk and sought survival by amalgamating into regional groups.

There has been a veritable revolution in publishing due to the huge expansion of 'paperbacks' (pioneered between the wars by Sir Alan Lane of Penguins). There was an increase in new fiction titles published from 3,697 in 1950 to 4,198 in 1975,

The Beatles

Teddy boys and girls at a dance

but the gigantic increase was in educational books (respectively from 1,984 to 4,979), and in titles on economics, politics, art and architecture. Even when, by 1977, inflation had caused a massive increase in the cost of individual books (especially hardbacks) the trend continued. Much of a peripheral nature has been published (especially salacious novels and journals), but much good quality modern fiction, especially in the field of childrens' books, has also been produced.

A new egalitarian atmosphere was prevalent during the '60s. Heavy advertising aimed at the 'ordinary housewife' and the rising demand for consumer goods gave an image of classlessness. This was well illustrated by the large number of 'architect designed' houses (often called 'Georgian', presumably because of the style of window) that were built. Private builders, whether they were small or large construction firms, tended to build the same type of small compact house (it sold quickly) so that it became virtually impossible to distinguish between new houses in different parts of the country. The traditional regional styles appear to have been sacrificed to convenience, economy and the current demands of a 'consumer society'. The kitchen has been transformed by mass-produced fittings and labour-saving devices. Vacuum cleaners, spin driers, washing machines and electrical food mixers have become the norm. A great many houses have been converted to central heating—there are even 'do-it-yourself' kits for this, for the '60s saw a huge growth of 'do-it-yourself', partly in response to the rising cost of tradesmens' services.

It has been claimed that Britain is a classless society and that the 'age of the common man' has arrived, but sociologists have been quick to point out that differences in attitude between classes survive. Yet it has become increasingly difficult to distinguish between social classes among the under-thirties, either by dress, speech or behaviour. The 'B.B.C. English' of the 1940s seems to have been replaced by a preference for not very exact regional accents (again put down by some critics to the influence of television). Styles of dress have become not only very casual, but also 'unisex', in that a jumper and jeans are the normal dress for the young of both sexes—in sharp contrast to the sartorial excesses of the 'teddy boys' of the '50s. There was a great emphasis in the late '60s upon the freedom of the young (the age of majority was reduced to eighteen in 1969). There has been considerable discussion of a new 'permissiveness' in society extending beyond sexual permissiveness to simple matters of honesty (shop-lifting has become a serious problem). Much of this discussion has been sensationalised in the press and has been promoted by the publicity given to the high spending power of the young.

Whether there is actually more immorality, crime and violence in contemporary society than in previous generations is an impossible question to answer. Statistics show an increase—the percentage of illegitimate births in the 1930s was 4·8, in the 1970s it had risen to 9.2; offenders sentenced to Approved Schools were 155 in 1955, in 1965 there were 788 and in the 1970s an average of 5750 were sentenced to borstal training each year—but statistics do not tell the whole story. Circumstances are different today: it is still a new experience for most families to be able to buy such a range of goods (most of them, of course, through hire-purchase), and it will take time to adjust to this situation. There is also a greater willingness today to discuss subjects that our grandparents rarely mentioned among themselves, and never before the children. It may be doubted whether today's youth is any more depraved or lacking in 'character' than the youth of the 1870s: sex, pornography and violence have been common experience for a very long time indeed!

The Hovercraft

Transport changes

A transport revolution greater than any in the past has taken place during the last two generations. It has had three aspects: the means of transport (by land, sea and air), its availability to all social classes and its social and economic effects. Not only are many people today able to travel quickly over considerable distances, but a whole range of specialist manufacturing firms connected with transport provide employment for a vast number of people.

Since the '20s, transport by sea has seen not only the change from coal to oil-burning, but an increase in the size of merchant ships—in the case of oil tankers to a tremendous 'super' size. In the 1930s the luxury liner was a dream for most people; in 1969 the *Queen Elizabeth II* was recognised as the last of her line. On the other hand there has been a huge growth of small pleasure craft and yachts, and single-handed crossings of the Atlantic no longer earn gasps of amazement. A quite new development has been C. S. Cockerell's invention of the *Hovercraft* which has established itself as a firm competitor with cross-Channel ferries and in 1977 a hydrofoil service going from London to Zeebrugge (Belgium) in $3\frac{1}{2}$ hours was begun.

The aeroplane has captured long distance travel.

A disused railway—victim of the Beeching Axe

In the 1930s flight was for the wealthy (often still by airship), but the development of the turbo-jet and huge airliners has brought trans-Atlantic flight within the reach of ordinary people (especially with the advent of charter flights). Internal and continental flights compete with railways. Supersonic travel has become a commercial reality with the Anglo-French *Concorde*. But the big airliners have brought a new problem—atmospheric pollution and noise—people living under the flight-paths approaching airports have suffered badly from noise

Traffic wardens (often women) not only check that parking meters are properly used and prosecute offenders, they also help direct rush hour traffic

and vibration. *Concorde* has experienced particular difficulties in this respect and was at first refused a landing licence at New York. Space travel has also ceased to be science fiction. In the 1960s men walked on the moon; in the 1970s capsules have linked up in space with parent laboratories and men have spent a couple of months at a time in them. There have also been space probes to Mars and Venus.

Compared with these technological achievements, those of the Railway Age (see *page 49*) pale into insignificance. Indeed, by the 1960s it was possible to imagine a future without railways. Between the enforced amalgamations of 1923 (see *page 247*) and the Second World War, railways were not noted for innovation or managerial excellence. The great 'steam spectaculars' like The Cheltenham Flyer or the Silver Jubilee were deservedly famous, but they were individual trains not part of regular service. Despite growing competition from buses, lorries and cars, there was little change to diesel or electric traction and speeds for passenger trains remained slow—for freight even slower. When the railways were nationalised in 1948 and British Rail took them over, the railways were suffering not only from the effects of the war but from thirty years' refusal to modernise. The competition from road

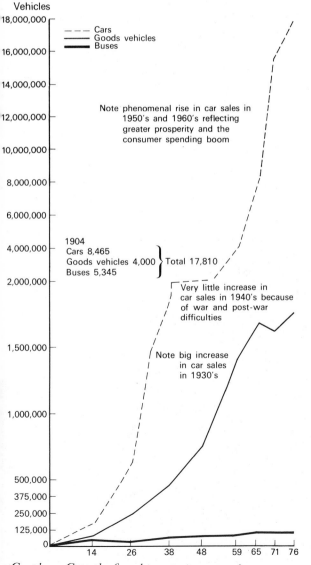

Graph 32 Growth of road transport, 1900–76

New architect-designed medium price-range housing

transport (the full effect of which no one could have foreseen in 1945) became a serious problem in the '50s. By 1954 an ambitious plan for conversion to diesel traction and electrification was begun: the Age of Steam was over. But by the 1960s losses were so serious that drastic economies were necessary. Under the *Beeching Plan* (1963), railways concentrated on the profitable inter-city routes and principal suburban lines, and on long-distance freight and heavy bulky loads for which special rolling-stock was designed. Local and unprofitable lines were closed. For social reasons the Government did not allow all the closures proposed by the 'Beeching Axe', but many lines disappeared, their tracks and bridges being removed: old track-ways and embankments are a common sight today. Some have been built over, some simply left; but others have been imaginatively developed as leisure areas, nature trails, walks and pony tracks.

However, technological developments in the 1970s showed that railways indeed had a future. New high-speed electrical signalling systems were introduced, freight containers were developed and huge marshalling yards controlled by computers. After extensive research, in 1976 the world's fastest regular eight-daily service at 125 m.p.h. (190 k.p.h) between London and Bristol and South Wales was introduced. No supplement was charged and no new track was needed (unlike similar trains abroad). A fast service (five hours) from London to Edinburgh was inaugurated in May 1978. The advanced passenger train (A.P.T.) is scheduled for a four-and-a-half-hour London to Glasgow service in 1979. However, inflation and rising costs were turning passengers away. The need for economies had already (in 1975) forced the Government to cancel work on the Channel Tunnel after twelve years of Anglo-French exploratory work.

Oddly enough, in the 1960s it took less time to fly from London to Paris than to get from the city centres to the airport by road. This was because of the congestion of urban roads by the tremendous growth in traffic (see *graph 32*). Today most adults drive and about fifty-six per cent of all households (1975) own a car—about ten per cent have two or more cars. Council estates are now provided with garages, and many 'architect designed' private houses incorporate a garage instead of a second ground floor room in order to economise on space.

Urban congestion rose to crisis point in the 1960s

Map 10 Motorways, 1978

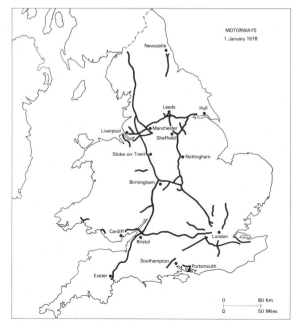

A multi-storey city car park

and in 1963 the *Buchanan Report*, 'Traffic in Towns', recommended a radical re-planning of towns to divide off principal roadways. At that time there were two types of traffic: local, including buses, and through traffic having to get through the town. By the '70s, they were joined by a third, the massive juggernaut lorries, often travelling from the continent. The greatest problem was the rush hour (between rush hours, roads are relatively quiet): but to provide roads adequate for the rush hour would be quite uneconomic. A number of solutions have been tried, some very radical, like constructing two-tier urban motorways (but these cause continuous disturbance to housing in the vicinity). Some big cities have divorced principal roadways from pedestrian areas. Most cities ban parking on main streets and urban 'clearways' and a number use parking meters, with traffic wardens to enforce regulations, on those streets where parking is allowed. Multi-storey car parks are one solution, and some cities have adopted one-way systems designed to speed up the flow of traffic (and to discourage through-traffic). More radical schemes involving banning the private car from inner-city areas while providing car parks on the edge and obliging people to travel in by public transport have been seriously considered. Since the 1930s the idea of by-pass roads to allow through-traffic to avoid congesting the city centres has been popular—but some by-passes are

long and this encourages drivers to risk a traffic jam by going through the city centre.

In the '60s a great deal of improvement was carried out on main roads to allow for greater speeds and safer motoring between towns. At the same time a completely new system of roads—*motorways* with limited access, designed for fast long-distance traffic—has been developed (see *Map 10*). Motorways frequently require major traffic intersections with a complex arrangement of bridges. The civil engineering involved in their construction has made as great an impact on the countryside and on people's minds as the railways before them.

With the massive growth of road transport has gone an increase in accidents. The belief that many accidents were caused by drunken drivers, led to the introduction (1967) of the 'breathalyser' to determine the amount of alcohol consumed by the driver concerned. The motorways, despite the permitted speed of 70 m.p.h. (112 k.p.h.), are less dangerous than main roads, possibly because there are no cyclists or pedestrians. And, strangely enough, most accidents occur in November and December, when motor traffic is not particularly heavy—indicating that the weather and the light may be important factors in the cause of accidents. Road casualties rose to a peak in 1972. Their decline since then is due to more stringent tests on cars over three years old (which have to carry an M.O.T. certificate), better braking systems, road improvements and greater awareness by the public of the need for maximum care.

Greater Leisure

In the last decade many people have begun to enjoy long paid holidays. Few enjoyed them before. The *Amulree Committee* (1938) was thought bold to recommend a week's paid holiday for the ordinary worker. By the 1950s most workers had two weeks paid holiday. By the 1970s this minor social revolution was racing ahead: we work fewer hours and have longer paid holidays than ever before (see *graph 33*). Greater leisure, allied with money to afford consumer goods, provides the conditions for gainful use of free time: but, simply because there are so many people and many of them have cars, quite intolerable pressures can result, like the long traffic jams on roads to the coast.

For some time now there has been concern that our countryside should be preserved from misuse and that ordinary people should have reasonable access to it. In 1949 the National Parks and Access to the Countryside Act was passed, creating the National Parks Commission. Ten National Parks

were established between 1950 and 1955, and twenty-seven areas of outstanding natural beauty were identified (see *Map 11*). The Parks are areas of wild country of great beauty; each is separately administered, but they are not museum pieces. People live and work there, and farming and industry continue within them, although the Commission exercises a strong control over building and any new workings. In 1968 the Countryside Commission was established to take over the National Parks and to extend its authority over the whole countryside in an endeavour to protect it against urban and industrial growth.

Within the National Parks are many education and adventure centres, including some large Youth Hostels, and much work is done to encourage the public to take a full and informed interest in the countryside. Motorways have made a great difference to the National Parks: they are no longer remote. Large numbers of people can travel to them quickly (the High Peak, of course, is very close to dense concentrations of people). The sudden build-up of cars, especially on a Sunday, creates particular problems over parking and access to service roads and it has proved necessary to enforce a one-way

A complex road intersection on the motorway

system around the Goyt reservoir in Derbyshire. Pressure of numbers creates a threat to beauty spots: they are no longer quiet; litter becomes a problem; the turf gets badly worn; holds in favourite climbs are damaged from overuse. The problem is reconciling interests. The National Parks are intended to provide the enjoyment of the countryside for the people. They are not commercial pleasure grounds. It is important that visitors observe the Country Code so that they do not cause damage, or danger to livestock. The interests of farmers and of the resident population has to be considered.

Provision of adequate leisure facilities for the growing amount of leisure time has been a major concern in the '70s. Increasing numbers visit country houses and castles, whether owned privately or in the care of the National Trust (founded in 1895) or of the Department of the Environment (formed in 1970). Long-distance footpaths have been established and many local bridlepaths are now clearly marked by signs. A large number of nature trails and nature reserves have been created and several local authorities have opened country parks to attract urban visitors to open spaces where organised activities are possible. Canals and other waterways have had a new lease of life as places for holidays and sailing. The British Tourist Authority (1969) does much to encourage foreign visitors (holiday travel is big business and earns a great deal of

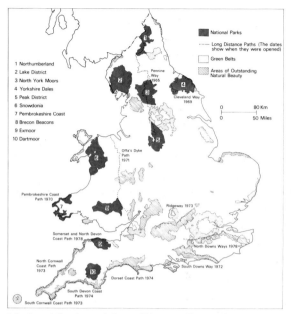

National Parks and Long Distance Footpaths. The map is evidence of successful efforts to preserve the countryside and to give the public access to areas of outstanding natural beauty

foreign currency). Since 1972 the number of foreign tourists has doubled to about 12 million, bringing in over £2,400 million in 1977.

Camping and caravanning grew amazingly in the '60s and '70s. The Camping Club of Great Britain had 52,000 members in 1960; by 1975 it had 157,000. A similar increase occurred in the Caravan Club

Graph 33 Greater leisure (a) Weekly hours worked by full-time adult manual workers, 1950–77
(b) Annual paid holiday, 1966–76

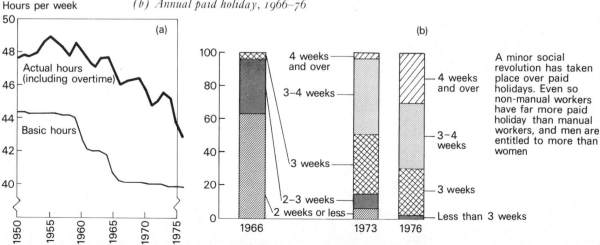

A minor social revolution has taken place over paid holidays. Even so non-manual workers have far more paid holiday than manual workers, and men are entitled to more than women

membership (44,000 increasing to 174,000)—although this may well be a response to the cost of accommodation rather than a desire for the joys of the outdoor life. Water sports have shown a huge increase, reflecting the affluence of the '60s—the Royal Yachting Association grew from 11,000 members (1960) to 36,000 (1975) and the Sub-Aqua Club from 4,000 to 21,000 in the same period. In urban areas, sports centres have made squash, basketball and badminton almost working-class games in the 1970s.

Problems of adjustment

The high wages, full employment and security offered by the post-war Welfare State has created a number of social strains, with which we are only today coming to grips. The most difficult for older professional people to accept is the growing 'class-lessness' of society. In their youth they were used to clear divisions between professional people and 'the working class': today these divisions, although they are still present, are blurred. The young have more money and greater leisure than ever before; they are also expected to express themselves openly, in a way their parents find unfamiliar. Many of these changes have been 'blamed' on the Welfare State. People complain that the young are less inclined to strive to achieve particular goals in life, and that they show less of a sense of personal responsibility and self-reliance, and come to lean on the Welfare State which is paid for by the heavy taxation of their parents. All this is very hard to instance precisely. Certainly there has been a rise in the indictable offences known to the police from 438,000 in 1955 to 1,235,000 in 1965 and to 2,136,000 in 1976; certainly there seems to be developing a distinct pattern of violent self-expression, especially by football crowds; certainly there is a great deal of vandalism to public property; even students since 1968 have assumed a new militancy demanding a say in the conduct of their courses. But this is not only confined to Britain, and it is not established that it results from the State assuming full responsibility for the physical, mental and moral develop-

Bank Holiday traffic jam on an Essex road

ment of its citizens (which is the philosophy of the Welfare State). After all, in providing so many services, the State is not acting from motives of promiscuous charity, but is making an investment in the future health of its citizens. The failure to do this in the past has meant incalculable loss in economic terms, and very great emotional stress and human suffering.

But if middle-class opinion has difficulty in perceiving the real nature of the social change that has taken place, working-class opinion experiences equal difficulty in adjusting itself, first to a new-found social security, and secondly to a degree of freedom never before experienced, resulting from high and secure wages and longer periods of leisure. The high level of unemployment in the later 1970s does not appear to have reduced self-confidence. It is quite impossible to say whether people work less hard than they did seventy years ago, simply because we cannot properly compare conditions in 1900 with those of today. But it does seem that the virtues Samuel Smiles encouraged are less often encountered today than formerly. Perhaps there has been a profound change in public attitudes: or perhaps it is that opportunities are greater today, and more people are able to fulfil their ambitions without being so unusual as to attract the pointed attention of society.

One of the clearest changes has been the rapid loss of class consciousness among the working class. Much of this is due to high incomes and full employment and the great success of the post-war Labour government in achieving so much social justice for so many of our citizens. This very success means that the Labour Party can no longer present itself as the defender of the rights of the under-dog and must seek out a new basis appropriate to the Welfare State it did so much to produce. It is not without significance that the only political movement really to capture the imagination and support of large numbers of serious minded young people over the last twenty years has been the Campaign for Nuclear Disarmament, organised quite independently of the older political parties, as something in

The behaviour of some fans among football crowds gave rise to serious concern throughout the 1970s. British Rail sometimes refused to run football specials because of the damage and disruption caused by hooligans and many leading clubs were fined by the Football Association because of the violence of some of their supporters

the nature of a protest against 'Establishment' politics.

Another sign that a different atmosphere was abroad came in 1968–9 when a series of student demonstrations and 'sit-ins' took everyone by surprise (a similar, more violent movement in France let to a serious political crisis—see *page 237*). It proved necessary to take the demonstrations seriously and to meet student demands. This *political activism* was normally concentrated in the sociology, arts and politics faculties, and was frequently disapproved of by the engineering students. Student unrest diminished in the '70s, but did not disappear —the London School of Economics was frequently affected and there were also many sit-ins in 1977 in protest against higher tuition fees. The protests appeared to indicate a dissatisfaction with the normal pattern of political life. A similar explanation might be given for the rise to prominence in the 1960s of Welsh and Scottish Nationalism. It could be interpreted as a protest by the outer regions against excessive centralisation and bureaucracy imposed by the complex administration of the modern Welfare State. The exploitation of oil deposits in the seas around Scotland have added pressure for a devolution of local affairs onto separate assemblies for Scotland and for Wales—but fears that this might lead to a break-up of the United Kingdom, among other reasons, led to the failure of a Government Devolution Bill in 1977.

Although there are definite differences of attitudes between the two principal parties in Britain, the experience of Government since the war has led to a realisation that there is only a small range of possible alternatives in Government policies. Consequently, a new Government has found itself largely continuing what its predecessor began and this has led to what has been called *consensus politics*, which may help to explain why politics as a whole appears to have less appeal in the '70s. Alternatively, a common dissatisfaction with both main parties may reflect a genuine search for a new political spectrum looking to the future, rather than the past. However, by 1978 it seemed that consensus politics were coming to an end.

It is easy to exaggerate the affluence of the 1960s and early '70s (particularly when one contrasts it with the experience of other developed countries). Many of the more expensive goods were bought on hire-purchase (a significant number of people had to return goods, or went to jail because they could not keep up with payments). More was spent on food and drink than ever before (although the proportion has fallen in the '70s)—much of the cash for purchase was earned by working overtime. The cost of living has continued to rise steeply in the '70s, diminishing that sense of new-found affluence. In 1967 a Government survey showed half a million families had

Marching to Aldermaston, 1961

incomes below the level set for supplementary (social payments) benefits, and pressure groups like Child Poverty Action Group and Shelter have been active in the '70s, indicating the survival of poverty in an age of apparent affluence (confirmed by a Royal Commission Report in 1978). Old age pensions have been badly hit by the rise in prices, and many pensioners require further assistance from the Department of Social Security. In April 1978 a new and complicated pension scheme was launched. Private pension schemes will be linked to the state system and all pensioners will receive a pension which will be 'inflation proof' and consist of two parts: the first will be a 'flat-rate' pension (in the style of the 1948 scheme, see *page 262*), the second will be an earnings-related *additional* pension paid either by the state or a private pension scheme. The position of women will be greatly improved: for the first time interruptions in their working career due to motherhood will be compensated by a 'home responsibility protection', and they will be able to earn the same basic and earnings-related pension as men. This new and revolutionary scheme will mature only in 1998, when a pension will equal over half an average wage.

Although pockets of particularly bad conditions and near-poverty continue to exist, the situation is much easier for most people. The social benefits brought by the Welfare State have made Britain a better place to live in. Yet there exists a widespread feeling of dissatisfaction, a spiritual malaise some have called it; a feeling that something is lacking. This may be because we are not yet properly adjusted to the security given by the Welfare State. One historian put it like this:

'Man does not live by gas-central heating alone, even though the assumption of the advertisers, the most effective mass ideologists since the decline of the churches, seemed to be that he should.'

It is the task of the present generation to work out a healthy basis, not only for the physical conditions, but also for the spiritual condition of life. The answer is likely to lie not merely in the tremendous technological achievements of the age, not merely in the outlawing of poverty, but in the field of human relationships.

20 · The 1970s : a watershed

We recognised the 1880s as a watershed between the Great Changes of the period of the Industrial Revolution, and those of the next hundred years, during which Britain experienced changes quite as great, although she was the first 'mature' industrial nation of the world. Since the second world war, indeed, the pace of these changes has been so great that we have not yet adjusted ourselves to them. However, the 1970s have developed a peculiar character that indicates that a hundred years after the watershed of the 1880s we are now experiencing a still greater one. We have yet to come to terms with our greatly reduced position in world affairs, and we have entered into a quite new rôle as a member of the E.E.C. For nearly twenty years our economy has performed poorly in contrast to that of Western Europe, and the affluence that characterised the '60s seems to have passed. The complexities of administration have grown so much that vigorous demands for greater participation by ordinary people have had to be met. There seems also to be a change in attitude as to what people can reasonably expect from society and what central and local government can achieve.

The loneliness of the aged

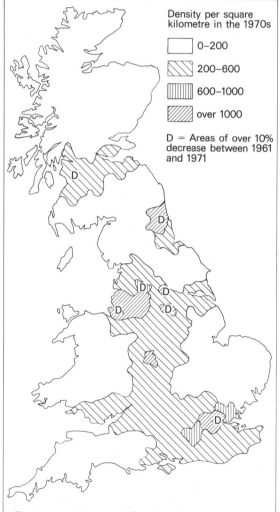

Density per square kilometre in the 1970s

- 0–200
- 200–600
- 600–1000
- over 1000

D = Areas of over 10% decrease between 1961 and 1971

The great conurbations, especially in their centres, have been losing population since the 1950s largely because of rehousing schemes and the growth of New Towns and 'over-spill' towns

Map 12 The changing distribution of population in twentieth-century England. (Contrast the distribution shown here with that shown in Map 1)

Population changes

Just as the population explosion ushered in the period of the Great Changes (see *page 2*), so the pattern of population since the 1880s has led us to the watershed of today. For a hundred years there has been a decrease in the *rate of growth*, but the total population has increased. The decline of infant mortality (see *graph 34*) helps to explain this (although, as we have seen, in demography no simple explanation is ever likely to be adequate). The rate fell from 154 per thousand in 1900 to 18 per thousand in 1975, reflecting higher standards in midwifery, diet and general health, with better nursing and hospital services playing their part. X-rays have been used since 1895, and throughout the century there has been extensive immunising of children against the old 'killer' diseases of whooping cough, diphtheria and polio. The pharmaceutical industry has developed new and sophisticated drugs, like penicillin, the antibiotics, the sulphonamides and even more advanced drugs like those that induce fertility in women who previously could not have children. Since 1925 insulin has permitted diabetics to lead a normal life. But some drugs have been shown to have serious side effects, like thalidomide which caused limb malformations in infants (the Distillers Company paid heavy sums in compensation after a long legal battle). In the '60s remarkable

technological developments also helped doctors— the most notable being the 'kidney machine' that performs the action of the kidneys artificially. Transplant surgery has also made great progress— heart, spleen, kidney and lung transplants can now be performed and it is possible to donate vital organs when one dies to be 'stored' until needed by patients. Life-expectancy has increased from forty-six for males and fifty for females in 1900, to sixty-nine and seventy-five respectively in the 1970s. But new 'killer diseases' have appeared; cancer and heart

Graph 34 (a) Population growth, birth and death rates, 1881–2001 (estimated). Compare this with Graphs 1 and 2 and note how the population growth levels off
(b) Age structure of the population, 1881–2001 (estimated)

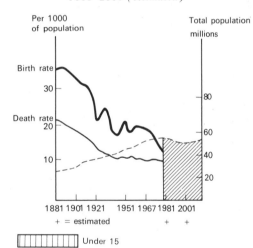

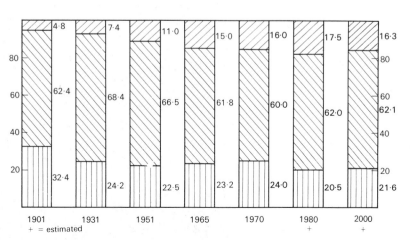

A declining working population will be burdened by extra taxation to provide for an increasing number of 'senior' citizens.
The age of retirement may be reduced to sixty or below before the end of the century.

diseases have replaced tuberculosis and pneumonia as the 'killers' of today.

The birth rate has fallen during the century, the steep decline from the levels of the 1870s being generally attributed to the adoption of effective means of birth control. It is undeniable that the middle class were using means of family limitation, but attempts to make these methods available to the poor were strenuously resisted in the 1920s. It seemed that what was sensible for the better off was a licence for unbridled profligacy for the poor. The extension of birth control is probably also a consequence of the rise of the feminist movement; for the modern mother has no wish to be burdened by continual pregnancies; and with the development of the 'pill' she herself may control the size of her family. The average family in 1860 had six children; by the 1970s it had two. But contraception may not be the only reason for the decline in births. Several sociological surveys have recently revealed that working-class families do not always practise family limitation, and yet do not have appreciably more children than other families.

There have been significant changes in the age structure of the population—we have now what is called an 'aging population'. This presents difficult sociological and administrative problems, particularly because the growing number of retired people throws an increasing burden upon the working population, for they need more medical aid and attention than the rest of the community. This has to be paid for by taxing the wage-earners. The Government is faced with the need to maintain an acceptable level of employment and provide proper welfare services and facilities for greater leisure. There has been a change in the distribution of the population (see *Map 12*) so that today the pattern is beginning to resemble that of pre-industrial England. But the distinction between town and country (urban and rural conditions) is far less than it has ever been: indeed, most people are likely to live out their lives in what is really an urban environment. There is over twice as much urban land today as there was in 1900, and the continued preference for small individual houses, so that each

family might have a home of its own, increases the pressure, as does the spread of 'commuter land'. In the '60s various Government schemes encouraged firms to *disperse* their head offices, and sometimes their factories, away from London to the big towns of the provinces (the civil service has led the way in this policy).

But a different problem is now faced by the *conurbations* (huge sprawling urban areas around major cities; it is usual to identify seven of them, see *graph 35*). At the beginning of the century the conurbations were growing rapidly but each now has extensive grey areas (see *page 265*) which have tended to attract a high proportion of immigrants from the New Commonwealth in search of cheap accommodation (see *page 295*). The social problems of these vast 'inner city' areas are increased because there has been a movement out of the conurbations during the last twenty years. In 1951 they had a population of 187 million (thirty-eight per cent of the total population) and this had shrunk to 173 million in 1974 (about thirty-three per cent of the total population, living in some three per cent of the total land area). In the rest of the country the population during these years increased by twenty-three per cent. Major problems of local government administration arise from this, for the conurbations are metropolitan counties (see *Map 9*) which have to meet the cost of a multitude of services from a declining population.

However, during the 1970s it became clear that the population as a whole was actually *declining*. In 1976 a decrease over the previous year of 13,000 was recorded; the birth rate has been falling since 1964 and in 1976 reached the lowest point since the 1930s. This reflects not only the more widespread availability of contraceptives (in the 1970s, for the first time, they have been openly on sale on the counters of chemists), but also the determination of young people to decide the size of their families and to concentrate the period of building up the family into a short time, so that the mother can go out to work. There has been a marked decrease in the number of families who want a third child. There has also been a decline in the number of

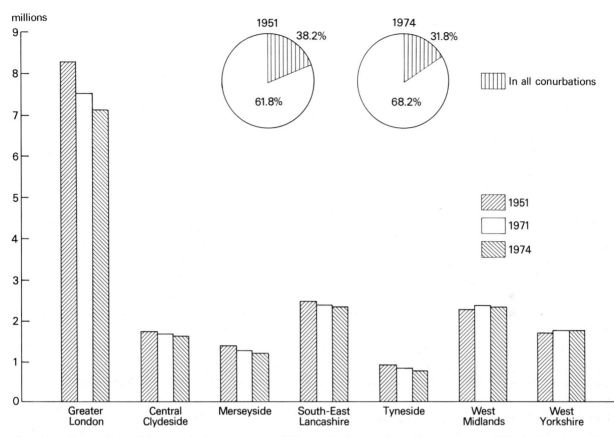

Graph 35 *Populations of the conurbations, 1951–74. (Changes in boundaries make comparisons difficult after 1974, but the trend has continued)*

pre-marital conceptions and of illegitimate births. The number of legal abortions also has an impact on the birth rate. At the same time as the birth rate has been falling, there has been an increase in the number of retired people (see *graph 34*). By 1978, however, it seemed that the birth rate decline had levelled off.

The change in the pattern of the population presents a number of important problems. In December 1976, the Central Policy Review Staff (C.P.R.S.—popularly called the Government's 'think-tank') urged big shifts in the pattern of spending by the social services to meet the new situation that was emerging. Plans for the development of education were seriously modified in 1976, resulting in a significant reduction in the number of colleges of education and increased unemployment among teachers: the expansion of the '60s was reversed. Forecasts of expenditure on social services also had to be altered. The proportion of retired

people has been increasing: these require adequate leisure activities, more medical attention and social welfare; particularly as many live alone. The increasing tax burden to support young and old will rest heavily upon the shoulders of the rising generation throughout the remainder of the century.

New-Commonwealth immigrants.

Since the '50s there has been a growing awareness of the increase in immigration and this has led to hostility, especially towards the immigrants from the New Commonwealth. A good deal of ignorance and racial prejudice lies behind the hostility. New-Commonwealth immigrants make a substantial contribution to the economy, especially in hospitals, the railways, the post office and local government. They do *not* add a disproportionate burden to the social services. Only on education and child-care does expenditure tend to be higher on immigrants than on the total population, but this reflects the age structure of the immigrants who tend to be young people and so, as a group, would be expected to show a higher fertility rate than the community as a whole. In any case, the birth rate among them is fast declining (5·9 per thousand in 1970 reducing to 5·2 in 1974).

However, substantial numbers of New-Commonwealth immigrants have tended to settle in the 'grey areas' of big towns in the Midlands, South Yorkshire and the London area, giving perhaps an exaggerated impression of their numbers. There was considerable agitation against coloured immigration, led notably by Enoch Powell (from whom has come the word 'Powellism') and concern was expressed that Britain would begin to suffer from a racial problem. In 1961 and 1968 controls on immigration were strengthened and in 1971 the Immigration Act allowed certain dependants of immigrants to settle in this country, but restricted work permits to the same conditions as applied to aliens (foreigners) from outside the E.E.C.

But racial discrimination has to be avoided and the immigrants have to be integrated into the community. For this reason a *Race Relations Board* and a *Community Relations Commission* were created in 1968 to prevent discrimination on grounds of race or colour. Their task was made more difficult by the sudden entry of many refugees from Uganda and East Africa—a Uganda Resettlement Board was established in 1972 to deal with this particular emergency. But for all the genuine concern for better relations, there is a definite problem in the poor opportunities open to young adult immigrants

Commonwealth immigrants at Heathrow Airport, London, 1968

and their children. They suffer a far higher unemployment rate and are expected to occupy lower status jobs than their English contemporaries. A report by the Community Relations Commission (1974) expressed the fear that *alienation* (rejection of accepted attitudes and standards) was growing among them, beginning at school because of inadequate provision and career advice, and continuing after school when they found great difficulty getting any but unskilled jobs. By 1977 the Department of Employment was suggesting that job prospects for the children of immigrants might be better, but they would have 'to fight for better jobs'. Race relations remains a problem for the future, particularly as New-Commonwealth citizens are gradually increasing as a percentage of the home population (2·1 in 1967, rising to 3·3 in 1975). The Race Relations Board and the Community Relations Commission were incorporated into a new *Commission for Racial Equality* in 1977.

Sex equality

The 1970s was a decade that saw sex equality brought into the legal system. Some women began to use the abbreviation 'Ms.' and 1975 was officially called 'International Womens' Year'. Already sociologists had shown that husbands were taking a greater part in running the home (*joint-conjugal roles*, they call it) and the number of working wives was increasing. The 'pill' and other means of contraception allowed wives a greater control over the size of their families, and the opportunity for a legal abortion (after the 1967 Abortion Act) relieved the burden of unwanted pregnancies. All these signs show an extension of the potential independence of women. In 1964 the Married Women's Property Act established a wife's right to an equal share in the family income, and the 1970 Matrimonial Proceedings and Property Act gave her a direct interest in her husband's property. The Divorce Reform Act (1969) allowed irretrievable breakdown of a marriage as sufficient grounds for divorce, and in 1973 this was extended to allow divorce without a judicial hearing, after a separation

lasting two years, provided both parties agreed and there were no dependent children. In 1977 the new procedure for undefended divorce amounted to little more than filling in a form. In 1973 equal rights for both parents were allowed over the guardianship of children. Within the family the woman was fast gaining equality.

In employment this was reflected in the Equal Pay Act (1970, becoming effective in 1975), the Equal Opportunities Commission set up under the Sex Discrimination Act (1975) and in the Employment Protection Act (1975) outlawing dismissal for pregnancy and requiring the payment of a maternity allowance. Yet, for all the legislation, discrimination on grounds of sex remains. It begins at school and continues through adult life, although the worst features have been removed. Women tend to marry and to interrupt their careers to have babies; but this does not explain their failure to rival men in management posts throughout industry, commerce, Government and education.

A new permissiveness or a classless society?

The '60s and '70s have often been regarded as more lax than other decades—partly because of the increased accent on young people with lots of money, which they were encouraged to spend by mass advertising (the phrase 'youth culture' was frequently used). Youth demanded (and was given) greater freedom than before—the 1969 Family Law Reform Act allowed marriage at eighteen without parental consent, and the 1970s have seen the lowest average age of marriage since records began 140 years before. Sex education has become a normal part of the school curriculum, even at primary level.

But the common idea that sexual morality is lower than ever before has not been borne out by the facts. Illegitimate births leapt from 4·9 per cent in 1951 to 8·4 per cent in 1972 but have risen only slightly since, despite the disappearance of the stigma of shame that used to attach to the unmarried mother. Premarital conceptions actually dropped from fifty-five per cent of all births to women under twenty in 1951 to fifty-one per cent in 1976. Even the number of abortions, which had risen from 62,000 in 1970 to 111,100 in 1973, dropped back to 103,300 in 1976. Marriage seems as popular as ever, despite the decline in church attendance.

Crime rates, however, give great cause for concern. Crimes of violence showed a rapid growth in the '60s and '70s. Crowd behaviour has also become unreliable—it seems almost impossible for there to be a big football match without violence and brutality among a small minority of supporters. Special measures against Manchester United and Chelsea supporters were announced in April 1977. Theft has become a more common crime, especially shop-lifting—as the frequent notices and even closed-circuit televisions in shops demonstrate— whilst the success rate of the police in clearing up cases has declined, even though police numbers have increased. Prison accommodation has been stretched to the limit and over-crowding is now a serious problem. In 1975 there were 1,154 prisoners serving life sentences (about ten times the number in most other west European countries). So great was the concern over the rise in the number of prisoners that in 1974 magistrates and judges, by means of a community service order, were permitted to sentence criminals over seventeen to do unpaid community work.

The most far reaching sign of social change in the '70s has been the increased consumer spending arising out of higher wages and greater leisure. Wage rates showed a peculiar pattern, for there has been a definite narrowing in the gap between the wages of labourers on the one hand and those of managers on the other (this is called a shrinking in *differential payments* and it affects as much the gap between skilled tradesmen and labourers as between management and labour). Indeed in 1975, some thirty per cent of workers' households had a higher income than those of professionals.

	Average worker	*Junior manager*	*Senior manager*
1970	£1,400	£3,000	£6,000
1975	£2,900	£5,400	£10,000
Difference in take-home pay:	+8%	−5%	−16%

(allowing for inflation and tax increases)

At a superficial level, it looks as though classes are drawing closer together in taste, dress and behaviour. It has become progressively more difficult to distinguish between social classes. To some extent the retail revolution has promoted this. The popularity of frozen foods and 'convenience' foods (processed foods requiring a minimum of cooking) has added to the tendency, although the trend to smaller families, smaller kitchens and the need for 'T.V. snacks' played their part. The advertising of

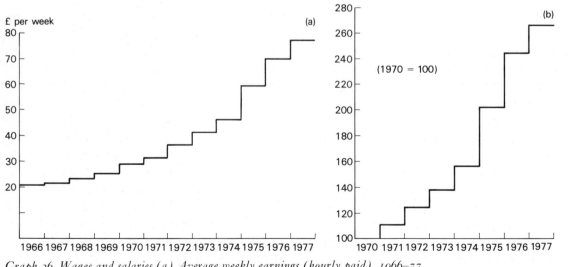

Graph 36 Wages and salaries (a) Average weekly earnings (hourly paid), 1966–77
(b) Average salaries (non-manual), 1970–77

consumer durables also helped towards the image of 'classlessness'—in the 1970s dishwashers and freezers have not been restricted to the middle class. Leisure activities point in the same direction—caravans and boats have appeared on council estates, and the provision of sports centres in big towns has made squash a popular working-class game. Many more families go abroad for holidays but there has been a change in the popularity of various holiday countries—Spain and France are now favoured and Switzerland and Italy have fallen badly behind. This partly reflects the different type of holiday-maker going abroad, and partly the skill of packaged-tour operators in securing low-cost holidays in Spain.

But all those pointers are only on the surface. Sociologists are at pains to tell us that we remain as much a class-dominated society as we have always been. Social classes behave differently: the working class tend to marry earlier, to have the first child earlier and to have larger families than the middle class (although the working-class birth rate is falling). They tend to occupy rented accommodation and to have less educational qualifications. The middle class tend to smoke less and to go on to higher education; they also tend to be absent from work (and school) far less—although there does not appear to be any significant difference in terms of what sociologists call 'job satisfaction'.

Problems of Government and industry

In the early 1970s there were a number of big strikes that gained a great deal of publicity, and there was much public resentment against the activities of the Government in its attempts to overcome the economic problems with which the country was faced. Journalists often spoke of Britain becoming 'ungovernable' but it was less this than a recognition of the limits to which a *collectivist* state could be stretched in a free society. In the second half of the decade there has been greater emphasis upon widespread participation in decision-making, a change of emphasis that may have important implications for the later years of the century.

Today, the Government, whatever its party, must play a central part in industry and commerce because of its major task of managing the economy. Throughout the '60s and '70s, the struggle to maintain a favourable balance of payments (sometimes endangered by strikes like the 1972 dock strike) has dominated policies, and latterly the extremely rapid rate of inflation has aggravated the situation. Since the creation of Neddy (see *page 232*), Government, C.B.I. and T.U.C. have held close and confidential discussions about economic policy. However, in the '70s there has been hostility between Government and trade unions because of the restraint on wage bargaining involved in a prices and incomes policy.

Hopeful of securing greater stability, the Heath

Graph 37 Working days lost by industrial action, 1965–77

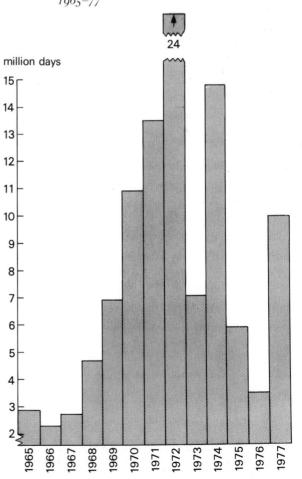

million days

government passed the Industrial Relations Act in 1971 (see *page 254*), setting up a National Industrial Relations Court and requiring all unions to register for their activities to be regarded as lawful. Most unions argued that industrial relations should not be determined by external forces, and backed by the T.U.C., refused to register and staged a one-day token strike against the Act. The crisis burst in February 1972, when the coalminers struck over a pay claim. At the time the Central Electricity Generating Board still depended upon coal to produce sufficient electricity to maintain the National Grid, despite the fact that many new power stations burnt oil, gas or even used nuclear energy. The miners' position was very strong—made stronger by the fact that power stations were too complex to be run by enthusiastic amateurs (so there could be no question of using volunteers as in 1926—see *page 222*). Furthermore, train drivers refused to deliver coal to the power stations and miners developed a 'flying picket' of men, going from power station to power station to ensure that no coal got through. The Government declared a State of Emergency, but by March they had surrendered and agreed to a pay increase outside the pay guidelines, decided by an enquiry under Lord Wilberforce (although their Civil Contingencies Unit established to run the National Grid in any future crisis was not dismantled).

Meanwhile, the Amalgamated Union of Engineering Workers was involved with the National Industrial Relations Court: it refused to recognise the Court, following T.U.C. policy, and it was repeatedly fined for contempt during 1972 until finally the Court, in 1973, seized £100,000 of the union's funds. A major crisis was provoked and only the payment of the fine by anonymous donors averted a national engineering strike (the funds were restored to the union). Twice the Government had been defeated in confrontations with the unions. However, under the Counter-Inflation Act (1973), a Pay Board and a Price Commission were appointed to control wages and prices. The miners argued that theirs was a special case and demanded higher wages than Government policy allowed, beginning

an overtime ban in November. But by that time the whole situation had been transformed because of the war in the Middle East and the very steep rise in oil prices that produced something of an 'energy crisis'. As in 1972, the power stations were dependent on coal, and the Government once more declared a State of Emergency with severe restrictions on the use of heating and lighting in public buildings, and a speed limit of 50 m.p.h. (80 k.p.h.) on roads to save petrol. The railwaymen began an overtime ban which deepened the crisis. After Christmas the Government imposed a three-day working week to conserve fuel. It was a national crisis: production was badly affected and the value of sterling fell sharply. As in 1926 the Government had taken on the unions—but in February 1974 it was the unions who won.

A general election was held, fought on newly drawn constituency boundaries that were thought to favour the Conservatives. The result was deadlock, but Labour took office, offering the chance of better relations through a 'social contract' with the unions to secure wage restraint voluntarily. The Industrial Relations Act (1971) was repealed and the Pay Board and the National Industrial Relations Court were abolished in July 1974. The 'social contract' worked as a temporary measure and efforts were made to sustain it, particularly as a far greater economic crisis gripped the nation in 1976; but by the spring of 1977, with prices rising and living standards beginning to drop, the 'contract' was under severe pressure from the union rank and file (particularly over differentials for skilled workers). There was even serious talk of a police strike over pay. The lesson of 1974 was that there was a limit to what a British Government could do: the way forward lay in co-operation between Government, T.U.C. and C.B.I.

In actual fact, the Heath Government had begun by seeking that co-operation. In the early 1970s it appeared that so far as running the economy was concerned, there was little difference between the parties: both were committed to close control. In 1971, for example, the Conservative Government had taken over the bankrupt Rolls-Royce engineering firm. In 1972, a Minister for Industrial Development was appointed to pursue policies similar to those of the previous Labour Government, but assuming greater powers under the Industry Act (1972), and through the Price Commission (1973). The Government could even demand that certain firms should reveal their future investment plans to Government inspectors. Nineteenth-century ideas of *laissez-faire* seemed dead: it appeared no longer meaningful even to talk of a 'free' economy.

In the 1970s there has been a retreat from the agreed policy of 'full employment' (see *page 231*), and the Government permitted unemployment to rise to over six per cent in 1976 and 1977 with the highest levels in the 'development areas' that had suffered in the 1930s. Skilled men and managers were affected as well as the unskilled. A 'job creation programme' was started, often using young unemployed people to do socially desirable jobs, and in 1972 a Training Opportunities Scheme run by the Department of Employment began, which had over

Graph 38 Total unemployment, 1966–77

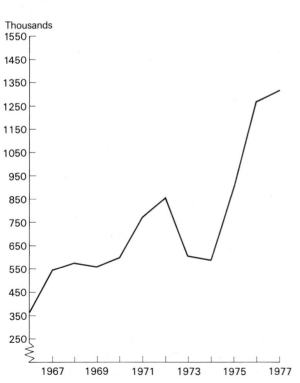

Thousands

60,000 on its courses by 1975. New-style Job Centres began to replace the old Employment Exchanges from 1973. It has been widely recognised that not only do the young and the unemployed need training, but skilled men need *retraining* simply because the nature of the technology of industry is changing so rapidly (steel-making provides an excellent example of this rapid change). In January 1974 a Manpower Services Commission was established under the Employment and Training Act (1973) for the purpose of gaining a better distribution of manpower and encouraging mobility (movement to new jobs) and retraining—it was spending £26 million in 1976 and was a good example of co-operation between Government, T.U.C., C.B.I. and local authorities.

One of the results of changes in fashion, or shifts in the economic strength of an industry, is the closure of works. The '70s have seen a number of these closures, the workers being made redundant (redundancy payments have been required by law since 1965). On several occasions the local *shop stewards* (workers' representatives) organised 'sit-ins', occupying the factory and refusing to leave, as in the case of the Upper Clyde Shipbuilders in July 1971. Where the work force was determined to keep the factory open (and so preserve their jobs even at the cost of wage cuts, or sometimes receiving no wage at all), the Government was occasionally prepared to back the workers with financial help. Sometimes a 'sit-in' persuaded a firm to reconsider closing, as in the case of some of the Plessey factories in 1977. Occasionally, a workers' co-operative was formed, with Government help, through the Industrial Development Advisory Board set up under the 1972 Industry Act. In 1974, £39 million was allocated to a workers' co-operative at Kirkby Manufacturing and Engineering after a protest sit-in against closure. In 1975, the workers at Meriden, Coventry, resisted closure and continued to make motor-cycles on their own initiative: they formed a workers' co-operative, received a Government loan and in 1977 were made quite independent. The principle of the Government entering the world of industry that had been illustrated by the Rolls-Royce case (1971) was being extended.

A new chapter in economic history is opening because of the growth of really large-scale enterprises. International corporations have developed which can affect the employment prospects of a whole area, and their plans for future development can affect those of the Government. The Government itself, as we have seen, has become increasingly involved in industry. In 1975 the *National Enterprise Board*, with Lord Ryder as chairman, was created as a Government agency with £1,000 million at its disposal to promote industrial efficiency, to provide employment, especially in the *development areas*, and to extend public ownership in profitable manufacturing industries by acquiring a majority holding or actual ownership of firms. This is a long step from piece-meal help to certain industries in distress, or small grants to assist research which the Department of Scientific and Industrial Research (D.S.I.R.) has made quite frequently over the past fifty years: it is an indication of the change in rôle that is taking place in the relative positions of Government and industry. By 1977 the Board controlled British Leyland, Rolls-Royce, Ferranti, Data Recording Instruments, and held a significant interest in other important companies, involving a commitment of many millions of pounds. This is in addition to direct Government intervention with particular firms. For example, in 1975 the American Chrysler corporation threatened to close its factories in Britain and to concentrate production in Europe. The Government prevented this by offering a loan of £162·5 million until 1980 in order to save the many jobs that would have been lost. In 1977 the company signed a long-term planning agreement with the Government. A further development in the same direction is the creation of the British National Oil Corporation (1975) to control new concessions for the exploitation of North Sea oil (see *page 306*) so that an adequate share (perhaps up to eighty per cent ultimately) of the massive profits that are anticipated should return to the British tax-payer for the money invested in discovering the oil. But this new departure in Government policy not only has importance for the future of industry, it also

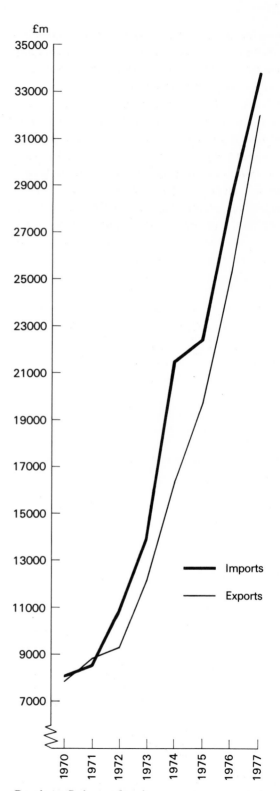

Graph 39 Balance of trade, 1970–77

means that the power of Parliament to control expenditure is very much reduced, for industrial and commercial decisions cannot wait whilst committees of M.P.s examine the accounts.

If Government, management and the leaders of the trade unions now discuss their problems and their plans more than they have ever done in the past, it is important that the rank and file union members do not hinder plans by serious unofficial strikes (the unofficial strike over differentials by the highly skilled toolmakers in British Leyland in March 1977 endangered the whole future of the firm). There have been many suggestions of ways to reduce unofficial strikes. The most contentious were the proposals of the *Bullock Report* (January 1977) on industrial democracy. It recommended that workers should be represented on an equal basis with shareholders on the boards of large public companies, with a real opportunity to influence decision-making. This was a radical suggestion. The C.B.I. rejected it on the grounds that, although they were prepared for consultation and participation in industry, the actual planning of future developments and some aspects of the running of

Graph 40 Retail prices, 1962–78

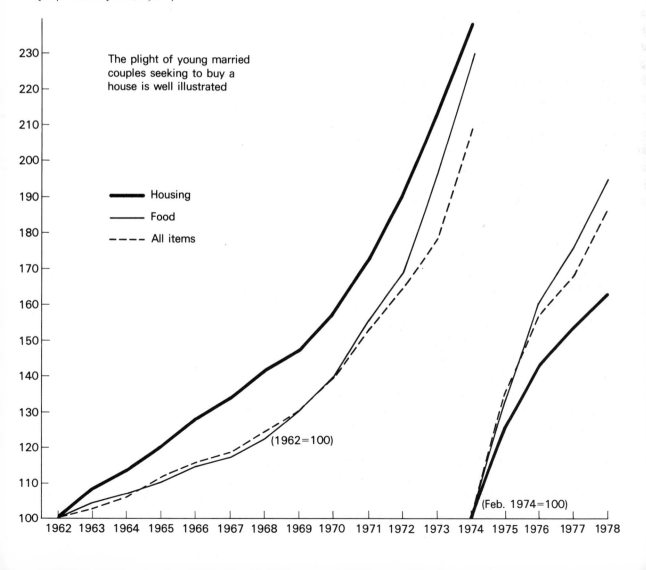

The plight of young married couples seeking to buy a house is well illustrated

—— Housing
—— Food
– – – – All items

(1962=100)

(Feb. 1974=100)

firms required expertise that workers did not have, and were unlikely to develop without actually ceasing to be workers and joining the managerial staff in their own right. They also were worried that trade unions would gain almost too much control of companies, because it was proposed that the unions should nominate the worker-directors. There was much force in these arguments, and there did not appear to be great support for worker-directors from ordinary workers or from some of the large unions. Understandably, the Government, while welcoming the Report, hesitated to act on it. The Report proposed a single board for each company; an alternative proposal was for a two-tier system, a larger board with one third elected members from the shop floor, to advise and deal with general matters, particularly those affecting working conditions and production, and a small board, not elected, to control policy and planning. This proposal had much more support from the C.B.I. and was, indeed, in line with schemes already operating in four E.E.C. member countries. Consultation between workers and management (industrial democracy, as we call it, or *co-determination in industry* as other E.E.C. countries call it) is a declared aim of E.E.C. policy. Clearly, it will become a part of the British scene, but not before the 1980s. In May 1978 a Government White Paper proposed moderate ways of putting workers in board rooms, which were more favourably received. The old nineteenth-century simple division of master and man is passing.

But, to bring Government, T.U.C. and C.B.I. into close consultation does not necessarily guarantee prosperity. Despite the appearance of affluence in the '60s, our industrial growth since 1960 has been poor and far less than that of most of our European neighbours. In the 1960s Government policy was simply stated: full employment, a satisfactory balance of payments, stable foreign exchange rates, price stability and economic growth. The economic crises of the '60s and the still greater ones of the '70s have meant a modification of these aims. In the mid '70s the prime concern was the control of inflation galloping away at over twenty per cent and almost the highest in western Europe. With

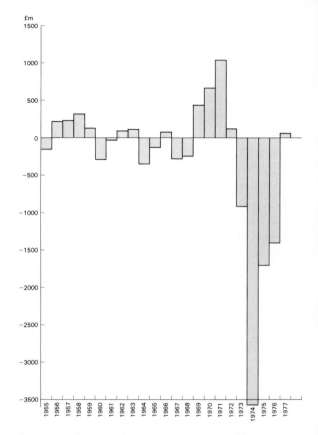

Graph 41 *Balance of payments, 1955–77. The severe economic crisis of the mid-1970s is well illustrated. So is the recovery—not due to North Sea oil which had only just begun to flow by 1977*

economic growth dropping by 1976 the Government faced a crisis as great as that of 1931. Full employment (see *page 231*) was no longer a priority; unemployment was 6 per cent in 1976, and a declining standard of living was the common experience. One estimate suggested that the average man's real wages fell by 64 per cent between 1970 and 1976.

Inflation was largely the cause. The steep rise in commodity prices in the early '70s, and particularly the rise in the price of oil after 1973 were main factors in this. By 1973 wage demands to keep up with prices (sometimes running at claims for thirty per cent increases) had become an important factor pushing upwards the rate of inflation. Another factor was the rapid growth in the money supply between 1970 and 1973, and the growth of Government expenditure in the same period. By 1973 the

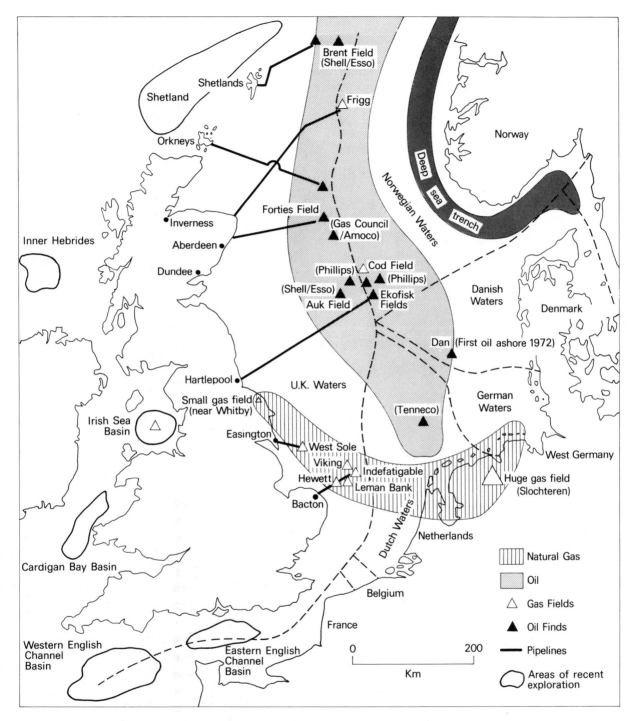

Map 13 Oil in home waters

Government appeared to have lost control and the attempt to induce an economic expansion in that year failed. The competitive performance of our industry also seemed to be declining, although exports held firm.

But it was the balance of payments that brought us to the verge of bankruptcy in 1976. The advantages of devaluation in 1967 (see *page 232*) were not. sustained and by 1972 the pound was allowed to 'float' (this meant effectively a devaluation of some sixteen per cent, but as it no longer had a fixed exchange rate, one cannot talk of *devaluation* after 1972, only of a *decline in purchasing power*). A world trade slump, higher oil prices and the increasing prices of our exports meant a growing deficit on our balance of payments in 1974 and 1975 and the pound fell as foreign bankers became increasingly concerned. One wit said that the Government was intending that the pound should fall to $1.776 on

4 July 1976, to commemorate the bicentenary of the American Revolution, but it dropped even lower than that, and bankers began to wonder how effective the pound sterling was as a reserve currency for use in foreign exchange dealings.

The crisis year was 1976. The T.U.C. accepted pay restraint as part of the 'social contract' and the Government desperately sought a huge loan of $39 billion over two years from the International Monetary Fund. By January 1977 this had been secured, and at the same time a further Basle Agreement was arranged (see *page 232*) for the phasing out of sterling as a world reserve currency, thus to some degree relieving the pressure of speculation that had helped to provoke crises in the past. However, very strict conditions were imposed by the I.M.F. for its loan and the Government was obliged to cut public spending locally and centrally very severely. The Welfare State was proving too costly. Enoch

North Sea Oil. Drilling platforms extract the oil from the sea bed and discharge it into tankers or by pipeline direct to the refinery

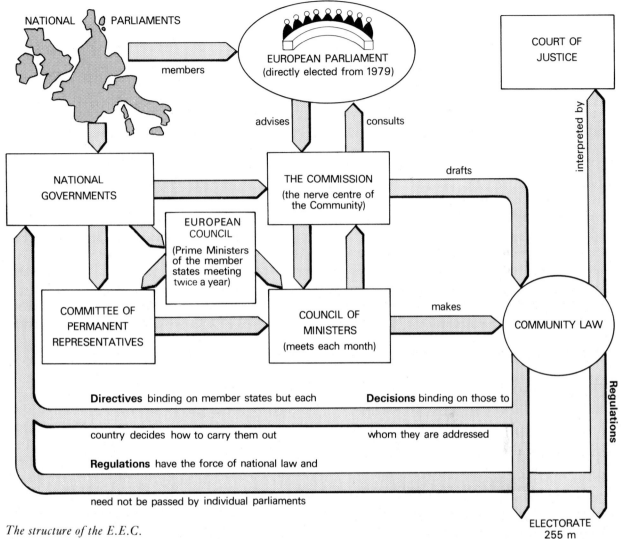

NATIONAL PARLIAMENTS

members

EUROPEAN PARLIAMENT
(directly elected from 1979)

COURT OF
JUSTICE

advises   consults

interpreted by

NATIONAL
GOVERNMENTS

THE COMMISSION
(the nerve centre of
the Community)

drafts

EUROPEAN
COUNCIL

(Prime Ministers
of the member
states meeting
twice a year)

COMMITTEE OF
PERMANENT
REPRESENTATIVES

COUNCIL OF
MINISTERS
(meets each month)

makes

COMMUNITY LAW

Regulations

Directives binding on member states but each   **Decisions** binding on those to

country decides how to carry them out   whom they are addressed

Regulations have the force of national law and

need not be passed by individual parliaments

ELECTORATE
255 m

The structure of the E.E.C.

Powell once remarked that there was 'an almost inevitable tendency of mass democracy towards inflation': the experience of the '70s has seemed to prove him right. But the severe measures taken by the Government were intended to promote a national recovery which would restore to the economy high levels of output, employment and real wages, and a vigorous, profitable and expanding industry.

There was a bright spot on the horizon, even in the midst of the economy measures. One of the principal causes of the world slump had been the steep rise in oil prices since the Middle East war of 1973. In common with the industrially developed nations, we have imported vast quantities of oil as a vital source of power. But in the '70s it became clear that in the continental shelf that surrounds Britain there is a vast store of oil to be exploited (see *map 13*). Exploration and production oil rigs of great size and cost were anchored in the North Sea and the first oil to come ashore by pipe-line flowed in 1976. New wealth and employment will come to Scotland and other parts of the country near to production areas, and the oil produced will go far towards making us self sufficient in oil (perhaps even an exporter) in the 1980s. This will have an immediate effect on our balance of payments and

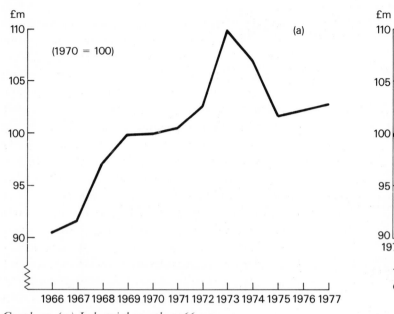

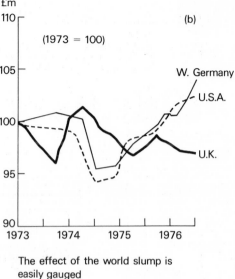

The effect of the world slump is
easily gauged

Graph 42 (a) Industrial growth, 1966–77
(b) Britain's changes in Gross National Product compared with other countries

help us towards a new prosperity in the next decade. (Another source of energy that might be developed in the 1980s could be power from the waves).

Britain and the E.E.C.

Britain's membership of the Common Market will have profound effects upon Government policy in many fields, not least in the management of the economy. For example, an immediate objective of the E.E.C. is the removal of tariffs between member states and the adoption of a common tariff in trade with the rest of the world (a common external tariff, C.E.T.). A more distant objective is monetary union: fixed exchange rates between the currencies of member states as the first step to adopting a common currency for the whole area. It is also intended that the financial and monetary policies of each member state should harmonise with the general policy of the Community, and the Commission at the centre of the Community (see *diagram on page 307*) will have power to alter the levels of taxation and expenditure within member states. Clearly, our joining a growing European Community

will have tremendous effects on our way of doing things.

Britain's relatively poor economic performance in the '70s has been a major point of concern for the E.E.C. (despite our rapid increase in trade with other members), and we have been linked with Italy and Ireland as the poorer members of the Community. We have a reputation for not working hard, for taking frequent holidays and going on strike. The reputation is partly due to the popular press giving considerable coverage to important strikes, and poor labour relations has been called the 'English disease'. Some industrialists have been reported as deciding not to invest in a British factory because of the prevalence of strikes; and this has been taken as a sign of Britain's industrial decline. But the reputation is by no means deserved, even though Britain lost more days over strike action in the early '70s than any other member country except Italy. A study by the Department of Employment in 1976 demonstrated that ninety-five per cent of British factories were, in fact, strike-free in 1971–3, a period of considerable industrial unrest, so that our bad reputation arises from big strikes in a few major industries. It is surprising how widespread

GOING METRIC-IN THE SHOPS

How to take it easy

Going metric is easier in practice than it sometimes sounds. All it really means is that you will be coming across more and more things being sold in metric quantities: metres for lengths, litres for liquids, and kilograms for weights. Some well-known things have gone metric recently and they may have caught your eye. Fabrics, for instance, are now sold by the metre; liquids like cooking oils and

soft drinks in litres. Cornflakes now come in ½ kilogram packs, and from the middle of the year sugar will be in the shops in kilogram bags. It's quite probable that you have bought some of these things in metric already.

Here are some facts about metric weights and measures, and some simple rhymes which may help you remember comparisons between the new and the old.

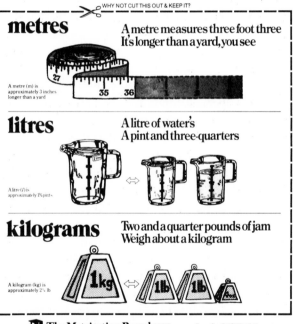

WHY NOT CUT THIS OUT & KEEP IT?

metres
A metre measures three foot three
It's longer than a yard, you see

A metre (m) is approximately 3 inches longer than a yard

litres
A litre of water's
A pint and three-quarters

A litre (l) is approximately 1¾ pints

kilograms
Two and a quarter pounds of jam
Weigh about a kilogram

A kilogram (kg) is approximately 2¼ lb

The Metrication Board 22 Kingsway, London WC2B 6LE

By 1977 trade labels were printed in both imperial and metric measurements; but the general public were slow to adopt metrication, and the Metrication Board was faced with a far more difficult problem of public relations than there was over decimalisation (see page 235)

is the idea that Britain's industry as a whole is declining. Despite the high rate of unemployment in the '70s, Britain has a better employment record than most other E.E.C. members.

The '70s have been lean years for the Community. The impetus of economic growth that characterised the '60s has been lost in the face of the world slump

and the crisis over the high price of oil. The hopes of reaching economic and monetary union in the early 1980s, and of making significant progress towards common political institutions began to fade in the mid-'70s. The 1976 report by M. Tindemans, Prime Minister of Belgium, made this clear, and progress towards granting greater powers to the central administration of the Community, at the expense of national sovereignty (the retention of control over the internal affairs of one's own country) will be slower than was once hoped.

Britain has made considerable strides towards close union with the Community, however. Decimalisation (see *page 235*) and the adoption of standard measurements (S.I.) are tokens of this, although progress towards full metrication (adopting continental weights and measures for goods in the shops, for example) is proving more difficult than was expected. In 1973 an important tax change was introduced. Our own purchase tax on articles in the shops (which allowed the Chancellor considerable room to influence the economy, simply by altering the level on particular articles in demand) was replaced by a Value Added Tax (V.A.T.), at first at ten per cent then reduced to eight per cent (1974) on most articles. This was in line with E.E.C. policy, but it reduces the area within which a Chancellor can manoeuvre when seeking to influence spending habits—luxury goods can no longer be made more expensive by simply increasing the purchase tax on them (although there have been special luxury rates of V.A.T.).

Membership of the Community is already affecting the pattern of Government and is likely to affect it further in the future. Civil service departments have developed specialist units to deal with Community matters and there is a constant inter-change of officials with those at Brussels, where the Commission of the Community has its headquarters. Community *directives* or *regulations* produced by the Commission are already curtailing the power of parliament in some areas of policy, notably in agriculture, internal trade, company law, insurance and regional aid. Parliament has not yet evolved a proper means of dealing with legislation proposed by the Commission and has little control over ministers and permanent representatives negotiating in Brussels. The problem of parliamentary control will be a major one in the '80s. This will become particularly pressing when the European Parliament is composed of members who have been directly elected. Since its establishment in 1958, the European Parliament has been composed of representatives selected from the members of parliament of each country in the Community, who have attended on a part-time basis. The Parliament has received little publicity in this country, and indeed has not played a major rôle in the development of the Community; but this is likely to change, for in September 1976, the Foreign Ministers of the Nine signed a document committing members to holding direct elections by May or June 1978. In the event, largely because of British delays, the elections were deferred until 1979. 'Direct election' means that the electorate votes for a candidate who would then sit as their own member in the European Parliament. When it has full-time members with the authority of direct election behind them, the European Parliament is likely to occupy a far more significant place in the way in which the decisions of the Community are taken and this can only diminish the power of each member country's parliament. But direct elections raise a number of problems: for example the very size of the constituency; the United Kingdom will have eighty-one members (in common with France, West Germany and Italy), which will mean some constituencies will have over half a million people. There is also concern that the British method of election—the 'first past the post' system—may not be quite suitable and that some form of *proportional representation* would be more appropriate. The cost of elections is also a problem—the Referendum of 1975 (see *page 238*) cost £10¼ million: would European elections cost more?

If Greece, Spain and Portugal enter the E.E.C. in the 1980s it will affect the balance of the Community quite as much as a directly elected parliament will alter the political institutions. These southern European countries are all agricultural and poor. They may impose new burdens that the Community will find hard to bear; but their entry might well be a means of preserving the new-found democracy in these countries.

Today, Britain benefits from the Community's social and regional funds and, because of the high rate of the 'green pound' (see *page 240*), from some aspects of the C.A.P. (Common Agricultural Policy). But the C.A.P. has brought a new feature into British life in that agricultural prices are now partly determined in Brussels and not just by the local conditions in the market. The old simple ideal of the classical economists that prices should constantly adjust themselves to the accepted level of a free market (see *page 85*) has passed away to be succeeded by a centrally controlled price structure that will permeate the whole economy of the Community. We have moved a very long way from the *laissez-faire* views of a hundred years ago.

Further Reading

A full bibliography for a book covering the breadth of this volume would stretch to many pages, and so the following list is restricted to those volumes that students will find most useful in following up any particular problem. Many of the works contain their own bibliographies, and your teacher will be able not only to advise you about the books listed but also to suggest others. Do try to read some of the novels written about the time you are studying— they often throw a powerful light upon conditions then. There are also learned periodicals, and other periodicals like *Punch*, *The Illustrated London News*, and newspapers which your big city library may store. *History Today* contains some interesting articles, *Transport History* and the *Journal of Industrial Archaeology* are also useful. Go to your local Records Office Museum and ask the Curator about *archives* to illustrate the subjects with which you are dealing. Remember that there is really no limit to the variety of sources the historian uses when he is investigating a period or a particular problem.

The Growth of the Eighteenth-Century Economy
ASHTON, T. S., *The Industrial Revolution, 1760-1830*, Oxford U.P., 1948 (*Home University Library*)
CAMPBELL, R. H., *Scotland since 1707*, Blackwell, 1965
DEANE, P., *The First Industrial Revolution*, Cambridge U.P., 1965
HOBSBAWM, E. J., *Industry and Empire*, Weidenfeld and Nicolson, 1968
MATHIAS, P., *The First Industrial Nation*, Methuen, 1969
SAW, R., *The Bank of England*, Harrap, 1944

Changes in the Countryside
CHAMBERS, J. D. and MINGAY, G. E., *The Agricultural Revolution, 1750-1880*, Batsford, 1966
HAMMOND, J. L. and B., *The Village Labourer*, Longmans, 1966
HOBSBAWM and RUDE, *Captain Swing*, Lawrence and Wishart, 1969
ARCH, JOSEPH, *The Story of His Life, by Himself*, MacGibbon and Kee, 1966
ASHBY, M. K., *Joseph Ashby of Tysoe 1859-1919*, Cambridge U.P., 1961 (for late nineteenth-century conditions)

The Shrinking Provinces
COLEMAN, T., *The Railway Navvies*, Hutchinson, 1965, Penguin 1968
HADFIELD, C. *British Canals*, 2nd edn. David and Charles, 1962
JACKMAN, W. T., *The Development of Transportation in Modern England* (2 vols.), Cass, 1962
NOCK, O. S., *The Railways of Britain*, Batsford, 1962
ROLT, L. T. C., *Telford*, Longmans, Green & Co. Ltd., 1958
ROLT, L. T. C., *Brunel*, Longmans, Green & Co. Ltd., 1957
ROLT, L. T. C., *George and Robert Stephenson*, Longmans, 1960
THORNTON, R. H., *British Shipping* 2nd edn., Cambridge U.P., 1959

Industrial Changes in the Nineteenth Century
ASHTON, T. S. and SYKES, J., *The Coal Industry in the Eighteenth Century* 2nd edn., Manchester U.P., 1964
BRACEGIRDLE, B., *Archaeology of the Industrial Revolution*, Heinemann, 1974

CHECKLAND, S. G., *The Rise of Industrial Society in England 1815–1885*, Longman, New Edition, 1971

CHALONER, W. H., *People and Industries*, Cass, 1963

CHAMBERS, J. D., *The Workshop of the World*, Oxford U.P., 1961

COURT, W. H. B., *The Rise of Midland Industries, 1600–1838*, Oxford U.P., 1938

HARVIE, C. (ed), *Industrialisation and Culture*, 1830–1914, Open University, 1974

KINGSFORD, P. W., *Engineers, Inventors and Workers*, Edward Arnold, 1964

MURPHY, B., *A History of the British Economy 1740–1970*, Vol. II 1740–1970 Longman, 1973

MOSS, M. and HUME, J. R., *Workshop of the British Empire*, Heinemann, 1977

REEVE, R., *The Industrial Revolution 1750–1850*, University of London Press 1971 (*London History Series*)

THOMIS, M., *Responses to Industrialisation*, David and Charles, 1976

Social Life in the Eighteenth and Nineteenth Centuries

BOTT, A., *Our Fathers*, Heinemann

BRANCA, P., *Silent Sisterhood: Middle Class Women in the Victorian House*, Oxford U.P., 1976

BRIGGS, A., *Victorian People*, Penguin, 1970

BURNETT, J., *A History of the Cost of Living*, Pelican, 1968

BURNETT, J., *Plenty and Want*, Pelican, 1968

BURNEY, F., *Diary*, Dent, 1968 (*Everyman Series*)

BYNG, J., *The Torrington Diaries*, Eyre and Spottiswoode, 1954

COBBETT, W., *Rural Rides*, (first published 1830) 2 Vols, Dent (*Everyman Series*)

DEFOE, A., *Tour Through the whole Island of Great Britain, 1724–27*, Harrap, 1950

DONCASTER, I., *Changing Society in Victorian England*, Longmans, 1966

GEORGE, M. D., *England in Transition*, Penguin, 1969

GEORGE, M. D., *London Life in the Eighteenth Century*, Penguin, 1966

HAMMOND, J. L. and B., *The Bleak Age*, Pelican, 1947

HAMMOND, J. L. and B., *Lord Shaftesbury*, Cass, 1969

JONES, R. B., *The Hanoverians*, Hart Davis, 1972

MINGAY, G. E., *English Landed Society in the Enghteenth Century*, Routledge, 1963

MINGAY, G. E., *Rural Life in Victorian England*, Heinemann, 1977

MOSS, M., *Britain from Waterloo to the Great Exhibition*, Heinemann History Broadsheets, 1975

ROYSTON PIKE E., *Human Documents of the Victorian Golden Age*, Allen & Unwin, 1966

SAMUEL, R. (ed), *Village Life and Labour*, Routledge, 1975

THOMPSON, F. M. L., *English Landed Society in the Nineteenth Century*, Routledge, 1963

TURBERVILLE, A. S., (ed), *Johnson's England* (2 vols.), Oxford U.P., 1933

WILLIAMS, H., *A Century of Public Health in Britain*, Black, 1960

WOODFORDE, REV. J., *The Diary of a Country Parson 1758-1802*, ed. Beresford, Oxford U.P., 1949 (*World's Classics*)

Education

COWIE, E., *Education* (*Examining the Evidence — Nineteenth Century England*), Methuen, 1973

JONES, M. J., *The Charity School Movement*, new edn., Cass, 1963

LOWNDES, G. A. N., *The Silent Social Revolution*, Oxford U.P., 1967

PEDLEY, R., *The Comprehensive School*, Penguin, 1969

PETERSON, A. D. *A Hundred Years of Education*, 2nd edn., Duckworth, 1960

SEABORNE, M., *Education*, Vista Books, 1966 (some excellent illustrations)

Also the various reports that are referred to in this volume

Working-Class Movements and the Labour Party
BRIGGS, A., *Chartist Studies*, Macmillan, 1963
HOBSBAWM, E. J., *Labouring Men*, Weidenfeld and Nicolson, 1964
HOVELL, M., *The Chartist Movement*, ed. Tout 2nd edn., Manchester U.P., 1925
JENKINS, C. and MORTIMER, J. E., *British Trade Unions Today*, Pergamon, 1965
JONES, R. B., *The Victorians*, Hart Davis, 1975
LANSBURY, G., *My Life*, Constable, 1934
MOWAT, C. L., *The General Strike*, Edward Arnold, 1969
PELLING, H., *A History of British Trade Unionism*, Macmillan, 1963; Penguin, 1970
PELLING, H., *A Short History of the Labour Party 1900-60*, Macmillan, 1961
SMILES, S., *Self Help*, John Murray, 1958
THOMIS, M., *The Luddites*, Edward Arnold, 1970
T.U.C., *The History of the T.U.C.*, (Centenary volume), 1968

Social and Economic Changes in the Twentieth Century
BAGRIT, L., *The Age of Automation*, Penguin, 1966
BERTHOUD, R., *The Disadvantages of Inequality*, P.E.P. Report, 1976
BEVERIDGE, W. H., *Report on Social Insurance and Allied Services*, H.M.S.O.,1942
BRITAIN, *A Handbook*, H.M.S.O. (annually)
BRUCE, M., *The Coming of the Welfare State*, Batsford, 1961
Census 1971—Preliminary Report, H.M.S.O.
DORFMAN, G., *Wage Politics in Britain, 1945–67*, Charles Knight, 1974
FREEMAN, T.W., *Conurbations of Great Britain*, Manchester U.P., 1959
HOBMAN, D. L., *The Welfare State*, Murray, 1960
HOPKINSON, T., *Picture Post, 1938–50*, Pelican, 1971
JONES, C., *Immigration and Social Policy in Britain*, Tavistock, 1977
LONGMATE, N., *How we lived then*, Longman, 1971
MARTIN, I., *From Workhouse to Welfare*, Longman, 1974
MARWICK, A., *The Deluge*, Penguin, 1967
MARWICK, A., *Scotland in Modern Times*, Cass, 1964
MCMAHON, C., *Sterling in the Sixties*, Oxford U.P., 1964
MOWAT, C. L., *Britain Between the Wars 1918-40*, new edn., Methuen, 1955
The New Towns of Britain, H.M.S.O.
NOWELL-SMITH, S., *Edwardian England, 1901-1914*, Oxford U.P., 1951
OGILVIE, V., *Our Times—A Social History (1912–1952)*, Batsford, 1955
ORWELL, G., *The Road to Wigan Pier*, new edn., Secker and Warburg, 1959, Penguin
PREST, A. R. and COPPOCK, D. J. (eds), *The U.K. Economy*, Weidenfeld, 1976
PRIESTLEY, J. B., *The Edwardians*, Heinemann, 1970
ROLT, L. T. C., *Motoring History*, Studio Vista, 1964
SMITH, P. I., *The Wonderful Story of British Industry*, Ward Lock, 1951
SISSONS, M. and FRENCH, P., *The Age of Austerity, 1945-51*, Hodder and Stoughton, 1963
WILKINSON, E., *The Town that was Murdered*, Gollancz, 1939
WORSWICK, G. D. N. and ADY, P. H., eds., *The British Economy in the 1950's*, Oxford U.P., 1962
STEVENSON, J. and COOK, C., *The Slump*, Cape, 1977
WYMER, N., *Sport in England*, Harrap, 1954
YOUNG, M. (ed), *Poverty Report, 1974*, Temple Smith, 1974

Various source books are appearing, some of which can be useful. For example:

Exploring History (Macmillan Education): The Industrial Revolution; Houses and homes; Transport; Victorian Britain.

Then and There (Longman) A series of short topic books, edited by Marjorie Reeves: The Agrarian Revolution; Steamships and shipbuilders in the Industrial Revolution; The railway revolution; Liverpool and the American cotton trade; A textile community in the Industrial Revolution; A coal and iron community in the Industrial Revolution; Edwin Chadwick, poor law and public health; The Chartists; London life and the Great Exhibition 1851; Police and prisons; Learning and teaching in Victorian times; Robert Peel, Free Trade and the Corn Laws; The potato famine and Irish emigrants; A hundred years of medical care; The great dock strike 1889; Edwardian England; The motor revolution; Suffragettes and votes for women; The General Strike.

Then and There Sourcebook: The Industrial Revolution

Longman Secondary History Packs
The First Industrial Revolution: 5 packs: Textiles; Iron; Mining; Power and Machinery; Workshop and factory.
Social Problems arising from the Industrial Revolution: 5 packs: Population; Urbanisation; Housing and Living conditions of the working classes; Public Health; Poverty.
Transport: 5 packs: Canals and Rivers; Railways; Ships; Cars; Aeroplanes—space.
Towards Democracy: 5 packs: Protest movements; Trade Unions: the 19th century; Trade Unions: the 20th century; Parliamentary reform
(Each pack is available separately)

The Archive Series (Edward Arnold) Relevant titles include: Agriculture and society in Britain 1846–1914; The emancipation of women; Great Britain; British Trade Unionism; The general

strike, 1926; The Liberals and the Welfare State.

Various Records Offices are also producing archive material, e.g. Buckingham (Aylesbury) on elections, enclosure and the eighteenth-century squirearchy; Newcastle Department of Education on coal-mining, railways and travel; Manchester Public Library on Peterloo; Manchester Historical Association on poor relief.

Manchester Studies Unit at Manchester Polytechnic has a collection of local history archives (including tape transcripts) on the cotton industry and life in Manchester at the beginning of the century.

The Jackdaw series varies greatly in quality but contains many titles relevant to the period.

Visual Aids The Then and There filmstrips are boxed sets of full-colour filmstrips: The Industrial Revolution (4 strips); The Agrarian Revolution (3 strips); Victorian Social Life (4 strips).

Museums Many museums have much to offer in the field of economic and social history; try to visit them, as well as country-houses which may be in your neighbourhood: the good historian hunts down his own sources. Among the more important museums are: The National Railway Museum, Leeman Road, York YO2 4XJ; The Ironbridge Gorge Museum, Shropshire; The Victoria and Albert Museum, Cromwell Road, South Kensington, London SW7; North of England Open-air Museum, Beamish Hall, Stanley, Co. Durham.

(*History Teaching through Museums* by John Fairley (Longman) is a useful guide for teachers).

For more advanced study:
The following series are more advanced but contain source material: Sources of History (Macmillan); Seminar Studies in History (Longman); Society and Industry in the Nineteenth Century (Oxford); Studies in Economic and Social History (Macmillan for the Economic History Society).

Index

advertising, 80, 193, 257, 278, 280, 291, 298

affluence, 236, 288–91, 298–9

agriculture, 19–20, Chapter 3, 44, 57–8, 88–93, 238–40, 310
  depression (1873–96), 91, 176–8
  gang system, 35
  High Farming, 36–7, 57–8, 91
  government aid to, 238–40
  government subsidies to, 238
  marketing boards, 238
  C.A.P., 240, 310

air travel, 188–9, 243, 282–3

Albert, Prince Consort, 81–2, 110–11

Anti-Corn Law League, 36, 90–2, 164

apprenticeship, 7, 64, 95, 152, 271, 274

Arch, Joseph, 35–6, 178, 213

Assistance Board (1934), 211, 260

atmospheric theory of disease, 104, 106

atomic energy, 244

automation, 244–5

Bakewell, Robert, 27–8, 37

balance of payments, 12, 83, 176, 224–8, 230–3, 236, 254, 278, 304, 307

balance of trade, 12, 83, 176, 224, 226

bank rate, 228, 232

banks, 20, 21, 84–5, 173
  Bank of England, 21, 84–5, 227–8, 250
  corporate, 21
  county, 21, 84
  joint stock, 84
  private, 21, 84
  savings, 35, 84, 135

Basle Facility Agreement, 232, 306

Bazalgette, Joseph, 107

Beeching Plan (1963), 284

Bentham, Jeremy, 87, 125, 169

Bessemer, Sir Henry, 60, 71–2

Bevan, Aneurin, 262–3

Beveridge, Sir W., 202, 205, 231, 260–3

Beveridge Report (1942), 230–1, 260

bicycle, 189, 285

bingo, 195

birth control, 294, 297

blast furnace, 69, 71, 72

Booth, Charles, 199, 207

Booth, 'General' William, 137–8, 199

borstal, 203

Boulton, Matthew, 22, 43, 73–4, 79–80

Bow Street Runners, 127

Brassey, Thomas, 54, 58, 78, 84

Bridgewater, Lord, 45, 46, 58

Bridgewater canal, 46, 50

Bright, John, 89

Brindley, James, 46–8

B.B.C., 194, 248, 276, 278–9, 281

Brunel, I.K., 52–3, 58–9

Building Societies, 208, 264

Caird, Sir James, 34, 36, 38

C.N.D., 289

canals, 45–9, 52, 58
  effects of, 47–8
  disadvantages of, 48–9

Carlyle, Thomas, 9, 124, 162

Cartwright, Edmund, 66

Chadwick, Edwin, 34, 102, 106–8, 160, 198–9, 212

Chamberlain, Joseph, 109, 124, 150, 169, 172, 184, 210, 224–5, 227

Chamberlain, Neville, 207, 210–11, 228

chartism, 66, 91, 135, 162–4, 168

child labour, 63–4, 93–6, 98

chemical industry, 76, 173, 242

chimney sweeps, 93–5

cholera, 104–8

Christian Socialists, 135, 146, 165

Churchill, Sir W., 194, 199, 202, 222, 228, 230

cinema, 195, 278

civil service, 93, 165, 202, 210–11, 226, 276–8, 292, 294, 300–2, 309

Clean Air Act, 246

coaching, 39–40, 42–3, 52

coal, 39, 45, 49, 58, 68–71, 76, 121, 132, 221, 225–6, 228, 242–3, 300

Cobbett, William, 30, 133, 158

Cobden, Richard, 88, 89, 90–1, 172

Coke, T.W., 26–7

collectivist state, 93, 168–9, 226, 250–2, 292, 299, 300–3, 310

Combination Acts (1799–1800), 156, 159

Common Agricultural Policy (C.A.P.), 239–40, 310

commuters, 57, 184, 188, 294

computers, 244–5
  micro-processors, 245

consensus politics, 290, 299

Confederation of British industry (C.B.I.), 249, 299–303

Co-operative movement, 132, 135, 159, 166–7

Corn Laws, 36, 38, 88–92

cotton industry, 16, 20, 64–7, 78, 88, 176, 225, 247

cotton famine, 68
Crompton's mule, 65

dancing, 191
Darby, Abraham, 68–9
decimalisation, 235, 308
Defoe, Daniel, 25, 39–40
D.S.I.R., 274, 302
development ('depressed') areas, 225, 228, 249–50, 302
devaluation, 227, 232–3, 236, 306
Disraeli, Benjamin, 9, 57, 84, 91, 107-8, 118, 121, 165, 168, 177
diversification of industry, 12, 176, 178, 246–7
doctors
    eighteenth century, 4
    nineteenth century, 104–6
    twentieth century, 108, 262–3, 293–4,
dole, 192, 206, 210–11, 226
domestic system, 8, 30, 62–4, 66, 78, 95
domestic servants, 2, 30, 118, 121, 140, 181, 192
drovers, 25

economic 'doldrums', 206, 209, 225, 228, 271–6
Eden, Sir A., 4, 13
education, Chapter 2, 203, 271–6, 294, 299
    free places, 153, 198
    Grand Tour, 117, 139
    half-time system, 148, 198
    monitorial system, 141–2
    national system, 147–53
    payment by results, 149
    poor, 133, 140–7
    R.O.S.L.A., 272
    Revised Code, 150
    schools
        academies, 140
        Board, 150–3
        charity, 133, 140
        comprehensive, 271, 273–4

dame, 140
denominational, 141–2, 151–2
factory acts and, 96, 148
grammar, 144, 271–2
parochial day schools for industry, 140
public, 57, 145–6, 173, 271–2
Sunday, 8, 116, 141
technical education, 142, 146, 151–3, 271–2, 274
polytechnics, 274–5
Mechanics' Institutes, 142–3
wealthy, 139–40
women, 140, 146–7
universities, 139, 140, 146–7, 153, 274, 275–6, 290
egalitarianism, 192, 258, 261, 273, 280–1, 287, 289, 291
electricity, 173, 186–7, 209, 226, 242–4, 248
emigration, 3, 35, 58, 61, 84, 164
empire (and commonwealth) trade, 12, 13, 77, 84, 175–7, 224, 234–7
employers' associations, 174, 216, 247–8
employers' liability, 169, 200
enclosure, 23, 28–32, 41, 100, 119
Engels, Frederick, 1, 95
entrepreneurs, 62, 76–81
'Establishment', 92, 290
E.E.C., 233–40, 254, 292, 296, 304, 307–10
E.C.S.C., 235
E.F.T.A., 236
evacuation, 259
evacuation, 259
Evangelicals, 94, 133–4
Exchange Equalisation Account, 227

Fabians, 217–18
Factory Acts, 94–8, 148, 200–1
factory system, 62, 66–8, 78–9, 92–3, 100

F.B.I. (C.B.I.), 249
Festival of Britain (1951), 263
films, 195
First World War, 205, 224–5, 238, 241
food adulteration, 166
food habits, contemporary, 259, 260, 290, 298
football, 190
foreign competition, 170–3, 176
foreign exchange, 227, 230, 232–3, 304
foreign trade, 12–14, 18, 83, 175–6
Forster, W.E., 150–1
Fox, C.J., 19, 121
free trade, 12, 16, 38, 87–9, 91, 225–7
friendly societies, 165, 205, 214
full employment, 230, 231, 249, 301–3

game laws, 33
garden city, 185
gas industry, 76, 112, 184, 186, 246
Geddes 'axe', 226, 261, 271
G.A.T.T. (1947), 230, 232
George III, 13, 16–17, 42, 123, 133, 139
Germany, 72, 171–3, 176–7, 226, 234, 236, 238, 242, 247
Gilbert's Act, 31
Gilchrist-Thomas, S., 71
Gladstone, W.E., 56, 57, 85, 89, 91, 97, 165, 168
gothic revival, 115, 122, 124, 135
'Great Depression', 38, 84, 170–4, 176–7, 179, 238
Great Exhibition, (1851), 10, 34, 37, 75, 81–2, 152, 164, 168, 176, 263
Green Belt, 185, 267
'green' pound, 240, 310

Hanway, Jonas, 13, 93
Hardie, Keir, 158, 182, 218

harvests
  eighteenth century, 4
  nineteenth century, 33, 36,
    84, 177
  twentieth century, 239–40
Health of Towns Association,
  101, 106–7
Heath, Edward, 236, 251, 299,
  300
Hill, Octavia, 110, 207
hire purchase, 197, 227, 232,
  278, 289, 290–1
highwayman, 40
Hogarth, William, 7
holidays, 57, 286–7,
  with pay, 286
hospitals, 5, 198, 210
housing, 103–12, 116, 168, 184,
  196, 207–9, 263–71
  nineteenth century, 110,
    184–5, 207
  municipal (council), 184, 208,
    263–4, 267, 270
  private, 208–9, 264, 266, 269
Hudson, George, 55–8
Huskisson, William, 36, 88
hypermarket, 251

illegitimacy, 5, 281, 294, 297
immigrants, 8, 201, 266
  New Commonwealth, 266,
    295–7
immunisation, 260, 293
incomes policy, 232–3, 254,
  299–300, 303–4
income tax, 89, 200
industrial democracy, 301, 302–4
inflation, 23, 231–3, 236, 254,
  300, 304
inflationary spiral, 231–2, 240,
  254
inoculation, 6
iron industry, 68–70, 72, 78–80,
  115, 170
  mania, 69–70
inspectors
  factories, 96–7, 201
  schools, 147–8

insurance, 21, 60–1, 83, 135
I.M.F., 230, 232, 304
I.T.V., 278–9
invisible earnings, 83, 176,
  224–5
Irish, 8, 54

Jenner, Dr., 6
Jessop, William, 47, 50

Kartel, 171, 173, 247–8
Keynes, J.M., (Lord), 226,
  228–30, 249
King, Gregory, 3, 8, 9
Kingsley, Charles, 94, 134–5

Labour Party, 132, 164, 167,
  199, 208, 213–14, 216–19,
  223, 227, 230–3, 236–7,
  248–50, 261–3, 300–6
laissez-faire, 82, 84, 87–8, 92–3,
  97–8, 106, 169, 205, 246, 248,
  250, 300, 301, 310
Lansbury, George, 204, 210
leisure, 188–91, 286–8
Liberal Party, 91, 168, 179, 200,
  204, 218, 225
limited liability, 57, 85–6, 241
Lloyd George, David, 200, 205,
  209, 213, 219, 230, 255
Lloyd, Selwyn, 232, 254
local government
  county, 108, 111–12, 128,
    276–7
  town, 108–9, 112, 128, 276–7
Luddites, 66, 156–7

Macadam, J.L., 40, 42
MacDonald, Ramsey, 213, 218,
  223
machine tools, 74–6, 83, 173–5,
  243
Macmillan, H. (Lord), 236, 249
Malthus, Dr. Thomas, 3, 5, 33,
  87

managers, 16, 17, 173–5, 232,
  241–6
man-made fibres, 242
Manpower Services
  Commission, 301
Marshall Plan (1947), 234
Marshall, William, 24
Marx, Karl, 9, 215–17, 219
mass production, 62, 163, 191
means test, 210, 211
mercantilism, 11, 87, 88
Metcalfe, ('Blind Jack'), 41–2,
  51
methodism, 34, 130–2, 136, 138,
  141, 159, 217
metrication, 309
Mohocks, 2, 121
Montague, Lady Mary, 5
motor car, 42, 188–9, 243,
  284–5
motorways, 284–6
municipal utility, 112
Murdoch, William, 43, 73, 76

nabobs, 20
Napoleonic Wars, 23, 27, 29, 32,
  62, 78, 120, 132, 156, 158, 168
Nasmyth, J., 59, 74–5, 79
N.E.D.C. ('Neddy') (1962),
  232, 254, 299
National Enterprise Board,
  302
national grid, 187, 242–4, 300
National Health Service, 261–3
National Insurance,
  1911, 205, 209
  1920s, 206–7, 210–11
  1978, 291
National Plan (1965), 232, 254
National Parks, 286–7
nationalised industries, 248–50
Navigation Acts, 11, 13, 15,
  87–9
navvies, 47, 54, 78
newspapers, 193–4
New Towns, 185, 266, 267–71
Nightingale, Florence, 5, 117,
  146, 180

North Sea oil, 302, 304–7
O'Connor, Feargus, 163–4
Oglethorpe, James, 124
oil prices, 1970s, 233, 238, 302–4, 307–9
old-age pensions, 204–5, 207, 261–2, 291
Ombudsman, 278
Open University, 275–6
O.E.E.C., 235
Owen, Robert, 79, 80, 95, 159–60, 164, 166, 202, 219

parish, 31, 40, 95, 129
parliamentary reform, 57, 89, 154, 160
1832, 34, 154, 158
1867, 92, 164–5, 168
1884/5, 168
1918, 164, 183
1928, 183
Parsons, C.A., 60, 86, 187
paupers, 31, 33, 95
P.A.Y.E., 256
Peel, Sir Robert, 36, 85, 88–92, 125–8
'permissive' society, 281–2, 288–91, 297–8
Peterloo, 77, 158
Peto, S.M., 54, 78, 84
Pitt the Younger, William, 15, 16, 19, 88–9, 121, 156
Place, Francis, 77, 156
Plimsoll, Samuel, 61
police, 126–8, 163, 277, 298
political party organisation, 168–9
pollution, 244, 246
Poor Law, 32–5, 111, 203–4, 209–12
1834, 34, 160–2
poor rate, 32, 37, 89, 95, 209
poor relief, 3, 32
out-door, 3
in-door, 34
population, 2–8
birth rate, 3, 293–5
death rate, 3

distribution, 3, 7–8, 13, 30, 178, 292–6
growth, 2–8, 11, 23, 102, 108, 293–5
Powell, Enoch, 296, 307
poverty
rural, 30–5, 58, 158, 168, 180, 197–8
urban, 101–4, 109–11, 180, 184, 196–8, 207–12, 290–1
press, the, 193–4, 222, 280
press gang, 12, 120
Price Commission, 252
prison, 15, 34, 122, 124–6
prisoners, 34, 122, 125–6
public corporation, 194, 248, 249
public health, 8, 9, 103, 106–9

race relations, 295–7
radio, 245, 248, 279
railways, 44, 47, 49–58, 67, 71, 82–3, 163, 188, 247, 249, 283
battle of gauges, 53
impact, 57–8
mania, 54–6
twentieth century, 247, 283–4
rationalisation, 79, 175, 247–8, 250
rationing
1917, 205–6
1939, 255–8
real wages, 170–1, 298, 303
redistribution of incomes, 20, 199
refrigeration, 38, 178
registration of births and deaths, 96
R.P.M., 247, 251–2
retail 'revolution', 175, 250–2
'ribbon development', 209, 267
Ricardo, David, 87, 89, 159
Rickman, John, 4
oads, 39–44, 284–6
Rowntree, S., 199, 211

'St. Monday', 9, 63, 141
Salvation Army, 136–8
Self Help, 42, 133, 165, 289

Second World War, 229–30, 244, 255–61
Settlement Acts, 31–2
Shaftesbury, Lord, 93–4, 96, 107, 133, 148
Shuttleworth, Dr. K., 106, 147–8
slavery, 16, 96, 120, 130, 133
slave trade, 13, 16, 19
Smiles, Samuel, 42, 133, 143, 165, 289
Smith, Adam, 11, 12, 15, 87–8, 228
smuggling, 15, 16
Snow, Dr. J., 104–6
social mobility, 179, 218, 289, 298–9
S.P.C.K., 124, 130
Southwood-Smith, Dr., 98, 107
spas, 122–3
Speenhamland System, 32–4, 160
steam
carriages, 43–4
power, 66, 70, 72, 73, 74, 80, 100, 173
ships, 38, 58–61, 75, 177–8
steel, 20, 71–2, 170, 172, 242, 248, 250
Stephenson, George, 41, 50–1, 71
Stephenson, Robert, 51, 53
Stock Exchange, 2, 55, 86
strikes, 35–6, 159–60, 163, 165, 193, 219–23, 253–4, 299, 300, 307–8
General Strike, 222–3, 226, 252, 300
suffragettes, 146, 182–3
supermarkets, 251
'sweated' trades, 201–2
'Swing' riots, 34, 158

Taff Vale Case, 218
tariff reform, 172, 225–7
tariffs, 11, 16, 87–9, 224–8, 235, 239–40, 308
Television, 194, 278–9, 281, 298

Telford, Thomas, 41–2, 47, 53, 69–70
Ten Hours' Movement, 96–7
Tory Party, 89, 109, 132, 158
Tolpuddle Martyrs, 34, 160
Townshend, Viscount, 26
trade gap, 176–7, 225–6, 231
Trade Disputes Act
    1906, 218
    1927, 223
trade slumps, 77, 83–4, 88–9, 162, 177, 210, 226–7
trade unions
    agricultural, 35–6, 178, 214
    early, 156, 159, 184, 216
    New Model, 164–5, 213, 214
    'new unionism', 1880s, 213–16, 219
    Owenite, 159–60, 219
    twentieth century, 219–23, 253–4, 300–3
T.U.C., 165, 184, 216, 222–3, 249, 252–4, 299, 301, 303–6
trams, 187–8
Trevithick, R., 43, 49
truck shops, 54, 98

unemployment, 31, 162–3, 171, 204, 210–11, 221, 226–7, 289, 303
universities, 130, 139–40, 147, 152–3, 274–6
U.S.A., 3, 16, 36–7, 55, 57–61, 64, 68, 72, 84, 171, 173, 219, 225–7, 230, 234, 236, 242, 258, 302, 304
urban 'renewal', 265–7, 270–1
Utilitarians, 87, 106

vaccination, 5
V.A.T., 308–9
vertical integration, 70, 78, 248
Victoria, Queen, 9, 34, 52, 124, 146, 163, 166

water supplies, 103–8, 184
Waterloo, Battle of, 36, 106, 158
Watt, James, 43, 72–4, 79–80
Walpole, Horace, 114–15
weavers, 63–7
Webb, Sydney and Beatrice, 183, 199, 204, 217, 219

Wedgwood, Josiah, 20, 46, 79–81
Welfare State, 202–5, 207, 255, 259–63, 288–9, 291, 306
Wesley, John, 80, 131–2, 138
Whitley Councils, 202, 220
Whitworth, Sir J., 74, 175
Wilberforce, William, 17, 19, 90, 96, 133
Wilkinson, John, 20, 69–70, 73, 76
Wilson, Sir H., 232, 237, 300
wool, 62–4, 67
Women's Land Army, 239
women's rights
    nineteenth century, 146–7, 180–1
    twentieth century, 181–4, 191, 281, 297
workers' compensation, 200, 261
workers' co-operative, 301

Young, Arthur, 23, 24, 26, 33, 41, 46
Youth Employment Service, 202
Youth Hostels, 189, 286